Government by Judiciary

The Transformation of the Fourteenth Amendment

All persons born or naturalized in the United States . . . are citizens of the United States and of the State wherein they reside. No State shall make or enforce any law which shall abridge the privileges or immunities of citizens of the United States; nor shall any State deprive any person of life, liberty, or property, without due process of law; nor deny to any person within its jurisdiction the equal protection of the laws.

—Fourteenth Amendment, §1

Government by Judiciary

The Transformation
of the
Fourteenth Amendment

Raoul Berger

Harvard University Press
Cambridge, Massachusetts
and London, England
1977

Library of Congress Cataloging in Publication Data
Berger, Raoul, 1901–
  Government by judiciary: The transformation of
  the Fourteenth Amendment

  Bibliography: p.
  1. Judicial power—United States. 2. United
States. Constitution. 14th Amendment. I. Title.
KF5130.B4   347'.73'12   77-6777
ISBN 0-674-35795-7

To
Leon Green
Cherished friend and mentor

Acknowledgments

Eminent historians, social scientists, and lawyers have read portions or all of my manuscript and favored me with their suggestions. I do not name them in order to spare them the embarrassment of being associated with my views. Above all I am indebted to them for encouragement.

R.B.

Concord, Massachusetts
August 1977

Contents

Part I

Abbreviations

Annals of Congress	*Annals of Congress,* vol. 1 (1789; 2d ed. 1834, print bearing running head "History of Congress"
Bickel	ALEXANDER M. BICKEL, "The Original Understanding and the Segregation Decision," 69 Harvard Law Review 1 (1955)
Donald, *Sumner I*	DAVID DONALD, *Charles Sumner and the Coming of the Civil War* (1960)
Donald, *Sumner II*	DAVID DONALD, *Charles Sumner and the Rights of Man* (1970)
Elliot	JONATHAN ELLIOT, *Debates in the Several State Conventions on the Adoption of the Federal Constitution* (2d. ed. 1836)
Fairman, *History*	CHARLES FAIRMAN, *Reconstruction and Reunion 1864–1888,* vol. 6, part 1 of *History of the Supreme Court of the United States* (1971)
Fairman, Stanford	CHARLES FAIRMAN, "Does the Fourteenth Amendment Incorporate the Bill of Rights?," 2 Stanford Law Review 5 (1949)
Farrand	MAX FARRAND, *The Records of the Federal Convention of 1787* (1911)
Federalist	*The Federalist* (Modern Library ed. 1937)
Flack	HARRY FLACK, *The Adoption of the Fourteenth Amendment* (1908)
Globe	*Congressional Globe* (39th Congress, 1st Session 1886)
Globe App.	Appendix to *Globe*
Graham	HOWARD JAY GRAHAM, *Everyman's Constitution* (1968)
James	JOSEPH B. JAMES, *The Framing of the Fourteenth Amendment* (1965)
Kelly, Fourteenth	ALFRED H. KELLY, "The Fourteenth Amendment Reconsidered: The Segregation Question," 54 Michigan Law Review 1049 (1956)
Kendrick	BENJAMIN KENDRICK, *The Journal of the Joint Committee of Fifteen on Reconstruction* (1914)
Levy, *Against the Law*	LEONARD W. LEVY, *Against the Law: The Nixon Court and Criminal Justice* (1974)
Levy, *Warren*	LEONARD W. LEVY, ed., *The Supreme Court Under Earl Warren* (1972)
Lusky	LOUIS LUSKY, *By What Right?* (1975)
Poore	BEN P. POORE, *Federal and State Constitutions, Colonial Charters* (1877)
TenBroek	JACOBUS TENBROEK, *Equal Under Law* (1965)
Van Alstyne	WILLIAM W. VAN ALSTYNE, "The Fourteenth Amendment, the 'Right' to Vote, and the Understanding of the Thirty-Ninth Congress," 1965 Supreme Court Review 33

1

Introduction

> *My colleagues have learned to respect nothing but evidence, and to believe that their highest duty lies in submitting to it, however it may jar against their inclinations.*
>
> Thomas H. Huxley*

THE Fourteenth Amendment is the case study par excellence of what Justice Harlan described as the Supreme Court's "exercise of the amending power,"[1] its continuing revision of the Constitution under the guise of interpretation. Because the Amendment is probably the largest source of the Court's business[2] and furnishes the chief fulcrum for its control of controversial policies, the question whether such control is authorized by the Constitution is of great practical importance.

Those whose predilections are mirrored in a given decision find such judicial revision an exercise of statesmanship.[3] Others consider that a democratic system requires adherence to consti-

---

* T. H. Huxley, *Man's Place in Nature* (1863), quoted in Homer W. Smith, *Man and His Gods* 372 (1953).

1. Reynolds v. Sims, 377 U.S. 533, 591 (1964).

2. Felix Frankfurter, "John Marshall and the Judicial Function," 69 Harv. L. Rev. 217, 229 (1955).

3. For example, Anthony Lewis hailed the Warren Court as the "keeper of the national conscience," in "Historical Change in the Supreme Court," *The New York Times Magazine,* June 17, 1962, p. 7, in *Supreme Court Under Earl Warren* 73, 79, 81 (L. Levy ed. 1972). See also A. S. Miller and R. F. Howell, "The Myth of Neutrality in Constitutional Adjudication," 27 U. Chi. L. Rev. 661, 686, 689 (1960).

tutional limits, by courts no less than presidents.[4] This study
seeks to demonstrate that the Court was not designed to act,
in James M. Beck's enthusiastic phrase, as a "continuing constitutional convention,"[5] that the role assigned to it was far
more modest: to police the boundaries drawn in the Constitu-

4. Chief Justice Marshall stated in M'Culloch v. Maryland, 17 U.S. (4
Wheat.) 316, 421 (1819), "We admit, as all must admit, that the powers of the
government are limited, and that its limits are not to be transcended." "The
theory of our governments," said Justice Samuel Miller, "is opposed to the
deposit of unlimited power anywhere. The executive, the legislative, and the
judicial branches of these governments are all of limited and defined powers."
Loan Association v. Topeka, 87 U.S. (20 Wall.) 655, 663 (1874). "[W]ritten
constitutions," said Justice Stanley Matthews, "were limitations upon all the
powers of government, legislative as well as executive and judicial." Hurtado
v. California, 110 U.S. 516, 531–532 (1884).

5. In *The Constitution of the United States* (1922), Beck compared "the work
of the Supreme Court to that of a 'continuous constitutional convention'
which adapts the original charter by reinterpretation." Quoted in Leonard W.
Levy, *Judgments: Essays in American Constitutional History* 18 (1972). In his recent critique of the "Nixon Court," Levy states that the "Court is and must be
for all practical purposes a 'continuous constitutional convention' in the sense
that it must keep updating the original charter by reinterpretation." L. Levy,
Against the Law 29, 30 (1974). "Adaptation" and "reinterpretation" are euphe-
misms for "revision" or "rewriting" the Constitution, the function of a constitutional convention, not the Court. See Louis Lusky, *By What Right?* 21
(1975); Louis Henkin, "Some Reflections on Current Constitutional Controversies," 109 U. Pa. L. Rev. 637, 658–659 (1961).

Solicitor General Robert H. Jackson, later a Justice of the Court, did not
share Beck's enthusiasm; the pre-1937 Court, he said, "sat almost as a continuous constitutional convention which, without submitting its proposals to any
ratification or rejection, could amend the basic law." R. Jackson, *The Struggle
for Judicial Supremacy* x–xi (1941). Ward Elliott reports that Anthony Lewis
(who was a leader in the drive that led to the "reapportionment" decision)
asked Solicitor General Archibald Cox (who had filed a brief amicus for reapportionment in Reynolds v. Sims, supra note 1) when the Court announced its
decision, "'How does it feel like to be present at the second American Constitutional Convention?' Cox retained enough of his old perspective to answer,
'It feels awful.'" Ward Elliott, *The Rise of a Guardian Democracy* 370 (1974).
See infra Chapter 5 note 1.

tion.[6] A corollary is that the "original intention" of the Framers, here very plainly evidenced, is binding on the Court for the reason early stated by Madison: if "the sense in which the Constitution was accepted and ratified by the Nation . . . be not the guide in expounding it, there can be no security for a consistent and stable [government], more than for a faithful exercise of its powers."[7]

The present generation, floating on a cloud of post-Warren Court euphoria, applauds a Court which read its libertarian convictions into the Fourteenth Amendment, forgetting that for generations the Court was harshly criticized because it had transformed laissez faire into constitutional dogma in order to halt the spread of "socialism."[8] With Brahmin restraint, Justice Holmes commented, in fear of socialism, "new principles had been discovered outside the bodies of those instruments

---

6. See infra Chapter 16 at notes 20–28.

7. 9 James Madison, *The Writings of James Madison* 191 (G. Hunt ed. 1900–1910).

8. Joseph H. Choate comprehended that he could rely on the Court to react to the red flag of communism which he waved in Pollock v. Farmers Loan & Trust Co., 157 U.S. 429, 532 (1895). Justice Stephen Field responded in a concurring opinion: "The present assault upon capital is but the beginning. It will be but the stepping stone to others, larger and more sweeping, till our own political contests will become a war of the poor against the rich." Id. 607. On rehearing, Justice Henry B. Brown dissented, saying, "the decision involves nothing less than a surrender of the taxing power to the moneyed class . . . Even the spectre of socialism is conjured up." 158 U.S. 601, 695 (1895). In 1893 Justice David J. Brewer referred to "'the black flag of anarchism, flaunting destruction to property,' and 'the red flag of socialism, inviting a redistribution of property.'" XVI Proceedings of the N.Y. State Bar Assn. 37, 47 (1893), quoted in A. T. Mason, "Myth and Reality in Supreme Court Drama," 48 Va. L. Rev. 1385, 1393 (1962). Such citations can be multiplied.

Justice Black reminded the Court of "the extent to which the evanescent standards of the majority's philosophy have been used to nullify state legislative programs passed to suppress evil economic practices." Rochin v. California, 342 U.S. 165, 177 (1952), concurring opinion.

[constitutions] which may be generalized into acceptance of the economic doctrines which prevailed about fifty years ago.'"[9] In the economic sphere that finally made due process a "dirty phrase."[10] The logic whereby that process becomes sanctified when employed for libertarian ideals has yet to be spelled out.[11] Logic, it is true, must yield to history, but history affords the Court even less support than logic.

Commentary on the Court's decisions frequently turns on whether they harmonize with the commentator's own predilections. My study may be absolved of that imputation: I regard segregation as a blot on our society,[12] and before I began to study the reapportionment issue I was taken with the beguiling slogan "one man, one vote." But almost thirty-five years ago I wrote of a decision that responded to my desires that I liked it no better when the Court read my predilections into the Constitution than when the Four Horsemen read in theirs.[13] Against the fulfillment of cherished ideals that turns on fortuitous appointments must be weighed the cost of warping the Constitution, of undermining "the rule of law." The Court has shown in

9. O. W. Holmes, Jr., *Collected Legal Papers* 184 (1920).

10. Herbert Packer, "The Aim of the Criminal Law Revisited: A Plea for a New Look at 'Substantive Due Process,'" 44 S. Cal. L. Rev. 490 (1971). See infra Chapter 14 at notes 64, 77–78.

11. See infra Chapter 14 at notes 80–90; and see Robert G. McCloskey, "Due Process and the Supreme Court: An Exhumation and Reburial," 1962 S. Ct. Rev. 34, 44–45. Although McCloskey was very sympathetic to the Warren Court's goals, he concluded that the distinction does not stand up. Id. at 51. Chief Justice Stone, wrote Learned Hand, "could not understand how . . . when concerned with interests other than property, the courts should have a wider latitude for enforcing their own predilections that when they were concerned with property itself." L. Hand, "Chief Justice Stone's Conception of the Judicial Function," 46 Colum. L. Rev. 696, 698 (1946).

12. One reads with horror of the Negro lynchings and torture that found their way into the courts as late as 1938. Paul Murphy, *The Constitution in Crisis Times, 1918–1969* 95, 123 (1972).

13. Raoul Berger, "Constructive Contempt: A Post Mortem," 9 U. Chi. L. Rev. 602, 604–605, 642 (1942).

the past that the Constitution can also be twisted to frustrate the needs of democracy.[14] These statements raise a congeries of questions which have been the subject of interminable controversy to which Part II is addressed.

The task here undertaken is that of an historian, to attempt accurately and faithfully to assemble the facts; that effort constitutes its own justification. For a decade the revisionist historians[15] have been engaged in what has been described as an "extraordinary revolution in the historiography" of Reconstruction,[16] throwing fresh light on the reasons for its limited objectives and its failure. To some extent the legal studies of Charles Fairman in 1949 and Alexander Bickel in 1955[17] had shown that the objectives of the framers of the Fourteenth Amendment were limited. Like the revisionist historians, a lawyer too may take another look after the passage of about a quarter-century. Despite the wilderness of commentary, largely devoted to the due process clause, the historical warrant for desegregation, reapportionment, and incorporation of the Bill of Rights in the due process clause remains controversial.[18] Little

14. For a withering condemnation of the Court's antidemocritarian course before 1937 see Henry Steele Commanger, "Judicial Review and Democracy," 19 Va. Quarterly Rev. 417 (1943).

15. W. R. Brock, Eric L. McKitrick, C. Vann Woodward, David Donald, Harold M. Hyman, Michael L. Benedict. Their works are listed in the bibliography.

16. Alfred H. Kelly, "Comment on Harold M. Hyman's Paper" in *New Frontiers of the American Reconstruction* 40 (H. M. Hyman ed. 1966).

17. C. Fairman, "Does the Fourteenth Amendment Incorporate the Bill of Rights?" 2 Stan. L. Rev. 5 (1949); Alexander Bickel, "The Original Understanding and the Segregation Decision," 69 Harv. L. Rev. 1 (1955).

18. See Alfred H. Kelly, "Clio and the Court: An Illicit Love Affair," 1965 S. Ct. Rev. 119, 132, 134–135; A. H. Kelly, "The Fourteenth Amendment Reconsidered: The Segregation Question," 54 Mich. L. Rev. 1049, 1081 (1956); Howard J. Graham, *Everyman's Constitution* 314 (1968); William W. Van Alstyne, "The Fourteenth Amendment, The 'Right' to Vote, and the Understanding of the Thirty-Ninth Congress," 1965 S. Ct. Rev. 33; Robert J. Harris, *The Quest for Equality* 55–56 (1960).

analysis has been devoted to the role of the privileges or immunities clause in the original scheme of things;[19] nor have studies of the equal protection and due process clauses adequately explored what those terms meant to the framers.

In reconstructing the past, historians generally are compelled to rely on accounts written after the event by participants and witnesses, or on the hearsay versions of those who learned at second-hand what had occurred. Such writings are subject to the infirmities of recollection, or of bias arising from allegiance to one side or the other. The historical records here relied on—the legislative history of the Fourteenth Amendment—are of a far more trustworthy character, being a stenographic transcription of what was said in the 39th Congress from day to day by those engaged in framing the Amendment. It is a verbatim account of what occurred, recorded while it was happening, comparable to a news film of an event at the moment it was taking place and free from the possible distortion of accounts drawn from recollection or hearsay. What men say while they are acting are themselves facts, as distinguished from opinions about facts.[20] Such statements constitute a reliable record of what happened as the Amendment was being forged by the framers.

It needs to be emphasized that the records of the 39th Congress are free from the reproach often leveled at legislative history—that it is "enigmatic." A statement such as that of Charles P. Curtis, "It is a hallucination: this search for intent. The room is always dark"[21] simply cannot stand up against these records. Instead of sparse, cryptic remarks there are, for

19. The leading article, D. O. McGovney, "Privileges and Immunities Clause, Fourteenth Amendment," 4 Iowa L. Bull. 219 (1918) states (at 222 note 2), "this essay . . . might have been entitled the Rule of the Slaughter-House Cases."

20. In Justice Holmes' words, a "party's conduct" may "consist in uttering certain words." O. W. Holmes, *The Common Law* 132 (1923).

21. "A Better Theory of Legal Interpretation," 3 Vand. L. Rev. 407, 409 (1950).

example, with respect to suffrage, the unequivocal Joint Report of the Committee on Reconstruction which drafted the Amendment; explanations of the Amendment and the antecedent Civil Rights Act of 1866 by the committee chairmen who had them in charge, and by other members of the committees; statements by leaders of the Republican Party which sponsored both, accompanied by a virtually unanimous chorus of fellow Republicans. These are commonly regarded as the best evidence of legislative "intention."[22] Then there are repeated rejections, by heavy pluralities, of extremist efforts to put through legislation or amendments that would confer suffrage. Thus, the records richly confirm Justice Harlan's comment: "The history of the Fourteenth Amendment with respect to suffrage qualifications is remarkably free of the problems which bedevil most attempts to find a reliable guide to present decision in the pages of the past. Instead, there is virtually unanimous agreement, clearly and repeatedly expressed, that §1 of the Amendment did not reach discriminatory voter disqualifications."[23]

In short, the proof is all but incontrovertible that the framers meant to leave control of suffrage with the States, which had always exercised such control, and to exclude federal intrusion. On traditional canons of interpretation, the intention of the framers being unmistakably expressed, that intention is as good as written into the text.[24] It is, therefore, as if the Amendment

22. H. M. Hart and A. Sacks, *The Legal Process: Basic Problems in the Making and Application of Law* 1266 (1958). Justice Frankfurter stated, "It has never been questioned in this Court that Committee reports, as well as statements by those in charge of a bill or of a report, are authoritative elucidations of the scope of a measure." Schwegmann Bros. v. Calvert Distillers Corp., 341 U.S. 384, 399–400 (1951), dissenting opinion. See also Lusky 45.

23. Oregon v. Mitchell, 400 U.S. 112, 200 (1970), dissenting opinion. Van Alstyne, who is critical of Justice Harlan's view in Reynolds v. Sims (supra note 1), states: "in none of the other kinds of cases where it was brought to bear did it [the historical record] cast the kind of blinding light that Mr. Justice Harlan sees here." Van Alstyne 36.

24. "A thing may be within the letter of a statute and not within its meaning, and within its meaning though not within its letter. The intention of

expressly stated that "control of suffrage shall be left with the States." If that intention is demonstrable, the "one man, one vote" cases represent an awesome exercise of power, an 180-degree revision, taking from the States a power that unmistakably was left to them. That poses the stark issue whether such revisory power was conferred on the Court. Because the "intention" of the framers is so crucial to examination of this issue, because a commentator should not pit his mere ipse dixit against the Court's finding, for example, that the historical evidence respecting desegregation is inconclusive, it is not enough to retort that the evidence is overwhelming. It is necessary to pile proof on proof, even at the risk of tedium, so that the reader may determine for himself whether it is overwhelming or inconclusive.

Whether the "original intention" of the framers should be binding on the present generation—a question hereafter discussed—should be distinguished from the issue: what did the framers mean to accomplish, what did the words they used mean to them. That must be the historical focus, not what we should like the words to mean in the light of current exigencies or changed ideals. In the words of the eminent British historians H. G. Richardson and G. O. Sayles, "We must learn, not from modern theorists, but from contemporaries of the events we are studying." We should not impose "upon the past a creature of our own imagining."[25] One hundred and fifty years earlier Justice James Iredell, one of the first Founders to spell out the case for judicial review, stated, "We are too apt, in estimating a law

----

the lawmaker is the law." Hawaii v. Mankichi, 190 U.S. 197, 212 (1903); United States v. Freeman, 44 U.S. (3 How.) 556, 565 (1845); United States v. Babbitt, 66 U.S. 55, 61 (1861); Matthew Bacon, *A New Abridgment of the Laws of England,* "Statutes" I (5) (7th ed. 1832); infra Chapter 9 note 22.

25. "Parliament and Great Councils in Medieval England," 77 L. Q. Rev. 213, 224 (1961). Miller and Howell label it an "historicist fallacy" to "appraise a former historical era by the criteria of values that have become important since." Supra note 3 at 673.

passed at a remote period, to combine in our consideration, all the subsequent events which have had an influence upon it, instead of confining ourselves (which we ought to do) to the existing circumstances at the time of its passing."[26]

In an area of warring interpretations no useful purpose is served by delivering another ex cathedra opinion.[27] A commentator should spread before the reader the evidence on which his opinion is based and comment both on discrepant evidence and on opposing inferences.[28] Consequently, a polemical tone is inescapable; a student of history can no more avoid criticism of views which seem to him erroneous than did the chemists who disputed the tenability of the phlogiston theory of combustion. To avoid that responsibility is to court the charge of ignoring an influential body of contrary opinion, of selecting only the evidence that advances one's own argument, and, even worse, to cast the reader adrift on a sea of conflicting opinions.

Now that the dust has settled, a synthesis of the historical materials that bear on the three controversial areas will furnish some cross-illumination. No synthesis need undertake to trace in complete detail the development of the Amendment and its antecedent bills. Not only is there no need to duplicate the chronological labors that others have already performed, but to do so is to risk swamping the reader in a mass of detail that is bewildering rather than illuminating.[29] Instead my effort will be

26. Ware v. Hylton, 3 U.S. (3 Dall.) 199, 267 (1796). In "the construction of the language of the Constitution . . . as indeed in all other instances where construction becomes necessary, we are to place ourselves as nearly as possible in the condition of the men who framed that instrument." Ex parte Bain, 121 U.S. 1, 12 (1887).

27. It is unsatisfying to have the fastidiously detailed study of Fairman dismissed with the phrase that it is "in the opinion of this writer against the weight of the evidence." Kelly, Fourteenth 1081 note 106. As will develop, Kelly was altogether wrong.

28. Sir Herbert Butterfield, *George III and the Historians* 225 (1969).

29. See Bickel; Joseph B. James, *The Framing of the Fourteenth Amendment* (1956); and Harry Flack, *The Adoption of the Fourteenth Amendment* (1908).

to focus on the facts that seem to me crucial, to take account of discrepant facts, and to analyze views that are opposed to mine.

Following the lead of Howard Jay Graham and Jacobus tenBroek,[30] academicians have shown a growing tendency to attribute to the framers of the Fourteenth Amendment moral-legal conceptions formulated by some abolitionists during their crusade of the 1830s–1860s, and to read those conceptions of substantive due process and equal protection into the Amendment. Noble enthusiasm is no less prone to distort the vision than vulgar prejudice. In evaluating the historical facts we do well to bear in mind Flaubert's view that "personal sympathy, genuine emotion, twitching nerves and tear-filled eyes only impair the sharpness of the artist's vision."[31] Even more, the historian, in the words of C. Vann Woodward, has "a special obligation to sobriety and fidelity to the record."[32]

BACKGROUND

The key to an understanding of the Fourteenth Amendment is that the North was shot through with Negrophobia, that the Republicans, except for a minority of extremists, were swayed by the racism that gripped their constituents rather than by abolitionist ideology. At the inception of their crusade the abolitionists peered up at an almost unscalable cliff. Charles Sumner, destined to become a leading spokesman for extreme abolition-

---

Walter Bagehot considered that "history should be like a Rembrandt etching, casting a vivid light on important causes and leaving all the rest unseen, in shadow." Quoted in Van Wyck Brooks, *Days of the Phoenix* 135 (1957).

30. Graham; Jacobus tenBroek, *Equal Under Law* (1965). For discussion of the Graham-tenBroek neoabolitionist theory see infra Chapter 13.

31. 4 Arnold Hauser, *The Social History of Art* 76 (Vintage Books, undated). Hauser states that Flaubert's view was shared by the Goncourts, Maupassant, Gide, Valery, and others. "To get at the truth of our system of morality (and equally of the law)," said Holmes, "it is useful to omit the emotion and ask ourselves [how far] those generalizations . . . are confirmed by fact accurately ascertained." O. W. Holmes, Jr., *Collected Legal Papers* 306 (1920).

32. *The Burden of Southern History* 87 (1960).

ist views, wrote in 1834, upon his first sight of slaves, "My worst preconception of their appearance and their ignorance did not fall as low as their actual stupidity . . . They appear to be nothing more than moving masses of flesh unendowed with anything of intelligence above the brutes."[33] Tocqueville's impression in 1831–32 was equally abysmal.[34] He noticed that in the North, "the prejudice which repels the negroes seems to increase in proportion as they are emancipated," that prejudice "appears to be stronger in the States which have abolished slavery, than in those where it still exists."[35]

Little wonder that the abolitionist campaign was greeted with loathing! In 1837 Elijah Lovejoy, an abolitionist editor, was murdered by an Illinois mob.[35a] How shallow was the impress of the abolitionist campaign on such feelings is graphically re-

---

33. David Donald, *Charles Sumner and the Coming of the Civil War* 29 (1960).

34. "[W]e can scarcely acknowledge the common features of mankind in this child of debasement whom slavery has brought among us. His physiognomy to our eyes is hideous, his understanding weak, his tastes low; and we are almost inclined to look upon him as a being intermediate between man and the brutes." 1 Alexis de Tocqueville, *Democracy in America* 363 (1900). In the 39th Congress, Robert Hale of New York stated that the District of Columbia "contains a black population which, undoubtedly, approaches to the very extreme of ignorance and degradation . . . a population that has come into this District suddenly, just freed from slavery, with all the marks and burdens upon them that a state of slavery necessarily fixes upon its victims." *Cong. Globe,* 39th Cong. 1st Sess. 280 (1865–1866), hereinafter cited as *Globe.* In citations to the *Globe,* Senators will be identified as such; all others are representatives.

Even one sympathetic to the Negro cause, Senator Henry Wilson of Massachusetts, was constrained to hope in 1864 that "the school house will rise to enlighten the darkened intellect of a race imbruted by long years of enforced ignorance." Quoted in tenBroek, 164.

35. Tocqueville, supra note 34 at 365, 364.

35a. "[T]he abolitionists were regarded throughout most Northern circles as disagreeable and intemperate radicals and were heckled, harrowed, assaulted and even killed by Northern mobs." Dan Lacy, *The White Use of Blacks in America* 54 (1972).

vealed in a Lincoln incident. A delegation of Negro leaders had called on him at the White House, and he told them,

> There is an unwillingness on the part of our people, harsh as it may be, for you free colored people to remain with us . . . [E]ven when you cease to be slaves, you are far removed from being placed on an equality with the white man . . . I cannot alter it if I would. It is a fact.[36]

Fear of Negro invasion—that the emancipated slaves would flock north in droves—alarmed the North.[37] The letters and diaries of Union soldiers, Woodward notes, reveal an "enormous amount of antipathy towards Negroes"; popular convictions "were not prepared to sustain" a commitment to equality.[38] Racism, David Donald remarks, "ran deep in the North," and the suggestion that "Negroes should be treated as equals to white men woke some of the deepest and ugliest fears in the American mind."[39]

36. Woodward, supra note 32 at 81. "In virtually every phase of existence Negroes found themselves systematically separated from whites [in the North, 1860] . . . in most places he encountered severe limitations to the protection of his life, liberty, and property." Leon Litwack, North of Slavery: The Negro in the Free States 91–97 (1961), quoted in C. Vann Woodward, "Seeds of Failure in Radical Race Policy" in Hyman supra note 16 at 126.

37. Woodward, "Seeds," supra note 36 at 127, 128, 131, 132. Senator Thomas A. Hendricks of Indiana stated, "The policy of the State has been to discourage their immigration . . . to protect white labor. The presence of negroes in large numbers tends to degrade and cheapen labor, and the people have been unwilling that the white laborer shall be compelled to compete for employment with the Negro." Globe 2939. The Freedmen's Bureau and Civil Rights Acts "were intended not only to protect the freedmen but also to secure a contented black labor force who . . . stayed in the South." Morton Keller, Affairs of State 65, 143 (1977).

38. Woodward, supra note 32 at 82, 83. Senator James R. Doolittle of Wisconsin reported that "four out of five" Wisconsin soldiers "voted against Negro suffrage." Globe 2165.

39. David Donald, Charles Sumner and the Rights of Man 202, 252 (1970). An Illinois Radical, John F. Farnsworth, said " 'Negro equality' is the everlasting

One need not look beyond the confines of the debates in the 39th Congress to find abundant confirmation. Time and again Republicans took account of race prejudice as an inescapable fact. George W. Julian of Indiana referred to the "proverbial hatred" of Negroes, Senator Henry S. Lane of Indiana to the "almost ineradicable prejudice," Shelby M. Cullom of Illinois to the "morbid prejudice," Senator William M. Stewart of Nevada to the "nearly insurmountable" prejudice, James F. Wilson of Iowa to the "iron-cased prejudice" against blacks. These were Republicans, sympathetic to emancipation and the protection of civil rights.[40] Then there were the Democratic racists who unashamedly proclaimed that the Union should remain a "white man's" government.[41] In the words of Senator Garrett Davis of Kentucky, "The white race . . . will be proprietors of the land, and the blacks its cultivators; such is their destiny."[42] Let it

---

skeleton which frightens some people." *Globe* 204. William E. Niblack of Indiana reminded the Congress that in 1851 Indiana ratified a Constitution that excluded Negroes from the State by a vote of 109, 976 to 21,084. *Globe* 3212.

"A belief in racial equality," said W. R. Brock, "was an abolitionist invention"; "to the majority of men in the midnineteenth century it seemed to be condemned both by experience and by science." "Even abolitionists," he states, "were anxious to disclaim any intention of forcing social contacts between the races." Brock, *An American Crisis: Congress and Reconstruction* 285, 286 (1963). See infra, Derrick Bell, Chapter 10 at note 6. Racism, Phillip Paludan states, was "as pervasive during Reconstruction as after. Americans clung firmly to a belief in the basic inferiority of the Negro race, a belief supported by the preponderance of nineteenth-century scientific evidence." P. S. Paludan, *A Covenant with Death* 54 (1975). See also Keller, supra note 37. Many Republican newspapers in the North opposed "equality with the Negroes." Flack 41. See also Keller, id. at 51, 58, 65.

40. *Globe* 257, 739, 911, 2799, 2948.

41. John W. Chanler of New York, *Globe* 48, 218; Senator James W. Nesmith of Oregon, id. 291; Aaron Harding of Kentucky, id. 448; Senator Hendricks of Indiana, id. 880; Senator Garrett Davis of Kentucky, id. 246–250. The sympathetic reformer, Senator William M. Stewart of Nevada, stated, the "white man's government . . . should not be scoffed at; that it was a prejudice in the country that no man has a right to disregard." Id. 1437.

42. Id. 935.

be regarded as political propaganda, and, as the noted British historiographer Sir Herbert Butterfield states, it "does at least presume an audience—perhaps a 'public opinion'—which is judged to be susceptible to the kinds of arguments and considerations set before it."[43] Consider, too, that the Indiana Constitution of 1851 excluded Negroes from the State, as did Oregon,[44] that a substantial number of Northern States recently had rejected Negro suffrage,[45] that others maintained segregated schools.[46] It is against this backdrop that we must measure claims that the framers of the Fourteenth Amendment swallowed abolitionist ideology hook, line, and sinker.[47]

The framers represented a constituency that had just emerged from a protracted, bitterly fought war, a war that had left them physically and emotionally drained. It had begun with a commitment to save the Union and had gone on to emancipate the slaves. Now the war-weary North was far from anxious to embark on fresh crusades for the realization of still other abolitionist goals.[48] While emancipation largely hit slavery in the South, eradication of inequality, as Vann Woodward remarked, required "a revolution for the North as well,"[49] a revolution for which most Republicans were utterly unprepared. Then too, the fact that Republicans and Democrats had been pretty evenly matched over the years, that some districts definitely were swing areas, led Republicans in those areas to be cautious of affronting their constituents.[50] Many moderate and conservative Repub-

---

43. Butterfield, supra note 28 at 226; compare Stewart, supra note 41.

44. For Indiana see supra note 39; for Oregon, see Fairman, Stanford 32 note 58.

45. See Van Alstyne's summary, infra Chapter 4 at note 16.

46. See infra Chapter 7 at note 41. As late as 1859 the Ohio Court rejected an attack on segregated schools. Van Camp v. Board of Education, 9 Ohio 407.

47. For additional details see infra Chapter 13.

48. Donald, *Sumner II* 232–233; see also id. at 158.

49. Woodward, supra note 32 at 79; see infra Chapter 10 at note 6.

50. David Donald, *The Politics of Reconstruction* 12–13, 61–62 (1965).

licans, as we shall see, were acutely aware of the impact on elections of sweeping radical claims for political, let alone, social, equality for the blacks.[51] While most men were united in a desire to protect the freedmen from outrage and oppression in the South by prohibiting discrimination with respect to "fundamental rights," without which freedom was illusory, to go beyond this with a campaign for political and social equality was, as Senator James R. Doolittle of Wisconsin confessed, "frightening" to the Republicans who "represented States containing the despised and feared free negroes."[52]

A striking reflection of Northern sentiment was furnished by Thaddeus Stevens, the foremost Radical leader. According to his biographer, Fawn M. Brodie, he

> sensed . . . that talk of "social equality" was dangerous politics. When he heard that the ex-slave Frederick Douglass . . . had paraded arm-in-arm with editor Theodore Tilton, he wrote . . . "A good many people here are disturbed by the practical exhibition of social equality in the arm-in-arm performance of Douglass and Tilton. It does not become radicals like us to particularly object. But it was certainly unfortunate at this time. The old prejudice, now revived, will lose us some votes."[53]

As Stevens revealed, most Republicans were politicians first and ideologues afterward.[54] Not civil rights for blacks but the dreaded take-over of the federal government by the South was their obsessive preoccupation. Emancipation brought the startling realization that Southern representation would no longer be limited in the House of Representatives to three-fifths of the

51. Speaking on June 4, 1966, James Wilson of Iowa said, "I know that many look forward to the fall elections and shiver in the presence of impartial suffrage." *Globe* 2948.

52. Donald, *Sumner II* 158.

53. *Thaddeus Stevens: Scourge of the South* 287 (1959).

54. See James 71.

blacks, as Article I, §3, provided. Now each voteless freedman counted as a whole person; and in the result Southern States would be entitled to increased representation and, with the help of Northern Democrats, would have, Thaddeus Stevens pointed out at the very outset of the 39th Congress, "a majority in Congress and in the Electoral College." With equal candor he said that the Southern States "ought never to be recognized as valid States, until the Constitution shall be amended . . . as to secure perpetual ascendancy" to the Republican party.[55] The North had not fought and quelled rebellion in order to surrender the fruits of victory to the unrepentant rebels. How to circumvent this possibility was the central concern of the Republicans, and it found expression in §2 of the Fourteenth Amendment, which reduced representation in proportion as the right to vote was denied or abridged. Unless we seize hold of the fact that, to borrow from Russell R. Nye, "what lies beneath the politics of the Reconstruction period, so far as it touched the Negro, is the prevailing racist policy tacitly accepted by both parties and by the general public,"[56] we shall fail to appreciate the limited objectives of the Fourteenth Amendment. That is the reality underlying the limited purposes of the framers of the Fourteenth Amendment, and which circumscribes the so-called "generality" of "equal protection" and "due process."

Proponents of a broad construction of the Amendment have assumed that advocates of a restricted construction have the

55. *Globe* 74; Samuel E. Morison, *The Oxford History of the American People* 714 (1965). Senator John Sherman of Ohio said, "never by my consent shall these rebels gain by this war increased political power, and come back here to wield that political power." *Globe* 745. "I would no more admit the rebels to control these States," said Senator Daniel Clark of New Hampshire, "than I would sail a ship with the mutinous part of a crew, and confine those who were faithful to the captain in the hold or put them in irons." Id. 835.

56. "Comment on C. V. Woodward's Paper," in Hyman, supra note 16 at 148, 151.

burden of proving that the framers' objectives were limited. The shoe is on the other foot; an interpretation that invades what had long been considered the exclusive province of the States, as, for example, criminal procedure, requires some justification. It is not enough in that situation that the words are capable of a broad meaning; the reservation to the States in the Tenth Amendment of powers not delegated to the federal government calls for a clear showing that the successor amendment was designed to curtail those reserved powers.[57] Over the years the Supreme Court, to be sure, has steadily eroded those reserved powers, but this simply represents another of the usurpations that bestrew the path of the Court. But the historian, looking to the Constitution itself, may not be blind to the fact that, in the words of Willard Hurst, the reservation "represented a political bargain, key terms of which assumed the continuing vitality of the states as prime law makers in most af-

57. The governing rule was laid down by Chief Justice Marshall: "an opinion which is . . . to establish a principle never before recognized, should be expressed in plain and explicit terms." United States v. Burr, 25 F. Cas. (No. 14,693) 55, 165 (C.C. Va. 1807). Long before it was stated, "statutes are not presumed to make any alteration in the common law, farther or otherwise than the act expressly declares: therefore in all general matters the law presumes the act did not intend to make any alteration; for if the parliament had had that design they would have expressed it in the act." Bacon's *Abridgment,* supra note 24, "Statutes" I (4). An analogous rule was applied to the Constitution in the Slaughter-House Cases, 83 U.S. (16 Wall.) 36, 78 (1872).

Such views were given striking reaffirmation in Pierson v. Ray, 386 U.S. 547, 554–555 (1967). After adverting to the common law immunity of judges from suits for acts performed in their official capacity, the Court stated, "We do not believe that this settled principle was abolished by §1983, which makes liable 'every person' who under color of law deprives another person of his civil rights . . . The immunity of judges [is] well established and we presume that Congress would have specifically so provided had it wished to abolish the doctrine." Thus the all-inclusive "every person" was curtailed because of an existing common law immunity; the express reservation of power to the States by the Tenth Amendment demands an even more exacting standard.

fairs."[58] No trace of an intention by the Fourteenth Amendment
to encroach on State control—for example, of suffrage and
segregation—is to be found in the records of the 39th Congress.
A mass of evidence is to the contrary, and, as will appear, the attachment of the framers to State sovereignty played a major
role in restricting the scope of the Amendment. "[W]e ought to
remember," Justice Holmes said, "the great caution shown by
the Constitution in limiting the power of the States, and should
be slow to construe the [due process] clause in the Fourteenth
Amendment as committing to the Court, with no guide but the
Court's own discretion the validity of whatever laws the States
may pass."[59] The history of the Amendment buttresses the flat
statement that no such jurisdiction was conferred.

"What, after all," asked Wallace Mendelson, "are the privileges and immunities of United States citizenship? What process
is 'due' in what circumstances? and what is 'equal protection?'"[60] Study of what the terms meant to the framers indicates
that there was no mystery. The three clauses of §1 were three
facets of one and the same concern: to insure that there would
be no discrimination against the freedmen in respect of "fundamental rights," which had clearly understood and narrow
compass. Roughly speaking, the substantive rights were identified by the privileges or immunities clause; the equal protection
clause was to bar legislative discrimination with respect to those
rights; and the judicial machinery to secure them was to be supplied by nondiscriminatory due process of the several States.
Charles Sumner summarized these radical goals: let the Negro
have "the shield of *impartial laws*. Let him be heard in court."[61]
That shield, it will be shown, was expressed in "equal protection of the *laws;* access to protection by the courts found expres-

58. *The Legitimacy of the Business Corporation in the Law of the United States*
140 (1970).
59. Baldwin v. Missouri, 28 U.S. 586, 595 (1930), dissenting opinion.
60. *The Supreme Court: Law and Discretion* 16 (1967).
61. *Globe* 675.

sion in "due process of law." The framers, it needs to be said at once, had no thought of creating unfamiliar rights of unknown, far-reaching extent by use of the words "equal protection" and "due process." Instead, they meant to secure familiar, "fundamental rights," and only those, and to guard them as of yore against deprivation except by (1) a nondiscriminatory law, and (2) the established judicial procedure of the State.

2

Privileges or Immunities

No State shall . . . abridge the privileges or immunities of citizens of the United States

THE "privileges or immunities" clause was the central provision of the Amendment's §1, and the key to its meaning is furnished by the immediately preceding Civil Rights Act of 1866,[1] which, all are agreed, it was the purpose of the Amendment to embody and protect. The objectives of the Act were quite limited. The framers intended to confer on the freedmen the auxiliary rights that would protect their "life, liberty, and property,"—no more. For the framers those words did not have the sprawling connotations later given them by the Court but, instead, restricted aims that were expressed in the Act. The legislative history of the Amendment frequently refers to "fundamental rights," "life, liberty, and property," and a few historical comments will show the ties between the two.

At Locke's hands, said Edward S. Corwin, natural law dissolves "into the rights of 'life, liberty, and estate,'" a derivation noted by Francis Bacon. The trinity was reiterated by Sir Matthew Hale[2] and sharply etched by Blackstone in his chapter on "The Absolute Rights of Individuals":

---

1. Act of April 9, 1866, ch. 21, 14 Stat. 27.
2. Edward S. Corwin, "The 'Higher Law' Background of American Constitutional Law," 42 Harv. L. Rev. 149, 365, 383 (1928).

these may be reduced to three principal or primary articles . . . I. The right of personal security [consisting] in a
person's legal and uninterrupted enjoyment of his life, his
limbs . . . II. . . . the personal liberty of individuals . . .
[consisting] in the power of locomotion, of changing situations or moving one's person to whatsoever place one's own
inclination may direct, without imprisonment, or restraint,
unless by due course of law . . . III. The third absolute right,
inherent in every Englishman . . . of property: which consists
in the free use, enjoyment and disposal of all his acquisitions,
without any control or diminution, save only by the laws of the
land.[3]

For Blackstone "due course of law" and the "laws of the land"
did not enlarge, they did not add to, the "absolute rights" of an
Englishman, but rather marked the sole means whereby those
rights might be diminished. These "absolute," "fundamental"
rights of "life, liberty, and property" referred, in sum, to (1)
personal security; (2) freedom of locomotion; and (3) ownership and disposition of property.

On this side of the water the opening Resolve of the First
Continental Congress affirmed that the Colonists "by the im-
mutable laws of nature, the principles of the British Constitution . . . 'are entitled to life, liberty, and property.'"[4] Blackstone, whose work was widely circulated in the Colonies, was
cited in Federalist No. 84 and paraphrased by Kent.[5] Instead of
the "absolute rights" of "life, liberty, and property" the Framers resorted to the terminology of Article IV, §2: "The Citizens

3. 1 William Blackstone, *Commentaries on the Laws of England* 129, 134, 138
(1765–1769). These "rights" were read to the House by James F. Wilson,
chairman of the House Judiciary Committee, in his exposition of the Civil
Rights Bill. *Globe* 1118.

4. Henry S. Commager, *Documents of American History* 83 (7th ed. 1963).

5. 1 James Kent, *Commentaries on American Law* 607 (9th ed. 1853): "The
absolute rights of individuals may be resolved into the right of personal security, the right of personal liberty, and the right to enjoy and acquire property."
This too was quoted by Wilson, supra note 3.

of each State shall be entitled to all Privileges and Immunities of Citizens in the several States." These words were construed "confiningly" by Justice Bushrod Washington on circuit, in *Corfield v. Coryell,* as comprising "fundamental" rights such as freedom of movement, freedom from discriminatory taxes and impositions, ownership of property, access to the courts.[6]

For the "principal spokesmen" and theorists of the abolitionist movement, Lysander Spooner and Joel Tiffany, "privileges and immunities" meant that a citizen has a right "to full and ample protection in the enjoyment of his personal security, personal liberty, and private property . . . protection against oppression . . . against lawless violence."[7] This echoes Blackstone's formulation and in large part anticipates the privileges embodied in the Civil Rights Act of 1866. The sponsors of the Act, Senator Lyman Trumbull and Representative James F. Wilson, chairmen respectively of the Senate and House Judiciary committees, cited Blackstone, Kent, and *Coryell,* as did others.[8] And John A. Bingham, draftsman of the Amendment, stated that he had drawn the "privileges or immunities" clause of the Fourteenth Amendment from Article IV, §2.[9]

THE CIVIL RIGHTS ACT OF 1866

The meaning and scope of the Fourteenth Amendment are greatly illuminated by the debates in the 39th Congress on the antecedent Civil Rights Act of 1866. As Charles Fairman stated, "over and over in this debate [on the Amendment] the correspondence between Section One of the Amendment and the Civil Rights Act is noted. The provisions of the one are treated as though they were essentially identical with those of the

---

6. 6 F. Cas. (No. 3230) 546 (C.C.E.D. Pa. 1823); the full quotation is set forth infra at notes 41–43.

7. TenBroek, 108, 110.

8. *Globe* 474–475, 1118, 2765.

9. Id. 1034.

other."[10] George R. Latham of West Virginia, for example, stated that "the 'civil rights bill' which is now a law . . . covers exactly the same ground as this amendment."[11] In fact, the Amendment was designed to *"constitutionalize"* the Act,[12] that is, to "embody" it in the Constitution so as to remove doubt as to its constitutionality and to place it beyond the power of a later Congress to repeal. An ardent advocate of an abolitionist reading of the Amendment, Howard Jay Graham, stated that "virtually every speaker in the debates on the Fourteenth Amendment—Republican and Democrat alike—said or agreed that the Amendment was designed to embody or incorporate the Civil Rights Act."[13]

10. Fairman, Stanford 44. It "was in these debates," said Alfred Kelly, that "the Radical [?] ideas as to how far federal guarantees of civil rights as against state action might properly extend, both by legislation and by constitutional amendment, were first clearly set down. The debates on the Civil Rights Act are also important . . . because the Civil Rights Act bore an extremely close relationship to the passage of the Fourteenth Amendment itself." Kelly, Fourteenth 1057.

11. *Globe* 2883.

12. Stevens, id. 2459; Kelly, Fourteenth 1071. Bingham strongly doubted the "power of Congress to pass" the Civil Rights Bill and insisted upon proceeding by amendment, id. 1291–1292; his doubts were shared by Henry J. Raymond, id. 2502, presumably, as Senator Henderson explained, because the Thirteenth Amendment went no further than to free the slaves. *Appendix to Globe* 122 (hereinafter *Globe App.*). John M. Broomall of Pennsylvania, Thomas D. Eliot of Massachusetts, and Senator James R. Doolittle of Wisconsin also thought it designed to remove constitutional doubts, id. 2498, 2511, 2896. Others like Stevens, James A. Garfield and Rufus P. Spalding of Ohio, and Senator Howard wanted to make the Act secure against repeal by a successor Congress, id. 2459, 2462, 2509, 2896. See also Henry Van Aernam of New York, id. 3069, Thayer, id. 2465. See also infra Chapter 6 at notes 18–19. For additional citations, see tenBroek 244 note 11.

13. Graham 291 note 73; Bickel 47; tenBroek 201, 203, 224; Benjamin Kendrick, *The Journal of the Joint Committee of Fifteen on Reconstruction* 350 (1914). Flack, a devotee of a broad construction of the Fourteenth Amendment, states, "nearly all said that it was but an incorporation of the Civil Rights Bill . . . there was no controversy as to its purpose and meaning." Flack 81, id. 54, 79.

Section 1 of the Civil Rights Bill provided in pertinent part,

That there shall be *no discrimination in civil* rights or immunities . . . on account of race . . . but the inhabitants of every
race . . . shall have the *same* right to make and enforce contracts, to sue, be parties, and give evidence, to inherit, purchase,
lease, sell, hold and convey real and personal property, and to
full and *equal benefit* of all laws and proceedings for the *security* of
person and property, and shall be subject to *like* punishment . . . and no other.[14]

The specific enumeration was in response to a sentiment expressed at the very outset by Senator John Sherman, who desired to secure such rights to the freedmen, "naming them, defining precisely what they should be."[15] Shortly stated,

14. Section 1 of the Bill is set out in *Globe* 474 (emphasis added); see also
supra note 1. It was anticipated by the Missouri Constitution of 1865: "no
person can, on account of color, be disqualified as a witness, or be disabled to
contract otherwise than as others are disabled, or be prevented from acquiring . . . property, or be liable to any other punishment for any offense
than that imposed upon others for a like offense . . . or be subjected in law,
to any other restraints or qualifications in regard to any personal rights other
than such as are laid upon others under like circumstances." 2 Ben P. Poore,
Federal and State Constitutions, Colonial Charters 1136 (1877).

"The master class looked upon any offense as more reprehensible (and
therefore subject to more severe penalties) when committed by a slave than
when committed by a white man." Kenneth M. Stampp, *The Peculiar Institution* 124 (Vintage Books, 1956).

15. *Globe* 42. In a letter to Sumner in 1865, Justin Morrill, soon to be Senator, doubtful whether his suggested words "civil rights, immunities, privileges [have] such a precise and definite meaning as to be practicable," asked
"must we specify, rights . . . to hold property, be a party and witness."
James 30.

A significant shift from the phraseology of the predecessor Freedmen's
Bureau Bill was made in the Civil Rights Bill; the former referred to "civil
rights or immunities . . . *including* the right to make and enforce contracts,"
etc., Bickel 8 (emphasis added); but the Civil Rights Bill phrase "no discrimination in civil rights" was deleted (see infra, Chapter 7 at notes 11–15), leaving
the provision that blacks should "have the same right to make and enforce
contracts," etc., a specific and exclusive enumeration. See infra at notes 15–17.

freedmen were to have the same *enumerated* rights (as white men), be subject to like punishment, suffer no discrimination with respect to civil rights, and have the equal benefit of all laws for the security of person and property. Patently these were limited objectives; the rights enumerated, said William Lawrence of Ohio, were the "*necessary incidents* of these absolute rights," that is, of "life, liberty, and property," lacking which those "fundamental rights" could not be enjoyed.[16] It was these "enumerated rights," "stated in the bill," said Martin Thayer of Pennsylvania, that were "the fundamental rights of citizenship."[17]

Section 1 of the Bill was a studied response to a perceived evil, the Black Codes,[18] which the Republicans averred were designed to set emancipation at naught, to restore the shackles of the prior Slave Codes, and to return the blacks to serfdom. The Bill was necessary, Senator Henry Wilson of Massachusetts said, because the new Black Codes were "nearly as iniquitous as the old slave codes."[19] Citing the prewar Slave Code of Mississippi, which prohibited the entry of a free Negro into the State, travel from one county to another, serving as a preacher, teaching slaves, and so on, Senator Trumbull stated that "the purpose of the bill . . . is to destroy all these discrimi-

16. *Globe* 1883, emphasis added. Senator Sherman said the Bill "defines what are the incidents of freedom." Id. 744. A leading Republican, Samuel Shellabarger of Ohio, explained that "those rights to contract, sue," etc. are "necessary . . . [for] the protection of the rights of person and property of a citizen." Id. 1293.

17. Id. 1151; fully quoted infra note 39.

18. For citations to collections of the Codes, see Bickel 14 note 35.

19. *Globe* 603. The Codes, Wilson said, "Practically made slaves of men we have declared to be free." Id. 39. They "set up elaborate systems of bound apprenticeship, labor restrictions, vagrancy laws, limits on property ownership and craft employment. They prescribed white supervision over almost every aspect of black lives . . . The bald declaration of Edmund Rhett of South Carolina—'the general interest both of the white man and of the negroes requires that he should be kept as near to the condition of slavery as possible' . . . —sums up the purpose of the Black Codes." Morton Keller, *Affairs of State* 203–204 (1977).

nations."[20] References to the Black Codes stud the debates:[21] they were described as "atrocious" and "malignant."[22] Samuel W. Moulton of Illinois, William Windom of Minnesota, Thomas D. Eliot of Massachusetts, and Senator Daniel Clark of New Hampshire considered that the Bill was needed to protect the Negro against "damnable violence" "wrong and outrage," "fiendish oppression," "barbarous cruelties."[23] As Senator John B. Henderson, a Republican from Missouri, stated, "though nominally free, so far as discriminating legislation could make him [the black] so he was yet a slave."[24] Republicans did not have to travel beyond the halls of Congress to savor Southern recalcitrance. Toward the close of the debates, Benjamin G. Harris of Maryland, an old-line Democrat, said,

> The States will still retain control and govern in their own way that portion of their population without leave asked of the United States. Mr. Speaker, all the efforts made here or elsewhere to educate the negro to an equality with the white man in the southern States, either civilly, socially or politically, are per-

20. *Globe* 474.

21. Senator Sumner, id. 95; Senator Timothy Howe of Wisconsin, id. 443; Ignatius Donnelly, id. 588; Senator Daniel Clark, id. 833; Burton C. Cook, id. 1124; William Higby, id. 2882. See the Opelusa Ordinance, id. 516–517. Senator Clark stated, the Master "will allow him no home, that he may become a vagrant. Becoming a vagrant, he will arrest him as a vagabond, and visit him with imprisonment and stripes . . . He will shut him off from the courts, seal his mouth as a witness." *Globe* 834. Cook stated, "Vagrant laws have been passed: laws which under the pretense of selling these men as vagrants, are calculated and intended to reduce them to slavery again." *Globe* 1123.

22. Senator Wilson, id. 603; Cook, id. 1123; James Wilson, "barbaric and inhuman," id. 1118.

23. Id. 631, 1159, 2773, 833. Whether the effects of the Black Codes were exaggerated or not is not nearly as important as the aversion to them; it "is incorporated by reference into congressional statements of objectives; it plays a large part in defining those objectives, regardless of the extent to which it was founded on reality and regardless of the motives which underlay its creation." Bickel 14.

24. *Globe* 3034.

fectly idle. The negro must be kept in subordination to the white man."[25]

So it proved.

The explanations of the Civil Rights Bill by the respective committee chairmen made its limited objectives entirely clear. Speaking to "civil rights and immunities," House Chairman Wilson asked,

> What do these terms mean? Do they mean that in all things, civil, social, political, all citizens, without distinction of race or color, shall be equal? By no means can they be so construed . . . Nor do they mean that all citizens shall sit on juries, or that their children shall attend the same schools. These are not civil rights and immunities. Well, what is the meaning? What are civil rights? I understand civil rights to be simply the absolute rights of individuals, such as "The right of personal security, the right of personal liberty, and the right to acquire and enjoy property."

quoting Chancellor Kent.[26] Of "immunities" Wilson said that a black should "not be subjected to obligations, duties, pains and

25. Id. 3172, 3174.

26. Id. 1117. Wilson quoted *Bouvier's Law Dictionary:* "Civil rights are those which have no relation to the establishment, support, or management of government." Id. Alfred Kelly states that Wilson "declared for a narrow interpretation of the measure in unequivocal terms." Kelly, Fourteenth 1066. But at another point he states that Wilson asserted *"vaguely* that civil rights were only the 'natural rights of man.'" Id. (emphasis added). Such "vagueness" is dispelled by Thayer's explanation infra. See also note 55 infra.

Josiah Grinnell of Iowa said, "A recognition of natural rights is one thing, a grant of political franchises quite another." TenBroek 170. Senator Howard stated, the purpose of the Civil Rights Bill "is to secure to these men whom we have made free the ordinary rights of a freeman and nothing else." Id. 504. "Wilson thus presented the Civil Rights Bill to the House as a measure of limited and definite objectives. In this he followed the lead of the majority in the Senate . . . And the line he laid down was followed by others who spoke for the bill in the House." Bickel 17.

penalties from which other citizens are exempted . . . This is
the spirit and scope of the bill, and it does not go one step
beyond."[27] M. Russell Thayer of Pennsylvania stated that "to
avoid any misapprehension" as to what the "fundamental rights
of citizenship" are, "they are stated in the bill. The same section
goes on to define with great particularity the civil rights and immunities which are to be protected by the bill." And, he added,
"when those civil rights which are first referred to in general
terms [that is, civil rights and immunities] are subsequently
enumerated, that enumeration precludes any possibility that the
general words which have been used can be extended beyond
the particulars which have been enumerated," that the Bill was
for "the protection of the fundamental rights of citizenship and
nothing else."[28] Wilson emphasized that the rights enumerated
were no "greater than the rights which are included in the general terms 'life, liberty, and property.'"[29] He did not proceed

27. *Globe* 1117.

28. Id. 1151. As Madison said in Federalist No. 41: "For what purpose
could the enumeration of particular powers be inserted, if these and all others
were meant to be included in the preceding general powers? Nothing is more
natural or common than first to use a general phrase, and to explain and qualify it by a recital of particulars. But the idea of particulars which neither explain nor qualify the general meaning . . . is an absurdity." Modern Lib. ed.
269 (1937). Lawrence, an Ohio Radical, said, "the privileges referred to in the
Constitution are such as are fundamental civil rights, not political rights nor
those dependent on local law." *Globe* 1836.

29. *Globe* 1295. While tenBroek, 110, defines privileges and immunities as
the right of a citizen to have "protection in the enjoyment of his personal security, personal liberty, and private property . . . protection against the ag-
gression of individuals, communities . . . and domestic states against lawless
violence exercised under the form of governmental authority," and while
Graham, 236, states the "abolitionist position" was to seek "protection for the
fundamental rights of life, liberty, and property," neither is really cognizant of
the fact that the Civil Rights Act, and hence the "constitutionalizing" Fourteenth Amendment, had enumerated and defined these rights in restricted
terms. I would also, therefore, take exception to Fairman's statement that
"vague aspirations" were hung on "privileges or immunities." Fairman, Stanford 139.

from the dictionary but responded to a sentiment unequivocally articulated by James W. Patterson of New Hampshire in a later discussion of the Fourteenth Amendment, for which he voted. I am opposed, he stated, "to any law discriminating against [blacks] in the security of life, liberty, person, property and the proceeds of their labor. These civil rights all should enjoy. Beyond this I am not prepared to go, and those pretended friends who urge political and social equality . . . are . . . the worst enemies of the colored race."[30]

Such views had been expressed in the Senate by Trumbull, who drafted the Bill: "The bill is applicable exclusively to civil rights. It does not propose to regulate political rights of individuals; it has nothing to do with the right of suffrage, or any other political right."[31] Commenting on *Corfield v. Coryell,* Trumbull stated that such cases had held that under the "privileges and immunities" of Article IV, §2, a citizen had "certain great fundamental rights, such as the right to life, to liberty, and to avail oneself of all the laws passed for the benefit of the citizen to enable him to enforce his rights." These were the rights with which the Civil Rights Bill would clothe the Negro.[32]

30. *Globe* 2699. Patterson voted for the Amendment, id. 2545. Windom said that under the Civil Rights Bill, the Negro "shall have an equal right, nothing more . . . to make and enforce contracts" and so on. "It does not . . . confer the privilege of voting," nor "social privileges. It merely provides safeguards to shield them from wrong and outrage and to protect them in the enjoyment of . . . the right to exist." Id. 1159.

31. Id. 599. As a prelude to the overriding of Johnson's veto, Trumbull stated, "the granting of civil rights does not . . . carry with it . . . political privileges . . . The right to vote . . . depends on the legislation of the various States." Id. 1757. He identified the rights "defined" in §1 as "fundamental rights belonging to every man as a free man." Id. 476. Bickel, 13, states that "Radicals and Moderates alike—who spoke in favor of the bill were content to rest on the points Trumbull had made. The rights to be secured by the bill were those specifically enumerated in section 1."

32. *Globe* 600, 474–475. Senator Henderson said that the Civil Rights Bill was "simply to carry out the provisions of the Constitution which confers upon the citizens of each State the privileges and immunities of citizens in the

Suffrage, said Senator Jacob M. Howard in later explaining the Fourteenth Amendment, is not "one of the privileges and immunities thus secured by [Article IV, §2 of] the Constitution"; it is not, said Senator William P. Fessenden of Maine, chairman of the Joint Committee on Reconstruction, a "natural right."[33] Trumbull stated that the Bill "has nothing to do with the right of suffrage, or any other political rights."[34] When Senator Willard Saulsbury, a Democrat of Delaware, sought specifically to except "the right to vote," Trumbull replied: "that is a political privilege, not a civil right. This bill relates to civil rights only."[35] And he reiterated that the Bill "carefully avoided conferring or interfering with political rights or privileges of any kind."[36] The views of Trumbull and Wilson were shared by fellow Republicans. The "only effect" of the Bill, said Senator Henderson, was to give the blacks the enumerated rights. "These measures did not pretend to confer upon the negro the suffrage. They left each State to determine the question for itself."[37] Senator Sherman said the bill "defines what are the incidents of freedom, and says that these men must be protected in certain rights, and so careful is its language that it goes on and defines those rights, the rights to sue and be sued [etc.] . . . and other universal incidents of freedom."[38] Thayer stressed that the bill did not "extend the right of suffrage," that suffrage was not a "fundamental right."[39] That the purpose of

---

several States." Id. 3035. As Lawrence stated, "It is idle to say that a citizen shall have the right to life, yet to deny him the right to labor, whereby alone he can live. It is a mockery to say that a citizen may have a right to live, and yet deny him the right to make a contract to secure the privilege and rewards of labor." Id. 1833.

33. Id. 704.
34. Id. 599.
35. Id. 606.
36. Id. 1760.
37. Id. 3034–3035.
38. Id. 744.
39. Id. 1151: "the words themselves are 'civil rights and immunities,' not political privileges; and nobody can successfully contend that a bill guaran-

the bill was to *prevent discrimination with respect to enumerated, fundamental not political or social rights,* was also stated in one form or another by Cook and Moulton of Illinois, Hubbell, Lawrence, and Shellabarger of Ohio, and Windom of Minnesota.[40]

Since *Corfield v. Coryell*[41] is cited on all hands, it will profit us to consider its bearing on the scope of "privileges or immunities." The actual holding was that the phrase did not confer on an out-of-state citizen the right to dredge for oysters in New Jersey waters. In passing, Justice Washington stated:

> We feel no hesitation in *confining* these expressions to those privileges and immunities which are, in their nature, *fundamental* . . . They may, however, be all comprehended under the following general heads: Protection by the government, the enjoyment of life and liberty, with the right to acquire and possess property of every kind and to pursue and obtain happiness and safety . . . The right of a citizen of one state to pass through, or reside in any other state, for purposes of trade, agriculture, professional pursuits,[42] or otherwise; to claim the benefit of the writ of habeas corpus; to institute and maintain actions of any kind in the courts of the state; to take, hold and dispose of

---

tying simply civil rights and immunities is a bill under which you extend the right of suffrage, which is a political privilege and not a civil right . . . [W]hen those civil rights which are first referred to in general terms are subsequently enumerated, that enumeration precludes any possibility that general words which have been used can be extended beyond the particulars which have been enumerated."

40. Cook, id. 1124; Moulton, id. 632; James R. Hubbell, id. 662; Lawrence, id. 1836; Shellabarger, id. 1293; for Windom, id. 1159, see supra note 30. Further details on the rejection of Negro suffrage are hereinafter set forth in the discussion of suffrage and the Fourteenth Amendment.

41. 6 F. Cas. at 551–552.

42. Emphasis added. Here Justice Washington spoke too loosely. If a State might deny a nonresident the privilege to dredge for oysters in its waters, all the more might it deny him the right to practice law in its courts. Bradwell v. State, 38 U.S. (16 Wall.) 130, 139 (1872) held that "the right to admission to practice in the courts of a State" is not a privilege of a United States citizen.

property, either real or personal; and an exemption from higher taxes or impositions than are paid by the citizens of the other state; may be mentioned as some of the particular privileges and immunities of citizens, which are clearly embraced by the general description of privileges deemed to be fundamental; to which may be added, the elective franchise,[43] as regulated and established by the laws or constitution of the state in which it is to be exercised . . . But we cannot accede to the proposition . . . that the citizens of the several states are permitted to participate *in all* the rights which belong exclusively to the citizens of any other particular state.

The last sentence alone militates against an "all-inclusive" reading of *Corfield*.[44]

In the main, these are the privileges and immunities enumerated in the Civil Rights Bill. Justice Washington's inclusion of the "elective franchise," as Charles Fairman remarked, was "plainly wrong."[45] Article IV hardly intended to enable a transient migrant to vote, and this after excluding him from dredging for oysters. From the beginning, admission to suffrage had been the province of the State, as Chief Justice Parker of Massachusetts held at about the same time as *Corfield,* being preceded by Judge Samuel Chase of Maryland.[46] Right or

43. The Supreme Court rejected this notion in Minor v. Happersett, 88 U.S. (21 Wall.) 162, 174 (1874): "This is more than asserting that [citizens] may change their residence and become citizens of the State and thus be voters. It goes to the extent that while retaining their original citizenship they may vote in any State." It must be borne in mind that Article IV, §2, applies to transient as well as permanent migrants.

44. Emphasis added. That last sentence is at odds with Alfred Kelly's statement that in the Corfield case "the rights incidental to national citizenship had been described in *all-inclusive* terms under the comity clause [Article IV,§2]." Kelly, Fourteenth 1059 (emphasis added).

45. Charles Fairman, *Reconstruction and Reunion, 1864–1888* 1122, vol. 6, pt. 1, of *History of the Supreme Court of the United States* (1971); see supra note 3.

46. Abbott v. Bayley, 6 Pick. 89, 91 (Mass. 1827); Campbell v. Morris, 3 H. & McH. 535, 554 (Md. 1797).

wrong, it was open to Congress to take a narrower view than that of Washington for purposes of the Act which the Fourteenth Amendment was to constitutionalize. Trumbull did just this, saying of Washington, "This judge goes further than the bill" in including the "elective franchise."[47] Graham dwells on the *Corfield* phrase "Protection by the government; the enjoyment of life and liberty . . . and to pursue and obtain happiness."[48] Here, too, the framers could choose to exclude protection for the "pursuit of happiness," but in truth it was to Trumbull's mind a synonym for property: "the great fundamental rights of life, liberty, and the pursuit of happiness."[49] And so it was read by Justice Bradley in the *Slaughter-House Cases:* the rights "to life, liberty and the pursuit of happiness are equivalent to the rights of life, liberty and property."[50] At any rate, the "pursuit of happiness" found no place in the Amendment; in its stead the framers substituted the bare word "property," clinging to the traditional trinity: "life, liberty, and property."

It remains to notice two earlier cases also cited in the debates. In *Campbell v. Morris* (1797), Judge Chase, before long to be a Supreme Court Justice, stated on behalf of the General Court of Maryland that counsel were agreed

> that a particular and limited operation is to be given to these words [privileges and immunities] and not a full and comprehensive one. It is agreed that it does not mean the right of election . . . The court are of opinion it means . . . the peculiar advantage of acquiring and holding real as well as personal property, that such property shall be protected and secured by the laws of the state, in the same manner as the property of the citizens of the state is protected. It means, such property shall not be liable to any taxes or burdens which the property of the citizens

47. *Globe* 475; see Senator Howard, supra at note 33.
48. Graham 332n.
49. *Globe* 475.
50. 83 U.S. (16 Wall.) 36, 116 (1872), dissenting opinion.

of the state is not subject to . . . It secures and protects personal rights.[51]

Mark that the emphasis is on freedom from discrimination, on equality with respect to described rights. In 1827, shortly after *Corfield,* Chief Justice Parker declared on behalf of the highest court of Massachusetts, in *Abbott v. Bayley,* that the privileges and immunities phrase confers a "right to sue and be sued," that citizens who remove to a second State "cannot enjoy the right of suffrage," but "may take and hold real estate."[52] Thus, long before 1866 courts had held that "privileges and immunities" were comprised of the rights Blackstone had enumerated; the framers, aware of Blackstone and the decisions, embodied those rights, and those rights only, in the Civil Rights Act of 1866.

That, however, is not the neoabolitionist reading of the history. So Alfred Kelly remarked, "Trumbull made it clear that his notion of the rights incidental to national citizenship were *exceedingly comprehensive* in character . . . Citing the dictum in *Corfield v. Coryell,* he argued that the rights of national citizenship included all 'privileges which are in their nature fundamental' . . . In short, he nationalized the comity clause [Article IV, §2] and turned it into a national bill of rights against the states, as the pre-war antislavery theorists had pretty generally done."[53] Such interpretations are poles removed from Trumbull's carefully restricted explanations. In the debates on the

51. Supra note 46.

52. Supra note 46. The Abbott and Campbell cases were quoted by Senator Trumbull, *Globe* 474, and at other points in the debates.

53. Kelly, Fourteenth 1062–1063, emphasis added. So too, Kelly reads Bingham's statement that "the protection given by the laws of the States shall be equal *in respect to* life, liberty, and property to all persons" as meaning "a very general requirement of equality on all state legislation of the most inclusive kind" (emphasis added). Id. 1074. There is also the fact that Bingham obtained the deletion of the "no discrimination in civil rights" clause because it was "oppressive." Infra Chapter 7 at notes 13–14.

Civil Rights Bill, Trumbull made no mention of the Bill of
Rights, but tied the "privileges and immunities" phrase to "certain great fundamental rights such as the right to life, to liberty," and the benefit of laws passed for the enforcement of
those rights, explicitly excluding "political" rights. His fellows
even more clearly viewed the enumerated rights as restrictive.[54]
As the citations to Blackstone and Kent show, "fundamental,"
"natural" rights had become words of received meaning.[55] Ten-
Broek himself states that "the area of disagreement" about
"privileges and immunities was not large, since their natural
rights foundation was generally accepted"; they were "the natural rights of all men or such auxiliary rights as were necessary
to secure and maintain those natural rights. They were the
rights to life, liberty, and property. They were the rights to contract, and to own, use and dispose of property."[56]

Nevertheless, tenBroek remained fuzzy as to the meaning of
"fundamental" rights as is shown by his citation to Senator
Henderson. After noting Henderson's explanation of the purpose of the Civil Rights Act, to give the rights *therein enumerated*
(which he read into the record), and his reference to "those fundamental rights of person and property which cannot be denied
to any person," tenBroek concludes: "This was the *sweeping*
view of those who sponsored . . . the Fourteenth Amend-

54. Supra at notes 31–32, 36–38, 26–30.

55. In his 1965 article Kelly himself stated, "Ultimately Revolutionary
natural-rights theorists insisted liberty was derived from a state of nature, but
it had long before been given a very positive and specific content. It was to be
found . . . above all in the common law as expounded by Coke and Blackstone in all their commentaries. The 'rights of Englishmen' were not vacuous;
instead they were quite well-developed and specific. The notion of pulling
new natural rights from the air to allow for an indefinite expansion can hardly
be considered to be within the original spirit of the amendment." Kelly, "Clio
and the Court: An Illicit Love Affair," 1965 S. Ct. Rev. 119, 154–155. They
had been crystallized by Blackstone, supra note 3. Madison, for example,
stated in the First Congress that "Trial by jury cannot be considered . . . as a
natural right." 1 *Annals of Congress* 437.

56. TenBroek 122–123, 236.

ment.[57] Henderson, however, had emphasized that the "only effect" of the Civil Rights Bill was to give the blacks the rights there listed, that because the "negro is the object of that unaccountable prejudice against race" the "country is not prepared" to give them more.[58]

The Graham–tenBroek–Kelly writings have muddied analysis; they are not true to the historical facts. Shortly restated, those facts are that the "fundamental" rights which the framers were anxious to secure were those described by Blackstone—personal security, freedom to move about and to own property; they had been picked up in the "privileges and immunities" of Article IV, §1; the incidental rights necessary for their protection were "enumerated" in the Civil Rights Act of 1866; that enumeration, according to the framers, marked the bounds of the grant; and at length those rights were embodied in the "privileges or immunities" of the Fourteenth Amendment. An argument to the contrary, it may be stated categorically, will find no solid ground in the debates of the 39th Congress.

57. Id. 231–232, emphasis added.
58. *Globe* 3034, 3035. Like tenBroek, Graham, 276, stated that "the evidence in the debates is overwhelming that racial discrimination *very broadly conceived* was the framers' target." Emphasis added. Compare his statement infra, Chapter 7 at note 41.

3

The "Privileges or Immunities of a Citizen of the United States"

NARROW as was the protection afforded blacks by the "privileges or immunities" clause, it was at least designed to shield them from violence and oppression. Even that limited goal was soon aborted when the Supreme Court divorced the rights of "a citizen of the United States" from the freedom from the discrimination proscribed by the Amendment. Consequently, the provision has become the all-but-forgotten clause of the Constitution.[1] In the *Slaughter-House Cases* the Supreme Court grounded this view in part on the differentiation between the declaration in the first sentence of §1 that "all persons born or naturalized in the United States . . . are citizens of the United States and of the State wherein they reside" and the second-sentence provision that no State "shall abridge the privileges or immunities of a citizen of the United States." From this Justice Miller deduced that a

1. Colgate v. Harvey, 296 U.S. 404, 443 (1935), Justice Stone dissenting. D. O. McGovney showed that a goodly number of Justice Miller's "national" privileges (infra note 3) can be enforced under some specific, direct constitutional grant. "Privileges and Immunities Clause, Fourteenth Amendment," 4 Iowa L. Bull. 219, 223 (1918). Hence, as Stanley Morrison remarked, "the effect of the decision was to make the privileges and immunities clause practically a dead letter." "Does the Fourteenth Amendment Incorporate the Bill of Rights?" 2 Stan. L. Rev. 140, 144 (1949).

The clause has received little scholarly attention.

"citizenship of the United States and a citizenship of a State
. . . are distinct from each other," and that §1 secured only
the privileges of a "citizen of the United States."[2] So meager
was his catalog of those privileges as to move Justice Field to
exclaim that if this was all the privileges or immunities clause
accomplished, "it was a vain and idle enactment."[3] *Slaughter-
House* was a five-to-four decision, and Field was joined by
Chief Justice Chase and Justices Bradley and Swayne in an
opinion that took more accurate account of the framers' intention than did that of Miller.

Preliminarily it will be useful to pull together a few strands
that tie the privileges or immunities of §1 to the specific enumeration of the Civil Rights Act of 1866. There is first the correspondence to the Civil Rights Bill's "civil rights and immunities," "privileges" being narrower than "civil rights," which
had been deleted at Bingham's insistence.[4] Second, Chairman
Trumbull explained that the Bill had been patterned on the
"privileges and immunities" of Article IV, §2, and its construction by Justice Washington. Third, in introducing the prototype
of §1, Bingham said that the "privileges or immunities" had
been drawn from Article IV; fourth, Senator Howard similarly
referred back to the Article.[5] Speaking after Howard, Senator
Luke P. Poland stated that §1 "secures nothing beyond what was

2. 83 U.S. (16 Wall.) 36, 74 (1872).

3. Id. 96. Among the rights Justice Miller enumerated were the right to
come to the seat of government, to assert claims against it, to have access to its
seaports, courts, and offices, to have protection abroad, to assemble and petition, to use navigable waters, to become a citizen of another State by residence. Id. 79.

It is anomalous that a "citizen of the United States" is limited to these
scanty rights whereas as a "citizen of a State" he may continue to invoke in a
sister State the broader rights secured to him by Article IV, §2. Chambers v.
Baltimore & Ohio R.R., 207 U.S. 142, 148 (1907); Blake v. McClung, 172
U.S. 239, 254 (1898).

4. Infra Chapter 7 at notes 11–16.

5. Supra Chapter 2 at notes 6, 9, 32, 33; *Globe* 2765.

intended by" the original privileges and immunities provision.[6] More important is the all but universal identification of §1 with the Civil Rights Act. Why, then, were not the terms of the Act incorporated bodily in §1? Constitutional drafting calls for the utmost compression, avoidance of the prolixity of a code;[7] "the specific and exclusive enumeration of rights in the Act," as Bickel remarked, presumably was considered "inappropriate in a constitutional provision."[8] In sum, the words "privileges or immunities," it is safe to say, were designed to secure "person and property" against violence and oppression by the rights auxiliary to such protection. How was this design separated from the "privileges or immunities of a citizen of the United States"?

Justice Miller correctly stated that Article IV, §2, did not "profess to control the powers of State governments over the rights of its own citizens." Its sole purpose was to require that the rights granted by a State to its "own citizens . . . the same, neither more nor less, shall be the measure of the rights of citizens of other States within your jurisdiction."[9] Without mentioning "citizens of the United States," the courts had construed Article IV to mean that a migrant citizen from one State would enjoy the "fundamental rights" accorded by a sister State to its own citizens.[10] This the framers understood; the cases were quoted, explained, and used as a platform for the Civil Rights Bill.[11] The task, however, was not one of outright adoption but

6. *Globe* 2961.

7. Cf. M'Culloch v. Maryland, 17 U.S. (4 Wheat.) 316, 407 (1819). In the First Congress, Abraham Baldwin, a Framer, commenting on a proposed amendment that "the President should not turn out a good officer," said that such minute regulation "would have swelled [the Constitution] to the size of a folio volume." 1 *Annals of Congress* 559.

8. Bickel 61.

9. 83 U.S. at 77.

10. Corfield v. Coryell, 6 F. Cas. (No. 3230) 546 (C. C. E. D. Pa. 1823). Abbott v. Bayley, 6 Pick. 89, 91 (Mass. 1827).

11. Trumbull, *Globe* 474, 475, 600; Senator R. Johnson, id. 505; Senator Davis, id. 595–596; Kerr, id. 1269.

of adaptation. For the Negro did not become a migrant by emancipation; generally speaking, he remained in the same State. But he had experienced a transmigration, from that of a slave, a nonperson,[12] to a freeman, and the framers meant to secure to this transmigrant the rights that Article IV, §2, had guarantied to a migrant citizen.

Early on, James A. Garfield of Ohio stated, the goal was that "personal liberty and personal rights are placed in the keeping of the nation, that the right to life, liberty, and property shall be guarantied to the citizen in reality . . . We must make American citizenship the shield that protects every citizen, on every foot of our soil."[13] That motive manifestly was at the heart of the Civil Rights Bill: "all persons born in the United States . . . are hereby declared to be citizens of the United States," and it went on to proscribe "discrimination in civil rights or immunities among the inhabitants of any State."[14] A citizen of the United States who was an "inhabitant" of a State was to be free from discrimination. The bill, Chairman Wilson stated, "refers to those rights which belong to men as citizens of the United States and none other."[15] Raymond of New York said that it provided protection for "citizens of the United

12. Roscoe Conkling described a slave as "A man, and yet not a man. In flesh and blood alive; politically dead." Now emancipated, "They are not slaves, but they are not, in a political sense, 'persons.'" *Globe* 356.

13. *Globe App.* 67.

14. *Globe* 474; *Globe App.* 315.

15. Id. 1294. Wilson distinguished these "fundamental" rights from rights under State laws, like the right to attend school, to serve on a jury. Kelly labels this a "restrictive interpretation which actually anticipated the dual citizenship doctrine of the 'privileges and immunities' clause of the Fourteenth Amendment in the *Slaughterhouse Cases.*" Kelly, Fourteenth at 1069. Compare Kelly's own "restrictive" view, supra Chapter 2 note 52. Kelly completely misreads Wilson. In tune with the limited Republican goals, he emphasized that "citizens of the United States, as such, are entitled to . . . life, liberty, and the right of property." *Globe* 1294. His object was to protect Negroes from violence and oppression whereas Justice Miller rejected even those rights, leaving blacks at the mercy of their former masters.

States . . . against anticipated inequality of legislation in the several States."[16] Cook of Illinois understood the bill to provide "that as between citizens of the United States there shall be no discrimination in civil rights or immunities. When these rights which are enumerated in this bill are denied to any class of men on account of race or color, when they are subject to a system of vagrant laws which sells them into slavery or involuntary servitude, which operates upon them as upon no other part of the community, they are not secured in the rights of freedom."[17]

In the Senate, Trumbull stated that *Corfield v. Coryell* "enumerates the very rights belonging to a citizen of the United States which are set forth in the first section of the bill."[18] Senator Garrett Davis of Kentucky understood full well what Trumbull was about, and therefore proposed to substitute the Article IV, §2, formula—"The citizens of each State shall be entitled to all the privileges and immunities of citizens in the several States"—explaining that it would apply "only when a citizen of one State goes into another State," whereas, he stated, Trumbull "proposes now to apply his bill to every citizen of the United States . . . where that citizen is domiciled in the State in which he was born." In other words, Trumbull would legislate "for the resident Negro in Kentucky, born there, who has always lived there, and who intends to remain there," to which, he stated, *Corfield* has no application.[19] Thus, Davis sought to restrict the bill exactly as Justice Miller later did, but his proposal was stillborn. Instead, Trumbull reasoned from *Corfield* that were a law to declare a "person born in the United States a citizen of the United States, the same rights [listed in *Corfield*] would then appertain to *all* persons who were clothed

---

16. *Globe* 1266.

17. Id. 1124. Shellabarger also referred to "the ordinary rights of national citizenship, such as the right of . . . holding land, and of protection." Id. 2104.

18. Id. 475.

19. Id. 595, 596.

with American citizenship."[20] After President Johnson's veto of
the bill, Trumbull again stated that "citizens of the United
States" have "fundamental rights . . . such as the rights enumerated in this bill," among them, citing Blackstone, that
"restraints introduced by law should be *equal to all*" and,
quoting Kent, "the right of personal security, the right of personal liberty, and the right to acquire and enjoy property."[21] In
short, the Senate rejected the Davis-Miller view in favor of a
United States citizenship that would clothe *residents* of a State

20. Id. 600. The Civil Rights Bill, said Raymond, "is intended to secure
these citizens against injustice that may be done them in the courts of those
States within which they may reside." Id. 1267. There were, however, some
who did not appreciate the difference between Article IV, §2 and §1 of the
Amendment; for example, Senator Poland stated that the privileges and immunities clause of §1 "secures nothing beyond what was intended by the original provision" of Article IV, §2. Id. 2961.

21. Id. 1757. Justice Field quoted Senator Trumbull's explanation of the
Civil Rights Bill (id. 474): "any statute which is not equal to all, and which deprives any citizen of civil rights, which are secured to other citizens, is an unjust encroachment upon his liberty"; he noted that the Fourteenth Amendment "was adopted to obviate objections which had been raised and pressed
with great force to the validity of the Civil Rights Act," and concluded that
"A citizen of a State is now only a citizen of the United States residing in that
State. The fundamental rights . . . now belong to him as a citizen of the
United States." 83 U.S. at 92, 93, 95. Corfield v. Coryell, he stated, "was cited
by Senator Trumbull with the observation that it enumerated the very rights
belonging to a citizen of the United States set forth in the first section of the
act, and with the statement that all persons born in the United States, being
declared by the act citizens of the United States, would thenceforth be entitled
to the rights of citizens, and that these were the fundamental rights set forth in
the act." Id. 98. What Article IV "did for the protection of the citizens of one
State against hostile and discriminating legislation of other States," Field
summed up, the "Fourteenth Amendment does for the protection of every citizen of the United States against hostile and discriminating legislation against
him in favor of others, whether they reside in the same or different States." Id.
100–101. Field was faithful to the legislative history, and it is remarkable that
successor judges and scholars did not further explore the path he marked.
When, however, he came to substantive due process he forgot about those
limited goals.

with the "fundamental rights" theretofore conferred on migrants.

Did these views, expressed in connection with the Civil Rights Bill, carry over into the Fourteenth Amendment? Here there is more than the intention to constitutionalize the Civil Rights Act. Frederick E. Woodbridge of Vermont stated that the proposed Bingham prototype was "intended to enable Congress . . . to give all citizens the inalienable rights of life and liberty, and to every citizen in whatever State he may be . . . that protection for his property which is extended to the other citizens of the State."[22] George R. Latham of West Virginia understood the Fourteenth Amendment "privileges and immunities of citizens of the United States" to "provide that no State shall make any discrimination in civil rights of citizens of the United States on account of race . . . the 'civil rights bill' which is now a law . . . covers exactly the same ground."[23] So, too, John M. Broomall of Pennsylvania stated, "We propose, first, to give power to the Government . . . to protect its own citizens within the States," a proposition for which the House had "already voted . . . in the civil rights bill."[24] Ephraim R. Eckley of Ohio also stressed the need to provide "security for life, liberty and property to all citizens of all the States."[25] And Senator Howard referred to the privileges and immunities of Article IV, quoted *Corfield* to explain the terms, and stated that these rights "are secured to the citizens solely as a citizen of the United States."[26] Apart from Garrett

22. *Globe* 1088.
23. Id. 2883.
24. Id. 2498.
25. Id. 2535.
26. Id. 2765. So the amended §1 was understood by Senator Stewart: "It declares that all men are entitled to life, liberty, and property, and imposes upon the Government the duty of discharging these obligations." Id. 2964. After Howard proffered his citizenship definition, Windom summarized the privileges or immunities of §1 as meaning "Your life shall be spared, your liberty shall be unabridged, your property shall be protected." Id. 3169. See also

Davis' abortive attempt to limit this objective, no one, so far as I could find, disputed that the purpose of both the Civil Rights Act and the Amendment was to guarantee to "citizens of the United States," whether they were migrants to or residents of a State, the enumerated fundamental rights.

In the process of hammering out the Amendment, the framers had lost sight of the definition of citizenship contained in the Civil Rights Bill, so it was late in the day when Senator Benjamin F. Wade of Ohio remarked anent the word "citizen" in §1, "that is a term about which there has been a great deal of uncertainty in our government." To "put the question beyond cavil," he proposed to "strike out the word 'citizen' [in what is now the second sentence of §1], and substitute all persons born in the United States."[27] Howard advanced a counterproposal, the present introductory sentence, "All persons born in the United States . . . are citizens of the United States and of the State wherein they reside." Wade then withdrew his proposal.[28] Presumably the Howard formulation struck Wade as a satisfactory substitute for, not a repudiation of, his own proposal. Although the Negro had been emancipated, the *Dred Scott* decision threw a shadow over his citizenship;[29] the matter had been a source of interminable argument. Trumbull wished "to end that very controversy, whether the Negro is a citizen or not."[30] Howard stated that his definitional amendment of §1 "settles the great question of citizenship and removes all doubt as to what persons are or are not citizens of the United States." And

Bingham: "rights of every person," id. 2542; Farnsworth: §1 "might as well read . . . 'No State shall deny to any person within its jurisdiction.'" Id. 2539.

27. *Globe* 2768–2769.

28. Id. 2869. Compare with supra at note 26.

29. Referring to the Dred Scott holding that a Negro could be neither a citizen of a State nor of the United States, Justice Miller said, "To remove this difficulty primarily . . . the first clause of the first section was framed . . . That its main purpose was to establish the citizenship of the negro can admit of no doubt." 83 U.S. 72.

30. *Globe* 1285.

he further explained, "we desired to put this question of citizenship and the *rights* of citizens and *freedmen* under the civil rights bill beyond the legislative power" of those who would "expose the freedmen again to the oppression of their old masters,"[31] thus confirming that his definition was not a sub rosa abandonment of the paramount goal throughout: protection of the resident Negro against State discrimination. In the House, Thaddeus Stevens of Pennsylvania regarded the Howard interpolation as an "excellent amendment, long needed to settle conflicting decisions."[32] This limited purpose of Howard's definition throws doubt on Miller's view that it was designed to demark the rights of a citizen of the United States from those of a State citizen. Against the manifest purpose of the framers, of which Justice Miller was well aware,[33] his reliance on a rule of construction—to express at one point is to exclude at another—should carry little weight.[34] Rules of construction are useful guides where other light is lacking, but they are not meant to dim or extinguish available light. The cardinal purpose of interpretation, it cannot too often be emphasized, is to ascertain and effectuate, not defeat, the intention of the framers. Once that purpose is ascertained, it may not be thwarted by a rule of construction.[35]

31. Id. 2890, 2896 (emphasis added). Howard stated that his interpolation "is simply declaratory of the law already." Id. 2890. Trumbull had quoted Chief Justice Marshall's statement that "A Citizen of the United States, residing in any state of the Union, is a citizen of that state." Gassies v. Ballon, 31 U.S. (6 Pet.) 761, 762 (1832); *Globe* 1756.

32. *Globe* 3148.

33. Infra at notes 39–40. "It is too clear for argument," said Justice Miller, "that the change in phraseology was adopted understandingly and with a purpose." 83 U.S. 75. That is quite true; but the purpose is that expressed by Trumbull, Stevens, Howard, and Fessenden, not exclusion from the benefits that had been so carefully wrought.

34. Howard, whose purpose Miller sought to ascertain by this rule, stated that it is "a dangerous principle of construction." *Globe* 4001.

35. For example, "The rule of '*ejusdem generis*' is applied as an aid in ascertaining the intention of the legislature, not to subvert it when ascertained." United States v. Gilliland, 312 U.S. 86, 93 (1941). The *expressio unius* rule

In sum, the purpose of the framers was to protect blacks from discrimination with respect to specified "fundamental rights," enumerated in the Civil Rights Act and epitomized in the §1 "privileges or immunities" clause. To achieve that purpose they made the black *both* a citizen "of the United States and of the State in which he resides." They did not intend by the addition of State citizenship to *diminish* the rights they had been at such pains to specify, but the better to *secure* them. The notion that by conferring dual citizenship the framers were separating said rights of a citizen of the United States from those of a State citizen not only is without historical warrant but actually does violence to their intention. Fessenden stated that the definition was framed "*to prevent a State from saying* that although a person is a citizen of the United States he is not a citizen of the State."[36] He did not mean to safeguard State citizenship in order to leave blacks at the mercy of Southern States. It was precisely their abuse of the freedmen that led to the Amendment.

Justice Miller next stressed the serious consequences that would follow adoption of a construction contrary to his own; the effect would be to "degrade the State governments by subjecting them to the control of Congress" in unwonted manner. He read "No State shall make or enforce any law which shall *abridge* the privileges or immunities of citizens of the United States" as transferring "the entire domain of civil right" from the States to the federal government, so that Congress could even "pass laws *in advance,* limiting and restricting the exercise of legislative power by the States."[37] Here Miller imported a term into the clause; "abridge" presupposes preliminary State action; before such abridgment there is nothing upon which to act "in advance." Moreover, Congress was confined to *corrective* measures, as Miller was aware: "If, however, the States did not

---

"serves only as an aid in discovering the legislative intent when that is not otherwise manifest." United States v. Barnes, 222 U.S. 513, 519 (1912).

36. *Globe* 2897.

37. 83 U.S. 77–78 (emphasis added).

conform their laws to its [the Amendment's] requirements, *then* by the fifth section . . . Congress was authorized to enforce it by suitable legislation."[38] It was emphatically not authorized to promulgate a general code "in advance."

Miller himself found that "the existence of laws in the States where the newly emancipated negroes reside, which discriminated with gross injustice and hardship against them as a class, was the evil to be remedied"—that is, the Black Codes.[39] The "one pervading purpose," he stated, was "protection of the newly-made freeman and citizen from the oppression of those who had formerly exercised unlimited dominion over him."[40] Consequently, the Amendment did not encompass "all legislation,"[41] but only discriminatory legislation with respect to specified rights, as Justice Field pointed out: "What, then, are the

38. Id. 81 (emphasis added). For the "corrective" purpose of §1, see infra Chapter 10 at notes 68–92.

39. 83 U.S. 81. Miller referred to the "black codes" and recapitulated some of their harsh provisions; id. 70.

40. Id. 71, 81. Miller also stated, "We doubt very much whether any action of a State not directed by way of discrimination against the negroes as a class . . . will ever be held to come within the purview of this [equal protection] provision." Id. 81. If this be read as excluding protection for whites, it runs counter to the history of the Civil Rights Bill. Senator Trumbull explained that the Bill "applies to white men as well as to black men. It declares that all persons . . . shall be entitled to the same civil rights." *Globe* 599; see also *Globe* 41, 158, 516. And the Amendment speaks in terms of "persons," in order, Bingham stated, to include "aliens" and "strangers," i.e., whites. Infra Chapter 11 at notes 91–92.

41. Justice Miller's "all legislation" is the more surprising because he noted that "privileges and immunities" was lifted out of Article IV of the Articles of Confederation, where it was particularized—"all the privileges of trade or commerce." Here, he commented, "we have some of these specifically mentioned, enough perhaps to give some general idea of the class of civil rights meant by the phrase." 83 U.S. 75. Self-evidently the privileges subsumed under "trade or commerce" are but a segment of the matters embraced by "all legislation." And his quotation of the Corfield enumeration again suggests that Miller was substituting "statesmanship" for hard-nosed legal interpretation.

privileges and immunities which are secured against abridgment by State legislation? In the first section of the Civil Rights
Act Congress has given its interpretation of these terms
[which] . . . include the right 'to make and enforce contracts . . .' "[42] The correction of discriminatory laws with
respect to the enumerated "fundamental rights" would hardly
constitute the "court a perpetual censor upon all legislation of
the States, on the civil rights of their own citizens."[43] When
Miller held that "the citizen of a State" must look to the State
for protection,[44] he aborted what he himself had declared to be
the "pervading purpose": to protect the Negro from the "evil"
of the Black Codes, Codes that handed the Negro back to their
oppressors.

Paradoxically, Justice Miller was ready to protect Negroes
from "gross injustice and oppression" by resort to the equal
protection clause.[45] How, one wonders, did "equal protection"
escape the blight that struck down "privileges or immunities"?
It equally "degrad[ed] the State governments by subjecting
them to the control of Congress"; it too constituted a "great departure from the structure and spirit of our institutions."[46] And
whereas the limits of "privileges or immunities" can be discerned in the rights specified in the Civil Rights Act which §1
incorporated, there is no clue whatever to the rights comprehended by the Miller formula—equal protection against "gross
injustice and hardship." One of the ironies that bestrews the
path of the Court is that the censorship abjured by Miller under

42. Id. 96. The Court's statement in Buchanan v. Warley, 245 U.S. 60, 77
(1917), that "The Fourteenth Amendment makes no attempt to enumerate the
rights it was designed to protect. It speaks in general terms, and those are as
comprehensive as possible," overlooks the framers' limited purposes, plainly
expressed in the enumeration of the Civil Rights Act which the Amendment
incorporated.

43. 83 U.S. 78.

44. Id. 75.

45. Id. 81.

46. Id. 78.

"privileges or immunities" really became unlimited under the converted due process clause.[47]

No discussion of *Slaughter-House* may fail to take account of Justice Bradley's dissent. Where Field won the concurrence of three associates, Bradley stood alone; where Miller held that protection of the citizen was for the State, Bradley propounded a theory of "absolute" rights that neither State nor nation may invade.[48] That theory, as will hereinafter appear, can draw small comfort from the intention of the framers; and he himself stated with respect to the preexisting Article IV, §2: "It is true that courts have usually regarded [it] . . . as securing only equality of privileges with the citizens of the State in which the parties are found."[49] In holding that the Amendment was designed to assure similar equality with respect to specified rights among residents of a State, Justice Field staked out a position midway between the extremes of Miller and Bradley, one that honestly reflected the intention of the framers.

There remain some remarks by Senator Trumbull in 1871, which Graham reads as a denial "that the Fourteenth Amendment authorized Congress to protect citizens in their rights of person and property in the States. Such an interpretation [Trumbull] declared, would mean 'annihilation of the States.'"[50] Little weight has been attached by the Supreme Court to postenactment remarks, even of the Congress itself.[51] When they contradict representations made by the speaker during the enactment process, upon which others have been led

---

47. Consequently I would dissent from Justice Frankfurter's reference to the "mischievous uses to which that [privileges and immunities] clause would lend itself if its scope were not confined to that given to it by all but one of the decisions beginning with the Slaughter-House Cases." Adamson v. California, 332 U.S. 46, 61–62 (1947), concurring opinion.

48. 83 U.S. 114–115.

49. Id. 118.

50. Graham 133.

51. Rainwater v. United States, 356 U.S. 590, 593 (1958).

to rely, they should be treated with special reserve.[52] Consider, too, the circumstances that gave rise to Trumbull's 1871 remarks. President Grant, Graham recounts, "had just called for a second Force Bill to cope with extralegal suppression of Negro rights. The problem . . . had risen not in the contemplated or familiar form of discrimination by carriers, theaters and inns but in the infinitely more tangled context of Southern whites fighting misrule and military government." Trumbull "flatly declined to go along with the latest proposal"; the tug of new political considerations shaped his version of the past. Now he maintained that the protection afforded by the Fourteenth Amendment was no greater than that accorded by Article IV, §2, that that section "did not have reference to the protection of those persons in individual rights in their respective States, except so far as being citizens of one State entitled them to the privileges and immunities of citizens in every other"; and that the "fourteenth amendment does not define the privileges and immunities of a citizen of the United States any more than the Constitution orginally did."[53]

This was only half the story. Trumbull did not mention his rejection of that very argument by Garrett Davis, that he had read the judicial definitions of the Article IV, §2, privileges and immunities to the framers and patterned the Civil Rights Bill on *Corfield v. Coryell,* that he adapted the Article IV, §2, conception—a migrant citizen was entitled to the same fundamental rights as a resident citizen—to the transmigrant black so suddenly released from slavery, named him a citizen of the United States to assure him of the same rights the migrant enjoyed under Article IV. To say in these circumstances that the Fourteenth Amendment "does not define the privileges and immunities" is therefore a half-truth. The terms, in lawyers' jargon,

---

52. Cf. Raoul Berger, *Congress v. The Supreme Court* 48 (1969); Raoul Berger, "Judicial Review: Counter Criticism in Tranquillity," 69 Nw.U.L. Rev. 390, 399–401 (1974).

53. Graham 324, 326, 325.

had become "words of art"; in borrowing them (with the exclusion of suffrage), Trumbull· expressly gave them the
meaning which courts had given under Article IV and which he
had carefully spelled out in the Civil Rights Bill. It follows that
Trumbull's 1871 argument that "the privileges and immunities
belonging to a citizen of the United States as such are of a national character," that "National citizenship is one thing and
State citizenship another"[54]—the precursor of the *Slaughter-
House* dichotomy—was a repudiation of his own explanation to
the framers, his enumeration of specific rights in the Bill that
were to belong to "citizens of the United States." He could
change *his* mind but he could not change that of the 39th
Congress which had adopted the Civil Rights Act on the
strength of his representations and then went on to incorporate
the Act in the Amendment.

54. Id. 528.

4

Negro Suffrage Was Excluded

NO area of Negro rights considered by the 39th Congress was so extensively discussed as Negro suffrage.[1] The issue was crucial to the maintenance of Republican ascendancy, a goal boldly proclaimed by Stevens at the very outset. Such ascendancy, the mass of Republicans believed, was to be assured through the reduction of Southern representation in the House of Representatives in proportion as a State denied or abridged suffrage, the device embodied in §2 of the Amendment.[2] Some strongly doubted whether the rebel ruling class, outnumbered by blacks, could be induced to "divest itself of the government and hand it over to a subject and despised caste."[3] But it was more important, Senator George H. Williams of Oregon, member of the Joint Committee, candidly avowed, to limit

1. Van Alstyne 36; James 21.

2. Supra Chapter 1 at notes 55–56. Roscoe Conkling of New York likewise acknowledged that the "representation" proposal "was primarily for party and sectional advantage." Kendrick 204; see also id. 207 and infra note 4.

3. Donnelly remarked, "To pass this law and then hope that South Carolina, moved by the hope of future power, would do justice to the negro is absurd. She has 291,000 whites and 412,000 blacks. To pass such a law would be for the governing power to divest itself of the government and hand it over to a subject and despised caste . . . The same is true, more or less, of all the South." *Globe* 378. Julian of Indiana likewise placed little hope in "representation" as an inducement to the grant of suffrage because southern "scorn of an enslaved and downtrodden race is as intense as ever. They hate the negro." *Globe* 58. Boutwell of Massachusetts admitted "the possibility that ultimately those eleven States may be restored to representative power without the right of franchise being conferred [by them] upon the colored people." *Globe* 2508.

Southern representation than to provide "that negroes anywhere should immediately vote."[4] The fact that Negro suffrage
was unmistakably excluded from the ambit of the Civil Rights
Bill, which proceeded on a parallel track with debate on "representation," lends substance to his avowal. The intention to exclude suffrage from the Amendment as well[5] need not rest entirely on its incorporation of the Civil Rights Act, for there is
ample affirmative evidence of that purpose.

Chief Justice Warren held in *Reynolds v. Sims,* a State reapportionment case, that "the right of suffrage can be denied by a
debasement or dilution of the weight of a citizen's vote just as
effectively as by wholly prohibiting the free exercise of the franchise." The premise, he said, that a State may not deny suffrage
was derived from a "conception of political equality . . . [that]

---

4. *Globe App.* 94. Ward Elliott remarks, "The post-Civil War Radical Republicans, as a group, cared very little for the black vote until they came to believe that it would help to secure their position . . . against a Democratic resurgence. Once convinced that they would profit from the black vote, they
passed the Fifteenth Amendment." *The Rise of a Guardian Democracy* 2 (1974);
see also id. 204. Section 2 "was not primarily devised for the protection of
Negro rights and the provision of Negro equality. Its primary purpose . . . was to put the southern states" under northern control. C. Vann
Woodward, "Seeds of Failure in Radical Race Policy," in *New Frontiers of the
American Reconstruction* 135 (H. M. Hyman ed. 1966). Aaron Harding of Kentucky tauntingly asked "if there is a single man among you who would vote
for negro suffrage if he believed the negroes would vote the Democratic
ticket? Not one, and you know it." *Globe* 449. Although McKee of Kentucky
favored the limitation of representation, he opposed Negro suffrage in the
District of Columbia because he did not believe "that this race, coming immediately out of bondage, is fit for all rights of citizens." Id. 452. When John
Bright expressed "reservations about enfranchising this large unlettered electorate," Sumner wrote, "Without them, the old enemy will reappear . . ."
Quoted in Donald, *Sumner II* 201.

5. As Michael Les Benedict justly remarks, the §2 curtailment of representation was "necessary only if Republicans did not intend to force black suffrage on the reluctant South." *A Compromise of Principle: Conservative Republicans and Reconstruction 1863–1869* 136 (1975).

can mean only one thing—one person, one vote."[6] Equality,
however, did not carry that meaning for the framers;[7] and in a
powerful dissent, Justice Harlan reproached the Court "for its
failure to address itself at all to the Fourteenth Amendment as
a whole or to [its] legislative history."[8] Even one who regards
the reapportionment decisions with favor, Carl Auerbach,
lamented that "the failure of the Court to mention, let alone
deal with, [Harlan's] argument is indeed, as he charged, remarkable and confounding."[9] Another proponent of those
decisions, William Van Alstyne, states that "the majority seems
tacitly to have conceded the argument."[10] In 1970 Justice Harlan
amplified his dissent in *Oregon v. Mitchell*;[11] both of his dissents
are models of scholarly exactitude. Having combed the debates
for myself, I can confirm his accuracy and scrupulousness in
drawing inferences from the facts; one can only complain that
he left so few gleanings for those who came after. Since his discussion in the two opinions covers many pages, and since it is
contained in law reports that only scholarly specialists are likely
to consult, I have undertaken to compress the materials into
smaller compass, particularly because they furnish the spring-
board for much that is to follow.

THE GRANT OF SUFFRAGE WAS EXCLUDED FROM §1

Senator Sumner labeled the right to vote "the Great Guarantee; and *the only sufficient Guarantee*,[12] without which, said Senator Samuel C. Pomeroy of Kansas, the Negro "has no secu-

6. 377 U.S. 533, 555, 558 (1964).
7. See W. R. Brock, *An American Crisis: Congress and Reconstruction* (1963).
This will be discussed infra Chapter 10.
8. 377 U.S. at 590.
9. C. Auerbach, "The Reapportionment Cases: One Person, One
Vote—One Vote, One Value," 1964 S. Ct. Rev. 1, 75.
10. Van Alstyne 36.
11. 400 U.S. 112, 152 (1970).
12. *Globe* 685.

rity."[13] Similar sentiments were expressed by James A. Garfield and James M. Ashley of Ohio, George S. Boutwell of Massachusetts, Ignatius Donnelly of Minnesota, and William A. Newell of New Jersey—Republicans all.[14] Nevertheless, as Senator Trumbull emphasized, it was not included in the Civil Rights Bill. Why not? Because, in the words of David Donald, it was "political dynamite."[15] The reasons have been so admirably compressed by Professor Van Alstyne as to bear quotation in extenso. He notes that the Joint Committee considered a forthright proposal to abolish "any distinctions in political or civil rights . . . on account of race" and states,

> The decision was made, however, not to propose a limited, single purpose amendment; not to advertise the particular issue of Negro suffrage and to dispose of it through a provision instantly invalidating the laws of all states where equal suffrage regardless of race was denied. The reluctance of the Republicans bluntly to dispose of the issue in this fashion is readily explainable; there was not sufficient prospect that the necessary number of votes would ratify such an amendment.
>
> There were, in 1866, but five states in the nation that permitted Negroes to vote on equal terms with whites: Maine, Massachusetts, New Hampshire, Rhode Island, and Vermont. Together, these states contained a mere 6 per cent of the Negro population. New York also permitted Negro suffrage, but only for those possessed of at least a $250 freehold estate, an added "qualification" that whites were not obliged to satisfy. No other state permitted Negroes to vote, regardless of qualification. Moreover, in late 1865, shortly before the Thirty-ninth Congress convened, Connecticut, Minnesota, and Wisconsin

13. Id. 1182. Senator Yates of Illinois declared "suffrage . . . the only remedy," id. 3037.

14. Id. 2462, 2882, 310, 589, 867.

15. Donald, *Sumner II* 202. Senator Garrett Davis of Kentucky stated, "Negro suffrage is political arsenic. If it is not, why do not the free States open wide their throats and gulp down the graceful and invigorating draught?" *Globe* 246.

voted down impartial suffrage by popular referendum. The Territory of Colorado defeated a referendum for impartial suffrage by a wide margin in September, 1865, and was, nevertheless, admitted to the Union by Congress.

The admission of Colorado, with its ban on Negro voting, followed the admission of Nevada, which had a similar ban, and was in turn, followed by the readmission of Tennessee on July 24, 1866. The readmission of Tennessee [*after* submission of the Fourteenth Amendment with its equal protection clause for ratification] was accomplished, moreover, with complete awareness that its general assembly had, on June 5, 1865, restricted the franchise to white males only. Indeed, all these facts were well known to the Congress, and were gleefully recited by some of the Democrats who challenged the Republicans to dare make an issue of Negro suffrage.

All these things and more had a conspicuous and significant influence on the Thirty-Ninth Congress.[16]

Indeed they had! They explain why the framers rejected Negro suffrage, as may immediately be gathered from two statements among many. Senator Pomeroy stated: "This nation . . . has not yet reached the point of giving all men their rights by a suffrage amendment; three-fourths of the States are not ready."[17] In opening the debate on the Amendment, Senator Jacob Howard stated on behalf of the Joint Committee, "it was our opinion that three-fourths of the States . . . could not be induced to grant the right of suffrage, even in any degree or under any restriction, to the colored race."[18] These views were repeated in the Final Report of the Joint Committee on Reconstruction.[19]

16. Van Alstyne 69–70. See also infra Chapter 5 at note 74. "The off-year state elections of 1867," during which ratification of the Fourteenth Amendment was debated, "made clear the popular hostility to black suffrage in the North." Morton Keller, *Affairs of State* 81 (1977).

17. *Globe* 1182.

18. Id. 2766.

19. Infra Chapter 5 at note 49.

If Negro suffrage was unacceptable to the great mass of Republicans, how can we read into the general terms "equal protection" the very grant they could not swallow? Van Alstyne also notes a number of proposals that would expressly abolish distinctions "in the exercise of the legislative franchise on account of race or color" (including one by Sumner that was rejected by a vote of 38 to 8),[20] and explains that "there was not sufficient prospect that the necessary number of States would ratify such an amendment." Are we to impute to the framers an intention to shroud in ambiguity the Negro suffrage they dared not "advertise" by a "blunt," unequivocal proposal? Something of the sort is suggested by Van Alstyne,[21] but there is no evidence of representations that the Fourteenth would mean one thing in 1866 and the very thing then "feared" in the future. A legislative intention to have words mean one thing in 1866 and the opposite in the future is so remarkable as to call for strict proof, not speculation, particularly when disclosure spelled political disaster.[22] But let me defer comment on this "open-ended" theory, fathered by Alexander Bickel, embraced by Alfred Kelly and Van Alstyne, and then picked up by Justice Brennan, to a later chapter, and for the moment permit the framers to speak for themselves. Because the suffrage issue is so vital for my subsequent discussion of the scope of judicial review, because in the eyes of Justice Brennan the historical record is "vague and imprecise,"[23] it is essential by copious doc-

20. Van Alstyne 69.

21. See infra Chapter 6 at note 53.

22. In an analogous situation Van Alstyne states, "It is even likely, by way of conjecture, that had the subject [reapportionment] been discussed there might have been a disavowal of an intention to apply the Equal Protection Clause to malapportionment, at least at that time . . . [But] hypothetical answers to hypothetical questions never actually entertained at the time would be a most dubious basis for expounding the content of 'equal protection' one hundred years later." Van Alstyne 85.

23. Oregon v. Mitchell, 400 U.S. 112, 278. Justices White and Marshall joined in this opinion.

umentation to establish firmly the deliberate exclusion of
Negro suffrage.

Negro Suffrage Was Unacceptable. With but "6% of the
Negro population," New England's advocacy of Negro suffrage, Senator Edgar Cowan of Pennsylvania acidly lectured
Sumner, came cheap: "he simply had no understanding of what
it is to live in a community surcharged with an idle, dissolute,
vicious, ignorant negro population just emerged from slavery."[24] At the other end of the political spectrum, the Radical
leader Thaddeus Stevens, also of Pennsylvania, wrote, "In my
county are fifteen hundred escaped slaves. If they are specimens
of the negroes of the South, they are not qualified to vote."[25]
Stevens told Robert Dale Owen, "We haven't a majority, either
in our committee or in Congress, for immediate suffrage; and I
don't believe the States have yet advanced so far that they would
ratify it."[26] William Lloyd Garrison, the indomitable abolitionist, "came out against the forcing of Negro suffrage upon the
South."[27]

The Republicans were keenly alive to the situation. Very
early in the session, Roscoe Conkling explained,

> The northern states, most of them, do not permit negroes to
> vote. Some of them have repeatedly and lately pronounced
> against it. Therefore, even if it were defensible as a principle for

24. Donald, *Sumner II* 158. Sumner himself had stated that "one must not
assume 'that a race, degraded for long generations under the iron heel of
bondage, can be taught at once all the political duties of an American citizen' . . . he thought that most of the negroes, free and contented, would
remain in the South as 'a dependent and amiable peasantry.'" Donald, *Sumner I* 235. But after 1864 he shifted because, as he wrote, "Without them,
the old enemy [slave oligarchy] will reappear . . . and in alliance with the
Northern democracy, put us all in peril again." Donald, *Sumner II* 201.

25. Fawn M. Brodie, *Thaddeus Stevens: Scourge of the South* 211 (1959);
C. Vann Woodward, *The Burden of Southern History* 92 (1960).

26. James 101.

27. Brodie, supra note 25 at 230–231.

the Central Government to absorb by amendment the power to control the action of the States in such a matter, would it not be futile to ask three-quarters of the States to do for themselves and others, by ratifying such an amendment, the very thing most of them have already refused to do in their own cases?[28]

Senator Fessenden, chairman of the Joint Committee, said of a suffrage proposal, there is not "the slightest probability that it will be adopted by the States . . . [it] would not commend itself to anybody."[29] Sumner's own Massachusetts colleague, Senator Henry Wilson, a leading Radical, commented on Senator Henderson's proposal of suffrage without distinction of race, "I cannot think . . . there is any hope of adoption after the indications of the last six months."[30] Another Senator who favored Negro suffrage, Doolittle of Wisconsin, said, "out of New England there are not three States in this Union, neither Nevada nor Colorado, nor any of the new States or the old States that will vote for an amendment . . . by which negro suffrage shall be imposed upon the States."[31] Similar remarks were made by still others.[32] On July 21, 1866, shortly after the Amendment passed the Congress, Sumner proposed an amendment to a bill for admission of Tennessee that "there shall be no denial of the electoral franchise, or of any other rights, on account of color or race, but all persons shall be equal before the

28. *Globe* 358. Nathaniel Banks of Massachusetts stated, "The public opinion of the country is such at this precise moment [May 1866] as to make it impossible we should do it." Id. 2532.

29. Id. 704.

30. Id. 1256.

31. Id. 2143. Senator Henderson stated, "the country is not yet prepared" to grant Negro suffrage. Id. 3035. Senator Sherman said, "no man can doubt . . . there was a strong and powerful prejudice in the Army and among all classes of citizens against extending the right of suffrage to negroes." *Globe App.* 127.

32. See: Senator Lane of Kansas, *Globe* 1799; Garfield and Ashley of Ohio, id. 2462, 2882; Senators Howard, Poland, and Sherman, id. 2766, 2963, and *Globe App.* 131.

law." It was voted down without debate, 34 to 4.[33] This background lends meaning to Senator Howard's assurance that "the *first section of the proposed amendment* does not give . . . the right of voting. The right of suffrage is not, in law, one of the privileges or immunities thus secured"[34]—an echo of assurances during debate on the Civil Rights Bill. Bingham likewise stated that "The amendment does not give . . . the power to Congress of regulating suffrage in the several States."[35] In any event, how can we attribute to the ratifiers approval of Negro suffrage when midway in the course of ratification, in the elections of April 1867, Bingham's own State, Ohio, "overwhelmed a negro suffrage amendment by 40,000? In every state where the voters expressed themselves on the Negro suffrage issue they turned it down."[36]

Attachment to State Sovereignty.   Notwithstanding that the States' Right doctrine had been badly tarnished by its association with secession, a potent factor in the exclusion of Negro suffrage was a deep-seated attachment to State sovereignty. That this was no mere rationalization for Negrophobia may be gathered from the objection of Senator James W. Grimes of Iowa to a national livestock quarantine measure: "Let us go back to the original condition of things, and allow the States to take care of themselves."[37] On the eve of the Civil War, Lincoln stated in his First Inaugural Address, "The right of each State to order and control its own domestic institutions according to its own judgment exclusively is essential to the balance of

33. *Globe* 4000. His similar motion on July 27 respecting Nebraska was rejected 34 to 5, id. 4222.

34. Id. 2766 (emphasis added).

35. Id. 2542.

36. Woodward, supra note 4 at 137.

37. *Globe* 2446. Senator Henry Anthony of Rhode Island asserted that "he would rather have cholera itself than such a bill." P. S. Paludan, *A Covenant With Death* 48 (1975).

powers on which the perfection and endurance of our political fabric depends."[38] So Story had earlier stated,[39] and this view was reiterated by Republicans like Thomas T. Davis, Robert S. Hale, and Giles W. Hotchkiss of New York[40] and Latham of West Virginia. Congress, Latham said, "has no right to interfere with the internal policy of the several states."[41] "The proposition to prohibit States from denying civil or political rights to any class of persons," said Conkling, "encounters a great objection on the threshold. It trenches upon the principle of existing local sovereignty . . . It takes away a right which has been always supposed to inhere in the States."[42] Bingham, a leader in the Negro cause, stated that "the care of the property, the liberty, and the life of the citizen . . . is in the States and not in the federal government. I have sought to effect no change in that respect."[43] It was because of the prevalence of such senti-

38. Quoted in *Globe* 2096. Governor (soon to be Senator) Yates of Illinois stated in 1865, "I am for unlimited state sovereignty in the true sense, in the sense that the State is to control all its municipal and local legislation and I would be the first to resist all attempts upon the part of the Federal Government to interpose tyrannical usurpation of power in controlling the legislation of States." Paludan, supra note 37 at 34.

39. The State "police power extends over all subjects within the territorial limits of the States and has never been conceded to the United States." Prigg v. Pennsylvania, 41 U.S. (16 Pet.) 539, 625 (1842), quoted in *Globe* 1270. Samuel S. Marshall of Illinois stated, "It is a fundamental principle of American law that the regulation of the local police of all the domestic affairs of a State belong to the State itself, and not to the Federal Government." *Globe* 627.

40. *Globe* 1083, 1085–1086, 1063; infra Chapter 10 at notes 77–78.

41. *Globe* 1295–1296.

42. Id. 358; see also Delano, *Globe App.* 158; Charles A. Eldredge, *Globe* 1154.

43. *Globe* 1292. He repeated, "I have always believed that the protection in time of peace within the State of all the rights of person and citizen was of the powers reserved to the States." Id. 1293. Commenting earlier on Hale's view that "the citizens must rely upon the State for their protection," he said, "I admit that such is the rule under the Constitution as it now stands." Id. 1093. Such reiteration testifies to pervasive uneasiness about the impairment of State sovereignty, uneasiness shared by his fellow Ohioan, Chief Justice Salmon

ment that Trumbull, defending the Civil Rights Bill after President Johnson's veto, felt constrained to reassure the Senate that the Bill "in no manner interferes with the municipal regulations of any State which protects all alike in their rights of person and property."[44]

This sentiment emerges even more sharply when suffrage is in issue, as when Conkling stated that interference therewith "meddles with a right reserved to the States . . . and to which they will long cling before they surrender it."[45] Early in the session, the Radical leader Stevens said of a proposed amendment to reduce State representation in proportion to a denial of Negro suffrage: "I hold that the States have the right . . . to fix the elective franchise within their own States. And I hold that this does not take it from them . . . How many States would allow Congress to come within their jurisdiction to fix the qualification of their voters? . . . You could not get five in this Union."[46] In the Senate, Chairman Fessenden stated, "everybody has admitted from the foundation of the Government down to the present day that the power to fix the qualifications of voters rested with the States," and that the proposed "representation" provision "leaves it just as it was before, and does not change it."[47] After stating his preference for Negro

---

Chase, who regretted that the Joint Committee had gone too far: "Even the loyal people in Northern states, he feared, might oppose the amendment because of its threat to state rights." James 118. This was a man of "radical tendencies." Id.

44. *Globe* 1761.

45. Id. 358; see also Thomas N. Stillwell of Indiana, id. 670; Senator Cowan, id. 1286; Shellabarger, id. 1293; Senator Poland, id. 2962.

46. Id. 536. Senator Lane of Indiana, who favored strong measures against the rebels, said, "the right to determine the qualifications of electors is left with the several States . . . I do not believe that Congress has a right to interfere between [Indiana] and the people and fix the qualifications of voters." Id. 740.

47. Id. 1279, 1278; see also id. 704. This assurance was meaningless if §1 conferred suffrage.

suffrage, Senator Doolittle said that "the Federal Government had no right or constitutional power to impose on a State negro suffrage . . . the right of a State to determine that question was one of the reserved rights of every State." Like Stevens, he averred that "out of New England" no three States would vote for an amendment "by which negro suffrage shall be imposed upon the States."[48] Although Senator Henderson of Missouri was an advocate of Negro enfranchisement, he too stated that he was "not now ready to take away from the States the long-enjoyed right of prescribing the qualifications of electors in their own limits."[49] "The Radical leaders," Flack stated, "were aware as any one of the attachment of a great majority of the people to the doctrine of States rights . . . the right of the States to regulate their own internal affairs."[50] These sentiments were accurately summarized by Justice Miller in 1872, shortly after adoption of the Fourteenth and Fifteenth Amendments:

we do not see in those amendments any purpose to destroy the main features of the general system. Under the pressure of all the excited feeling growing out of the war, our statesmen have still believed that the existence of the states with power for domestic and local government . . . was essential to the working of our complex form of government.[51]

48. Id. 2143.

49. *Globe App.* 120.

50. Flack 68. "One reason the Reconstruction of the South loomed so high to northerners," Harold Hyman concluded, "was less that blacks were involved than that every one understood the pre-eminence of states . . . in affecting all their citizens' lives." H. M. Hyman, *A More Perfect Union* 426 (1973). In "early 1865 virtually unhampered state powers were considered fundamental for liberty, federalism and democracy." Id. 301. "A heavy phalanx of Republican politicos, including Sherman and Trumbull . . . were states rights nationalists, suspicious of any new functional path the nation travelled." Id. 304. "No one reading the debates carefully," said Graham at 312, "will question the framers' devotion to federalism, even the extreme Radicals."

51. The Slaughter-House Cases, 83 U.S. (16 Wall.) 36, 82 (1872).

This "commitment to traditional state-federal relations meant," in the words of Alfred Kelly, that "the radical Negro reform program could be only a very limited one."[52] That it was in fact a program "limited" to a ban on discrimination with respect to "fundamental rights" from which suffrage was excluded is confirmed by §2.

THE EFFECT OF §2

The framers' intention to leave control of suffrage in the States, untouched by §1, is confirmed by §2 of the Amendment. That section provides,

> Representation shall be apportioned among the several States according to their respective numbers, counting the whole number of persons in each State. But when the right to vote at any election . . . is denied . . . or in any way abridged . . . the basis of representation therein shall be reduced.[53]

The denial is not prohibited, it is not declared void, but as Eckley of Ohio put it, if a State "persists in withholding the ballot" from blacks, she will be "confine[d] . . . to the white basis of representation."[54] It is difficult to dispute Justice Harlan's conclusion that §2 "expressly recognizes the State's power to deny 'or in any way' abridge the right . . . to vote."[55] Were this doubtful, doubts are dispelled by the

---

52. Kelly's remark in "Comment on Harold M. Hyman's Paper" in *New Frontiers of the American Reconstruction* 55 (H. M. Hyman ed.), written in 1966, constitutes to my mind a tacit repudiation of his earlier pieces. Hyman notes Republican unwillingness "to travel any road more rugged than the Civil Rights–Freedmen's Bureau extension–Fourteenth Amendment route that left the states masters of their fates." Hyman, supra note 50 at 470; see also id. at 440, 448.

53. For earlier variants, see James, Index "Representation."

54. *Globe* 2535.

55. Reynolds v. Sims, 377 U.S. 533, 594.

"blinding light" of the legislative history.[56] Since that is disputed by Van Alstyne and Justice Brennan, the evidence must be permitted to speak for itself, unfiltered by a commentator's paraphrase.

Bingham, a leading Republican member of the Joint Committee, the pillar of the neoabolitionists, said, "we all agree . . . that the exercise of the elective franchise . . . is exclusively under the control of the States . . . The amendment does not give, as the second section shows, the power of regulating suffrage in the several States."[57] Instead, as he said of a predecessor proviso, it "offers an inducement to those States . . . to make the franchise universal."[58] On the Senate side, Chairman Fessenden said of an earlier provision, H.R. No. 51, couched in terms of racial discrimination respecting suffrage, "It takes the Constitution just as it finds it, with the power in the States to fix the qualifications of suffrage precisely as they see fit . . . If in the exercise of the power you [States] have under the Constitution you make an inequality of rights, then you are to suffer such and such consequences."[59] When illness prevented Fessenden from explaining §2, Senator Howard stated: "The second section leaves the right to regulate the elective franchise with the States, and does not meddle with that right." Later he added: "We know very well that the States retain the power which they have always possessed of regulating the right of suffrage . . . the theory of this whole amendment is to leave the power of regulating the suffrage with . . . the

56. Van Alstyne, 36, refers to "the kind of blinding light that Mr. Justice Harlan sees here."

57. *Globe* 2542.

58. Id. 432.

59. Id. 1279. Fessenden explained the Committee's espousal of the "representation" provision subsequently embodied in §2: "we cannot put into the Constitution, owing to existing prejudices and existing institutions, an entire exclusion of all class distinctions." Id. 705. The effect of the proposed amendment, he stated, "is simply to leave the power where it is, and leave it perfectly in the power of the States to regulate suffrage as they please." Id.

States."[60] Senator Yates of Illinois recognized that "we do not obtain suffrage now"; Senator Doolittle of Wisconsin stated, the "amendment proposes to allow the States to say who shall vote"; Senator Poland of Vermont would have preferred that "the right of suffrage had been given at once," but realized it was not "practicable"; Senator Howe of Wisconsin likewise preferred to say "no man shall be excluded from the right to vote" to saying "hereafter some men may be excluded from the right of representation."[61]

In the House, Blaine of Maine stated, "The effect contemplated . . . is perfectly well understood, and on all hands frankly avowed. It is to deprive the lately rebellious States of the unfair advantage of a large representation in this House, based on their colored population, so long as that people shall be denied political rights. Give them the vote or lose representation."[62] Conkling stated that the Joint Committee rejected proposals "to deprive the States of the power to disqualify or discriminate politically on account of race or color" and preferred "to leave every State perfectly free to decide for itself . . . who shall vote . . . and thus to say who shall enter into its basis of representation." "[E]very State," he reiterated, "will be left free to extend or withhold the elective franchise on

60. Id. 2766, 3039. Senator Wilson of Massachusetts stated that the "right to vote . . . has been regulated by the State in every State . . . from the beginning of the Government." Id. 1255. Senator Yates of Illinois did "not deny the power of the States to regulate suffrage." Id.

61. *Globe* 3038, 2943, 2963–2964, *Globe App.* 219. Senator Henderson had proposed an amendment to the "representation" proposal, prohibiting discrimination with respect to suffrage (id. 702), but he later supported "representation" because "the country is not yet prepared" for Negro suffrage. Id. 3035. Senator Reverdy Johnson, probably the most open-minded of the Democrats, understood the Amendment to concede "to the States . . . the exclusive right to regulate the franchise" so that the United States would "be impotent to redress" exclusion of blacks. *Globe* 3027. Another Democrat, Senator Davis, stated that the measure "shrinks from . . . openly forcing suffrage upon the States, but attempts by a great penalty to coerce them to accept it." *Globe App.* 240. See also Senator Hendricks, *Globe* 2939.

62. Id. 141.

such terms as it pleases, and this without losing anything in representation if the terms are impartial to all." And he summed up, "every State has the sole control, free from all interference, of its own interests and concerns," spelling out that if New York chose to withhold suffrage, "her right cannot be challenged."[63] Stevens, co-chairman of the Joint Committee, stated that the right of a State to disfranchise "has always existed under the Constitution" and the proposed "representation" provision "acknowledges it." He repeated that "the States have the right . . . to fix the elective franchise" and that the proposed representation provision "does not take it from them." In fact, he preferred the reduction of representation to an "immediate declaration" that "would make them [Negroes] all voters"; he did not "want them to have the right of suffrage" until they had been educated in "their duties . . . as citizens."[64] Although Garfield expressed his "profound regret" that the Joint Committee had been unable to "imbed . . . [suffrage] as a part of the fundamental law of the land," he stated, "I am willing . . . when I cannot get all I wish to take what I can get."[65] Similarly, John F. Farnsworth of Illinois stated, "I should prefer to see incorporated into the Constitution a guarantee of universal suffrage; as we cannot get the required two-thirds for that, I cordially support this proposition as the next best."[66]

Nathaniel P. Banks of Massachusetts congratulated the Joint Committee for "waiv[ing] this matter in deference to public opinion," and George F. Miller of Pennsylvania stated, "This amendment will settle the complication in regard to suffrage and representation, leaving each State to regulate that for itself."[67] Against this mass three Democrats raised the possibility in the House that the amendment might affect suffrage qualifi-

63. Id. 357, 358, 359.
64. Id. 428, 536.
65. Id. 2462.
66. Id. 2540.
67. Id. 2532, 2510.

cations.[68] On the other hand, leading Democrats—Senators Reverdy Johnson and Garrett Davis—better understood that it left suffrage to the States.[69] These historical materials, which by no means exhaust the quotable statements,[70] seem to me, as to Robert Dixon and Ward Elliott, "overpowering," "overwhelming."[71] In discreetly skirting the issue the Court tacitly acknowledged their unimpeachability. The rebuttal thus eschewed by Chief Justice Warren was undertaken by Professor Van Alstyne, and it emboldened Justice Brennan to pick up the cudgels in a later case, *Oregon v. Mitchell.*

Before examining the Warren and Brennan opinions it is desirable to consider in this setting the argument against reapportionment and its relation to suffrage.

68. Niblack, Benjamin M. Boyer of Pennsylvania, and Andrew J. Rogers of New Jersey. Justice Harlan comments on these statements in Oregon v. Mitchell, 400 U.S. at 181–182.

69. Supra note 61.

70. See supra note 55 at 626–632. Samuel McKee of Kentucky, who supported the Amendment, stated, "this House is not prepared to enfranchise all men." *Globe* 2505. William D. Kelley of Pennsylvania said, "Could I have controlled the report of the Committee of Fifteen, it would have proposed to give the right of suffrage to every loyal man." Id. 2469. Boutwell of Massachusetts stated, "The proposition in the matter of suffrage falls short of what I desire . . . I demand . . . the franchise for all loyal citizens." Id. 2508. But like others of the same persuasion, he voted for the Amendment.

Broomall understood §2 "to limit the representation of the several States as those States themselves shall limit suffrage." Id. 2498. Lawrence said that the "representation" amendment "does not propose to extend the right of suffrage to or to withhold it from any class of people . . . It does not propose to disturb the commonly received construction of the Constitution which leaves to the State the right to determine who shall or shall not be voters." Id. 404. G. F. Miller of Pennsylvania conceded "to each State the right to regulate the right of suffrage . . . they ought not to have a representation for" excluded persons. The Amendment "leav[es] each State to regulate that for itself." *Globe* 2510. See also Thayer, id. 282; Eliot, id. 2511.

71. Robert Dixon, "Reapportionment in the Supreme Court and Congress: Constitutional Struggle for Fair Representation," 63 Mich. L. Rev. 209, 212 (1964); Elliott, supra note 4 at 127.

5

Reapportionment

BAKER v. Carr (1962), the unprecedented reapportionment decision, said
Paul Kauper, opened a "new chapter of
judicial adventurism."[1] When the issue was once again presented in *Reynolds v. Sims,* Justice Harlan wrote a dissent that to
my mind is irrefutable. The majority of the Court made no pretense of meeting his historical demonstration; it remained for
William Van Alstyne to essay a rebuttal. Harlan's reliance on
the legislative history to establish the "original understanding,"
Van Alstyne writes, pertains solely to "exclusive state power

---

1. Paul Kauper, "Some Comments on the Reapportionment Cases," 63
Mich. L. Rev. 243, 244 (1964). In more restrained diction, Archibald Cox instances the reapportionment cases as a "dramatic" example of "reading into
the generalities of the Due Process and Equal Protection Clauses notions of
wise and fundamental policy which are not even faintly suggested by the
words of the Constitution, and which lack substantial support in other conventional sources of law." *The Role of the Supreme Court in American Government* 100 (1976).

Reapportionment may have been "wise," but did it represent the kind of
emergency situation that at best arguably excuses judicial revision? Philip
Kurland considers that "reapportionment of the state and local legislatures
was not among the more pressing problems in post–World War II America."
Politics, the Constitution and the Warren Court 83 (1970). For an extended and
persuasive demonstration that reapportionment was not necessary, see Ward
Elliott, *The Rise of a Guardian Democracy* (1974).

69

over suffrage qualifications" and has no bearing on "the separate issue of malapportionment"; "there was almost no mention of the subject."[2] That fact alone gives one pause: how can a revolution in *Northern* apportionment be based on nonmention?

The dominant purpose of the 39th Congress was to maintain Republican hegemony by reducing Southern representation; and only secondarily did they think to secure the "person and property" of the Negro from oppression.[3] There were repeated disclaimers of any intention to interfere with State sovereignty beyond those objectives. Moreover, while Negro suffrage was predominantly a Southern problem, reapportionment would invade long-established State practices with respect to *white* voters in the North.[4] But Van Alstyne argues that to read malapportionment in the equal protection clause "is to say *only* that among the enfranchised [white] elite," qualified by the State to vote, "no invidious distinction shall be permitted. The States may be as capricious as they please in withholding the ballot but not in perpetuating elites within the elite."[5] That is

2. Van Alstyne 78–79.

3. Supra Chapter 1 at note 55; Chapter 4 at note 4; Kendrick 207; cf. Van Alstyne 57.

4. Chief Justice Warren, Alfred Kelly states, "carefully neglected the far more important fact that every one of the state legislatures that sent delegates to Philadelphia was grossly malapportioned by any 'one man, one vote' standard, and the state conventions that ratified the Constitution were in every instance set up on the same rule of apportionment." "Clio and the Court: An Illicit Love Affair," 1965 S. Ct. Rev. 119, at 136–137. Justice Story, commenting on the possible introduction of a clause "to regulate the State elections of members of State legislatures" stated, "It would be deemed a most unwarrantable transfer of power, indicating a premeditated design to destroy the State governments. It would be deemed so flagrant a violation of principle as to require no comment." 1 Joseph Story, *Commentaries on the Constitution of the United States* §819 (5th ed. 1905).

5. Van Alstyne 80. Stevens stated that "This section [2] allows the States to discriminate *among the same class,* and receive proportionate credit in representation." *Globe* 2460 (emphasis added). So too, the antecedent Civil Rights Bill, Shellabarger stated, "does not prohibit you from discriminating between citi-

a tremendous "only." Republicans who shrank from interfering with State control of Negro suffrage in the South would scarcely have dared to impose on the North a radical reconstruction of white apportionment patterns.[6] Certainly there was no disclosure that such intrusion was contemplated;[7] there is in fact striking evidence that malapportionment was an accepted

---

zens of the same race . . . as to what their rights to testify, to inherit . . . shall be." *Globe* 1293.

6. With reference to a bill introduced by Sumner in March 1867, David Donald states, "Disturbed by the revolutionary changes Sumner hoped to bring about in the South, Republican Congressmen were horrified that he proposed to extend them to the North as well," among them to secure "the elective franchise to colored citizens." Donald, *Sumner II* 299. Bickel, 16 note 40, states that "Conservative Republicans who considered the Freedmen's Bureau Bill [applicable only in the South] an appropriate concession to offer to the Radicals, evidently felt quite differently about a statute which might be applied in their constituencies." "[N]ational enfranchisement of the Negro—which meant Negro voting in the North—was out of the question." William Gillette, *The Right to Vote: Politics and the Passage of the Fifteenth Amendment* 32 (1965). See also H. M. Hyman *A More Perfect Union* 470 (1973).

7. When the Amendment was submitted to the States for ratification, "the northern press," states Flack at 145, "with few exceptions, if any, took the view that the first section of the Amendment re-enacted or gave authority for, the Civil Rights Bill." He quotes a speech of Trumbull in Chicago: §1 "was a reiteration of the Civil Rights Bill"; and one of Sherman in Cincinnati: "the first section embodied the Civil Rights Bill"; id. 148.

Justice Black, that fervent advocate of reapportionment (Wesberry v. Sanders, 376 U.S. 1 (1964)), stated in his earlier attempt to read corporations out of the Fourteenth Amendment that "the people were not told they [were ratifying] an amendment granting new and revolutionary rights to corporations." Connecticut General Ins. Co. v. Johnson, 303 U.S. 77, 86 (1938), dissenting opinion. Compare supra Chapter 1 note 57. Justice Field, dissenting in Ex parte Virginia, 100 U.S. 339, 362–363 (1879), stated that the provision for Negro jurors was "a change so radical . . . [as] was never contemplated by the recent amendments. The people, in adopting them did not suppose they were altering the fundamental theory of their dual system of government." As we have seen, the framers actually contemplated the continued exclusion of Negro jurors. But the selfsame Field had no difficulty in advocating the tremendous alteration embodied in substantive due process.

practice. Speaking with respect to reduced representation, Blaine of Maine said,

> if you cut off the blacks from being enumerated in the basis of representation in the southern States the white population of those States will immediately distribute Representatives within their own territory on the basis of white population. Therefore the most densely populated negro districts will not be allowed to offset the most densely populated white districts . . . Do you suppose that the upland districts of Georgia and South Carolina, inhabited largely by whites, will, in the event of adoption of this amendment, allow the distribution of Representatives to be made on the basis of the whole population? By no means. They will at once insist on the white basis within the State.[8]

Not a hint that this would be unlawful, but, rather, clear recognition that States were free to apportion representation to suit themselves. Although, as Van Alstyne notices, this would leave "areas populated by non-voters without representation (and not merely without a vote in the choice of 'their' representatives),"[9] Bingham replied, "no possible amendment . . . will answer the purpose unless it is followed by further legislation."[10]

---

8. *Globe* 377. Malapportionment was fastened on the Constitution from the outset by the compromise which permitted three-fifths of the voteless Negro population to be counted for purposes of representation in the House of Representatives. Thereby, as John Quincy Adams remarked, "Every planter South of the Potomac has three votes in effect for every five slaves he keeps in bondage; while a New England farmer who contributes ten-fold as much to the support of the Government has only a single vote" (Nov. 8, 1804). Quoted in Samuel F. Bemis, *John Quincy Adams and the Foundation of American Foreign Policy* 123 note 37 (1949). The result was to give the South twenty-five additional members and to "enable the slave power to keep its grip on the nation." Samuel F. Bemis, *John Quincy Adams and the Union* 417, 446 (1956). Malapportionment was also embedded in the Constitution by the provision for two Senators from each State, although, as Thomas Hartley remarked in the First Congress, "their proportions are as ten to one." 1 *Annals of Congress* 481.

9. Van Alstyne 79 note 142.

10. Id.

Bingham thus confirms Blaine's recital of the plenary State power over apportionment and implies that the "representation" (§2) proposal was not designed to meet this situation. Van Alstyne's comment that "Blaine's remarks were directed only to the apportionment of congressional rather than state representation" implausibly suggests that the States would be readier to surrender control over their own internal patterns—a suggestion that is incompatible with the pervasive attachment to State sovereignty.

Blaine's remarks did not reflect a fleeting improvisation, but responded to established practice. Earlier he had stated: "As an abstract proposition no one will deny that population is the true basis of representation; for women, children and other non-voting classes may have as vital an interest in the legislation . . . as those who actually cast the ballot." But, he noted, recognizing existing practice, as had Federalist No. 54 and James Wilson long before,[11] "the ratio of voters to population differs very widely in different sections, from a minimum of *nineteen per cent* to a maximum of *fifty-eight per cent*."[12] Even that uncompromising abolitionist Charles Sumner was reconciled to such practices because they reflected "custom and popular faith," and could not be changed "unless supported by the permanent feelings and conditions of the people."[13] Then, too, in the con-

11. Infra at notes 26–27, 69–70.
12. *Globe* 141.
13. "The true basis for representation, Sumner declared in a speech to the [Massachusetts] convention on July 7 [1853], should ideally be founded 'absolutely upon equality' so as to make all men, in the enjoyment of the electoral franchise, whatever their diversity of intelligence, education or wealth, and wheresoever they may be within the Commonwealth, whether in small towns or populous city, 'absolutely equal at the ballot box.' But, he swiftly backtracked, this system of equal representation could not be advantageously instituted 'unless supported by the permanent feelings and conditions of the people.' As the practice of giving Massachusetts small towns disproportionate influence had sprung 'from custom and popular faith, silently operating with internal power, not from the imposed will of a lawgiver' . . . no radical change in the admittedly inequitable system should be tried at present, but in-

gressional debate of June 1868 (that is prior to ratification of the
Fourteenth Amendment), on the readmission of the Rebel States,
Farnsworth pointed out that the Florida apportionment provision gave "to the sparsely populated portions of the State the
control of the Legislature." But Ben Butler responded that the
Senate Judiciary Committee "have found the [Florida] constitution republican and proper," as did the Senate, the House Committee on Reconstruction,[14] and the House itself, thus reaffirm-
ing that such malapportionment did not violate the guarantee of
a "republican form of government," nor the equal protection
clause which was the work of Butler and his fellows. The Blaine,
Sumner, and Butler statements constitute hard evidence which
is not overcome by mere speculation.[15] Since, moreover, most
of the States were malapportioned, it is a strained assumption
that by ratification they surrendered a right they had exercised
from the outset, and of which surrender they were totally unap-
prised.[16]

---

stead the rural towns should be given more representation so as to protect the
Commonwealth against the 'commercial feudalism' of the big cities." Donald,
Sumner I 246, quoting 3 Sumner, *Works* 229–258. See supra note 4.

14. Quoted in Reynolds v. Sims, 377 U.S. 533, 605 (1964). Stevens likewise
stated that the several constitutions had been pronounced "republican in
form." Id. 604 note 42.

15. See Van Alstyne, quoted infra at note 17. "[T]o quarrel with the records without abundant cause is to engage in a desperate cause." H. G. Richardson and G. O. Sayles, "Parliament and Great Councils in Medieval
England," 77 L. Q. Rev. 213, 235–236 (1961). Roughly speaking, unless testimony is inherently incredible it must be countered by evidence, not speculation. Phillips v. Gookin, 231 Mass. 250, 251, 120 N.E. 691 (1918); Messon
v. Liberty Fast Freight Co. 124 F.2d 448, 450 (2d Cir. 1942); Eckenrode v.
Pennsylvania R. Co., 164 F.2d 996, 999 note 8 (3d Cir. 1947); cf. Miller v.
Herzfeld, 4 F.2d 355, 356 (3d Cir. 1925); Magg v. Miller, 296 F. 973, 979
(D.C. Cir. 1924).

16. After cataloging the "malapportioned" States, Justice Harlan asked,
"Can it be seriously contended that the legislatures of the States, almost
two-thirds of those concerned, would have ratified an amendment which
might render their own State constitutions unconstitutional?" 377 U.S. at 603.

When Van Alstyne dismissed Harlan's reading of the §2 phrase "or in any way abridged" because "once the congressional history" of this phrase is "canvassed . . . it becomes clear that the phrase had nothing at all to do with malapportionment," he scuttled his whole case. For, by the same token, the history of the equal protection clause likewise "had nothing at all to do with malapportionment." "There is," he states, "no evidence that §2 was applicable to abridgment of the right to vote resulting from malapportionment of state legislatures." "It is even likely," he avers, "that had the subject been discussed there might have been a disavowal of an intention to apply the Equal Protection Clause to malapportionment." But "hypothetical answers to hypothetical questions . . . would be a most dubious basis for expounding the content of 'equal protection' one hundred years later."[17] There is no need to speculate because Blaine and others plainly recognized malapportionment as an existing practice that was left untouched. I, too, prefer to eschew speculation, particularly when it is unnecessary. One

17. Van Alstyne 80, 81, 85. Alfred Kelly also dismisses Harlan's argument; "it neglected one embarrassing fact: both the provision of §2 and the extensive debate . . . were directed at the possibility of a state's limiting Negro franchise and not to the problem of district legislative apportionment, an entirely different historical question." Kelly, "Clio," supra note 4 at 137. Notwithstanding the difference, Chief Justice Warren built his reapportionment case on "one man, one vote." Because of this "embarrassing fact" Kelly charges that Harlan "indulged in a bit of law office history of his own." Id. That charge, as the above analysis of the same argument by Van Alstyne demonstrates, is without foundation. Nor is Kelly the man to cast stones.

He recorded that when he was retained in the desegregation case to file an historical brief for the NAACP (Kelly, Fourteenth, 1049n), he "manipulated history in the best tradition [?] of American advocacy, carefully marshalling every scrap of evidence in favor of the desired interpretation and just as carefully doctoring all the evidence to the contrary, either by suppressing it when that seemed plausible, or by distorting it when suppression was not possible." Kelly, "Clio," supra note 4 at 144. That is an astonishing admission from a *scholar* who upbraids the Court because it "carefully selected the materials designed to prove the thesis at hand, suppressing all data that might impeach the desired historical conclusion." Kelly, "Clio," supra note 4 at 126.

who would bring an unmentioned departure from settled practice within the perimeter of the Amendment has the burden of
proof, made heavier here by (1) the fact that Negro suffrage, on
which the Court rested its case for reapportionment, was
unmistakably excluded; (2) the plainly expressed attachment of
the framers to State sovereignty and their intention to intrude
no further than the limits of the Civil Rights Act; and (3) the
presumption that a diminution of powers reserved to the States
by the Tenth Amendment will be clearly stated.[18]

In one form or another, Van Alstyne would put asunder what
the Warren Court hath joined; he would jettison the Court's
"one man, one vote" postulate. Granting arguendo State power
"with respect to outright denials of the right to vote," he asks,
"is it equally so with respect to partial disfranchisement
through malapportionment?"[19] The simple answer is that the
greater includes the less.[20] If a State may altogether *deny* the
vote, it may *dilute* it. It was in these terms that Chief Justice
Warren rationalized reapportionment: the Constitution, he
held, protects the right to "vote," the "right to have one's vote

18. See supra Chapter 1 note 57. "An alleged surrender . . . of a power of
government . . . must be shown by clear and unequivocal language; it
cannot be inferred from . . . any doubtful or uncertain expressions." Bel-
mont Bridge v. Wheeling Bridge, 138 U.S. 287, 292–293 (1891).

Even where States were forbidden to legislate with respect to a particular
subject and Congress was empowered to enforce the prohibition, Justice
Bradley rejected the assumption that "this gives Congress power to legislate
generally upon that subject" as "repugnant to the Tenth amendment." Civil
Rights Cases, 109 U.S. 3, 15 (1883). In the Slaughter-House Cases, 83 U.S. (16
Wall.) 36, 78 (1872), Justice Miller rejected a construction which would subject
States "to the control of Congress, in the exercise of powers heretofore universally conceded to them" in the absence of "language which expresses such
a purpose too clearly to admit of doubt." One may differ with his construction of the Fourteenth Amendment, but the fact remains that he was neither
the first nor last to state that rule.

19. Van Alstyne 80.

20. "Nothing is more evident than that the greater must include the
less." Minor v. Happersett, 88 U.S. (21 Wall.) 162, 175 (1874).

counted." And "the right of suffrage can be denied by a debasement or dilution of the weight of a citizen's vote just as effectively as by wholly prohibiting the free exercise of the franchise."[21] His premise—that the Constitution, that is, the Fourteenth Amendment, protects the right to vote—is contradicted by historical facts. But his logic is impeccable and may be stated inversely: given a right to deny suffrage, it follows that there is a right to dilute it.

REPUBLICAN FORM OF GOVERNMENT

One of the "other" powers invoked by radical extremists was the guarantee of a "republican form of government."[22] Senator Sumner, its leading advocate, could do no better than to find it "obscure" and to write in 1865 that "the time has come to fix meaning to those words."[23] They were not wrapped in obscurity by the Founders. In the Federal Convention, Edmund Randolph stated that "a republican government must be the basis of a national union; and no state in it ought to have it in their power to *change* its government into a monarchy."[24] This was echoed by Madison in Federalist No. 43: "the superin-

21. Reynolds v. Sims, 377 U.S. 533, 554, 555. "The fundamental issue, as [Solicitor General Archibald Cox] puts it, is whether the State law 'arbitrarily and unreasonably apportions its legislature so as to deny the real meaning of the right to vote, i.e. effective participation in democratic government.'" Phil C. Neal, "Baker v. Carr: Politics in Search of Law," 1962 S. Ct. Rev. 252, 285.

My study of the "republican form of government" guarantee, infra at notes 22–47, persuaded me that the Founders had no intention of interfering with State control of suffrage. Justice Stewart's opinion (concurring and dissenting in part) in Oregon v. Mitchell, 400 U.S. 112, 288–290 (1970), pulls together the other textual and historical materials that confirm me in that view.

22. Van Alstyne 49–51.

23. Hyman, supra note 6 at 469. Sumner early invoked the "republican form of government" guarantee to secure blacks against "denial of rights, civil or political," and to make them "equal before the law." *Globe* 92.

24. 1 Max Farrand, *The Records of the Federal Convention of 1787* 206 (1911) (emphasis added).

tending government ought clearly to possess authority to defend the system against aristocratic or monarchical innovations . . . [the members of the Union have] the right to insist that the *forms* of government under which the compact was *entered* should be substantially *maintained.*" The guarantee "supposes a *preexisting* government of the *form* which is to be guaranteed. As long, therefore, as the *existing* republican forms are *continued* by the States they are guaranteed by the federal Constitution."[25] Although Federalist No. 52 stated that the "definition of the right of suffrage is very justly regarded as a fundamental act of republican government," it concluded that the right must be left to the States because "the different qualifications in the different States [could not be reduced] to one uniform rule."[26] Finally, Federalist No. 54, alluding to the allocation of representation according to the number of inhabitants, added, "the right of choosing their alloted number in each State is to be exercised by such part of the inhabitants as the State itself may designate . . . In every State, a certain proportion of inhabitants are deprived of this right by the Constitution of the State."[27]

Fessenden therefore stood on solid ground when he rebutted Sumner's reliance on the guarantee, saying, "in the very instrument in which the fathers provided that the United States should guaranty to every State a republican form of government they recognized the existence of slavery unmistakably . . . Did they then consider that the obligation to guaranty a republican form of government extended thus far, giving Congress the right to interfere in Virginia to examine her constitution?" When Sumner argued that the guarantee places Congress under a duty to "see that every man votes who ought to vote," said Fessenden, "he goes considerably further than those who made the Constitution ever intended to go." If a State "should choose to have a

25. Federalist 282, 283 (emphasis added).
26. Id. 341–342.
27. Id. 356.

monarchy, or the controlling portion of the people should choose to have an oligarchy, it then becomes the duty of Congress to interfere."[28] Such was the view of the Fathers, and it was reiterated by other leaders in the 39th Congress. Meeting a query whether a State would "cease to be republican" if it excluded a race from the franchise, Conkling responded that this "has always been permitted with universal acquiescence by the courts and the nation."[29] On the admission of Tennessee without provision for Negro enfranchisement, Bingham said in July 1866 that if this was in violation of the guarantee, then Tennessee was in the company of many Northern States. His critics were defeated by a vote of 125 to 12.[30] In the Senate, Trumbull stated, "most of us are here under republican forms of government, just like this in Tennessee."[31]

One of the dissentients, William Higby of California—whom Van Alstyne quotes as saying that no "State which excludes any class of citizens [from voting] on account of race or color is republican in form," and that he was opposed to H.R. No. 51 because "it gives a power to the States to make governments that are not republican in form,"[32]—revealed tellingly that he was merely engaged in wishful thinking. He admitted that by his disenfranchisement test his own State of California is "not republican in form": "I do not believe there is a single State in the Union, except it may be one of the New England States, which is an exception to that general rule . . . Now, sir, I am aware that the practice has been very differ-

---

28. *Globe* 706. David Donald comments that Sumner's program met with little favor in his own Massachusetts, that it "was not taken seriously," and that his "Republican colleagues greeted his resolutions and bills" with "total silence." Donald, *Sumner II* 234, 235, 240, 243.

29. *Globe* 358–359.

30. Id. 3980. Two of Van Alstyne's dissentients, Higby and Kelley, were among the twelve who voted against the admission.

31. Id. 3988.

32. Van Alstyne 50.

ent . . . from the establishment of the Government."[33] When Ralph Hill of Indiana stated that, in placing the guarantee in the Constitution, the Framers "spoke with reference to such governments as then existed, and such as these same framers recognized for a long time afterwards as republican governments," Higby replied: "that is a very good answer. It is an answer from a standpoint of seventy-five years ago. I speak from the standpoint of the present time."[34] Like our contemporary apologists for a judicial revisionary power, Higby would displace the established, original meaning with his own new one. Given that the Northern States discriminated against voting by blacks, "they were as subject to reconstruction by the federal authority" as was the South. For Radicals, "this whole argument contained political dynamite";[35] and Higby himself admitted, "I do not know that there are half a dozen in this House who will sustain me."[36] Like the 125 to 12 vote on the admission of Tennessee, Higby's concession underscores the framers' indifference to the dissentient views on which Van Alstyne largely pitches his case.

Is it to be wondered that the Court, as Carl Auerbach noted, "agreed in Baker v. Carr that 'any reliance' on the Guarantee clause would be futile?" Auerbach pointed out that the Court "never adequately answered Mr. Justice Frankfurter's argument that the equal protection claim it held to be justiciable was 'in effect a Guarantee Clause claim masquerading under a different label.' In fact the Court was being asked 'to establish an appro-

33. *Globe* 427.

34. Id. Shellabarger admitted that although the Southern States disenfranchised blacks, they have "been by common consent regarded as republican and constitutional." Id. 405. See also Thomas A. Jenckes of Rhode Island, id. 387. Replying to Sumner's argument that the limitation of suffrage to whites in the Colorado constitution violated the "republican form of government," Senator Stewart stated, "Nineteen of the free States now exclude blacks from the franchise." Id. 1330–1331.

35. Donald, *Sumner II* 202.

36. *Globe* 427.

priate form of government . . . for all the States in the Union.'"[37] Congress, as Auerbach noticed, had expressed its judgment, in one form or another, "as to the nature of a republican form of government," and it is Congress, not the Court, *Luther v. Borden* held, to whom that function is confided.[38] Where is the evidence that the framers who rejected the argument that Congress had power over State suffrage by virtue of the "republican form of government" guarantee meant to confer that power by the "equal protection" clause? It speaks

37. Auerbach, "The Reapportionment Cases: One Person, One Vote— One Vote, One Value," 1964 S. Ct. Rev. 1, 85. "Yet to rest the *Reapportionment Cases* on the Guarantee Clause creates difficulties of its own which must be evaluated . . . Historically the system of legislative representation prevailing in a State was intended to be subject to the requirements of the Guarantee Clause while, as we saw, the Equal Protection Clause was not originally intended to deal with this matter." Id. Paul Kauper likewise was critical of the conversion of equal protection to the guarantee of a republican form of government. "This is the central issue in these cases—what form of government is compatible with a representative form of government—and the guarantee of a republican form of government is the explicit constitutional provision relevant to the problem." Kauper, supra note 1 at 244.

38. Auerbach, supra note 37 at 86; 48 U.S. (7 How.) 1 (1849). Auerbach notices the "serious difficulty" posed by the fact that "Congress has admitted states into the Union and declared their forms of government to be 'republican,' even though their constitutions authorized systems of apportionment that the Court would now declare unconstitutional. It would be awkward for the Court to say not only that it has a role in enforcing the Guarantee Clause but that it also may overrule the expressed judgment of Congress as to the nature of a republican form of government" (in an area which Luther v. Borden held was not for the Court but for Congress). "The Court," Auerbach continues, "thinks it has avoided this contradiction of Congress by resting on the Equal Protection Clause . . . but the Court's explanation is not very satisfactory." Id. 86.

Auerbach finds solace in Justice Frankfurter's statement that "if the 'changing circumstances of a progressive society' for which the Constitution was designed 'yield new and fuller' import to the language of the Equal Protection Clause, they also yield new and fuller import to the language of the Guarantee Clause." Id. 87. Yet Frankfurter could not extend the "new and fuller import" to the reapportionment cases.

volumes that Sumner, who employed "equality before the law" in a school desegregation case (wherein Chief Justice Shaw held against him),[39] should have turned to the "republican form of government" guarantee in the 39th Congress. After passage of the Amendment he proposed that the admission of Tennessee and Nebraska be conditioned upon no denial of suffrage, a confession that the "equal protection" clause did not preclude such denials.[40]

Van Alstyne attaches considerable weight to Bingham's "unusually rewarding" appeal to "a republican form of government," which Bingham translated as a guarantee of the "right of franchise."[41] His view was not shared by influential Republicans, and in the course of the debates he shifted his position, stating, "we all agree . . . that the exercise of the elective franchise . . . is exclusively under the control of the States."[42] Shortly thereafter he changed course on the very "republican form" guarantee. He had moved for the admission of Tennessee, and Boutwell proposed "a condition precedent" that would require Tennessee to establish "suffrage for all male citizens," without which, he argued, Tennessee would not have a "republican form of government" because of the exclusion of 80,000 blacks.[43] Boutwell was twitted by Bingham: "Why does not the gentleman move for an expulsion of Missouri from representation?" "When [the blacks] shall vote rests with the people of the State. There I leave it." And, he concluded, with respect to the exclusion of Negroes, "So does Ohio, so does Pennsylvania, and so, also, do a majority of the States." Boutwell was voted down 125 to 12.[44]

39. Cf. Donald, *Sumner I* 180; Kelly, Fourteenth 1056.

40. Senator Sumner proposed as a condition upon the admission of Tennessee that there should be no denial of suffrage; the proposal was rejected by a vote of 34 to 4. Several days later a similar Sumner proposal respecting the admission of Nebraska was defeated by a vote of 34 to 5. *Globe* 4000, 4232.

41. Van Alstyne 51–52; *Globe* 431.

42. *Globe* 2542.

43. *Globe* 3950, 3975–3976.

44. Id. 3978–3979, 3980.

Bingham is invoked still again by Van Alstyne:

> The second section excludes the conclusion that by the first section suffrage is subjected to congressional law; save indeed, with this *exception,* that as the right in the people of each State to a republican government and to choose their Representatives in Congress is of the guarantees of the Constitution, by this amendment a remedy might be given directly for a case supposed by Madison, where *treason* might change a State government from a republican to a despotic government, and thereby deny suffrage to the people.[45]

Although Van Alstyne finds this statement "puzzling," it suffices to read the words in their ordinary sense: §2 shows that Congress was given no control of suffrage by §1, except in a case of a treasonable shift to a despotic government which does away with all voting. Manifestly, a change from representative government to a dictatorship calls for effectuation of the guarantee. But what light does this shed on the general control of suffrage? No subtle elucidation of this passage can cancel out Bingham's flat-footed statement that "the exercise of the elective franchise is exclusively under the control of the States," at a time when he completely abandoned the "guarantee" as a limitation on State control of suffrage.[46] The Supreme Court confirmed the views of the framers in 1874: "All the States had governments when the Constitution was adopted . . . These governments the Constitution did not change. They were accepted precisely as they were . . . Thus we have unmistakable evidence of what was republican in form."[47] Unless some special magic was deemed to inhere in the words "equal protection"—a supposition hereinafter examined—the evidence, to my mind, that suffrage was excluded from the Amendment is all but incontrovertible.[48]

45. Van Alstyne 62–63; *Globe* 2542; emphasis added; see supra at note 25.
46. *Globe* 2542; and supra at notes 43–44.
47. Minor v. Happersett, 88 U.S. (21 Wall.) 162, 175–176.
48. "It is clear," said the Court in Minor v. Happersett, id. at 171, "that the

The Report of the Joint Committee on Reconstruction, which Stevens, Boutwell, and Bingham signed, furnishes a conclusive summation:

> Doubts were entertained whether Congress had power, even under the amended Constitution, to prescribe the qualifications of voters in a State, or could act directly on the subject. It was *doubtful*, in the opinion of your committee, whether the *States would consent to surrender* a power they had always exercised, and to which they were attached. As the best if not the only method of surmounting the difficulty, and as eminently just and proper in itself, your committee came to the conclusion that political power should be possessed in all the States exactly in proportion as the right of suffrage should be granted, without distinction of color or race. This it was thought *would leave the whole question with the people of each State,* holding out to all the advantage of increased political power as an inducement to allow all to participate in its exercise.[49]

To "leave the whole question with the people of each State" is to say that §1 left suffrage untouched and that §2 was merely "an inducement [to the States] to allow all to participate in its exercise."

Constitution [Fourteenth Amendment] has not added the right of suffrage to the privileges and immunities of citizenship as they existed at the time it was adopted."

49. Report of the Joint Committee on Reconstruction, 39th Cong., 1st Sess. (undated, 1866) xiii (emphasis added). At an early stage Conkling stated that the Committee rejected a proposal "To deprive the States of the power to disqualify or discriminate politically on account of race" and instead approved a proposal "To leave every State perfectly free to decide for itself, not only who shall vote, but who shall belong to the political community in any way." *Globe* 357. Chairman Fessenden stated that §2 "leaves the power where it is," i.e., with the States. *Globe* 705. When James M. Ashley of Ohio was asked by his Ohio colleague, Francis LeBlond, "why the gentleman yields the question of suffrage, as he does, in supporting the [representation] proposition of the Committee," he replied, "Because I cannot get it." Id. 2882.

CHIEF JUSTICE WARREN'S OPINION IN REYNOLDS V. SIMS

Chief Justice Warren made no allusion to Justice Harlan's historical demonstration of the limited scope of the Fourteenth Amendment, and instead struck off a new version of constitutional principle and history. He premised that "the right to vote freely for the candidate of one's choice is of the essence of a democratic society, and any restrictions on that right strike at the heart of representative government."[50] Were Warren drafting a new Constitution that principle would be unexceptionable. But that was not the established principle at the adoption of the Constitution; nor was it embodied therein. On the contrary, Federalist No. 54 recognized that "in every State, a certain proportion of inhabitants are deprived of this right by the constitution of the State."[51] In the 39th Congress itself, Fessenden said that "everybody has admitted from the foundation of the Government down to the present day that the qualification of voters rested with the States."[52] Such was the clear consensus in the 39th Congress.

Warren postulated that "the conception of political equality from the Declaration of Independence, to Lincoln's Gettysburg Address, to the Fifteenth, Seventeenth and Nineteenth Amendments can mean only one thing—one person, one vote."[53] But Lincoln also bowed to "the right of each State to order and control its own domestic institutions,"[54] and reminded a Negro delegation of the ineradicable prejudice toward blacks, who were "far removed from being placed on an equality with the white man."[55] And if we are to extract a principle from the Fifteenth and Nineteenth Amendments it is that Congress and the

50. 377 U.S. at 555

51. Federalist 356; see supra at notes 26–27; infra at notes 69–70.

52. *Globe* 1279.

53. 377 U.S. at 558. This was quoted from the opinion of Justice Douglas in Gray v. Sanders, 372 U.S. 368, 381 (1963).

54. Supra Chapter 4 at note 38.

55. Supra Chapter 1 at note 36.

people considered that express Amendments were needed to confer suffrage on Negroes and women, that absent these Amendments neither enjoyed "political equality."[56] The point was made by the Court itself in *Minor v. Happersett* (1874), wherein a woman claimed that the Fourteenth Amendment endowed her with suffrage: "after the adoption of the fourteenth amendment, it was deemed necessary to adopt a fifteenth . . . If suffrage was one of the privileges and immunities [of the Fourteenth], why amend the Constitution to prevent its being denied on account of race."[57]

The Seventeenth Amendment likewise speaks against Warren, for it provides, with respect to the popular election of Senators that "the electors in each State shall have the qualifications requisite for electors of the most numerous branch of the State

56. As Justice Harlan stated, "the very fact that constitutional amendments were deemed necessary to bring about federal abolition of state restrictions on voting by reason of race (Amendment XV), sex (Amendment XIX) . . . is itself forceful evidence of the common understanding in 1869, 1919 . . . that the Fourteenth Amendment did not empower Congress to legislate in these respects." Oregon v. Mitchell, 400 U.S. at 202, dissenting and concurring in part.

57. 88 U.S. (21 Wall.) 162, 175. In United States v. Cruikshank, 92 U.S. 542, 555 (1875), Chief Justice Waite reaffirmed that "the fifteenth amendment has invested the citizens of the United States with a *new constitutional right,* which is exemption from discrimination in the exercise of the elective franchise on account of race. From this it appears that the right of suffrage is not a necessary attribute of national citizenship" (emphasis added).

After indicating that "the 15th and 19th amendments prohibit a State from overweighting or diluting votes on the basis of *race* or *sex,*" Chief Justice Warren, quoting a prior opinion, asked, "How then can one person be given twice or ten times the voting power of another person . . . merely because he lives in a rural area." 377 U.S. at 557. Given that discrimination in favor of "rural areas" is historically deep-rooted, orthodox analysis would conclude: because the Fifteenth and Nineteenth govern only "race and sex," not "rural areas." My citation of old cases does not betray a weakness for ancient vintages but responds rather to the weight long given to interpretations contemporary with or close to the event, particularly when they confirm the intention of the framers as disclosed by the legislative history. See infra Chapter 10 note 66.

legislature," qualifications, it will be recalled, that were under exclusive State control from the beginning and were left in place by the Fourteenth Amendment.

Reliance upon the Declaration of Independence to which the Radical left frequently appealed in the 39th Congress, might be dismissed with the remark of neoabolitionist tenBroek: "'All men are created equal' proclaimed the Declaration of Independence. All men? Well not quite all—not negro slaves like those owned by Jefferson, among others."[58] To import the Declaration into the Constitution is to overlook their totally different provenance. The Declaration was a product of rebels and revolutionaries; the Constitution came twelve years later, in no small part as a recoil from the "excesses" of popularly controlled legislatures.[59] Men of substance felt threatened and, in the words of John Dickinson, sought to protect "the worthy against the licentious."[60] TenBroek noted that "Equality was the dominant note in the Declaration," whereas a "stronger position" was accorded in the Constitution to "property,"[61] including property in slaves as the fugitive slave clause testifies. There is no blinking the fact, as Kent Newmeyer recently reminded us, that the Constitution was "racist."[62] Jefferson himself, author of the Declaration, predicted emancipation, but wrote: "it is equally certain that the two races will never live in a state of equal freedom . . . so insurmountable are the barriers which nature, habit and opinions have established between them."[63] Stevens powerfully summarized this history at the outset of the 39th Congress:

58. TenBroek 14.

59. Raoul Berger, *Congress v. The Supreme Court* 10–11 (1969).

60. Quoted in Gordon Wood, *The Creation of the American Republic 1776–1787* 475 (1969).

61. TenBroek 16.

62. "Book Review," 19 Am. J. Legal Hist. 66, 67 (1975). Kelly, however, regards efforts to prove that "the Constitution was exclusively a 'white man's document'" and "to discount the Declaration of Independence" as a lapse into "a priori, fiat technique." Kelly, "Clio," supra note 4 at 126 note 26.

63. Quoted in 1 Alexis de Tocqueville, *Democracy in America* 378n (1900).

Sir, our fathers made the Declaration of Independence; and that
is what they intended to be the foundation of our Government.
If they had been able to base their Constitution on the principles
of that Declaration it would have needed no amendment during
all time, for every human being would have had his rights; every
human being would have been equal before the law. But it so
happened when our fathers came to reduce the principles on
which they founded this Government into order, in shaping the
organic law, an institution hot from hell appeared among
them. . . . It obstructed all their movements and all their actions, and precluded them from carrying out their own principles into the organic law of this Union.[64]

It needs also to be borne in mind that the Declaration was
drawn by the Continental Congress, a league of independent
States, each of which jealously guarded its independence.[65] One
of the reasons advanced by Senator Poland for §1 of the Fourteenth Amendment was doubts as to Congress' power to
"destroy all such partial State legislation" as violated the "principles" of the Declaration of Independence.[66] Senator Howard,
a favorite of the neoabolitionists, stated that he could not discover the Negro right to vote in the Declaration of Independence and that, "notwithstanding the Declaration of Independence, it is the right of every organized political community to
regulate the right of suffrage."[67] Manifestly, Warren's appeal to
the Declaration as a guiding principle of constitutional construction is out of tune with the historical facts.

A word about his appeal to James Wilson's 1791 Lectures in
Philadelphia: "all elections *ought* to be equal. Elections are equal,
when a given number of citizens, in one part of the State,
choose as many representatives, as are chosen by the same

---

64. *Globe* 536.
65. See Raoul Berger, *Executive Privilege: A Constitutional Myth* 103–107
(1974).
66. *Globe* 2961.
67. Id. 2175.

number of citizens, in any other part of the state."[68] This stated an ideal, not a constitutional requirement. When Wilson turned to the Article I, §2, provision that "the Electors in each state shall have the qualifications requisite for Electors of the most numerous Branch of the State Legislature," he said, "the regulation is generous and wise. It is generous for it *intrusts* to . . . the several *states,* the very important power of ascertaining the qualifications" of the Electors. It was evidence of confidence, "that this foundation should be continued or altered by the States themselves."[69] Wilson was thoroughly aware of the disparate State exclusions from suffrage, having made a survey of the different State constitutions, even noticing that Connecticut provided power to exclude freemen, "according to the sentiments which others entertain concerning their conversations and behavior . . . a power of very extraordinary nature." And he praises "the wisdom . . . which rested one of the principal pillars of the national government upon the foundations prepared for it by the governments of the several states."[70] Warren's use of Wilson affords striking illustration of the "lawyers history" so justly condemned by Alfred Kelly.

Warren's pervasive error, to my mind, is to substitute twentieth-century logic for the framers' intention, so clearly expressed in the legislative history: "Logically, in a society *ostensibly grounded* on representative government, it would seem reasonable that a majority of the people in a State would elect a majority of that State's legislators."[71] "Ostensibly grounded"

68. Quoted in 377 U.S. at 564 note 41 (emphasis added). The quotation appears at 1 James Wilson, *The Works of James Wilson* 406 (R. G. McCloskey ed. 1967).

69. 1 Wilson, supra note 68 at 407 (emphasis added).

70. Id. at 409, 411.

71. 377 U.S. at 565 (emphasis added). Ward Elliott justly states that in Reynolds v. Sims the Court fabricated a "fundamental principle of 'one person, one vote' that was exactly the reverse of text and stated intent of the equal protection clause." Elliott, supra note 1 at 129. As a professor, Solicitor General Robert J. Bork wrote, "Chief Justice Warren's opinions in this series of [state legislative apportionment] cases are remarkable for their inability to

refuses to come to terms with the historical fact that suffrage
and apportionment were the province of the States. Once again
is demonstrated the wisdom of Holmes' aphorism, "a page of
history is worth a volume of logic."[72] That history was summarized with crystal clarity in the Report of the Joint Committee on Reconstruction.[73]

JUSTICE BRENNAN'S OPINION IN OREGON V. MITCHELL

Justice Brennan recognized that "racial prejudice in the
North" was a most "significant" obstacle in the path of equal
suffrage":

> Only five New England States and New York permitted any
> Negroes to vote as of 1866 . . . and extension of the suffrage
> was rejected by the voters in 17 or 19 popular referenda held on
> the subject between 1865 and 1868. Moreover, Republicans suf-
> fered some severe election setbacks in 1867 on account of their
> support of Negro suffrage . . .
>   Meeting in the winter and spring of 1866 and facing elections
> in the fall of the same year the Republicans thus faced a difficult
> dilemma: they desperately needed Negro suffrage in order to

---

muster a single respectable supporting argument. The principle of one man,
one vote . . . runs counter to the text of the fourteenth amendment, the history surrounding its adoption and ratification and the political practice of
Americans from Colonial times up to the day the Court invented the new formula." "Neutral Principles and Some First Amendment Problems," 47 Ind.
L.J. 1, 18 (1971).

72. New York Trust Co. v. Eisner, 256 U.S. 345, 349 (1921). Dissenting in
a reapportionment case, Justice Stewart stated, "these decisions mark a long
step backward into that unhappy era when a majority of the members of this
Court . . . convinced themselves and each other that the demands of the
Constitution were to be measured not by what it says, but by their own notions of wise policy . . . What the Court has done is to convert a particular
political philosophy into a constitutional rule." Lucas v. Colorado General Assembly, 377 U.S. 713, 747–748 (1964).

73. Supra at note 49.

prevent total Democratic resurgence in the South, yet they feared that by pressing for suffrage they might create a reaction among northern white voters that would lead to massive Democratic electoral gains in the North. Their task was thus to frame a policy that would prevent total Democratic resurgence and simultaneously would serve as a platform upon which Republicans could go before their northern constituents in the fall. What ultimately emerged as the policy and political platform of the Republican Party was the Fourteenth Amendment.[74]

Why could not the Republicans in Congress tell their constituents that unless Negro suffrage was granted Republican hegemony was doomed? Unless Northern voters preferred Democratic resurgence to Negro suffrage, the interests of Republican voters and members of Congress were one and the same. In fact the framers *shared* the prejudices of their Northern constituency, to recall only George W. Julian's statement in the House: "The real trouble is *we hate the Negro.*"[75] If the Republicans entertained a secret design to slip suffrage into the Amendment over voter opposition in order to hang on to office, they were betraying their constituency, and for this firm evidence needs to be adduced.

Given the framers' awareness of voter antipathy to suffrage, one would expect Justice Brennan to resolve all doubts in favor of those sentiments. Instead he substitutes twentieth-century speculation for historical fact to effectuate his own predilections and commits the very sin he incorrectly lays at Harlan's door: "historical analysis is flawed by ascription of 20th century meanings to the words of 19th century legislators."[76] For example, Harlan's "view would appear to allow a State to exclude any unpopular group on the basis of its political opinions."[77] But if State control over suffrage was plenary, if the Amend-

---

74. Oregon v. Mitchell, 400 U.S. at 255–256, dissenting in part.
75. *Globe* 257. Similar statements are collected supra Chapter 1 at note 40.
76. 400 U.S. at 251.
77. Id. 252 note 4.

ment left States free to exclude Negroes on account of their color, they were equally free to exclude others for their "political opinions," unpalatable as that appears to twentieth-century thinking. It will be recalled that James Wilson noticed the Connecticut provision for exclusion of freemen, "according to the sentiments which others entertain concerning their conversations and behavior . . . a power of very extraordinary nature." Historical analysis must proceed from the 1866 facts, not reason backward from 1970 predilections. Justice Brennan would substitute his choices for those of the framers; because we dislike a policy today, it does not follow that it is unconstitutional. That standard was rejected both by the Founders and by Chief Justice Marshall.[78]

Justice Brennan's opinion runs to some 38 pages; refutation, as is well-known, requires more space than bare assertion; hence only a sampling of the Brennan opinion can here be analyzed. A few examples, however, should suffice to disclose Justice Brennan's preference for speculation over fact. Section 1 began, he notices, as a "provision aimed at securing equality of 'political rights and privileges'"; but the Joint Committee rejected an express reference "to political and elective rights"; it dropped all references to "political rights" and spoke in terms of "privileges and immunities" and equal protection of "life, liberty, and property" by a vote of seven to six. Commenting on these facts, Justice Brennan stated, "the breakdown of the committee vote suggests that . . . no change in meaning was intended," because the "substitute was supported by men of all political views," among them Howard and Boutwell, "who had earlier sought to make the section's coverage of suffrage explicit," and Stevens and Fessenden.[79] But Boutwell, Fessenden, Howard, and Stevens later agreed that the Amendment did not grant suffrage and signed the Joint Committee Report that so stated. To deduce that Bingham merely "sought to do

78. See infra Chapter 14 at notes 103–104.
79. 400 U.S. 257–260.

no more than substitute for his earlier specific language more general language,"[80] ignores the repeated *rejection* of the specific proposals. General language may be construed to comprehend specific language that was earlier approved; but when specific language was rejected, evidence is required to explain why the rejected specific was now embodied in the general, evidence, not speculation. Then, too, Bingham cannot be lifted out of the mainstream of Republican statements that the Amendment *did not* confer suffrage; in fact he himself so stated.[81]

At the instigation of Robert Dale Owen, a reformer, Stevens had submitted a proposal that after July 4, 1876, "no discrimination shall be made . . . as to . . . the right of suffrage because of race." This provision was deleted by the Joint Committee, Justice Brennan notes, but "the reasons for the rewriting are not entirely clear." He notices, however, that in 1875 Owen furnished Stevens' explanation: "several state delegations held caucuses which decided that the explicit references to 'negro suffrage,' in any shape, ought to be excluded from the platform."[82] Is this not a "clear" explanation? By Brennan's own testimony the Republicans feared to endanger the Fall elections by the submission of Negro suffrage. He reasons, however, "Perhaps the changes in §1 of the Amendment were thought by the Committee to be mere linguistic improvements which did not substantially modify Owen's meaning."[83] The fact is that the 1876 provision was dropped to avoid alienating the electorate. That the "changes" were not "thought by the Committee to be mere linguistic improvements" is once more demonstrated by the unequivocal statement in its Report that suffrage had proven impossible of achievement and was left in the control of the States.

80. Id. 260.

81. See infra at notes 91–93.

82. 400 U.S. at 260–262. This incident is more fully discussed infra Chapter 6 at notes 38–41.

83. 400 U.S. at 263.

At "the very least," states Justice Brennan, "the Committee must have realized that it was substituting for Owen's rather specific language Bingham's far more elastic language—language that, as one scholar [Alexander Bickel] has noted, is far more 'capable of growth' and 'receptive to "latitudinarian" construction.'"[84] Because, Brennan amplified, "political considerations militated against clarification of issues and in favor of compromise," because "much of the North . . . opposed Negro suffrage, and many Republicans in Congress had to seek reelection from constituencies where racial prejudice remained rampant," "what Republicans needed, in the words of Wendell Phillips . . . was 'a party trick to tide over the elections and save time.'"[85] This is the Bickel "open-ended" theory which I shall hereafter examine; and I shall also collate the evidence which repels the conclusion that the framers purposely employed "elastic language" to dupe the voters.

For Justice Brennan "the purpose of §1 in relation to the suffrage emerges out of the debates . . . with an equal obscurity."[86] As exhibit #1 he instances Howard's statement that "the first section of the proposed amendment does not give to either of these classes the right of voting," which is "not as unambiguous as [it] initially appear[s]." This is because after stating that "the right of suffrage was not one of the privileges and immunities protected by the Constitution . . . he read into the record an excerpt from . . . Corfield v. Coryell . . . which listed the elective franchise as among the privileges and immunities."[87] But Senator Trumbull, after calling attention to this *Corfield* listing, had pointed out that suffrage was *not* included in the Civil Rights Bill.[88] One might deduce that Howard felt no need to repeat such a statement after twice stating

84. Id.
85. Id. 272, 273.
86. Id. 263.
87. Id. 263–264.
88. Supra Chapter 2 at notes 47, 31.

that the Amendment did not grant suffrage. Moreover, if an ambiguity be assumed, it was cured by his final statement: "the theory of this whole amendment is to leave the power of regulating the suffrage . . . with the States . . . and not to assume to regulate it."[89]

For exhibit #2, Justice Brennan turns to Bingham's "completely incongruous statement": "the exercise of the elective franchise though it be one of the privileges of a citizen of the Republic, is exclusively under the control of the States."[90] Now Bingham was a confused thinker, as I shall show, but on one thing he was clear: the Amendment did not confer suffrage. At a later point he said: "We all agree . . . that the exercise of the elective franchise . . . is exclusively under the control of the States . . . The amendment does not give, as the second section shows, the power of regulating suffrage in the several States." He further stated, "the second section excludes the conclusion that by the first section suffrage is subjected to congressional law."[91] Thereafter Bingham vigorously defended the exclusion of Negro suffrage from the Tennessee Constitution. When Boutwell objected during the debate on the readmission of Tennessee that in consequence it did not have a "republican form of government," Bingham replied that whether a black "shall vote rests with the people of [Tennessee]. There I leave it . . . I ask the gentlemen to weigh well the question when they come to vote, whether Tennessee shall be rejected only because the majority exercises the same power as to colored suffrage claimed for and exercised by all the other States."[92] This was after Congress submitted the Amendment with its "equal protection" clause to the people, and Bingham was upheld by a vote of 125 to 12,[93] an irreducible fact that speaks more loudly

89. *Globe* 3039; and see supra Chapter 4 at note 34.
90. 400 U.S. at 264.
91. *Globe* 2542.
92. Id. 3978, 3979.
93. Id. 3980.

than all of Justice Brennan's speculations. Here were materials
that cured the "ambiguity,"[94] that dissipated the "obscurity"
conjured up by Justice Brennan, of which he took no notice.
And why lean so heavily on the alleged "ambiguities" of two
leaders when the vast majority of the leadership and rank and
file affirmed or recognized that suffrage was excluded from the
Amendment?

Then there is Brennan's citation of Sumner, who was all but
ostracized in the Senate, whose proposals were regularly voted
down by very large majorities;[95] and his appeal to Stevens'
statement that the Amendment "merely allowed 'Congress to
correct the unjust legislation of the States, so far that the law
which operates upon one man shall operate *equally* upon all.'"[96]
Stevens sought equality with respect to the rights enumerated in
the Civil Rights Act, from which suffrage was excluded. But on
the issue of suffrage, he stated, "I hold that the States have the
right . . . to fix the elective franchise within their own States.
And I hold that this ["representation" proposal] does not take it
from them . . . How many States would allow Congress to
come within their jurisdiction to fix the qualifications of their
voters . . . You could not get five in this Union."[97] It was on
Stevens' motion that the Joint Committee adopted a reduction
of representation proposal; and it rejected Boutwell's motion to
"abolish" any distinction.[98]

Justice Brennan also refers to three Democratic opponents of
the Amendment who, more or less clearly, saw in it a grant of

94. 400 U.S. at 264.
95. Supra note 40; infra Chapter 7 at note 40. For rejection of another
Sumner proposal see supra Chapter 4 at note 20. A "deep estrange-
ment . . . existed between Sumner and his Republican colleagues . . . More
and more Senators came to distrust, when they did not detest, him." Donald,
Sumner II 248. See also supra notes 6 and 28.
96. 400 U.S. at 266.
97. *Globe* 536.
98. Kendrick 51, 55.

suffrage.[99] Opponents of a measure, particularly those who seek to discredit it, are given slight credence, as I shall show; their testimony is not employed to define its scope.[100] What are we to think of Brennan's reference to Senator Stewart, who, "while unhappy that the Amendment did not directly confer suffrage, nevertheless could 'support this plan' because it did 'not preclude Congress from adopting other means by a two-thirds vote'"?[101] Of course Congress could later propose *another* amendment by a "two-thirds vote"; Stewart plainly had no reference to Congressional implementation by statute, for that could be done by majority vote, given authorization by the Amendment.

Finally, Justice Brennan takes over Van Alstyne's critique of Harlan's alleged view that "§2 is specifically concerned with voting rights, and it provides an exclusive remedy that precludes or preempts application of §1."[102] Apparently this is based on Harlan's reference to the "Court's utter disregard of the second section which expressly recognized the State's power to deny the right . . . to vote and its express provision of a remedy for such denial or abridgment."[103] This unduly exalts a loose, passing reference to "remedy." Remedies are given for "wrongs"; it is no "wrong" to exercise the "recognized . . . power to deny the right . . . to vote." Then, too, since §1 conferred no suffrage, §2 obviously created no remedy for a nonexistent right. Certainly it gave no "remedy" to the black who was denied a vote. Senator Stewart, a Republican, sardonically commented that §2 relieves the Negro "from misrepresentation in Congress by denying him any representation what-

99. 400 U.S. at 267. Brennan also cites two other Democrats, Boyer of Pennsylvania and Senator Hendricks of Indiana, id. 274.

100. Infra Chapter 9.

101. 400 U.S. at 268.

102. Id. at 276–277; Van Alstyne 39.

103. Reynolds v. Sims, 377 U.S. at 594.

ever."[104] Justice Brennan explains that §2 "was of critical importance in assuring that, should the Southern States deny the franchise to Negroes, the Congress called upon to remedy that discrimination would not be controlled by the beneficiaries of discrimination themselves."[105] The truth is that §2 was the core of the Republican program because, as Brennan himself states, the Republicans needed to "prevent total [Democratic] resurgence," "massive electoral gains in the North." Reduction of representation when Negro suffrage was denied was deemed more important than endowing blacks with the vote; perceptive Republicans doubted whether the South would be "induced" to enfranchise Negroes and thus lose control.[106] Section 2, therefore, was not so much a "remedy" to enforce rights which §1 had not granted as a mechanism to preserve Republican hegemony. Forlorn hopes that the South could thereby be "induced" to confer suffrage were doomed to disappointment.

Enough has been set forth to exhibit Justice Brennan's strange preference for minority Democrats and dissentient radicals like Sumner over the Republican leadership and its followers who enacted the measure and whose utterances are virtually ignored by him, his preference for "ambiguous" utterances rather than the crystal-clear explanations of the self-same speakers, and for speculation over the mass of stubborn evidence to the contrary.[107] Future historians, I confidently predict, will not prefer the "history" of Brennan to that of Harlan.

104. *Globe* 2801. See also Senator Reverdy Johnson, supra Chapter 4 note 61.

105. 400 U.S. at 277.

106. Supra Chapter 4.

107. Unless evidence is inherently incredible, it must be countered by evidence, not speculation. Supra note 15.

6

The "Open-Ended" Phraseology Theory

We cannot put into the Constitution, owing to existing prejudices and existing institutions, an entire exclusion of all class distinctions.

Senator William P. Fessenden*

THE "open-ended" theory, shortly stated, is that the framers dared not submit Negro suffrage and the like to the electorate in 1866 and therefore discarded "specific" terms, as Justice Brennan put it, in favor of "far more elastic language—language that, as one scholar [Alexander Bickel] has noted, is far more 'capable of growth' and 'receptive to "latitudinarian" construction.'"[1] This is the classic invocation to extraconstitutional power,[2] power to revise the Constitution under the theory that the framers gave a "blank check to posterity."[3] Bickel had cautiously advanced the theory as an hypothesis; it found favor in scholarly circles,[4] and more posi-

---

* *Globe* 705. Fessenden was co-chairman of the Joint Committee on Reconstruction, which drafted the Amendment.

1. Oregon v. Mitchell, 400 U.S. 112, 263 (1970).

2. Cf. T. C. Grey, "Do We Have an Unwritten Constitution?" 27 Stan. L. Rev. 703, 712–713, 709 (1975); see infra note 9.

3. "The Constitution is not a blank check to posterity." Ward Elliott, *The Rise of Guardian Democracy* viii (1974). For a similar statement by Justice Black see infra Chapter 11 note 27.

4. Dean Francis Allen stated, "There is evidence that those who drafted Section 1 intended that the meanings of these phrases should evolve and expand with the passage of time and changes of circumstance." "The Constitution: The Civil War Amendments: XIII–XV," in D. Boorstin, *An American Primer* 161, 165 (1966). Carl Auerbach likewise noticed general agreement that

tively formulated variants were profferred by Alfred Kelly and Willian Van Alstyne. It has since been enshrined in an opinion by Justice Brennan; and Justice Black, jumping off from Brennan's paraphrase, announced that it made "the history of the Fourteenth Amendment . . . irrelevant to the present problem."[5] The theory is therefore deserving of close analysis.

Alexander Bickel   At the time the "desegregation" case, *Brown v. Board of Education,*[6] was first argued before the Supreme Court, Bickel was a law clerk of Justice Frankfurter, who assigned to him the task of compiling the legislative history of the Fourteenth Amendment, a task he performed brilliantly. When he delivered his memorandum in August 1953 he stated in a covering letter:

> It was preposterous to worry about unsegregated schools, for example, when hardly a beginning had been made at educating Negroes at all and when obviously special efforts, suitable only for the Negroes, would have to be made . . . It is impossible to conclude that the 39th Congress intended that segregation be abolished; *impossible* also to *conclude* that they *foresaw* it might be, *under the language* they were adopting.[7]

In 1962 he again wrote:

> Was it the intention of the framers . . . to forbid the states to enact and enforce segregation statutes? If one goes to the histori-

---

the original understanding did not comprehend "immediate" suffrage but that Congress wittingly chose "language capable of growth." "The Reapportionment Cases: One Person, One Vote—One Vote, One Value," 1964 S. Ct. Rev. 1, 75–76. Wallace Mendelson said that due process and equal protection "doubtless were designed to have the chameleon's capacity to change their color with changing moods and circumstances." *Justices Black and Frankfurter: Conflict in the Court* viii (1961).

5. 400 U.S. at, 139–140.

6. 347 U.S. 483 (1954).

7. Richard Kluger, *Simple Justice* 654 (1976) (emphasis added).

cal materials with this specific question, the only answer is in the negative. The framers did not intend or expect then and there to outlaw segregation, which, of course, was a practice widely prevalent in the North.[8]

Upon the termination of his clerkship Bickel wrote a farewell letter to Frankfurter in which he adverted to the "living Constitution" dictum of Marshall.[9] But when he revised his memorandum for publication in 1955 he sought more solid footing. Were the amendment a statute, he concluded, a "Court might very well hold" on the basis of the evidence "that it was foreclosed from applying it to segregation in the public schools." Apart from the "immediate effect of the enactment," he asked, "what if any thought was given to the long-range effect" in the future—a possibility he had labeled "impossible" in 1953. Noting the shift from "equal protection in the rights of life, liberty and property" to "equal protection of the laws, a clause which is plainly capable of being applied to all subjects of state legislation,"[10] he asked,

Could the comparison have failed to leave the implication that the new phrase, while it did not necessarily, and certainly not ex-

8. A. Bickel, *The Least Dangerous Branch* 100 (1962).

9. Kluger, supra note 7 at 655. Professor Robert McKay "finds the answer in the fact that it is not a statute but in Chief Justice Marshall's words, 'a *constitution* we are expounding.'" Quoted in Louis Pollak, "The Supreme Court Under Fire," 6 J. Pub. L. 428, 440 (1950). That Marshall has been utterly misconstrued down the years is shown infra Chapter 21 at notes 1–28. Here it may be noted that the plea for "growth" is in truth a claim for judicial power to revise the Constitution. In one of the great paradoxes of our time, Justice Black, that supreme "revisionist," dismissed "rhapsodical strains, about the duty of the Court to keep the Constitution in tune with the times. The idea is that the Constitution must be changed from time to time and that this Court is charged with the duty to make those changes . . . The Constitution makers knew the need for change and provided for it" by the amendment process of Article V. Griswold v. Connecticut, 381 U.S. 479, 522 (1965), dissenting opinion.

10. This shift is discussed infra Chapter 11 at note 35.

pressly, carry greater coverage than the old, was nevertheless roomier, more receptive to "latitudinarian" construction? No one made the point with regard to this particular clause. But in the opening debate in the Senate, Jacob Howard was frank to say that only the future could tell what application the privileges and immunities would have.

So, too, Reverdy Johnson, a Democrat, "confessed his puzzlement about the same clause."[11] How does the Howard-Johnson "puzzlement" about "privileges or immunities" advance the argument that "due process" and "equal protection" were understood to be open-ended? Neither Johnson nor Howard expressed uncertainty as to the meaning of *those* terms, and the implication is that there was none, an implication I shall flesh out in subsequent chapters. And given the Republican commitment to a "limited" program of protection for "enumerated" rights,[12] why did Bingham, who had insisted on deletion from the Civil Rights Bill of the words "civil rights" as "oppressive," too "latitudinarian,"[13] now, as author of the Amendment's §1, resort to phraseology that was "roomier, more receptive to 'latitudinarian' construction?" No explanation of his turnabout has been offered, and when we descend from speculation to the facts we shall find that they offer no support for the Bickel hypothesis.

Bickel states that some Republicans referred to "the natural rights of man,"[14] but those rights had been specified in the Civil Rights Act, and the Act was understood to exclude suffrage and desegregation of schools, as Bickel himself noted.[15] The Act,

11. Bickel 60–61.

12. See Kelly infra Chapter 13 at note 53; Thayer supra Chapter 2 at note 28.

13. See infra Chapter 7 at notes 11–17, and 21.

14. Bickel 61.

15. "Natural rights" had acquired a settled common law meaning; supra Chapter 2 note 55. "The obvious conclusion, to which the evidence, thus summarized, easily leads is that section 1 of the fourteenth amendment, like section 1 of the Civil Rights Act of 1866, carried out the relatively narrow ob-

with its restrictive "enumeration" of the rights to be protected, was represented to be embodied in the Amendment. A repudiation of such representations by the framers, in the teeth of their attachment to State sovereignty, their respect for the rights reserved to the States by the Tenth Amendment, needs to be proved, not assumed. And as will appear, the words "equal protection of the laws" evolved side by side with the framers' limited objectives and gave perfect expression to their central goal: to prevent discriminatory legislation with respect to the enumerated rights, and those alone.

Howard knew well enough what "privileges or immunities" comprised. He stated, "we may gather some intimation of what probably will be the opinion of the judiciary by referring to . . . Corfield v. Coryell." He quoted therefrom the reference to those "privileges and immunities which are in their nature fundamental . . . They may be comprehended under the following general heads: protection by the Government, the enjoyment of life and liberty, with the right to acquire property" and so on.[16] The correlation between these rights, the "privileges and immunities" of Article IV, §2, and the Civil Rights Act had been explained by Trumbull. After Howard's speech, Reverdy Johnson moved to strike the "privileges or immunities" clause because he "did not understand what will be the effect of that"; but his motion fell to the ground,[17] testimony that the Senate did not share his doubts. The "puzzlement" of Howard and Johnson cannot cancel out the repeated association of "privileges or immunities" with "security of person and property"; it cannot vitiate the all but universal understanding that the Amendment was to embody the Civil Rights Act, reiterated

---

jectives of the Moderates, and hence, as originally understood, was meant to apply neither to jury service, nor suffrage, nor miscegenation statutes, nor segregation." Bickel 58.

16. *Globe* 2765.

17. Id. 3041. Just before Johnson spoke, Senator James A. McDougall of California stated that the Civil Rights Act "was simply to carry out the 'privileges and immunities'" provision of Article IV, §2. Id. 3035.

after Howard spoke. The Act, said Latham, "covers exactly the same ground as this amendment." Senator Doolittle said it "was the forerunner of this constitutional amendment, and to give validity to which this constitutional amendment is brought forward," a view also expressed by Henry Van Aernam of New York.[18] The "privileges or immunities" clause, Senator Poland stated, "secures nothing beyond what was intended by the original provision [Article IV, §2] of the Constitution."[19] In fact, Senator Howard undercuts Bickel, for toward the close of the debates he stated, "the first section of the proposed amendment does not give . . . the right of voting. The right of suffrage is not in law, one of the privileges . . . thus secured."[20] With respect to suffrage, the "Great Guarantee," Howard was quite clear that it was excluded; that concept, at least, could not in future change its skin.

Bickel noticed that the "no discrimination in civil rights" sentence of the Act had been deleted because Republicans "who had expressed fears concerning its reach . . . would have to go forth and stand on the platform of the fourteenth amendment." "It remains true," he said, "that an explicit provision going further than the Civil Rights Act would not have carried in the 39th Congress." And he noted that the Republicans drew back from "a formulation dangerously vulnerable to attacks pandering to the prejudice of the people." But, he asked, "may it not be that the Moderates and Radicals reached a compromise permitting them to go to the country with language which they could, where necessary, defend against damaging alarms raised by the opposition but which at the same time was sufficiently elastic to permit reasonable future advances?"[21] Talk of a

18. Id. 2883, 2896. Van Aernam stated the Amendment gives "constitutional sanction and protection to the substantial guarantees of the civil rights bill." Id. 3069.

19. Id. 2961.

20. Id. 2766.

21. Bickel 61–62. Earlier Flack had put the matter more bluntly: the "main purpose [of the Radical leaders] in proposing the first section of the Amend-

"compromise" between Moderates and Radicals on "vague" language is without factual basis. Consider the "radical" opposition to readmission of Tennessee because its constitution excluded Negro suffrage, voted down by 125 to 12; or the rejection of Senator Sumner's suffrage proposal by 34 to 4.[22] What need was there to "compromise" with so insignificant a group? Senator Sherman told a Cincinnati audience in September 1866, while the Amendment was up for ratification, "we defeated every radical proposition in it."[23]

Bickel's theory, to speak plainly, is that the compromisers concealed the future objectives that they dared not avow lest the whole enterprise be imperiled; it is an elegant reformulation of conspiratorial purpose. To begin with, this theory posits that the 39th Congress harbored designs not shared by the voters, when, in fact, as Morton Keller remarks, "most congressional Republicans were aware of (and shared) their constituents' hostility to black suffrage."[24] Anticipating that his hypothesis might be "disparaged as putting forth an undisclosed, conspiratorial purpose such as has been imputed to Bingham and others with regard to the protection of corporations,"[25] Bickel invoked statements by Stevens and the Joint Committee Report to the effect that the Amendment's "imperfections" may be cured by "further legislation, enabling acts," by "legislative wisdom"[26]—hardly a warrant for *judicial* changes! What mem-

---

ment was to increase the power of the Federal Government very much, but to do so in such a way that the people would not understand the great change intended to be wrought in the fundamental law of the land." Flack 69. But, he observed, "had the people been informed of what was intended by the Amendment, they would have rejected it." Flack 237.

22. Supra Chapter 5 at note 30; Chapter 4 at note 33.

23. James 167; see also infra Chapter 13 at notes 38–45.

24. Morton Keller, *Affairs of State* 67 (1977); and see infra Chapter 13 at notes 16–17.

25. Bickel 63.

26. Id. "Perhaps the passage of the Civil Rights Act of 1875 ultimately is the most decisive indication of the conviction of a large majority of the Radicals that *Congress* might properly forbid state caste and segregation legislation

ber of the 39th Congress would conclude that by such words was meant that Congress had conferred sub rosa for the future the suffrage it dared not propose in the present? Bickel himself torpedoed that inference.

Observing that Stevens stated the Amendment "falls far short of my wishes . . . but . . . is all that can be obtained in the present state of public opinion . . . I . . . *leave it to be perfected by better men in better times,*" Bickel states; "In all probability, the disappointment of Thaddeus Stevens centered on failure to make *any* provision for negro suffrage, immediate *or prospective.*"[27] Disappointment over failure to provide for prospective suffrage rules out an open-ended design to authorize such provision in the future. What Stevens meant by "further legislation" does not need construction. As Senator Stewart stated, the Amendment "does not preclude Congress from adopting other means by a two-thirds vote [another amendment] when experience shall have demonstrated . . . the necessity for a change of policy,"[28] as it did before long in recommending the Fifteenth Amendment. Studied ambiguity also collides with Fessenden's suggestion of a change because "there is a little obscurity or, at any rate, the expression in section 4 might be construed to go further than was intended."[29] A "blank check to posterity" is likewise refuted by Chairman

---

under the amendment [§5], but again this law implied congressional power and discretion, not necessarily the existence of prior mandatory rights enforceable under the amendment alone." Kelly, Fourteenth 1085 (emphasis added). See infra Chapter 12.

27. Bickel 45–46 (emphasis added); cf. Globe 2459. Stevens stated "prospective" suffrage would be unacceptable; infra at notes 27, 38–41. In explaining §2, Stevens stated, "True it will take two, three, possibly five years before they [Southern States] conquer their prejudices sufficiently to *allow* their late slaves to become their equals at the polls." *Globe* 2459 (emphasis added). This speaks against a §1 power in the future to compel States to grant suffrage; and it is confirmed by Stevens' statement that "The large stride which we in vain proposed is dead." *Globe* 2460.

28. *Globe* 2964.

29. Id. 2941.

Wilson's statement: "I fear that comprehensive statesmanship which cares for posterity as well as for itself will not leave its impress upon the measure we are now considering."[30]

There are also several disclaimers of concealed objectives, of playing a trick upon an unsuspecting people.[31] Charged with "indirection," Fessenden said:

> where a legislator avows his object and his purpose, states what he wishes to accomplish and the mode by which he is to accomplish it, he is [not] to be charged, although it operates indirectly, with what is properly understood by the term "indirection," which conveys the idea of a trick, a contrivance, to do something by taking advantage of others which you cannot do if you make plain to their senses what is the object.[32]

Shortly after congressional approval of the Amendment, and during the warm-up for the elections of 1866, a leading Radical, Congressman Robert C. Schenck of Ohio, averred the Democrats "are afraid that it may have some concealed purpose of elevating negroes . . . [to] make them voters. It goes to no such length."[33]

"Equal protection," as will appear, emerged from the framers' intention to outlaw *laws* which discriminated against blacks with respect to the "coverage of the Civil Rights Act." "Indeed," Bickel himself concluded, *"no specific purpose* going beyond the [limited] coverage of the Civil Rights Act is suggested; rather an awareness on the part of the framers that it was *a constitution* they were writing, which led to a choice of language

30. Id. 2947.

31. In his famous attempt to read corporations out of the Fourteenth Amendment, Justice Black said, "A secret purpose on the part of the members of the Committee, even if such would be the fact, however, would not be sufficient to justify any such construction." Connecticut General Ins. Co. v. Johnson, 303 U.S. 77, 87 (1938), dissenting opinion. Cf. infra Chapter 8 at notes 77 and 95.

32. *Globe* 1275.

33. Fairman, Stanford 74–75.

capable of growth."[34] His appeal to the "awareness" of the
framers assumes what needs to be proved—that there was in fact
such a "choice." Such speculation is rebutted by the very limited
objectives of the Civil Rights Act, embodied in the Amendment,
the absence of explanation for a change of direction, and the fact
that "due process" and "privileges or immunities" were deemed
to be used in their established sense. If there was such a
"choice,"[35] it cannot harbor a purpose they confessedly dared not
submit. Senator Howard, who has been regarded as "one of the
most reckless of the radicals," one who "served consistently in
the vanguard of the extreme negrophiles,"[36] explained to the
Senate that he would have preferred to

> secure suffrage to the colored race to some extent at least . . .
> But sir, it is not a question what you, or I, or half a dozen other
> members of the Senate may prefer in respect to colored suf-
> frage . . . the question really is, what will the Legislatures of
> the various States . . . do in the premises; what is likely to
> meet the general approbation of the people. The Committee

34. Bickel 63 (emphasis added). Yet Bickel noted that "equal protection"
had a limited meaning for the "Moderates, led by Trumbull and Fessenden,"
the right "of benefitting equally from the laws for the security of person and
property." Id. 56.

35. Bickel also builds on the fact, that §1 of the Fourteenth Amendment
deals with discrimination "whether or not based on color" and "this feature of
it could not have been deemed to be included in the standard identification of
section 1 with the Civil Rights Act," an indication of future breadth. Id. 60.
But §1 of the Civil Rights Act likewise provided that "the inhabitants of every
race and color . . . shall have the same right," and the debates show that its
coverage extended to whites. As Bickel noticed, Senator Trumbull stated that
"this bill applies to white men as well as black men. It declares that all
persons . . . shall be entitled to the same civil rights." *Globe* 599; Bickel 14
note 36. In any event, inclusion of whites does not broaden the protection for
property and personal security which the Act provided for both blacks and
whites.

36. Kendrick 192.

were of the opinion that the States are not yet prepared to sanction so fundamental a change.[37]

How is Bickel's "undisclosed" purpose to be reconciled with the fact that an attempt to provide for Negro suffrage *after 1876* was rejected? Robert Dale Owen, a pro-suffrage reformer, had brought a proposal which Stevens placed before the Joint Committee. Section 2 of the proposal provided that after July 4, 1876 (a fitting anniversary for enfranchisement), "no discrimination shall be made . . . as to . . . the right of suffrage."[38] Owen's reason for the "prospective suffrage," he explained to Stevens, was that "the negro is, for the present, unprepared wisely to use the right of suffrage."[39] When this provision was noised about, Stevens told Owen,

> members from New York, from Illinois . . . from Indiana held, each separately, a caucus to consider whether equality of suffrage, present *or prospective*, ought to form a part of the Republican programme for the coming canvass. They were afraid . . . some of them . . . might lose their elections . . . [E]ach one of these caucuses decided that negro suffrage, *in any shape*, ought to be excluded.[40]

In consequence, the 1876 proposal was dropped and the Committee substituted a "new section simply eliminating from the basis of representation persons to whom the vote was denied,"[41] the present §2. Add to this Senator Howard's statement of the Joint Committee's opinion that "three-fourths of

37. *Globe* 2766.
38. Bickel 41–42; Kendrick 83–84.
39. Kendrick 298. This view was shared by Senator Fessenden, *Globe* 704; William A. Newell of New Jersey, id. 867; and Stevens himself, supra Chapter 4 at note 64. See also C. Vann Woodward, *The Burden of Southern History* 92 (1960).
40. Kendrick 302 (emphasis added).
41. Bickel 43.

the States . . . could not be induced to grant the right of suffrage, *even in any degree* or under any restriction, to the colored
race,"[42] and we have solid evidence which overcomes speculation that there was an unrevealed purpose to confer broader
powers in the future.

Alfred Kelly Kelly does not follow Bickel's theory of a
behind-the-scenes "compromise" between Radicals and Moderates, but suggests that the Radicals attempted, baldly stated,
to hoodwink the Moderates. He regards it as "highly probable"
that the Civil Rights Act "was not intended to bar racial segregation and classification laws." But he finds that

> The intent of certain Radical leaders to go beyond the restrictive
> enumeration of the Civil Rights Act and to incorporate a series
> of expansive guarantees in the Constitution is quite
> clear . . . the *best evidence* of this is the language of the guaran-
> tees which Bingham and the other authors of the Fourteenth
> Amendment incorporated in the first section. The guarantees
> they finally adopted—privileges and immunities, due process
> and equal protection—were not at all derived from the Civil
> Rights Act, which . . . had used the restricted enumerative de-
> vice. Instead, the authors derived their guarantees deliberately
> from the prewar Radical antislavery movement.[43]

A Constitution, Chief Justice Marshall stated, cannot have "the
prolixity of a code";[44] there the drive is for the most compressed utterance. Moreover, the terms of §1 were far from
"vague and amorphous."[45] "Privileges or immunities" was

42. *Globe* 2766 (emphasis added).

43. Kelly, Fourteenth 1069, 1071 (emphasis added).

44. "A constitution, to contain an accurate detail of all the subdivisions of
which its great powers will admit . . . would partake of the prolixity of a
legal code, and could scarcely be embraced by the human mind." M'Culloch
v. Maryland, 17 U.S. (4 Wheat.) 316, 407 (1819); cf. Bickel 61.

45. Kelly, Fourteenth 1071.

drawn from Article IV, §2, via the Civil Rights Bill, which adopted the established judicial construction.[46] An abolitionist departure needs to be proved, not assumed by reference to "expansive" language. Bingham himself repudiated such notions when he declared that the meaning of "due process" was to be found in the decisions of the courts.[47] That his conception of "equal protection" did not go beyond the ban on discriminatory laws with respect to the enumerated "fundamental rights" is again demonstrated by his defense of Tennessee's disenfranchisement of blacks, regretting that though "We are all for equal and exact justice . . . justice for all is not to be secured in a day."[48]

Next Kelly notices a "curious ambiguity . . . in the Radicals' advocacy of the measure . . . It was as though the Radical leaders were avoiding a precise delineation of legal consequences," this on the basis of their resort to the "technique of lofty, expansive and highly generalized language."[49] Why such avoidance? He explains that

> there was a substantial block of moderate Republicans who had not yet committed themselves entirely to the Radical position . . . if [Bingham et al.] drove home too far the proposition that this amendment would undoubtedly consummate the destruction of all caste and class legislation . . . moderate Republican support might be alienated and the requisite two-thirds majority necessary to the amendment's adoption might not be obtained. Political strategy called for ambiguity not clarity.[50]

---

46. Andrew J. Rogers charged that §1 "is no more nor less than an attempt to embody in the Constitution . . . that outrageous and miserable civil rights bill"; later he stated that it "simply embodied the gist of the civil rights bill." *Globe* 2538; *Globe App.* 229; quoted in Bickel 48, 54. This was the all but universal view; supra Chapter 2 at notes 10–13.

47. Infra Chapter 11 at notes 36–37.

48. *Globe* 3979.

49. Kelly, Fourteenth 1077.

50. Id. 1084.

Stripped of fig leaves, the Kelly rationale would give the Amendment a meaning which the radicals had concealed even from their Moderate confreres! In truth, there is no evidence of a concealed purpose. How did Bingham's "lofty generalizations" become freighted with a cargo he had severely condemned as "oppressive" and "unjust" when he insisted upon deletion of the words "civil rights" from the Civil Rights Bill?[50a] Although Bingham was given to windy oratory,[51] his own words show that he did not regard "due process," "equal protection," and "privileges or immunities" as "lofty generalizations," but rather as terms of known and limited content. For example, he explained that "privileges or immunities" was drawn from Article IV, §2, that "due process" had been judicially defined. Then, too, Bingham and Stevens are an odd couple to conspire to pull the wool over the eyes of their colleagues. On the floor of the House in the 39th Congress, Stevens said to Bingham: "In all this contest about reconstruction I do not propose either to take his counsel, recognize his authority, or believe a word he says."[52]

William Van Alstyne   After downgrading some statements in the debates, Van Alstyne nevertheless concludes that "the case can safely be made that there was an original understanding that §1 of the proposed Fourteenth Amendment would not itself *immediately* invalidate state suffrage laws severely restricting the right to vote." But, he states, "we cannot safely declare that there was also a clear, uniform understanding that the *open-*

50a. Infra Chapter 7 at notes 11–21.

51. For example, by way of prelude to a quotation from Kent, who had frequently been cited without florid panegyrics, Bingham must needs gild the lily: "one of those grand intellects who during life illustrated the jurisprudence of our country, and has left in his works a perpetual monument of his genuis, his learning, and his wisdom." *Globe* 1292. It is instructive to compare the flow of such effusions with the spare, lean style of Fessenden, Trumbull, and Hale. See also infra Chapter 8 note 54.

52. *Cong. Globe,* 39th Cong., 2d Sess. 816 (Jan. 28, 1867). See also infra Chapter 13 at notes 30–36; Kluger, infra Chapter 7 note 20.

ended phrases of §1 . . . would foreclose a *different application in the future* [because invalidation of State Negro suffrage laws] was avoided . . . from *fear* that such an amendment would not be ratified and that its Republican sponsors would be *turned out of office* at the next congressional election."[53] Van Alstyne reverses the normal order of proof, that a departure from the norm was intended, that what was unmistakably excluded in 1866 was to be embraced in 1966. For such extraordinary drafting *proof,* not speculation, is required.

In an attempt to offer some proof Van Alstyne argues that Congress had based its authority to enact the Civil Rights Act on the fact that it was "appropriate legislation to enforce the mere ban on 'slavery' in §1 of the Thirteenth Amendment." He continues: "fresh from their own experience in developing new applications of the Thirteenth Amendment . . . the Radicals could scarcely have failed to foresee that the still broader contours of the Fourteenth Amendment would offer greater possibilities for the future."[54] Undeniably some appealed to the Thirteenth Amendment for constitutional authority to enact the Civil Rights Act. But there was vigorous opposition. Conkling declared that "Emancipation vitalizes only natural rights, not political rights."[55] And most Republicans held that natural rights did not include the right to vote. Senator Henry Wilson, a Massachusetts Radical, stated that the Thirteenth Amendment "was never understood by any man in the Senate or House to confer upon Congress the right to prescribe or regulate the suffrage in any State . . . If it had been supposed that it gave that power the amendment would never have passed the Congress, never have received the sanction of the States."[56] Considerable

53. Van Alstyne 72; emphasis added.
54. Id. 74–75.
55. *Globe* 356.
56. Id. 1255. "George Ticknor Curtis typified a large stream of conservative constitutionalism in his argument that the Thirteenth Amendment diminished states' powers not one whit beyond abolition." H. M. Hyman, *A More Perfect Union* 428 (1973). Senator Cowan, a Conservative Republican from

impetus to the Fourteenth Amendment was given by Bingham's insistence that there was no constitutional authority for the Civil Rights Bill and that an amendment was required.[57] And the fact that Congress went on to enact the Fourteenth Amendment refutes the view that the Thirteenth was conceived to be "open-ended," to authorize legislation going beyond emancipation.

Even "more significance" is attached by Van Alstyne to what he views as an important parallel between the Civil Rights Act and the Fourteenth Amendment.[58] When Bingham objected that the "no discrimination in civil rights" sentence of the Act was oppressive and invaded States' Rights,[59] the Committee deleted the sentence, and Chairman Wilson explained, "I do not think it materially changes the bill, but some gentlemen were apprehensive that the words we propose to strike out might give warrant for a latitudinarian construction not intended."[60] In contrast, Van Alstyne points out, although "several of the Democrats declared . . . that the Privileges and Immunities Clause would eventually be applied to suffrage . . . the Republicans declined to limit the language of §1 [of the Amendment] to avoid such application." The moral he draws is that the "Civil Rights Act was, of course, a statute; a law not ex-

---

Pennsylvania, stated that the Thirteenth Amendment was understood merely "to liberate the negro slave from his master." *Globe* 499. On the other hand, Senator Howard, a member of the Judiciary Committee that drafted the Thirteenth Amendment, understood it to authorize the Civil Rights Bill. *Globe* 503.

57. *Globe* 1291.

58. Van Alstyne 75.

59. *Globe* 1291; see Chapter 7 at notes 12–15. Van Alstyne, 76, states that "In spite of the declarations that the bill would not affect voting rights, even Bingham was not satisfied. He moved to strike out the opening general phrase . . . he doubted both the *wisdom* and constitutionality of legislating with respect to the franchise" (emphasis added). Since Bingham was the architect of §1 of the Amendment, how did he become the vehicle of smuggling an undisclosed provision for suffrage into the section?

60. *Globe* 1366; Van Alstyne 77.

pected to 'endure for ages to come.' The Fourteenth Amendment was something else again."[61] A more prosaic explanation can serve. Bingham was an influential Republican with a following, and the deletion of the "civil rights" sentence, regarded as gratuitous, was a small price to pay for bringing him into camp; whereas the objections of "several Democrats" could safely be ignored because their votes could be written off.[62] The Republicans, who had been assured both during enactment of the Civil Rights Bill and consideration of the Amendment that neither purported to grant suffrage, needed no express exception to make that plain. The established rule is that if a thing is within the intention of the framers, it is as good as written in the text.[63]

The hypotheses of Bickel, Kelly, and Van Alstyne seem to me a speculative fabric that collapses under the fact, made so clear by the framers, that they did not mean to confer Negro suffrage, present *or prospective*. And the theory runs into another formidable obstacle. During the ratification process, in the summer election campaign of 1866, the Republicans repeatedly assured the people that, in the words of Senator John Sherman of Ohio, the Amendment "was an embodiment of the Civil Rights Bill," itemizing several of its provisions. A similar assurance was given by Senator Lane of Indiana.[64] Congressman Schenck of Ohio repudiated "a concealed purpose" to confer Negro suffrage; his Ohio colleague Columbus Delano stressed that the Amendment was designed to make citizens "safe in the South."[65] Logan of Illinois said it was meant to permit the citi-

61. Van Alstyne 73, 77.
62. Democratic Senator Saulsbury's proposal to add to the Civil Rights Bill "except the right to vote in the State" was rebuffed by Senator Trumbull: "This bill relates to civil rights only, and I do not want to bring up the question of negro suffrage in the bill." *Globe* 606; Van Alstyne 76; cf. supra at note 17.
63. Supra Chapter 1 note 24.
64. Fairman, Stanford 77, 74.
65. Id. 74, 75.

zen "to sue and be sued, to own property, to have process of
court," a reminder of the limited objectives of the Civil Rights
Act, accompanied by a specific disclaimer that §1 "gives the
negro the right of suffrage."[66] These and still other representations collected by Charles Fairman militate against a concealed purpose to go beyond the confines of the Act.

Finally, be it assumed that there was an undisclosed purpose,
the question arises whether "ratification" extends to objectives
that were not disclosed, that were in fact expressly disclaimed.
The doctrine of ratification premises that the principal knows
what he is ratifying; without full disclosure there can be no ratification.[67] And there is the larger issue of political morality.
Ours is a generation insistent on full disclosure, for example, in
the marketing of corporate securities. To accept dissimulation
as a means of obtaining a constitutional amendment would be
to condone lower morals in the halls of Congress than is demanded in the marketplace.[68]

66. Id. 70. James, 179, said, "statements of congressmen before their constituents definitely identify the provisions of the first section of the amendment with those of the Civil Rights Bill."

67. Infra Chapter 8 at note 93. See supra note 21.

68. Justice Douglas wrote, "The principle of full disclosure has as much
place in government as it does in the market place." Douglas, "Stare Decisis,"
49 Colum. L. Rev. 735, 754 (1949).

7

Segregated Schools

THE "desegregation" decision in *Brown v. Board of Education*[1] was, as Richard Kluger called it, an act of "Simple Justice,"[2] a long overdue attempt to rectify the grievous wrongs done to the blacks. For the legal historian, however, the question is whether the Fourteenth Amendment authorized the Supreme Court to perform that act.[3] For the Court, like every agency of government, may act only within the limits of its constitutional powers. As Lee stated in the Virginia Ratification Convention, "When a question arises with respect to the legality of any power, exercised or assumed," the question will be, "*Is it enumerated in the Constitution?* . . . It is otherwise arbitrary and unconstitutional."[4]

In his illuminating study of the way in which the desegregation case was handled in the Supreme Court, Kluger asks, "Could it be reasonably claimed that segregation had been outlawed by the Fourteenth when the yet more basic emblem of

1. 347 U.S. 483 (1954).

2. Richard Kluger, *Simple Justice* (1976); hereinafter Kluger.

3. "The result," Archibald Cox stated, "can only be described as a revolution in constitutional law." *The Role of the Supreme Court in American Government* 57 (1976).

4. 3 Jonathan Eliot, *Debates in the Several State Conventions on the Adoption of the Federal Constitution* 186 (1836); Berger, *Congress v. The Supreme Court* 13–16.

citizenship—the ballot—had been withheld from the Negro under that amendment?"[5] Given the rampant racism in the North of 1866—which still has to loose its grip—it needs to be explained how a North which provided for or mandated segregated schools[6] was brought to vote for desegregation in the Amendment.

When the "desegregation" case came to the Court in 1952, Justice Frankfurter assigned the task of compiling the legislative history of the Amendment to his brilliant clerk, Alexander Bickel,[7] who was destined to become one of the foremost authorities in the field of constitutional law. Upon completing the assignment, in August 1953, Bickel delivered his memorandum to Frankfurter with a covering letter in which he stated: "it is impossible to conclude that the 39th Congress intended that segregation be abolished; impossible also to conclude that they foresaw it might be, under the language they were adopting."[8] When he later published a revision of that memorandum, he concluded: "there is no evidence whatever showing that for its sponsors the civil rights formula had anything to do with unsegregated schools. Wilson, its sponsor in the House, specifically disclaimed any such notion."[9] Wilson, chairman of the House Judiciary Committee and the House Manager of the Bill, who could therefore speak authoritatively, had advised the House that the words "civil rights . . . do not mean that all citizens

5. Kluger, 635.
6. Infra at notes 24–25.
7. Kluger 599, 653.
8. Id. 654. Kluger states that the Bickel memorandum held that "the legislative history, while revealing no evidence that the framers of the amendment had intended to prohibit school segregation, did not foreclose future generations from acting on the question, either by congressional statute or by judicial review." Id. 655; see also 634. But this is at odds with Bickel's covering letter, supra Chapter 6 at note 7. In fact, as will shortly appear, the framers deliberately *excluded* school segregation from the ambit of the Civil Rights Bill and therefore of the Amendment.
9. Bickel 56.

shall sit on juries, or that their children shall attend the same schools. These are not civil rights."[10] Wilson's statement is proof positive that segregation was excluded from the scope of the bill.

Another piece of evidence, which Alfred Kelly, one of the historians drawn into the case by the NAACP,[11] considered "very damning," was the "removal of the 'no discrimination' clause from the Civil Rights Bill." The bill, he stated, "was amended specifically to eliminate any reference to discriminatory practices like school segregation . . . it looked as if a specific exclusion had been made."[12] The deletion was made at the insistence of John A. Bingham, the architect of the Fourteenth Amendment, whom neoabolitionists regard as the conduit through which abolitionist concepts of substantive due process and equal protection were poured into the Amend-

10. *Globe* 1117. Wilson's statement is more fully quoted supra Chapter 2 at note 26. He later reiterated that the limited objectives of the bill did not extend to "setting aside the school laws and jury laws." *Globe* 1294.

11. Kluger 626.

12. Id. 635. Among the legal historians drawn into preparation of the briefs by the NAACP was Howard Jay Graham. Id. 625–626. "He was particularly troubled by Representative Wilson's insistence during the phase of the debates dealing with the 'no discrimination' clause that the Civil Rights Bill was not intended to outlaw separate schools. That negative reference, Graham reported, was unfortunate, particularly since he was House Manager of the . . . bill." Id. 634–635.

The "key session" of the NAACP "giant conference running for three days and nights" was "devoted to the papers of [Howard] Jay Graham and Alfred Kelly on the troubling relationship between the Civil Rights Act of 1866, which had been specifically stripped of its broad 'no discrimination' language, and the Fourteenth Amendment, created in its immediate aftermath and conceived, as many historians believed, simply to constitutionalize the rights act." Id. 637. The paper Kelly delivered was on "the damning modification of the Civil Rights Bill in the House and its apparent identity in purpose with the Fourteenth Amendment." He recounted that he "didn't understand the relationship between advocacy and history at that point" and considered the problem "nearly insurmountable." Id. 637.

ment.[13] Roughly speaking, he moved for instructions to the Judiciary Committee to strike the "no discrimination" sentence of the bill,[14] in order to render it "less oppressive and therefore less objectionable." The enactment of laws "for the general government of the people" was reserved to the States; "civil rights," he continued, "include and embrace *every* right that pertains to a citizen as such," including "political rights." On this view the Bill, according to Bingham, proposed "simply to strike down by congressional enactment every state constitution which makes a discrimination on account of race or color *in any* of the civil rights of the citizen." With "some few exceptions every state in the Union does make some discrimination . . . in respect of civil rights on account of color." Hence the "no discrimination" sentence "must be stricken out or the constitutions of the States are to be abolished by your act." Deletion of this sentence would remove what he considered the Bill's "oppressive and I might say its unjust provisions," all of which adds up to a States' Rights manifesto. Bingham's censure, however, does not extend to the *enumerated* rights that follow the "no discrimination" clause; these he quotes with approval, but asserts that the needed reform should be accomplished "not by an arbitrary assumption of power, but by amending the Constitution . . . expressly forbidding the States from any such abuse [that is, denial of said specified rights] in the future."[15] In short, the enumerated rights should be protected by Amendment against State abuse, whereas the "civil rights," which embraced any and every right, should be excised because "oppressive." In this Bingham was in accord with the restricted objectives of almost all of his Republican colleagues who spoke to the measure.[16] Bickel therefore correctly concluded that, "Bingham while committing himself to the

13. TenBroek 145–148; Graham 280, 283.
14. The bill is set out in pertinent part supra Chapter 2 at note 14.
15. *Globe* 1291–1293 (emphasis added).
16. E.g., Wilson, supra at note 10.

need for safeguarding by constitutional amendment the specific rights enumerated in the body of section 1, was anything but willing to make a similar commitment to 'civil rights' in general."[17]

Not without cause was this regarded gloomily in the camp of the NAACP. Kluger relates:

> In calling for the deletion, Bingham, the former abolition theorist, had openly acknowledged that the bill as drafted would have prohibited statutes such as school segregation. Since that broad language was in fact deleted from the final form of the bill and since many of the proponents of the Fourteenth held that the amendment had no purpose beyond constitutionalizing the Civil Rights Act, it had therefore seemed to Kelly, [Thurgood] Marshall, Ming, and others in the NAACP camp that they could not reasonably argue that the framers intended the amendment to prohibit school segregation.[18]

Finally, a "light" broke through, "a really plausible interpretation" dawned on Kelly: "Bingham's objection to the 'no discrimination' was based solely on the apparent lack of constitutional authority for so sweeping a congressional enactment."[19] This was a "light" that failed. Kelly completely overlooked Bingham's separation between the too-inclusive "civil rights," which were deleted, and the enumerated rights, which, because they also trenched on traditional State governance, required an amendment. Justice Black understood this if Kelly did not.[20]

17. Bickel 24.

18. Kluger, 640–641. The noted historian Henry Steele Commager had advised the NAACP that "The framers of the amendment did not, so far as we know, intend that it should be used to end segregation in schools." Id. 620.

19. Id. 641.

20. Justice Black, for whom Bingham is the authoritative expositor, recognized that Bingham objected to the Civil Rights Bill because "it would actually strip the states of power to govern, centralizing all power in the Federal Government. To this he was opposed." Adamson v. California, 332 U.S. 46, 100 (1947), dissenting opinion.

More important, Chairman Wilson confirms that the deletion was merely designed to repel a "latitudinarian" construction:

> Some members of the House thought, in the general words of the first section in relation to civil rights, it might be held by the courts that the right of suffrage was included in those rights. To obviate that difficulty and the difficulty growing out of any other construction beyond the specific rights named in the section, our amendment strikes out all of those general terms and leaves the bill with the rights specified in the section.

The deletion, Wilson further explained, was made because "some gentlemen were apprehensive that the words we propose to strike out might give warrant for a latitudinarian construction not intended."[21]

To Kelly, who later defended the desegregation decision, Bickel's view "seems a very doubtful reading of Bingham's position. It ignores his extensive extremist antislavery background as well as his position in Congress as one of the strong Radical Republicans."[22] But neither Bingham's background nor his

---

Kluger, 641, relates, "One hurdle in the way of [Kelly's] reading of Bingham's intention was a later speech of Thaddeus Stevens, the most powerful man in the House and a strong ally of Bingham. Among other things, Stevens said that a principal purpose of the Fourteenth Amendment had indeed been to re-enact and therefore insure the constitutionality of the Civil Rights Act (even shorn of its broad 'no discrimination' language)—an apparent concession to those who wished to interpret the amendment narrowly. But Kelly concluded that the apparently damaging portion of Stevens' speech had to be considered against the larger political picture and the clear drift of Stevens' generally radical utterances." One thing he was plainly not so radical about was desegregation in the schools. See infra at note 39.

21. *Globe* 1366.

22. Kelly, Fourteenth 1068 note 73. In this very article, however, Kelly concluded, "It seems highly probable, then, that the Civil Rights Act, as finally passed, was not intended to ban state racial segregation and classification laws. The main force of the Conservatives' attack on the 'no discrimination' clause was that it would indeed destroy all race classification laws." Id. 1069–1070.

Bingham's remarks have been subject to varying interpretations, see Bickel position had dissuaded him from opposition to Negro suffrage.[23] Moreover, as Bickel informed Justice Frankfurter, "It was doubtful that an explicit 'no discrimination' provision going beyond the enumerated rights in the Civil Rights Bill as finally enacted could have passed in the Thirty-Ninth Congress."[24] At this time "Eight [Northern] states either provided for separate schools or left it up to local communities to adopt that practice if they wished. Five states outside the old Confederacy either directly or by implication excluded colored children entirely from their public schools."[25] Kluger comments, "If Congress and state legislatures had understood that the amendment was to wipe away the practices, surely there would have been more than a few howls."[26] With suffrage unequivocally barred there was no reason to infer that desegregation, a far more touchy matter, was required.

Then there was another thorny fact: "Congress had permitted segregated schools in the District of Columbia from 1864 onward."[27] Sumner's "long fight to abolish segregated Negro schools in the District of Columbia" had been "unavailing."[28] With good reason did Judge E. Barrett Prettyman hold in *Carr v.*

---

27 note 54; Kelly, Fourteenth 1068. Bickel sums up, "Whatever the ambiguities of his speech, one thing is certain. Unless one concludes that Bingham entertained apprehensions about the breadth of the term 'civil rights' and was unwilling at this stage, as a matter of policy, not constitutional law, to extend a federal guaranty covering all that might be included in that term, there is no rational explanation for his motion to strike it." Bickel 25–26. Certainly Wilson so understood; supra at note 21.

23. E.g., supra Chapter 5 at notes 42–43.

24. Kluger, 654–655.

25. Id. 633–634.

26. Id. 635.

27. Id. The problem also troubled Justice Jackson, infra at note 43.

28. Kelly, Fourteenth 1085. For example, when Senator Wilson proposed to allocate funds for the public schools in the District of Columbia, explaining that existing law provided "for the establishment of colored schools" in the District, and the funds would be divided pro rata, Reverdy Johnson asked for and received assurance that "there is no authority to have a mixture of children in any one school." *Globe* 708–709.

Corning[29] that congressional support for segregated schools in
the District of Columbia contemporaneously with the adoption
of the Amendment (and the Civil Rights Act) was conclusive
evidence that Congress had not intended §1 of the Amendment
to invalidate school segregation laws. Kelly too lightly dismissed
this: "technically the parallel is not constitutionally precise or
apposite."[30] To the contrary, the parallel is both "precise and
apposite." It has long been the rule that laws dealing with the
same subject—in pari materia—must be construed with
reference to each other, "as if they were one law."[31] The
Amendment originated as a congressional Joint Resolution, so it
is entirely appropriate to look to the light shed contemporaneously by the District of Columbia bills on the meaning of the
Resolution. In truth, it is unrealistic to presume that a Congress
which has plenary jurisdiction over the District and yet refused
to bar segregation there would turn around to invade State
sovereignty, which the framers were zealous to preserve, in
order to impose a requirement of desegregation upon the States.
The difference was fully appreciated by Senator Henry Wilson, a
Radical Republican from Massachusetts, who introduced a bill
providing for suffrage in the District of Columbia, but lamented
that in "dealing with the States," State "constitutions block up
the way and we may not overleap the barriers."[32]

The relation of mixed schools to the limited objectives that
were expressed in the Civil Rights Act was lucidly summarized
by John L. Thomas of Maryland:

> As a freeman, he is entitled to acquire and dispose of real and
> other property . . . to have his life, liberty, and person pro-

29. 182 F.2d 14, 17 (D.C. Cir. 1950).

30. Kelly, Fourteenth 1085.

31. United States v. Freeman, 44 U.S. (3 How.) 556, 564 (1845). See also
infra Appendix I note 46.

32. I copied Wilson's statement from the debates but have lost the citation
and have been unable to locate it in the circa 4500 three-column pages. The
reader may give it such credence as it deserves.

tected by the same laws that protect me . . . so shall he not only have the right to enforce his contract, but to that end shall be received as a witness in a court of justice on the same terms . . . It would be an outrage . . . [if] we were to refuse to throw around them such legal guards as will prove their only protection and secure to them the enforcement of their rights.

I will go even further . . . and will vote for all measures to elevate their condition and to educate them separate and apart from the whites . . . [B]ut when it comes to placing him upon the same social and political level as my own race, I must refuse to do it.[33]

There is yet other evidence that the framers had no intention of striking down segregation. The Senate gallery itself was segregated, as Senator Reverdy Johnson mordantly remarked.[34] The Carl Schurz report *Education of the Freedmen* spoke throughout of " 'colored schools,' 'school houses in which colored children were taught.' There were no references to unsegregated schools, even as an ultimate objective."[35] Instead there was a pervasive assumption that segregation would remain. Referring to the burning of black schools in Maryland, Josiah B. Grinnell of Iowa said, give them schoolhouses and "invite schoolmasters from all over the world to come and instruct them." Senator Daniel Clark of New Hampshire stated, "you may establish for him schools." Ignatius Donnelly of Minnesota stated, "Educate him and he will himself see to it that the common schools shall forever continue among his people."[36]

33. *Globe* 263–264. For a similar expression by Patterson of New Hampshire, see supra Chapter 2 at note 30. So, too, Republican Senator Cowan of Pennsylvania was willing to secure to blacks "their natural rights" but not to desegregate the schools. *Globe* 500. See also Republican Thomas T. Davis of New York, infra Chapter 10 at note 21.

34. *Globe* 766: "Why is it that [you have] separate places for the respective races even in your own chamber? Why are they not put together?"

35. Bickel 10 note 29.

36. *Globe* 652, 834, 590; cf. Donnelly, id. 513. Recall Lawrence's exclusion of "political rights [and] those dependent on local law," as was the privilege of

Senator William P. Fessenden said of the "representation" proposal that was to become §2 of the Fourteenth Amendment: it "should serve as an inducement to the southern States to build school houses . . . and educate their colored children until they are fit to vote."[37] In vetoing the antecedent Freedmen's Bureau Bill, President Johnson noted that it provided for the "erection for their benefit of suitable buildings for asylums and schools," and objected that Congress "has never founded schools for any class of our own people."[38] Thaddeus Stevens "did not publicly object to the separation of the races in the schools although he was against segregation in theory . . . But he never pressed for legal enforcement of this kind of equality, as Charles Sumner did, believing it achievement enough that the South would have free schools at all."[39]

Additional light may be gathered from post-Fourteenth Amendment developments, part of Sumner's continuing campaign for desegrated schools. On March 16, 1867, Sumner moved to amend a Supplementary Bill to require "that State constitutions provide for a system of non-discriminatory public

---

attending public schools, supra Chapter 2 note 28, and Windom's statement that the Civil Rights Bill does not confer "the privilege of voting" nor "social privileges." Supra Chapter 2 note 30.

John F. Farnsworth feared that enfranchisement alone might not suffice if it were dependent on reading and writing qualifications, for the States may "exclude him from the schools." *Globe* 383. See also Frederick Pike of Maine, id. 407. Enfranchisement failed, as did attempts to open the schools. See infra note 40.

37. Kendrick 206.

38. *Globe* 916.

39. Fawn Brodie, *Thaddeus Stevens: Scourge of the South* 320 (1959). Stevens assured the electorate in September 1866 that the Amendment "does not touch social or political rights." James 201. Perhaps the reason, as Rogers noted, was that in "Pennsylvania there is a discrimination between the schools for white children and the schools for blacks. The laws there provide that certain schools shall be set aside for black persons," and inquired whether Congress has a right to "interfere with these statutes." *Globe* 1121. Senator Cowan of Pennsylvania objected to such interference. Id. 500.

schools." The motion failed; it "went beyond what majority sentiment would sustain."[40] Let an impassioned apostle of the incorporation of abolitionist ideology—Howard Jay Graham —sum up:

> There were many reasons why men's understanding of equal protection, as applied to educational matters, was imperfect in 1866 . . . Negroes were barred from public schools of the North and still widely regarded as "racially inferior" and "incapable of education." Even comparatively enlightened leaders then accepted segregation in the schools.[41]

40. Fairman, History 329. Sumner "placed little stress upon the Fourteenth Amendment guarantee of equal protection of the laws; too many of his colleagues who had helped draft that ambiguous document would reply that they had never intended to outlaw segregation . . . When Senator Morrill insisted upon learning exactly where in the Constitution the federal government was given control 'over matters of education, worship, amusement . . .' Sumner discovered authorization in the Sermon on the Mount and in the Declaration of Independence." Donald, *Sumner II* 532.

As late as December 1871 Sumner reintroduced a bill which had been adversely reported in 1870–1871: "He maintained that hotels, public conveyances and schools . . . should be opened equally to all." Flack 250. "Without this complementary bill," the Civil Rights Act "was imperfect, he declared," Flack 251. Though there was some contrariety of opinion, id. 253–265, the House, by a vote of 128 to 48, insisted on an amendment "striking out all reference to common schools," id. 275. Senator Morrill opposed the Sumner bill because the "Federal Government had no right to take cognizance of matters of education, amusement . . . it is without warrant in the Constitution," i.e., the Fourteenth Amendment. Id. 252–253.

41. Graham 290 note 70. Nevertheless Graham stated that "no one is obliged or disposed to grant—that an outright majority of 1866–1868 did regard race segregation in *their* public schools, as a peculiar form of race discrimination—as one which in *their* judgment, would remain unaffected by the Fourteenth Amendment." Id. 291.

Compare with the foregoing history, in considerable part earlier set forth by Alexander Bickel, Charles Black's recent statement: "I started, virtually [as of NAACP counsel], with Brown v. The Board of Education, a case which seemed to me then and still seems to me to have been as nearly syllogistic as a real law case can be. The Fourteenth Amendment, *in the clear light of its history,*

The "imperfect" "understanding of equal protection" in 1866 means that the framers did not conceive it in the vastly broadened terms given to the phrase by the Warren Court. How did this history fare in the Warren Court?

In his painstaking reconstruction of the progress of *Brown v. Board of Education,* Richard Kluger has furnished some fascinating glimpses behind the portals of the Supreme Court.[42] The case was first argued before the Vinson Court; Chief Justice Vinson "found it 'Hard to get away' from the contemporary view by its framers that the Fourteenth Amendment did not prohibit segregation." Jackson noted, "For 90 years segregated schools in the city [Washington] "[43] Frankfurter, "a keen observer of his colleagues' voting inclinations," listed Clark— along with Vinson, Reed, and Jackson—as "probable dissenters if the Court voted to overturn *Plessy* in the spring of 1953."[44] If they were to be brought about time was needed; a decision outlawing segregation by a divided Court would have produced tremendous shock waves.[45] With Bickel's aid Frank-

---

and without any straining or special pleading, forbade *all* discrimination against black people as such, however euphemized and however daubed with cosmetics." C. Black, "The Judicial Power as Guardian of Liberties," statement prepared for delivery at a Symposium on Constitutional Liberties in Modern America, Wayne State University, Detroit, Michigan, October 16, 1976, 2 (emphasis added). Chief Justice Warren's "syllogisms" are examined infra Chapter 13 at notes 56–60. Black's "clear . . . history" seemed "inconclusive" to Chief Justice Warren, who chose rather not to "turn back the clock to 1868." See infra at note 61.

42. Among other things, Kluger consulted the notes of Justices Burton, Frankfurter, and Jackson, and interviewed several of the Justices and the Justices' clerks. Kluger 788–789.

43. Id. 590.

44. Id. 612, 614; Plessy v. Ferguson, 163 U.S. 537 (1896), the "separate but equal" decision.

45. Kluger 600. "Nothing could have been worse, for the Court or the nation itself, than a flurry of conflicting opinions that would confuse and anger the American people." Id. 696. Desegregation could hardly have been imposed upon the nation by a divided Court; the stakes simply were too high.

furter framed five questions for reargument, which the Court submitted to counsel and put the case over to the next term.[46] The Frankfurter tactic paid off in an unexpected way: the sudden demise of Chief Justice Vinson just before the *Brown* reargument. How much that mattered may be gathered from Frankfurter's remark: "This is the first indication I have ever had that there is a God."[47] And that remark also reveals that men and votes, not the impalpable "consensus of society" picked up by judicial antennae, are what count.

The most interesting figure was Frankfurter himself. According to William Coleman, who had clerked for him a few years earlier and was the coordinator of research for the NAACP in the various States, Frankfurter "was for ending segregation from the very start."[48] A remarkable fact: Frankfurter, the sworn foe of subjective judgment, who disclaimed enforcement of his own "private view rather than the consensus of society's opinion,"[49] had made up his mind "from the day the cases were taken"[50] that segregation must go! This was before

---

Frankfurter "played a pivotal role in bringing about a unanimous Court" in Brown. Joseph P. Lash, *From the Diaries of Felix Frankfurter* 83 (1975).

46. Kluger 614–616.

47. Id. 656. As Justice Frankfurter was dressing for the Vinson funeral, Bickel overheard him murmuring, "An act of Providence, an act of Providence." Lash, supra note 45 at 83. Compare this with his condemnation of "Law" that turns on "contingencies in the choice of successors." Infra Chapter 17 note 44.

48. Kluger 624, 601. "When President Eisenhower appointed Earl Warren to the Chief Justiceship, Frankfurter took him to school on the issues in the *Brown* case in lengthy talks." Lash, supra note 45 at 83–84.

49. Infra Chapter 14 at note 50. In a file memorandum, the essence of which Frankfurter communicated to his brethren at a conference, he emphasized, "it is not our duty to express our personal attitudes towards these issues however deep our individual convictions may be. The opposite is true." Kluger 684.

50. Kluger 601. Bickel justly remarked that were the ultimate "reality" that judicial review spells nothing more than "personal preference," the judicial "authority over us is totally intolerable and totally irreconcilable with the theory and practice of political democracy." *The Least Dangerous Branch* 80 (1962).

hearing argument or reading briefs in a case of extraordinary
national importance.[51] Not that he was unaware of the constitutional obstacles. Kluger recounts that Frankfurter "had studied the history of the Fourteenth Amendment" and concluded
that "in all likelihood, the framers of the amendment had not
intended to outlaw segregation."[52] His conclusion must have
been greatly strengthened by the Bickel memorandum, which
he found so impressive that "he had it set up in type in the
Court's basement print shop and distributed among the Justices
a few days before the Brown reargument."[53] Bickel showed,
and his demonstration is yet to be successfully controverted,
that the 39th Congress meant to leave segregation "as is"—to
the States. After the distribution of the Bickel memorandum,
Jackson wrote a file memorandum dated February 15, 1954, in
which he stated: "despite my personal satisfaction with the
Court's [forthcoming] judgment, I simply cannot find, in sur-
veying all the usual sources of law, anything which warrants me
in saying that it is required by the original purpose and intent of
the Fourteenth or Fifth Amendment."[54] He told the Conference
that he would "file a separate concurring opinion" if the "Court
feigned that the Justices were doing anything other than declaring new law for a new day."[55] This, Kluger comments, was
asking the majority to admit that "there was no judicial basis
for its decision," that "it was acting in a frankly unjudicial
way."[56] Kluger considers it "a scarcely reasonable request to

51. Justice Jackson "was worried about how a Court decision outlawing
segregation could affect the nation's respect for 'a supposedly stable organic
law' if the Justices were now, overnight, as it were, to alter an interpretation of
the Fourteenth Amendment which had stood for more than three-quarters of
a century." Kluger 604.

52. Id. 598. Justice Tom Clark "had been surprised by the legislative history, since he had always thought that one of the avowed purposes of the
Fourteenth Amendment had been to abolish segregation." Id. 682.

53. Id. 653.

54. Id. 688–689.

55. Id. 681, 609.

56. Id. 690, 683.

make of the brethren."[57] Why not? What kind of "consensus of society" (which the Court purportedly effectuates) is it that cannot withstand the truth—that effectuation required "new law for a new day"? An adult jurisprudence for an age of "realism" surely called for an end to the pretense that it was the Constitution, not the Justices, who spoke.[58] Concealment suggests there may in fact have been no consensus.[59] Perhaps Jackson's insistence impelled Chief Justice Warren—after labeling the history "inconclusive"[60]—to state that "we cannot turn back the clock to 1868,"[61] a veiled declaration that the intention of the framers was irrelevant and that the Court was revising the Constitution to meet present-day needs.[62]

Justice Frankfurter, the professed devotee of "self-restraint," reached a similar conclusion, but in different rhetoric. He had

57. Id. 683.

58. A deterrent, in Justice Frankfurter's words, was that the decision required "the adjustment of men's minds and actions to the unfamiliar and unpleasant." Id. 615. See infra Chapter 14 notes 140, 143, Chapter 23 at notes 30–34.

59. Edmond Cahn welcomed judicial intervention precisely because no amendment could have been obtained. Infra Chapter 15 at note 14.

60. It had not seemed "inconclusive" to Vinson, supra at note 43; Frankfurter, supra at note 52; Jackson, supra at note 54; Clark, supra note 52; and probably not to Reed, Kluger 595–596, 680–692.

61. 347 U.S. at 489, 492. Brown told about Warren's "unabashed and primary commitment to justice and his willingness to shape the law to achieve it." Paul Murphy, The Constitution in Crisis Times, 1918–1969 312 (1972). For analysis of Warren's opinion see infra Chapter 13 at notes 56–61.

62. As Graham, 269, stated, Brown v. Board of Education was "decided with scant reference to the historical rebriefings or to framers' intent or original understanding. Rather, political and judicial ethics, social psychology —what the equal protection of the laws means, and must mean in our time, whatever it may have meant to whomsoever in 1866–1868—these were the grounds and the essence of Chief Justice Warren's opinion." "What it must mean in our time" is one way of saying that the Justices may revise the Constitution. Sumner did not rely on equal protection because he knew that many of the draftsmen would affirm "that they had never intended to outlaw segregation." Supra note 40.

asked, Justice Burton noted, "What justifies us in saying that what *was* equal in 1868 is not equal now?"[63] and in a file memorandum he formulated his own answer:

> the equality of laws enshrined in a constitution which was "made for an undefined and expanding future . . ." . . . is not a fixed formula defined with finality at a particular time. It does not reflect, as a congealed summary, the social arrangements and beliefs of a particular epoch . . . The effect of changes in men's feelings for what is right and just is equally relevant in determining whether a discrimination denies the equal protection of the laws.[64]

Although the framers were well aware of the nation's "expanding future," they nonetheless, for example, rejected suffrage, "present *or prospective*." They knew that Article V provided the means to avoid "congealment,"[65] as was before long evidenced by adoption of the Fifteenth Amendment. The real issue, therefore, was not whether the Constitution must be "congealed," but rather who was to make the change—the people or the Justices. Buried in Frankfurter's fine phrases is a

63. Kluger 601.

64. Id. 685. But compare Hamilton, infra Chapter 17 at note 15. Frankfurter's pronouncement that the clearly expressed intention of the framers cannot be regarded as "a fixed formula," cannot be "congealed," is incompatible with his insistence that "very specific provisions" such as the prohibition of "bills of attainder" must be read as "defined by history." Infra Chapter 21 at note 46. Why should an historical definition deserve more respect than the framers' own explanation of their intention? Courts, Frankfurter had stated, "are not designed to be a good reflex of a democratic society." Dennis v. United States, 341 U.S. 494, 525 (1951), concurring opinion.

65. In "recalling that it is a Constitution 'intended to endure for ages to come,'" Justice Black stated, "we also remember that the Founders wisely provided the means for that endurance: changes in the Constitution, when thought necessary, are to be proposed by Congress or conventions and ratified by the States. The Founders gave no such amending power to this Court." Bell v. Maryland, 378 U.S. 226, 342 (1964). See infra Chapter 17 at notes 15–22.

confession that the people could not be trusted to reflect the "changes in men's feelings" by an amendment, and that in consequence the Justices had to rewrite the Constitution. Even in a memorandum for his own use, Frankfurter could not bring himself to admit that he was "making new law for a new day," but sought to disguise the fact with "majestic generalities."

In Chapter 10 I shall show that the framers employed "equal protection of the laws" to express their limited purpose: to secure the rights enumerated in the Civil Rights Act, and those only, against *discriminatory* State *legislation*. With respect to those rights there could no longer be one *law* for whites and another for blacks. The limitless objectives that Frankfurter read into the phrase were utterly beyond the contemplation of the framers. For the stubborn fact is that racism was, and still remains, an ugly fact of American life;[66] as Jackson's file memorandum stated, "Neither North nor South has been willing to adapt its racial practices to its professions.[67] "It was into this *moral void*," Kluger states, "that the Supreme Court under Earl Warren now stepped,"[68] not to give effect to a national consensus, still less to the Fourteenth Amendment, but to revise it for the people's own good. But "the criterion of constitutionality," said Justice Holmes, "is not whether we believe the law to be for the public good."[69]

66. For 1866, see supra Chapter 1 at notes 36–46; for the present day, see infra Chapter 17 at notes 55, and note 55.

67. Kluger 688.

68. Id. 710, emphasis added.

69. Adkins v. Children's Hospital, 261 U.S. 525, 570 (1923), dissenting opinion.

8

Incorporation of the Bill of Rights in the Fourteenth Amendment

INVOCATION of the Bill of Rights against the States is of fairly recent origin,[1] whether it be regarded within the older framework of "adoption" or the more recent theory of "incorporation."[2] From the First Amendment's "Congress shall make no law" may be gathered that it was to apply exclusively to Congress, and it was held in *Barron v. Baltimore*[3] that the Bill of Rights had no application to the States, as in fact the First Congress, which drafted the Bill, had earlier made clear.[4] Justice

1. Henkin, "Some Reflections on Current Constitutional Controversies," 109 U. Pa. L. Rev. 637, 644; Lusky 159.

2. For the difference between "incorporation" and "absorption" see Felix Frankfurter, "Memorandum on 'Incorporation' of the Bill of Rights into the Due Process Clause of the Fourteenth Amendment," 78 Harv. L. Rev. 746, 747–748 (1965). For "adoption," see infra Chapter 14 at notes 99–122.

3. 32 U.S. (7 Pet.) 243 (1833).

4. It has been little noticed that, as Egbert Benson, speaking with reference to freedom of speech and press, said, all the Committee of Eleven to whom the amendments had been referred "meant to provide against was their being infringed by the [federal] Government." 1 *Annals of Congress* 732. Madison urged that "the State governments are as liable to attack these invaluable privileges as the General Government is, and therefore ought to be as cautiously guarded against." Id. 441. But his attempt failed. Charles Warren "The New 'Liberty' under the Fourteenth Amendment," 39 Harv. L. Rev. 431, 433–435 (1926). The drive was for protection against the federal government; as Thomas Tucker said, "Five important States have pretty plainly expressed

Harlan spoke truly in stating that "every member of the Court for at least the last 135 years has agreed that our Founders did not consider the requirements of the Bill of Rights so fundamental that they should operate directly against the States."[5] And for a long time the Supreme Court found that the Fourteenth Amendment had made no change in this respect.[6] By means of "selective" incorporation or adoption the Court has worked "a revolutionary change in the criminal process"[7] of the States. Some consider that the Court was "trying to legislate a detailed criminal code for a continental country."[8]

Historically the citizenry have relied upon the States for protection, and such protection was afforded before the Constitutional Convention by a Bill of Rights in virtually every state Constitution. It was not fear of State misgovernment but distrust of the remote federal newcomer that fueled the demand for a federal Bill of Rights which would supply the same protection against the federal government that State Constitutions

---

their apprehensions of the danger to which the rights of their citizens are exposed." 1 *Annals of Congress* 757. Elbridge Gerry observed; "This declaration of rights, I take it, is designed to secure the people against the maladministration of the [federal] Government." Id. 749. Earlier James Jackson asked, "Who are Congress, that such apprehensions should be entertained of them?" Id. 442. In presenting the amendments Madison explained that "the abuse of the powers of the General Government may be guarded against in a more secure manner." Id. 432. He added, "If there was reason for restraining the State Governments [by State constitutions] from exercising this power, there is like reason for restraining the Federal Government." Id. 439. The view that prevailed was that of Thomas Tucker: "It will be much better, I apprehend, to leave the State Governments to themselves, and not to interfere with them more than we already do." Id. 755.

5. Duncan v. Louisiana, 391 U.S. 145, 173 (1968), dissenting opinion in which Justice Stewart concurred.

6. The cases are discussed in Stanley Morrison, "Does the Fourteenth Amendment Incorporate the Bill of Rights?" 2 Stan. L. Rev. 140 (1949).

7. Lusky 161.

8. Anthony Lewis, "A Man Born to Act, Not to Muse," in Levy, *Warren* 151, 159.

already provided against the States. This was understood by the framers of the Fourteenth Amendment,[9] and their own attachment to State sovereignty led them to refrain from intruding beyond the ban on discrimination against blacks with respect to certain rights. All else, including suffrage, was left to the States. In particular, Chairman Wilson emphasized during the debates on the Civil Rights Bill, "We are not making a general criminal code for the States."[10] Since the Amendment indisputably was designed to "incorporate" the guarantees of the Civil Rights Act, evidence is required to show that the framers had moved beyond the limited purposes of the Act.

The architect of the "incorporation" theory, Justice Black, invoked some fragmentary history—utterances in connection with an explanation of "privileges or immunities" by two leading Republican spokesmen, Bingham, author of §1, and Senator Jacob M. Howard, who purported to express the views of the Joint Committee.[11] Such statements are not lightly dismissed, after the manner of Justice Frankfurter, because "Remarks of a particular proponent of the Amendment, no matter how influential, are not to be deemed part of the Amendment."[12] Accepted canons of construction are to the contrary; the paramount consideration is to ascertain the intention of the legislature. That intention may be evidenced by statements of

9. See infra, at notes 86–88. It can hardly be gainsaid that "The States have always borne primary responsibility for operating the machinery of criminal justice within their borders, and adapting it to their peculiar circumstances." Justice Harlan, 391 U.S. at 172. Cf. Justice Miller, supra Chapter 4 at note 51. For a century the federal system "permitted States, but forbade Washington, to protect and defend the civil and political rights of citizens." P. S. Paludan, *A Covenant with Death* 12 (1975).

10. *Globe* 1120.

11. Fairman states that "The rest of the evidence bore in the opposite direction, or was indifferent." Fairman, Stanford 65. I found no additional confirmation for Black.

12. Adamson v. California, 332 U.S. 46, 64 (1947), concurring opinion. Frankfurter himself later spoke to the contrary, supra Chapter 1 note 22.

leading proponents,[13] and, if found, is to be regarded as good as written into the enactment: "the intention of the lawmaker is the law."[14] But Black's history falls far short of the "conclusive demonstration" he thought it to be in his famous *Adamson* dissent.[15] The contrary, it may fairly be said, was demonstrated in Charles Fairman's painstaking and scrupulous impeachment of Black's history,[16] buttressed by Stanley Morrison's telling companion article.[17]

Absorption of one or another portion of the Bill of Rights—free speech, for example—antedated *Adamson*,[18] but

13. Wright v. Vinton Branch, 300 U.S. 440, 463 (1937); Wisconsin R.R. Comm. v. C. B. & Q.R.R. Co., 257 U.S. 563, 589 (1922); United States v. Federal Power Commission, 191 F.2d 796, 802 (4th Cir. 1951): "great weight must be accorded . . . to opinions expressed by members of the committees having the legislation in charge."

14. Supra, Chapter 1 note 24.

15. Adamson v. California, 332 U.S. at 74.

16. Fairman, Stanford.

17. Supra note 6; Lusky 162. Fairman "conclusively disproved Black's contention, at least, such is the weight of opinion among disinterested observers." A. Bickel, *The Least Dangerous Branch* 102 (1962). Levy states, however, that "Fairman's findings were basically negative. He did not disprove that the Fourteenth incorporated the Bill of Rights; he proved, rather, that there is very little evidence either that its framers intended that result or that the country understood that intention." Levy, *Judgments: Essays in American Constitutional History* 70 (1972). The proposition that "the Fourteenth Amendment incorporated the Bill of Rights" constitutes an invasion of rights reserved to the States by the Tenth Amendment, an invasion of such magnitude as to demand proof that such was the framers' intention. Levy would shift the burden of proof and require Black's critics to prove the negative before he *proved* the intention to incorporate. He himself stated that "Black did not merely misread history . . . he mangled or manipulated it." Levy, *Judgments,* id. at 68.

But Justice Black remained unconvinced. Duncan v. Louisiana, 391 U.S. 145, 165, concurring opinion. The Court itself, as Thomas Grey remarked, "clearly has declined" to accept "the flimsy historical evidence" mustered by Black for incorporation. "Do We Have an Unwritten Constitution?" 27 Stan. L. Rev. 703, 711–712 (1975).

18. In Gitlow v. New York, 268 U.S. 652, 666 (1925), the Court "assumed" arguendo that the free speech of the First Amendment is protected by

this was on a selective basis, under cover of due process. To Black this was an abhorrent claim to "boundless power under 'natural law' periodically to expand and contract constitutional standards to conform to the court's conception of what at a particular time constitutes 'civilized decency' and 'fundamental liberty and justice.'" Why, he asked, should the Bill of Rights "be 'absorbed' in part but not in full?"[19] The cure, he maintained, was "incorporation" en bloc. His condemnation was not, however, wholehearted, for he was ready to accept "selective" adoption if he could not obtain wholesale incorporation, suggesting that sacrifice of a desired result was more painful than "boundless power to expand or contract constitutional standards."[20] The words "privileges or immunities" seemed "an eminently reasonable way of expressing the idea that henceforth the Bill of Rights shall apply to the States."[21] The two concepts, however, are of entirely different provenance and deal with quite different matters. "Privileges or immunities" has its roots in Article IV, §2, which requires States to accord certain privileges to citizens of a sister State; the Bill of Rights, on the other hand, was designed to protect certain rights against the federal government. The debates in the First Congress contain not the faintest intimation that the "privileges and immunities" of Article IV were being enlarged or, indeed, that the Bill of Rights was in any way related to "privileges and immunities."

---

the due process of the Fourteenth. From that assumption grew the absorption of free speech into due process. See infra Chapter 14.

19. 332 U.S. at 69, 86. So too, "When the Court declares that one or the other of the Bill of Rights provisions is 'fundamental' and therefore incorporated, it draws only upon its own sense of what the Fourteenth Amendment *ought* to say." Lusky 163; see also id. 266.

20. 332 U.S. at 89. Black confirmed his compromise in Duncan v. Louisiana, 391 U.S. at 171, concurring opinion. For discussion of the legal consequences presented by the differentiation between "selective" and "full" incorporation, see Louis Henkin, "'Selective Incorporation' in the Fourteenth Amendment," 73 Yale L.J. 74 (1963).

21. Duncan v. Louisiana, 391 U.S. at 166, concurring opinion.

And, when Justice Bushrod Washington later enumerated those "privileges and immunities," he too made no reference to the Bill of Rights. To read the Bill of Rights into "privileges or immunities" is therefore no more "reasonable" than to read a "bill of attainder" into "habeas corpus."

In *Adamson*, Black appealed to "the original purpose of the Fourteenth Amendment,"[22] as disclosed by the Bingham-Howard statements. These statements had reference to the "privileges or immunities" clause, but that clause had been emasculated in the *Slaughter-House Cases*.[23] Hence Black relied on "the provisions of the Amendment's first section, separately, and as a whole" for incorporation of the Bill of Rights.[24] The "privileges or immunities" clause gains no fresh vitality as a component of the "whole" of §1. Reliance on the due process clause runs afoul of Black's statement in the *Adamson* case that in *Chicago, M. & St. P. R. Co. v. Minnesota* (1890)[25] the Court "gave a new and hitherto undisclosed scope for the Court's use of the due process clause to protect property rights under natural law concepts."[26] Substantive due process was fashioned in *Wynehamer v. The People* (1856) to bar abolitionist natural law claims and confine protection to property; and libertarian due process came long after economic substantive due process. No one in the 39th Congress intimated that the due process clause would incorporate the Bill of Rights; Bingham looked to the judicial

22. 332 U.S. at 90.
23. See supra Chapter 3.
24. 332 U.S. at 71.
25. 134 U.S. 418.
26. 332 U.S. at 79. Historically, due process meant service of process (e.g., a writ or summons) in due, i.e. proper, course. Infra Chapter 11 at notes 13–22. Dissenting in Harper v. Virginia Board of Elections, 383 U.S. 663, 675 (1966), Justice Black found "no constitutional support whatever" for the use of the due process clause as "a blank check to alter the meaning of the Constitution as written." For the 39th Congress' narrow view of due process, see infra Chapter 11 at notes 48–52.

decisions for the scope of due process, then purely procedural.[27] Speaking to the Bingham amendment, Chairman Wilson indicated that the due process clause was considered to furnish a "remedy" to secure the "fundamental rights" enumerated in the Civil Rights Act.[28] To transform it into a "source" of other unspecified rights is to set at naught the careful enumeration of rights in the Act, "constitutionalized" by the Amendment, which is incompatible with Black's invocation of the original purpose. In truth, expansion of due process to libertarian claims is largely a product of the post-1937 era; and "substantive equal protection" is a very recent concept indeed. Black's reliance on §1 "as a whole" can therefore be met with the adage "when nothing is added to nothing, the sum is and remains the same—nothing."

Bingham's remarks were addressed to H.R. No. 63, the antecedent Bingham amendment: "The Congress shall have power to make all laws which shall be necessary and proper to secure to citizens of each State all privileges and immunities of citizens in the several States (Art. IV, §2); and to all persons in the several States equal protection in the rights of life, liberty, and property (5th amendment)." This proposal, said Bingham, "stands in the very words of the Constitution . . . Every word . . . is today in the Constitution."[29] It is a mark of Bingham's sloppiness that "every word" was *not* "in the Constitution": "equal protection" was missing altogether. "[T]hese great provisions of the Constitution," he continued, "this im-

27. 13 N.Y. 378; infra Chapter 11 at notes 23–27, 36–37; Chapter 14 at notes 34–35.

28. Infra at note 36.

29. Kendrick 61; *Globe* 1034. Kendrick comments that when the Bingham amendment was reported to the House, "That body did not receive it with wild enthusiasm, and even denied it the privilege of being considered as a special order. Since to have placed it on the regular calendar would have meant its indefinite postponement, it was recommitted" in the hope of returning on a "more propitious occasion." Bingham "stood almost alone as its champion and defender" when he introduced it. Kendrick 215.

mortal bill of rights embodied in the Constitution, rested for its execution and enforcement hitherto upon the fidelity of the States."[30] As Fairman pointed out, the antecedent of his remark was Article IV, §2, and the Fifth Amendment due process clause which Bingham equated with "equal protection."[31] There is no reason to believe that his subsequent references to the Bill of Rights had broader compass.[32] Certainly his fellow Republicans did not so read his proposed amendment. The radical William Higby of California thought that the Article IV, §2, clause and the Fifth Amendment due process clause constituted "precisely what will be provided" by the Bingham amendment.[33] Another radical, Frederick E. Woodbridge of Vermont, stated: "It is intended to enable Congress by its enactments when necessary to give a citizen of the United States in whatever State he may be, those privileges and immunities which are guarantied to him under the Constitution [Article IV] . . . that protection to his property which is extended to other citizens of the State [due process clause]."[34] Bingham's reference to "the enforcement of the bill of rights, touching the life, liberty, and property . . . within every organized State . . ."[35] would convey to his fellows the technical meaning that had been attached to "life, liberty, and property" in the Civil Rights Bill debate.

Bingham, it will be recalled, had proposed his amendment to avoid doubts as to the constitutionality of the Civil Rights Bill. Wilson, chairman of the Judiciary Committee, joined issue: "in relation to the great fundamental rights embraced in the bill of

30. *Globe* 1034.

31. Fairman, Stanford 26.

32. "No one in debate ever runs down the list of the federal Bill of Rights." Id. 44; see also infra at notes 57–59.

33. *Globe* 1054.

34. Id. 1088. Price of Iowa understood the Bingham amendment "to give the same rights, and privileges, and protection to the citizen of one State going into another that a citizen of that State would have who had lived there for years," i.e., under Article IV, §2; *Globe* 1066.

35. Id. 1291.

rights, the citizen . . . is entitled to a remedy. The citizen is
entitled to the right of life, liberty and property. Now if a State
intervenes, and deprives him, without due process of law, of
those rights . . . " And he said, "I find in the bill of rights
which the gentleman desires to have enforced by an amendment . . . that 'No person shall be deprived of life, liberty and
property without due process of law.' I understand that these
constitute the civil rights . . . to which this bill relates."[36]
Implicit in Wilson's formulation is the assumption that no more
is needed; and that is likewise the implication of the Higby and
Woodbridge remarks about the Bingham amendment.

Far from accepting every word that fell from Bingham as
gospel, the framers gave his proposal a chilly reception. According to Kendrick, he "stood almost alone . . . a great
many Republicans, including particularly the entire New York
delegation, were opposed to the amendment."[37] He tried to
soften the opposition by arguing that to oppose his amendment
was "to oppose the grant of power to enforce the bill of rights,"
to perpetuate statutes of confiscation, of banishment, of
murder.[38] Bickel considers that Bingham "was suggesting to
those members who were alarmed that he had some definite
evils in mind, limited and distinct in nature."[39] When we add:
(1) the fact that Bingham's amendment was shelved argues
against adoption of his views;[40] (2) the fact that the Joint Committee's subsequent rejection of Bingham's motion to add to
Owen's proposed amendment the phrase "nor take private
property for public use without just compensation"[41] is incompatible with blanket adoption of the first Eight Amendments;
(3) the fact that Bingham made no reference to inclusion of the
Bill of Rights during debate on the final proposal which became

36. Id. 1294.
37. Kendrick 214–215; cf. Bickel 42–43; cf. Flack 59.
38. *Globe* 1090–1091.
39. Bickel 39.
40. Id. 40.
41. Id. 42; this was drawn from the Fifth Amendment.

§1 of the Amendment; (4) Wilson's emphasis during debate that the Civil Rights Bill embodied the very civil rights embraced by due process protection of life, liberty, and property; and (5) Wilson's assurances during that debate that "we are not making a general criminal code for the States"[42] (suggesting that what was unpalatable in the Bill would be no more acceptable in the Amendment)—it becomes apparent that beyond due process the framers had no intention to adopt the Bill of Rights.

Bingham was in fact utterly at sea as to the role of the Bill of Rights. At first he considered it to be binding upon the States. Thus, after reading the due process clause of the Fifth Amendment as the source of his own proposed amendment, he stated: "this proposed amendment does not impose upon any State . . . an obligation which is not now enjoined upon them by the very letter of the Constitution."[43] For this he appealed to the "supremacy clause" of Article VI, which makes the Constitution binding,[44] hurdling the preliminary question whether the Constitution made the Fifth Amendment binding on the States. Although he noted that *Barron v. Baltimore*[45] held that the Bill of Rights is "not applicable to and do[es] not bind the States,"[46] he stated on February 28: "A State has not the right to deny equal protection . . . in the rights of life, liberty, and property." On March 9 he stated:

> the care of the property, the liberty, and the life of the citizen . . . is *in the States,* and not in the Federal Government. I have sought to effect no change in that respect . . . I have advocated here an amendment which would arm Congress with the power to punish all violations by State officers of the bill of rights . . . I have always believed that *protection* . . . within

42. *Globe* 1120.
43. Id. 1034. The Bill of Rights, he said, is "to be enforced by State tribunals." Id. 1291.
44. Id. 1034.
45. 32 U.S. (7 Pet.) 243 (1833).
46. *Globe* 1089–1090.

the States of all the rights of person and citizen, was of the powers *reserved to the States*.[47]

Reservation of "protection" to the States runs counter to rejection of a State's denial of an existing "right to equal protection"; it is incompatible with State "violations" of the Bill of Rights. Apparently unaware that Article IV, §2, protected nonresident migrants, not residents,[48] Bingham said: "No State ever has the right . . . to abridge . . . the privileges and immunities of any citizen of the Republic." Shifting again, he stated: "we all agree . . . that the exercise of the elective franchise, though it be one of the privileges of a citizen of the Republic, is exclusively under the control of the States."[49] "Exclusive control" authorizes a State to "abridge" the privilege. In truth, as Morrison, concurring with Fairman, stated, Bingham's "many statements . . . are so confused and conflicting as to be of little weight."[50] This goes beyond the issue of credibility, which courts test by inconsistent statements. It poses the question: upon which of his conflicting explanations did the framers rely?

47. *Globe* 1089, 1292–1293; emphasis added. On February 28 he commented on Hale's statement "that the citizens must rely upon the State for their protection. I admit that such is the rule under the Constitution as it stands." *Globe* 1093. Consider too his statement, "although as ruled the existing amendments . . . *do not bind* the States, they are nevertheless to be enforced and observed in the States." *Globe* 1090 (emphasis added). As Fairman, *History* 334, pointed out, "civil status had been entirely a matter of State concern. Thus when Chancellor Kent discussed the 'Rights of Persons' to 'Personal Liberty and Security' . . . he told of State constitutions and laws." See also Fairman, id. 1368. Speaking of the First Amendment "right . . . to assemble," Chief Justice Waite stated, "For their protection in its enjoyment . . . the people must look to the States. The power for that purpose was originally placed there, and it has never been surrendered to the United States." United States v. Cruikshank, 92 U.S. 542, 552 (1875).

48. See supra Chapter 3 at notes 19–20.

49. *Globe* 2452. But earlier he stated, "I do not admit . . . that any State has a right to disfranchise any portion of the citizens of the United States." *Globe App.* 57.

50. Morrison, supra note 6 at 161; Fairman, Stanford 34–36.

How can "conclusive" legislative history rest on shifting sands?[51]

In the eyes of Justice Black, "Bingham may, without extravagence be called the Madison of the first section of the Fourteenth Amendment."[52] Shades of Madison! Bingham was a muddled thinker,[53] given to the florid, windy rhetoric of a stump orator, liberally interspersed with invocations to the Deity,[54] not to the careful articulation of a lawyer who addresses himself to great issues. Recall his location of the words "equal protection" in the Constitution from which they were notably absent. Hale attributed to Bingham the view that "there had been from first to last, a violation of the provisions of this bill of rights by the very existence of slavery itself,"[55] thereby, as

51. Or, as Fairman stated, "When other members were unable to find out what he meant, they can hardly be charged with consenting to his words." Fairman, id. 66.

52. 332 U.S. at 74. The "implied comparison seems a slur upon the sharp-minded Father of the Constitution. For Bingham is one who used ringing rhetoric as a substitute for rational analysis." Wallace Mendelson, "Mr. Justice Black's Fourteenth Amendment," 53 Minn. L. Rev. 711, 716 (1969).

53. Bickel charitably states Bingham was "not normally distinguished for precision of thought and statement." Bickel 25. Fairman considers him "an ardent rhetorician, not a man of exact knowledge or clear conception or accurate language." Fairman, *History* 462; see id. 1289.

54. Three specimens must suffice: late in a debate which had frazzled men's patience, he dwelt on "the departing sun shall have gilded with its last rays the dome of the capitol"; again, "I humbly bow before the majesty of justice, as I bow before the majesty of that God whose attribute it is." *Globe* 2542, 1293.

When he grasped that Barron v. Baltimore, 32 U.S. (7 Pet.) 243 (1833), held the Bill of Rights inapplicable to the States, he stated, "they are nevertheless to be enforced and observed in the States by the grand utterance of that immortal man, who, while he lived, stood alone in his intellectual power among the living men of his country, and now that he is dead, sleeps alone in his honored tomb by the sounding sea," namely, Daniel Webster. *Globe* 1089–1090.

55. Quoted in Fairman, *History* 1277; *Globe* 1065; compare this with Chapter 5 supra at notes 58–64. For Bingham, enfranchisement of the blacks conformed "exactly to the spirit of the Constitution and according to the declared intent of its framers." *Globe* 430. Yet he stated that "the grant of

Judge Hale doubtless was aware, converting the Bill into a repealer of several existing provisions that sanctioned slavery—and this in the teeth of the First Congress' express intention to exclude the States from the ambit of the Bill of Rights.[56]

Presumably the framers who listened to Bingham found his frequent shifts of position no less perplexing than they seem to us; consequently, they had an added incentive to cling to the vastly preponderant view that they were merely incorporating the limited provisions of the Civil Rights Act in the Amendment. Whatever be the weight that attaches to Bingham's utterances, it needs to be noted that even his admirers read them restrictively. So, Kelly states that his speech of February 29 "makes it clear that by 'bill of rights' Bingham meant both the guarantees of the comity clause and the guarantee of due process in the Fifth Amendment."[57] And tenBroek asks, "What Bill of Rights? Certainly not the first eight amendments to the Constitution. The answer is not left open to conjecture: the Bill of Rights that contain (1) the comity clause . . . which guarantees the privileges and immunities of citizens of the United States; (2) the due process clause of the Fifth Amendment; and (3) the requirement that all shall be protected alike in life, liberty, and property, not explicitly mentioned in either body or amendments . . . this was the 'immortal Bill of Rights' of

---

power" to "secure the enforcement of these provisions of the bill of rights in every State" "would have been [in the Constitution] but for the fact that its insertion . . . would have been utterly incompatible with the existence of slavery in any State." *Globe* 1090. Engulfed by a sea of rhetoric, he never paused to sort out his ideas.

56. The legislative history of the Bill of Rights leaves no doubt that the First Congress designedly excluded States from its operations. Supra note 4.

57. Kelly, Fourteenth 1073 note 88. Graham, 265, states, "no one even pretended that *all* the clauses and guarantees of the Bill of Rights ever could or would be enforced against the States." He concluded that the "odds appear heavily against" imputing to Bingham an intention to include "every clause of each of the eight Amendments," and accepts Fairman's proof that "the entire Bill of Rights was not incorporated," Graham 315 note 80, as does Bickel 5 note 13. What are the criteria for selection?

John A. Bingham."[58] Among the abolitionists themselves there was general agreement only about the due process clause and the First and Fourth Amendments; the "rights in the other amendments," tenBroek says, "received only casual, incidental, and infrequent reference."[59] Justice Black, therefore, would impute to Bingham views which far outran the abolitionist program that allegedly was the source of his inspiration. Before we marshall the evidence which further undermines attribution of Bingham's views to the framers, let us consider the companion remarks of Senator Jacob M. Howard.

By a caprice of fortune—the sudden illness of Chairman Fessenden—it fell to Senator Howard to act as spokesman for the Joint Committee in explaining the Amendment. Up to this point his participation in the debates on the Civil Rights Bill and the several aspects of the Amendment had been negligible. Poles removed from Chairman Fessenden, who "abhorred" extreme radicals, Howard, according to Kendrick, was "one of the most . . . reckless of the radicals," who had "served consistently in the vanguard of the extreme Negrophiles."[60] He had expended "fruitless efforts" to include the right to vote; he and Elihu B. Washburne of Illinois "had been the only Republicans to hold out for black suffrage to the end, all the others proved willing to abandon it."[61] That such a man should speak "for" a Committee in which the "non-radicals clearly outnumbered the radicals," in which, by the testimony of the co-chairmen Fessenden and Stevens, there "was very considerable difference of opinion,"[62] needs to be taken, in the words of the "immortal" Samuel Goldwyn, with "a bushel of salts."

On May 23 Senator Howard rose in the Senate, alluded to Fessenden's illness, and stated that he would present "the views and the motives which influenced the committee, so far as I

58. TenBroek 214.
59. Id. 127; cf. infra Chapter 11 at notes 48–52.
60. Kendrick 257, 192.
61. James 82; M. L. Benedict, *A Compromise of Principle* 170 (1975).
62. Benedict, id. 34; *Globe* 2332, 3148; James 59.

understand [them]." After reading the privileges and immunities listed in *Corfield v. Coryell,* he said, "to these privileges and immunities . . . should be added the personal rights guaranteed and secured by the first eight amendments."[63] That is the sum and substance of Howard's contribution to the "incorporation" issue. Justice Black assumed without more ado that Howard "emphatically stated the understanding of the framers."[64] No one, to be sure, rose to challenge Howard's remark, casually tucked away in a long speech.[65] "The argument from silence," as Alfred Kelly observed, "is always more than a little dangerous."[66] But was there really silence? Consider Senator Poland's subsequent statement: "Great differences have existed among ourselves; many opinions have had to yield to enable us to agree upon a plan." A similar statement had been made by Fessenden and repeated by the radical leader Senator Benjamin Wade.[67] Now, after the compromise of such differences about *known* objectives, we are asked to infer that there was unquestioning acceptance of a sweeping, brand-new element, which had received no consideration whatever! Then too, others who spoke after Howard, repeated that the goal was legitimation of the Civil Rights Act. So, Senator Poland observed, "The clause . . . that 'no State shall . . . abridge the privileges and

63. *Globe* 2764, 2765.

64. 332 U.S. at 73.

65. Flack once more relies on the argument from silence: "Howard's interpretation of the amendment was not questioned by any one . . . this interpretation must be accepted as that of the Committee, since no member of the Committee gave a different interpretation or questioned his statements in any particular." Flack 87. But see Trumbull infra p. 159.

66. Kelly, "Clio and the Court: An Illicit Love Affair," 1965 S. Ct. Rev. 119, 147. Fairman, Stanford 68–69, points out that no newspaper reported Howard's remarkable expansion of the privileges and immunities clause, notwithstanding that application of the Bill of Rights would cut a wide swath through State self-rule. He rightly remarks, "If Senator Howard's statement about Amendments I to VIII had really been accepted at the time, surely one would find it caught up and repeated in contemporary discussion." Id. 137.

67. *Globe* 2964, 2332, 2769–2770.

immunities of citizens of the United States' secures *nothing beyond* what was intended by the original [Article IV, §2] provision in the Constitution."[68] If this be not regarded as a delicately phrased repudiation of Howard's addition, at the very least it exhibits a more limited view than that of Howard by a respected Republican.[69] Senator Doolittle stated that the Civil Rights Bill "was the forerunner of this constitutional amendment, and to give validity to which this constitutional amendment is brought forward."[70] Such reminders of known and limited objectives were designed to reassure those whose consent had thus far been won; and they rob Howard's remark of uncontroverted standing.[71]

68. Id. 2961 (emphasis added). From Poland's statement, "the last two clauses were . . . in the Declaration of Independence and in the Constitution," Flack distills, "evidently meaning some or all of the first eight Amendments, since one of the clauses [due process] was taken from the Fifth Amendment." Flack 91. Reference to one Amendment does not warrant a deduction that *all* were intended; to the contrary the rule is that to enumerate one is to exclude others.

69. Fairman, Stanford 61, regards Poland's remarks as "quite inconsistent with Howard's speech."

70. *Globe* 2896. On January 30 Howard assured the Senate that the purpose "is to secure" to the blacks "the ordinary rights of a freeman and nothing else . . . There is no invasion of the legitimate rights of the States." Id. 504. Later, after his explanation of the Amendment, he stated that the Committee desired to put the rights conferred by the "civil rights bill beyond the legislative power [to repeal]." Id. 2896. Compare Senator Howe's approval of the Amendment on June 5 because it enumerated the rights of citizenship: to hold land, collect wages, sue, and testify. *Globe App.* 219.

71. To convert the loose statements of Bingham and Howard, as Justice Black did, into the proposition "that one of the chief objects" of §1 "was to make the Bill of Rights applicable to the States," 332 U.S. at 71–72, suggests that Black did not really take time to study the record but relied on the feeble and unsophisticated analysis of Flack. Id. at 72 note 5.

Kelly stated that among the "argument[s] for the Black thesis," which Fairman allegedly "ignores," is that Senator Trumbull talked "constantly about 'nationalizing' an already existing 'Bill of Rights' for the states, which he repeatedly asserted to be implicit in the Privileges and Immunities Clause of Article IV of the 'Old Constitution.'" Kelly, "Clio," supra note 66 at

Account must also be taken of expressions in the House after Howard's speech, for even if his words be taken to express the sentiment of the Senate, it must not be facilely assumed that it was shared by the House. Nothing was said about the Bill of Rights upon return of the measure to the House[72]—surely a remarkable silence about an extraordinary expansion of jointly accepted goals! Instead, George R. Latham, a West Virginia Republican, remarked "The 'civil rights bill' which is now a law . . . *covers exactly* the same ground as this amendment."[73] Henry Van Aernam of New York said that the Amendment gives "constitutional sanctions and protection to the substantial guarantees of the civil-rights bill."[74] The Latham–Van Aernam remarks, parenthetically, afford additional proof that the earlier Bingham remarks did not represent the thinking of the House. Also significant are Stevens' final remarks lamenting his failure to abolish "all" "inequality" and "distinctions" and explaining that he was constrained to accept so "imperfect a proposition" because he lived "among men and not among angels . . . who . . . do not choose to yield their opinions to mine."[75] It strains credulity to attribute to "men" who had rejected abolition of "all" distinctions readiness to swallow whole-hog reconstruction of their Northern institutions which had not even been discussed. Instead, the specific incorporation of one portion of the Bill of Rights—the due process clause—and the rejection of

---

132–133. Kelly's citation to *Globe* 474–475 does not sustain him. Trumbull made no reference to the Bill of Rights, confined his citations to Article IV, §2, and explained that the purpose of the Civil Rights Bill was "to destroy all these [enumerated] discriminations" against the Negroes. The Bill, he stated, "will have *no operation* in any State where the laws are equal, where all persons have the same civil rights without regard to color or race," *Globe* 476 (emphasis added), a statement that spells "hands off" internal State laws that are non-discriminatory and do not touch "civil rights."

72. Fairman, Stanford 65.
73. *Globe* 2883 (emphasis added).
74. Id. 3069.
75. Id. 3148.

another—the just compensation clause—gave the framers ample reason to conclude that "due process" alone was to be "incorporated."[76]

Flack's canvass of "speeches concerning the popular discussion of the Fourteenth Amendment" led him to conclude:

76. In his Adamson concurring opinion, Justice Frankfurter stated that adoption of the due process clause would be "a strange way of saying" that "every State must thereafter initiate prosecutions through indictment by a grand jury, must have a trial by a jury of twelve in criminal cases . . . after all, an amendment to the Constitution should be read in a 'sense most obvious to the common understanding *at the time of its adoption,*'" quoting Justice Holmes (emphasis added). Those "conversant with the political and legal history of the concept of due process . . . would hardly recognize the Fourteenth Amendment as a cover for the various explicit provisions of the first eight Amendments." 332 U.S. at 63. But no more would such readers guess that the due process clause would authorize judges to select "such provisions of the Bill of Rights as were 'implicit in the concept of ordered liberty.'" Id. 54. Even less would they guess that it would be a "cover" for substantive due process, which was all but unknown to the "common understanding." See infra Chapter 11. "It ought not to require argument," Frankfurter stated, "to reject the notion that due process of law meant one thing in the Fifth Amendment and another in the Fourteenth." Id. 66. Apart from such considerations, the courts were too little trusted by the framers of the Fourteenth Amendment to be entrusted with such vast discretion. Infra Chapter 12.

Although Frankfurter inveighed against a "selective incorporation" without a "calculus for determining which go in and which stay out" as throwing us "back to a merely subjective task," id. 65, he did not really appreciate that his "canons of decency and fairness which express the notions of justice of English-speaking . . . peoples," id. 67, were no less "subjective." Nowhere were those "canons" catalogued with even the specificity of the Bill of Rights, as Frankfurter himself acknowledged: "These standards of justice are not authoritatively formulated anywhere as though they were prescriptions in a pharmacopoeia." Id. 68. For comparison of the Black and Frankfurter approaches, see infra Chapter 14 at notes 44–73.

Writing in 1960, Miller and Howell prophetically stated that Justices Black and Douglas "fail either to realize or be concerned about the fact that if the fourteenth amendment should embrace the procedural rights of the Bill of Rights, the criminal jurisdiction of the fifty states might be entirely disrupted." "The Myth of Neutrality in Constitutional Adjudication," 27 U. Chi. L. Rev. 661, 680 note 76.

the general opinion held in the North . . . was that the Amendment embodied the Civil Rights Act . . . There does not seem to have been any statement at all as to whether the first eight amendments were to be made applicable to the States or not, whether the privileges guaranteed by those amendments were to be considered as privileges secured by the amendment.[77]

Senator Sherman, for example, told Cincinnati during the campaign for adoption that "the first section was an embodiment of the [Civil Rights] Act."[78] Fairman has collected remarks by five Senators and five Representatives, not one of whom "said that the privileges and immunities clause would impose Articles I to VIII upon the States."[79] We must assume that they knew of no such purpose; men of Sherman's stature may not be charged with a conspiracy to conceal the proposed imposition from the people—certainly not without substantial proof. There is no need to retrace Fairman's examination of the State ratification proceedings;[80] let it suffice that there is no intimation therein that ratification would produce radical changes in the States' judicial machinery, for example, the replacement of an information by a grand jury indictment, of a six-man jury by a jury of twelve.[81] If this was in fact the purpose of the framers,

77. Flack 153. This was quoted by Justice Black, 332 U.S. at 118, but he appeared oblivious to its implications.

78. Fairman, Stanford 77; see also supra Chapter 6 at notes 64–66.

79. Id. 78.

80. Id. 81 et seq. See Justice Harlan's dissent in Oregon v. Mitchell, 400 U.S. 112, 196 (1970).

81. Fairman collected examples of State constitutional provisions which "incorporation" would have abrogated and of which, of course, no intimation was given to the State ratifying conventions. Fairman, Stanford 81 et seq. As Justice Frankfurter stated in his concurring Adamson opinion, 332 U.S. at 64, "It could hardly have occurred to these States [which had no rigorous grand jury requirement] that by ratifying the Amendment they uprooted their established methods for prosecuting crime and fastened upon themselves a new prosecutorial system." For a similar expression by Justice Black in a corporate context, see infra at note 95. See also Justice Jackson, dissenting in Beauharnais v. Illinois, 343 U.S. 250, 292–293 (1952), quoted infra note 95.

honesty required disclosure.[82] None was made, and the reason, I suggest, is that no such purpose was entertained.

Then there is the remarkable fact that the cases which followed on the heels of the Fourteenth Amendment continued to hold the Bill of Rights inapplicable to State action, without mentioning the Amendment.[83] Oversight will not account for the omission; the Amendment had been widely discussed; bench and bar are alert to every new and relevant enactment; they would not be oblivious to the revolution worked by the alleged incorporation of the Bill of Rights.[84]

In sum, the framers were motivated by discriminatory denials of "fundamental rights" to the blacks.[85] No trace of a purpose to reconstruct Northern institutions for the protection of white inhabitants against the State will be found in the debates; the frequent expressions of jealous regard for State sovereignty repel such a purpose. When Judge Robert Hale insisted that "the American people have not yet found their State governments are insufficient to protect the rights and liberties of the citi-

82. After listening in 1871 to broad claims as to the scope of the Fourteenth Amendment, John B. Storm of Pennsylvania stated, "If the monstrous doctrine now set up as resulting from the provisions of the Fourteenth Amendment had ever been hinted at that Amendment would have received an emphatic rejection at the hands of the People." Quoted in Flack 236–237. Flack, who searched the newspapers of the period quite thoroughly, 332 U.S. at 109, comments, "no doubt [Storm] was right in saying that had the people been informed of what was intended by the Amendment, they would have rejected it." Flack 237, a point unnoticed by Justice Black.

83. Fairman, Stanford 132 et seq.

84. The point was made by Justice Frankfurter with respect to Twichell v. Pennsylvania, 74 U.S. (7 Wall.) 321 (1868), decided only a few months after adoption of the Fourteenth Amendment. Frankfurter, "Memorandum," supra note 2 at 750. See also Mendelson, supra note 52 at 721.

85. The "major inspiration for the 1866 law," says Kelly, "was the resentment and alarm that the enactment of the Black Codes . . . had produced among Radical Republicans." Kelly, "Clio," supra note 66 at 147. "All agree, however, regarding the racial motivation of the Amendment." Graham 274. This view was expressed in the Slaughter-House Cases, supra Chapter 3 at notes 39–40.

zen,"[86] Bingham translated this as "the citizens must rely upon
the State for their protection," and added, "I admit that such is
the rule under the Constitution as it now stands."[87] It cannot be
presumed that the States which, in Stevens' words, would not
"allow Congress to come within their jurisdiction to fix the
qualifications of their voters,"[88] would tolerate a federal over-
haul of their judicial processes that went beyond making them
available to Negroes. Such a presumption runs counter to Senator Trumbull's assurance that the "provisions of the
[Freedman's Bureau] bill in regard to holding courts . . . are
confined entirely to the rebellious States." "Certainly nobody
has ever complained," Senator Cowan said, "that a full and
exact measure of justice has not been meted out to him in all our
courts . . . I do object to extending it to the loyal States of the
North."[89] Subsequently, Trumbull twice stated that the Civil
Rights Bill had no application to a State that did not discriminate between its citizens.[90] The constant reiteration that the purpose of the Amendment was to constitutionalize the Civil
Rights Act, the frequent tributes to State sovereignty, and recognition of powers reserved to the States by the Tenth Amend-

86. *Globe* 1064–1065.

87. Id. 1093.

88. Id. 536; to the same effect see Conkling, id. 358. What Howard said,
"The Committee were of the opinion that the States are not yet prepared to
sanction so fundamental a change as would be the concession of suffrage to the
colored race," id. 2766, which would have its greatest impact in the South, is
even more applicable to wholesale revision of internal practices affecting
whites in the North. Latham, a West Virginia Republican, "denied that
Congress had a right to interfere with the internal policy of the States so as to
define and regulate the civil rights and immunities of the inhabitants thereof."
Id. 1295–1296. The requirement that State laws must not discriminate with
respect to certain enumerated rights was an enclave cut out of this general policy. See also the remarks of Hotchkiss, infra Chapter 10 at note 78.

89. *Globe* 334–335.

90. See Trumbull, supra note 71; infra, Chapter 10 at note 49. Bingham insisted on the deletion of no discrimination in "civil rights" because of its "oppressive" invasion of State sovereignty. Supra Chapter 7 at notes 11–17.

ment, in which Bingham joined,[91] unite to repel an inference that the framers intended to interfere with State conduct of its own affairs otherwise than is described in that Act. The pervasive attachment to federalism—State control of local institutions—Phillip Paludan repeatedly emphasizes, was "the most potent institutional obstacle to the Negroes' hope for protected liberty"[92]—and even more of an obstacle to federal encroachment on Northern States' control of their own white citizens. If there was a concealed intention to go beyond the Civil Rights Act, it was not ratified because, first, ratification requires disclosure of material facts,[93] whereas there was no disclosure that the Amendment was meant to uproot, for example, traditional State judicial procedures and practices; and, second, a surrender of recognized rights may not be presumed but must be proved. In truth, the Fourteenth Amendment "was presented to the people as leaving control of suffrage in state hands, as representing no change in previous constitutional conditions so far as protection of rights was concerned [beyond banning discrimination], as stripped of radical character."[94]

Let Justice Black himself, the unremitting champion of

91. We need to recall Chief Justice Stone's statement that the Tenth Amendment "states but a truism that all is retained which has not been surrendered." Its purpose was "to allay fears that the new national government might seek to exercise powers not granted, and that the states might not be able to exercise fully their reserved powers." United States v. Darby, 312 U.S. 100, 124 (1941).

92. Paludan, supra note 9 at 15, 13, 51, 54.

93. To bind a principal, ratification must be "with a full knowledge of all the material facts. If the material facts be either suppressed or unknown, the ratification is treated as invalid." Owings v. Hull, 34 U.S. (9 Pet.) 606, 628 (1835), per Justice Story. See also Bennecke v. Insurance Co., 105 U.S. 355, 360 (1881). There must be "an intention . . . to ratify." Flournoy v. Hewgley, 234 F.2d 213, 216 (10th Cir. 1956). To find ratification by implication, "the implication to ratify must be clear." United States v. Pan-American Petroleum Co., 55 F.2d 753, 771 (9th Cir. 1932); "implied ratification is not to be presumed." Id. 772.

94. Paludan, supra note 9 at 52.

"incorporation," sum up, substituting for his word "corporations" the words "judicial processes":

> The states did not adopt the Amendment with knowledge of its
> sweeping meaning under its present construction. No section of
> the Amendment gave notice to the people that, if adopted, it
> would subject every state law . . . affecting [judicial processes]
> . . . to censorship of the United States courts. No word in all
> this Amendment gave any hint that its adoption would deprive
> the states of their long recognized power to regulate [judicial
> processes].[95]

95. Connecticut General Ins. Co. v. Johnson, 303 U.S. 77, 89 (1938), dissenting opinion. It is a profound irony that Black should go on to broaden the
Fourteenth Amendment and curtail States' Rights beyond the wildest conceptions of the framers and ratifiers. Or should we rather regard "interpretation"
like a meandering river that conforms to a Justice's wandering predilections?
    My study of the debates and the history of the period leads me fully to
concur with Fairman: "The freedom that states traditionally have exercised to
develop their own systems of administering justice, repels any thought that
the federal provisions on grand jury, criminal jury, civil jury were fastened
upon them in 1868. Congress would not have attempted such a thing, the
country would not have stood for it, the legislatures would not have ratified."
Fairman, Stanford 137. As Justice Jackson said in a comparable situation, "We
are justified in assuming that the men who sponsored the Fourteenth Amendment in Congress, knew of such provisions then in many of their State Constitutions. Certainly they were not consciously cancelling them or calling
them into question, or we should have some evidence of it." Beauharnais v.
Illinois, 343 U.S. at 292–293, dissenting opinion.

9

Opposition Statements Examined

THE case for a broad reading of the Fourteenth Amendment has been rested in large part on statements by those who opposed both the Civil Rights Bill and the Amendment. That is a sharp departure from traditional canons of interpretation voiced by Thomas Jefferson; he looked for the "meaning" of the Constitution to the "explanations of those who advocated, not those who opposed it."[1] Like Jefferson, courts look to statements by the advocates of a measure and give short shrift to its opponents.[2] There are sound reasons for that view.

It beclouds analysis merely to identify Senators Willard Saulsbury, Garrett Davis, Thomas A. Hendricks, and Peter G. Van Winkle as "Conservatives,"[3] without adding that they were Democrats adamantly opposed to the Reconstruction

1. 4 Elliot 446.
2. Statements by "opponents" of a bill "cannot be relied upon as indicative of legislative intent." National Labor Relations Board v. Thompson Products, 141 F.2d 794, 798 (9th Cir. 1944). "If resort to legislative history is had, the statements of those who supported the legislation and secured its passage will be accepted in determining its meaning." Union Starch & Refining Co. v. National Labor Relations Board, 186 F.2d 1008, 1012 (7th Cir. 1951). See also Duplex Co. v. Deering, 254 U.S. 443, 474–475 (1921), and infra at notes 13 and 14.
3. Kelly, Fourteenth 1063, 1070.

measures, who wanted to keep the Negroes in subjection, and of whom Davis and Saulsbury were in the front rank of the assault. Among the opponents was Lovell H. Rousseau of Kentucky, an unabashed racist, who charged that the Freedmen's Bureau Bill "gave negroes the same privileges in railway cars and theaters, and there would be mixed schools."[4] Harry Flack comments that "no one questioned [Rousseau's] statements in regard to these things," and concludes: "Many believed that the negro would be entitled to sit on juries, to attend the same schools . . . It does not appear that *all* of these contentions were specifically contradicted. It would seem reasonable to suppose that . . . these rights could not be legally denied to them."[5] To begin with, there were, for example, a number of specific denials by proponents of the bill that it provided for Negro service on a jury;[6] it was hardly necessary to pop up like a jack-in-the-box with a retort to each such remark, particularly when the sponsors repeatedly underscored the limited objectives of the Bill. Why should any weight be given to the insistence by Andrew J. Rogers, Democrat of New Jersey, that the Bill would nullify school segregation, coming on the heels of Chairman Wilson's categorical denial, later reiterated, of any such effect?[7]

The length to which the approach of Flack has been carried

4. Cited in Flack at 16. A similar statement was made by John L. Dawson of Pennsylvania, *Globe* 541.

5. Flack 16–17, 40 (emphasis added).

6. Infra at notes 25–27.

7. Supra Chapter 7 at note 10. Rogers continued to insist that suffrage was a "civil right" within the meaning of the Civil Rights Bill, *Globe* 1122, although it had been carefully explained by Wilson and Trumbull that it was excluded. Thayer, who followed Rogers, stated, "nobody can successfully contend that a bill guarantying simply civil rights and immunities is a bill under which you could extend the right of suffrage, which is a political and not a civil right." Id. 1151. Rogers illustrates why opposition statements are unreliable. Speaking to §1 of the Amendment, he said, "This section . . . is . . . an attempt to embody in the Constitution . . . that outrageous and miserable civil rights bill," and that the "privileges or immunities" clause embraced the right to vote . . . to marry . . . to be a juror," *Globe* 2538, all of which had been

is illustrated by Alfred Kelly. After noting the various references to constitutionalization of the Civil Rights Act by the Fourteenth Amendment, he states: "All this might well imply that the first section of the proposed amendment was intended to be merely declaratory of the Civil Rights Act, and would not go beyond its rather restrictive guarantees. But a second theme was present in the House debates—the argument that the phraseology of the first section was expansive and 'revolutionary' in character, so that its precise meaning was susceptible to indefinitely broad interpretation." And who are the Congressmen avouched for this "revolutionary" reading? A group of Democratic worthies, Benjamin M. Boyer and Samuel J. Randall of Pennsylvania, and Rogers, the " 'bete noire' of the Radicals," says Kelly himself[8]—a man so far out that he was actually embarrassing to his more practiced Democratic colleagues.[9] It is astonishing to derive "revolutionary" principles

specifically denied by proponents of the bill and, with respect to suffrage, of the Amendment.

Senator Trumbull explained at one point that he did not reply to opposition assertions "because I thought we should soonest get action on the bill by voting silently upon them." Id. 399.

8. Kelly, Fourteenth 1078–1079. For similar reliance on an array of Democrats, see tenBroek 218–219. In Bell v. Maryland, 378 U.S. 226, 295 (1964), Justice Goldberg stated in a concurring opinion, "opponents . . . frequently complained, without refutation or contradiction, that these measures [Freedmen's Bureau Bill and Civil Rights Bill] would grant negroes the right of equal treatment in places of public accommodation," citing Senator Garrett Davis (Globe 936). On the same page, however, Senator Trumbull stated, "The original act [FBB] and this amendatory bill together were simply designed to protect refugees and freedmen from persecution." Shortly thereafter Chairman Wilson reiterated in the House that the Civil Rights Bill had limited aims, which did not, for example, extend "to setting aside the school laws and jury laws." Globe 1294.

9. Samuel S. Marshall, a fellow Democrat, said, "in many of the extreme views expressed by . . . [Rogers] . . . he does not . . . represent the Democratic portion of this House." Globe 1172. To which Rogers added, "I know that my views are somewhat in advance of those of some members on this side of the House." Id. See also Marshall, id. 1157; William E. Niblack of Indiana, id. 1158.

from the argumentative statements of the very foes who fought even moderate proposals tooth and nail.

Now the Democrats well knew that a broad segment of the Northern electorate was opposed to Negro equality, so their statements, as Charles Fairman noted, were calculated to render the bill "odious."[10] They sought to discredit it, not to make it the instrument of a "revolution" in Negro rights. For the Democrats, color prejudice, Eric McKitrick remarks, "was their greatest asset. All they needed to do was to keep it alive and exploit it in every way."[11] Fairman's admonition against "drawing inferences from a failure to deny such statements in such unreasonable partisan harangues"[12] reflects established interpretive practice most recently restated by the Supreme Court: "[remarks] made in the course of legislative debate or hearings other than by persons responsible for the preparation or the drafting of a bill are entitled to little weight . . . This is especially so with regard to the statements of legislative opponents who '[i]n their zeal to defeat a bill . . . understandably tend to overstate its reach.'"[13] Or, as it stated on another occasion: "An unsuccessful minority cannot put words into the mouths of the majority."[14]

Several broad constructions cannot, however, quickly be dismissed as calculated partisanship. Senator Edgar Cowan, a conservative Republican of Pennsylvania, read the bill to mean "that there shall be no discrimination made . . . none in any way," so that Pennsylvania officials could be punished for enforcing its school segregation laws.[15] The bill, however, was restricted to "civil rights," whose narrow scope was repeatedly emphasized. Then, too, the "no discrimination in civil rights"

10. Fairman, Stanford 138.

11. Eric McKitrick, *Andrew Johnson and Reconstruction* 58 (1960).

12. Fairman, *History* 1236.

13. Ernst & Ernst v. Hochfelder, 425 U.S. 185, 204 note 24 (1976). See also Justice Frankfurter, quoted in Kluger 668.

14. Mastro Plastics Corp. v. Labor Board, 350 U.S. 270, 288 (1956).

15. *Globe* 500.

phrase was later deleted, in order, Chairman Wilson explained, to obviate a "latitudinarian" construction.[16] Another statement, that of Senator Reverdy Johnson, a Democrat of Maryland and respected veteran lawyer, merits notice. He urged that because a Negro would now be authorized to enter into a contract, he could enter into a "contract of marriage" with a white woman and thereby the State miscegenation laws would be invalidated.[17] Tocqueville recorded that "in the North of the Union, marriages may be legally contracted between negroes and whites; but public opinion would stigmatize a man who should connect himself with a negress as infamous."[18] That attitude persisted; Stevens' Negro mistress horrified the abolitionists.[19] Few of the most ardent abolitionists would have dared argue for intermarriage at this time, because it would have wrecked their hope of securing the indispensable "fundamental rights" to blacks.[20] To attribute to the framers an intention by the word

16. *Globe* 1366; see Wilson, supra note 8.

17. *Globe* 505–506.

18. 1 Tocqueville, *Democracy in America* 364 (1900).

19. Fawn M. Brodie, *Thaddeus Stevens: Scourge of the South* 20 (1959).

20. Recall Stevens' perturbation upon learning that Theodore Tilton had walked arm-in-arm with ex-slave Frederick Douglass. Supra Chapter 1 at note 53; see also infra Chapter 10 at note 6. Rhode Island enacted a miscegenation statute in 1844. *Globe* 201. Lincoln stated in an address at Columbus, Ohio, September 1859, "I am not . . . in favor of bringing about in any way social and political equality of the white and black races . . . I am not . . . in favor of making voters or jurors of negroes, nor of qualifying them . . . to intermarry with white people." Id. 3214–3215. He faced up to the realities as President, supra Chapter 1 at note 36. Farnsworth of Illinois, replying to fears of intermarriage expressed by Rogers, said he would "very cheerfully join him in voting the restraining influence of a penal statute." *Globe* 204. Julian of Indiana expressed himself to the same effect. Id. 258. In 1867—while the Fourteenth Amendment was in the course of ratification—the Pennsylvania Supreme Court stated, "The natural law which forbids their intermarriage and that social amalgamation which leads to a corruption of races, is as clearly divine as that which imparted to them different natures." West Chester & Philadelphia Railroad Co. v. Miles, 55 Pa. at 209, 213. See also Morton Keller, *Affairs of State* 150 (1977).

"contract" to authorize intermarriage runs counter to all intendments. In the House, Samuel W. Moulton of Illinois flatly denied "that it is a civil right for a white man to marry a black woman or for a black man to marry a white woman."[21] Although a contract of marriage, strictly speaking, is a contract, marriage is not in ordinary usage conceived in terms of contract. Given the stated purposes of the bill, the association of contracts with other property rights, authority to contract could be read as a license for intermarriage only by a strained construction. Senator Johnson himself stated to Fessenden, "you do not mean to do that. I am sure that the Senator is not prepared to go to that extent."[22] Nevertheless, to forestall the possibility that a court might thus broadly construe the bill, he urged specific exclusion of intermarriage. It would be straining at a gnat to deduce from the omission to make such an exclusion that the bill contemplated the abolition of miscegenation laws. No court which, like Senator Johnson, would perceive that Congress did "not mean to do that," should so read the Act; for from the bloodletting case in Bologna in the Middle Ages, courts have striven to ascertain and effectuate the intention of the lawmaker.[23] Although President Johnson vetoed the Civil Rights Bill, he referred to "the enumeration of the rights

21. *Globe* 632.

22. Id. 506.

23. The question that underlies all "rules for the interpretation of statutes [or Constitutions] . . . is, what was the intention of the legislative body? Without going back to the famous case of the drawing of blood in the streets of Bologna, the books are full of authorities to the effect that the intention of the lawmaking power will prevail even against the letter of the statute . . . The intention of the lawmaker is the law." Hawaii v. Mankichi, 190 U.S. 197, 212 (1903). Blackstone refers to "the Bolognian law . . . 'that whoever drew blood in the streets should be punished with the utmost severity,' " which was held "not to extend to the surgeon, who opened the vein of a person that fell down in the street with a fit." 1 William Blackstone, *Commentaries on the Laws of England* 60.

to be enjoyed" and noted that it did not repeal "State laws on the subject of marriage between the two races."[24]

A similar objection, that of Columbus Delano, an Ohio Republican, was that the "equal benefit of all laws and proceedings for the security of person and property" would extend to the "right of being jurors." Mark that an Ohio Republican said to Chairman Wilson, "I presume that the gentleman himself will shrink from the idea of conferring upon this race now, at this particular moment, the right of being jurors." Wilson countered, "I do not believe it confers that right,"[25] and he reiterated that the limited objectives of the bill did not extend to "setting aside the school and jury laws."[26] Moulton also denied "that it is a civil right for any one to sit on a jury"; and Ohio Republican William Lawrence stated that the bill "does not affect any political rights, as that of suffrage, the right to sit on juries . . . That it leaves to the States to be determined each for itself."[27]

The positive explanations that the bill had restricted objectives are fortified by the fact that sweeping proposals to abolish *all* discriminatory classifications[28] repeatedly fell by the wayside, confirming that Congress with open eyes rejected a comprehensive ban against all discriminations. For example, early in the session, on January 12, 1866, Stevens submitted to the Joint Committee on Reconstruction that "*All* laws, state or federal, shall operate impartially and equally on all persons without regard to race or color."[29] On February 19, 1866, Senator Richard Yates of Illinois proposed that "No State shall . . . *in any*

24. *Globe* 1679–1680. The veto was overridden in both Houses. Id. 1809, 1861.

25. *Globe App.* 156–157.

26. *Globe* 1294.

27. Id. 632, 1832. Madison stated, "Trial by jury cannot be considered as a natural right, but a right resulting from a social compact." 1 *Annals of Congress* 437.

28. TenBroek at 205 collected some proposals.

29. Kendrick 46 (emphasis added).

manner recognize *any distinction* between citizens of the United
States or any State . . . on account of race," and renewed the
proposal on March 9, 1866, at which time it was decisively
voted down, 38 to 7.[30] Senator Sumner proposed that in the
rebel States "there shall be no denial of rights, civil or political,
on account of race." This, too, was rejected, 39 to 8;[31] a similar
proposal was made by Senator Henderson, and there were
others.[32] One and all came to naught.[33] At Bingham's insistence, it will be recalled, the phrase "There shall be no discrimination in civil rights" was deleted from the Civil Rights Bill,
leaving the express enumeration of protected privileges and immunities.[34] The plain fact, as Senator Fessenden, the respected
chairman of the Joint Committee said, was that "we cannot put
into the Constitution, owing to existing prejudices and existing
institutions, an entire exclusion of all class distinctions."[35]

In the teeth of this history, to import into the Civil Rights
Act views of abolitionists and opponents[36] that so plainly had

30. *Globe App.* 98; *Globe* 1287 (emphasis added).

31. *Globe* 1287 (emphasis added). Alfred Kelly said of these measures introduced by "the more enthusiastic Radicals" that the "significant" fact is they all
"resorted to sweeping and all-inclusive prohibitory language and not mere
enumeration alone." Kelly, Fourteenth 1060. Their "significance" resides,
rather, in the fact, to use his own words, that "all died early deaths," demonstrating that they were unacceptable to the dominant Republicans.

32. *Globe* 702; supra note 28.

33. As Frederick A. Pike of Maine said of Thomas Eliot's proposal that
"the elective franchise shall not be denied or abridged in any State on account
of race," "no amendment of that character can pass . . . It is useless to submit
such a one to the States when it is sure of rejection." *Globe* 406, 407.

34. Supra Chapter 7 at notes 13–17; supra at note 16.

35. *Globe* 705. A similar statement was made by Stevens, id. 537; see also
supra note 32.

36. Kelly tells us that the "mood of the Radicals . . . was 'revolutionary,'" they projected "changes in the southern social order going far
beyond the mere destruction of slavery"; "both the Civil Rights Act of 1866
and the Fourteenth Amendment were products of" this "general 'revolutionary' mood." Kelly, Fourteenth 1060–1061. It would also have required "something of a revolution" in the Northern "social order," for which

been rejected, is to thwart, not to effectuate, the intention of its framers. Bickel fairly summarizes the evidence: "The Senate Moderates, led by Trumbull and Fessenden, who sponsored this [civil rights] formula, assigned a limited and well-defined meaning to it," namely, "the right to contract" and so on, "also a right to equal protection in the literal sense of benefiting equally from the laws *for the security of person and property.*"[37] Even so, James G. Blaine recorded, "it required potent persuasion, reinforced by the severest party discipline, to prevent a serious break in both Houses against the bill"[38]—and this in spite of repeated assurances as to its limited scope. Subsequently, four defectors in the Senate could have defeated the Amendment.[39]

---

the Republicans were totally unprepared. As we have seen, the "revolutionary" proposals were beaten back time after time. Supra at notes 29–35.

37. Bickel 56 (emphasis added).

38. 2 Blaine, *Twenty Years of Congress* 171, quoted in Flack 19 note 22.

39. James 150.

10

"Equal Protection of the Laws"

IT has long been the habit of the Supreme Court to say that the Fourteenth Amendment "speaks in general terms, and those are as comprehensive as possible."[1] Its opinions are replete with references to the "majestic generalities" of the Fourteenth Amendment,[2] to the "vague contours" of the due process clause,[3] and the like. Even Judge Learned Hand, though later dubious whether the Amendment authorized the desegregation decision, had said, "history is only a feeble light, for the rubrics were meant to answer future problems unimagined and unimaginable."[4] And, though Negro suffrage was unmistakably excluded from the Amendment, no less a figure than Justice Holmes held that the equal protection clause self-evidently requires admission of Negroes to a Texas primary: "it seems hard to imagine a more direct and obvious infringement of the Fourteenth. That amendment . . . was passed . . . with a special

1. Strauder v. Virginia, 100 U.S. 303, 310 (1879).
2. Katzenbach v. Morgan, 384 U.S. 641, 649 (1966).
3. Infra Chapter 11 at notes 2–3; Chapter 14 at notes 40–43.
4. *The Spirit of Liberty* 172–173 (Dillard ed. 1969). Yet he could say of the Court's resumption of the "role of a third legislative chamber" in the context of the "desegregation" case, "I have never been able to understand on what basis it does or can rest except as a *coup de main.*" Hand, *The Bill of Rights* 55 (1962).

intent to protect blacks from discrimination against them."[5] Yet, as we have seen, the framers meant to outlaw discrimination only with respect to enumerated privileges. Even the abolitionists shrank from complete equality. Derrick Bell points out that "few abolitionists were interested in offering blacks the equality they touted so highly. Indeed, the anguish most abolitionists experienced as to whether slaves should be granted social equality as well as political freedom is well documented."[6]

It is the object of this and the succeeding chapter to show that the framers chose words which aptly expressed, and throughout were wedded to, their limited purposes; that there is virtually no evidence that the framers meant by resort to those words to open goals beyond those specified in the Civil Rights Act and constitutionalized in the Amendment.[7] If the terms of the Amendment are "vague," it is because the Court

5. Nixon v. Herndon, 273 U.S. 536, 541 (1927). Justice Matthews had earlier cited "the political franchise of voting" as a "self-evident" illustration of "fundamental rights" "because preservative of all rights," Yick Wo v. Hopkins, 118 U.S. 356, 370 (1886), a position that had been pressed by Sumner and others but had been rejected. Supra Chapter 4 at notes 12–14 et seq.

In the same opinion wherein Justice Frankfurter finds it impossible to swallow reapportionment, he states that "the controlling command of Supreme Law is plain and unequivocal" on the issue of Negro disfranchisement: "An end of discrimination against the Negro was the compelling motive of the Civil War Amendments. The Fifteenth expresses this in terms, and it is no less true of the Equal Protection Clause of the Fourteenth." Baker v. Carr, 369 U.S. 186, 285–286 (1962) citing Nixon v. Herndon, dissenting opinion. The invocation to Holmes cannot overcome the fact that the Fourteenth Amendment designedly withheld suffrage.

Holmes himself construed a statute "not to include a case that indisputably was within its literal meaning, but was believed not to be within the aim of Congress." American Security Co. v. District of Columbia, 224 U.S. 491, 495 (1912). There he *inferred* that "Congress meant no such result"; here we have proof positive that the framers meant to exclude suffrage.

6. Derrick A. Bell, Jr., "Book Review," 76 Colum. L. Rev. 350, 358 (1976). See Chapter 1 at notes 38, 39, 53.

7. See supra Chapter 5.

made them so[8] in order to shield the expanding free enterprise
system from regulation.

Analysis will be facilitated by a breakdown into subsidiary
questions: What privileges were to be protected? Was the protection to be absolute, that is, to guarantee certain rights to all,
or comparative, only to secure freedom from discrimination if
those rights were granted? Do the words confer upon Congress
a general power to legislate for the States or merely a power to
correct State violations? The materials that bear upon these
questions are so intermingled that it is not easy to disentangle
them for separate discussion. Some repetition is therefore
unavoidable, but an effort to isolate the several issues is well
worth the cost.

"Equal protection," it has been said, "had virtually no antecedent history."[9] Sumner believed that he may have been "the
first to introduce the words 'equality before the law' into American jurisprudence."[10] In truth, the concept that laws should
be general, nondiscriminatory in their application, is of long
standing. As Locke put it, rulers "are to govern by promulgated
established laws, not to be varied in particular cases, but to have
one rule for rich and poor."[11] A note to Blackstone stated generality in more limited terms: "*restraints* introduced by the law
should be equal to all."[12] Nor was selection of those entitled to
equal protection ruled out, as the very exclusion of black slaves
from the society attested. The Massachusetts Constitution of
1780 provided that *Christians* "demeaning themselves peaceably
shall be equally under the protection of law"; and, like the Civil
Rights Act of 1866, that Constitution confined protection to
"the enjoyment of his life, liberty and property according to

8. See infra Chapter 14 at notes 40–43.

9. Kelly, Fourteenth 1052.

10. Donald, *Sumner II* 149.

11. Quoted in R. J. Harris, *The Quest For Equality* 10 (1960).

12. 1 William Blackstone, *Commentaries on the Laws of England* 127n. The
Blackstone note was called to the attention of the 39th Congress by Senator
Trumbull. *Globe* 474.

standing laws."[13] As slaves, blacks were chattels, nonpersons singled out for grossly discriminatory treatment and oppression at every step. It would be little exaggerated to say that they were all but unprotected. Declared free by the Thirteenth Amendment, they continued to be treated like slaves,[14] so it was essential to insure that the laws which protected whites would also protect blacks from oppression. In the words of Senator James W. Nye of Nevada, the Negroes "have equal rights to protection—equalized protection under equalized laws."[15] This "equalized protection," it can not be overemphasized, was limited to the rights enumerated in the Civil Rights Act of 1866, as will now appear.

What Was Equal Protection to Protect?

The Civil Rights Act, it will be recalled, secured to blacks the *same* right to contract, to hold property, and to sue, as whites enjoyed, and the *"equal* benefit of all laws *for security of person and property."* "Political rights" were excluded.[16] In describing these aims the framers interchangeably referred to "equality," "equality before the law," and "equal protection" (but always in the circumscribed context of the rights enumerated in the Bill), so that it is reasonable to infer that the framers regarded these terms as synonymous. What is required, said Moulton of Illinois, is "that each State shall provide for equality before the law, equal protection to life, liberty, and property, equal right

13. Articles III and X; 1 Poore 957–958.

14. Supra Chapter 2 at notes 18–24; Conkling, *Globe* 356; Kenneth M. Stampp, *The Peculiar Institution* 124, 192–236 (1956).

15. *Globe* 1073, 1074.

16. Supra Chapter 2 at note 26 et seq. In 1797 Judge Samuel Chase had decided that the privileges and immunities clause of Article IV required a State to accord an out-of-State citizen the "same" protection for property and "personal rights" and the "same" exemptions from taxes and burdens it afforded to its own citizens. Campbell v. Morris, 3 H. & McH. 535, 554 (Md.).

to sue and be sued."[17] A leading Radical, Samuel Shellabarger of Ohio, said, of the Civil Rights Bill, "whatever rights *as to each of these enumerated* civil (not political) matters the State may confer upon one race . . . shall be held by all races in equality . . . It secures . . . *equality of protection in those enumerated civil rights* which the States may deem proper to confer upon any races."[18] So it was understood by Senator Hendricks, an Indiana Democrat: "To recognize the civil rights of the colored people as equal to the civil rights of the white people, I understand to be as far as Senators desire to go; in the language of the Senator from Massachusetts [Sumner] to place all men upon an equality before the law; and that is proposed in regard to their civil rights." He objected that "in the State of Indiana we do not recognize the civil equality of the races."[19] When Andrew Johnson combed the Bill for objections and vetoed it, he noted that §1 "contains an enumeration of the rights to be enjoyed" and that "perfect equality" was sought with respect to "these enumerated rights."[20] Thomas T. Davis, a New York Republican, expressed a widely shared feeling in stating, Negroes "must be made equal before the law, and be permitted to enjoy life, liberty, and the pursuit of happiness [property]," but he was against "the establishment of perfect equality between the colored and the white race of the South."[21] While James W. Patterson of New Hampshire was "opposed to any law discriminating against [blacks] in the security and protection of life, liberty, person and property," "beyond this," he stated, "I am not

17. *Globe* 1622.

18. Id. 1293 (emphasis added). Wilson called for a stop to "inhuman" discriminations and for "equality in the exemptions of the law." *Globe* 1118.

19. Id. 601–602.

20. Id. 1679–1680. Bickel concluded that the Moderate leadership—Trumbull and Fessenden—had in mind a "limited and well-defined meaning . . . a right to equal protection in the literal sense of benefitting equally from the laws for the security of person and property." Bickel 56.

21. Id. 1085.

prepared to go," explicitly rejecting "political and social equality."[22] Windom declared that the Civil Rights Bill conferred an "equal right, nothing more . . . to make and enforce contracts," and so on, but no "social privileges."[23] Thus, the concept of "equal protection" had its roots in the Civil Rights Bill and was conceived to be limited to the enumerated rights.

What reason is there to conclude that when the words "equal protection of the laws" were embodied in the Amendment they were freighted with a new cargo of meaning—unlimited equality across the board? The evidence points the other way. In an early version of the Amendment, provision was made for both "the same political rights and privileges and . . . equal protection in the enjoyment of life, liberty and property,[24] an indication that "equal protection" did not include "political rights and privileges," but was confined to "life, liberty, or property." Bingham proposed a substitute, H.R. No. 63, that would empower Congress "to secure . . . all privileges and immunities . . . (Art. IV, Sec. 2); and . . . equal protection in the rights of life, liberty and property (5th Amendment)."[25] "Political rights and privileges" had disappeared; in its place was "privileges and immunities." Neither "privileges and immunities," nor its antecedent, "civil rights" had included "political privileges."[26] Bingham explained that his proposal was aimed at "confiscation statutes . . . statutes of unjust imprisonment" of the "rebel states," the objects of the Civil Rights Bill. It would enable Congress to insure "that the protection given by the laws of the States shall be *equal in respect to* life, liberty and property to all persons."[27] Hale of New York asked him to point to the clause "which contains the doctrine he here announces."

22. Id. 2699.
23. Id. 1159. See also John Thomas, supra Chapter 7 at note 33.
24. Bickel 31.
25. Id. 33; Kendrick 61.
26. Supra Chapter 2 at notes 26–40.
27. *Globe* 1091, 1094 (emphasis added).

Bingham replied, "The words 'equal protection' contain it, and *nothing else.*"[28]

Among the statements indicating that §1 was considered to embody the objectives of the Civil Rights Act is that of Latham of West Virginia: "The 'civil rights bill,' which is now a law . . . covers exactly the same ground as this amendment."[29] Stevens explained that the Amendment

> allows Congress to correct the unjust legislation of the States *so far* that the law which operates upon one shall operate *equally* upon all. Whatever law punishes a white man for a crime shall punish the black man precisely in the same way . . . Whatever law protects the white man shall afford *equal protection* to the black man. Whatever means of redress is afforded to one shall be afforded to all. Whatever law allows the white man to testify in court shall allow the man of color to do the same. These are great advantages over their present [Black] codes . . . I need not enumerate these partial and oppressive laws . . . Your civil rights bill secures the same thing.[30]

As Bickel noted, the "evils to which the proposal was directed" hark "back to those which had been pointed to in support of the

28. Id. 1094 (emphasis added). This interchange with Hale about a provision described by Bingham as "equal *in respect to* life, liberty, and property" (emphasis added), is rendered by Kelly thus: "In other words, the amendment was to impose a very general requirement of equality on *all* state legislation of the most inclusive kind"! Kelly, Fourteenth 1074. "Life, liberty, and property," we have seen, had a limited connotation for the framers.

29. *Globe* 2883; see also supra Chapter 1 at notes 10–13; Chapter 8 at notes 68–70.

30. *Globe* 2459 (emphasis added). Van Alstyne comments on this passage, "Surely the right to vote is one essential protection that white men enjoyed and surely equal protection would require that black men enjoy it to the same extent." Van Alstyne 56. He substitutes twentieth-century logic for the intention of the framers, including Stevens, to exclude suffrage from both the Civil Rights Bill and the Fourteenth Amendment. See infra Appendix I at notes 21–33.

Civil Rights Bill."[31] In attributing to Stevens the view that the Amendment proposed "a congressional guarantee of equality with respect to *all* state legislation,"[32] Alfred Kelly misconceived Stevens' position. Very early in the session he had proposed that "*all* national and State laws shall be equally applicable to every citizen . . . that is the one I love . . . But it would not be wise to entangle the present proposition with that one. The one might drag down the other."[33] And when Stevens summed up his views on the Amendment, he said he had hoped that the people "would have so remodeled all our institutions as to have freed them from *every vestige of . . . inequality* of rights . . . that *no distinction* would be tolerated. . . . This bright dream has vanished . . . we shall be obliged to be content with patching up the worst portions of the ancient edifice."[34] Those patches went only to discriminatory punishments, deprivation of judicial redress and the like.

31. Bickel 47. Referring to an earlier Stevens interpellation in a Hale-Bingham colloquy, Kelly states that Stevens "made it clear" he proposed to go "far beyond the scope of the Civil Rights Bill." Kelly, Fourteenth 1073. That concerned a Bingham proposal that "Congress shall have power to make all laws . . . to secure equal protection in the rights of life, liberty, and property." Hale objected, and Stevens asked whether he meant Congress "could interfere in any case where the legislation of a State was equal, impartial to all? Or is it not simply to provide that, where any State makes a distinction in the same law between different classes of individuals Congress shall have power to correct such inequality." *Globe* 1063. The proposal really embodied the former alternative (see infra at notes 76–81 for discussion), and it had to be abandoned. For present purposes, the important thing is that equal protection was limited to "life, liberty, and property," and as the later Stevens statement, quoted supra at note 30, shows, he did not go beyond the rights enumerated in the Civil Rights Act.

32. Kelly, Fourteenth 1073. Apparently Kelly changed his views. In a 1965 article he stated that "so far as I know, there is no instance of any discussion on the floor of either House in terms of anything other than a proposal to guarantee against *certain* forms of *discriminatory* state action." Kelly, "Clio and the Court: An Illicit Love Affair," 1965 S. Ct. Rev. 119, 147 (emphasis added).

33. *Globe* 537.

34. Id. 3148 (emphasis added).

Senator Howard, a far less acute and careful lawyer than Stevens, delivered himself of a looser statement, but even he went on to qualify the general by his enumeration of particulars:

> The last two clauses of the first section of the amendment disable a State from depriving . . . any person . . . of life, liberty or property without due process of law, or from denying to him equal protection of the laws. This abolishes *all class* legislation in the States and does away with the injustice of subjecting one caste of person to a code not applicable to another. It prohibits the hanging of a black man for a crime for which the white man is not to be hanged. It protects the black man in his fundamental rights . . . with the same shield which it throws over the white man . . . . Ought not the time to be now passed when one measure of justice is to be meted out to a member of one caste while another and different measure is to be meted out to the member of another caste.[35]

By "fundamental rights" Howard was employing the familiar shorthand for the incidents of "life, liberty, or property," repeatedly so identified during the course of the Civil Rights Bill. That by "all legislation" he did not really mean "all" is demonstrated by his statement that §1 "does not . . . give . . . the right of voting"; it is not, he said, "one of the privileges or immunities."[36] One who confessed that suffrage was not granted can hardly have held out in the same breath that "all class legislation" would now be banned, including some for which even greater distaste had been exhibited—desegregation, miscegenation. Reflecting earlier comments on the Civil Rights Bill, Howard stated in the same context that the Amendment "establishes equality before the law," that it will prevent States from "trenching upon these rights and privileges," and will give blacks the "same rights and the same protection before the law"

35. Id. 2766 (emphasis added).
36. Id.

as it gives whites.[37] Patently both Stevens and Howard were addressing themselves to the oppressive discriminations perpetuated by the Black Codes.

Bingham himself contributed a telling bit of evidence against an interpretation of equal protection in unlimited terms. He it was who imported "equal protection" into the Amendment; speaking toward the close of the session in behalf of the admission of Tennessee despite its whites-only suffrage provision, he said: "One great issue has been finally . . . settled . . . [by the Amendment] the equality of all men before the law."[38] Manifestly an equality that excluded Negro suffrage was not unqualified as he recognized: "We are all for equal and exact justice . . . [but] justice for all is not to be secured in a day." When Joseph H. Defrees of Indiana, like Stevens, said that §1 of the Amendment "places all persons on an equality . . . *so far as* equal protection of the laws is concerned,"[39] he distinguished between full-scale equality and "equal protection of the laws." That distinction was underlined by Samuel Shellabarger who, speaking to the Civil Rights Bill, confined "equality of protection [to] the enumerated civil rights," if conferred upon whites. Similar remarks were made by Wilson and Moulton.[40] Limited equality was adopted because, as Senator Henderson of Missouri declared early in the session: "A bold declaration of man's equality cannot be carried."[41] His prediction was fulfilled

37. Id. To read Howard's "all legislation" literally is also to ignore the proposals to that effect that perished. Supra Chapter 9 at notes 28–35. These facts refute Kelly's statement that Howard "presented in no uncertain terms a powerful and convincing 'broad construction' of the force and scope of the first section," an "extremely latitudinarian interpretation of the due process clause, which he asserted would destroy all class legislation entirely." Kelly, Fourteenth 1081. Compare with note 32 supra.

38. *Globe* 3979.

39. *Globe App.* 227 (emphasis added).

40. Supra, Chapter 2 at note 26; supra at notes 17–18, 21–23.

41. *Globe App.* 119. See Senator Fessenden, supra Chapter 6, Epigraph. "One is driven by the evidence," Woodward states, to conclude that "popular convictions were not prepared to sustain" a "guarantee of equality." *The Burden of Southern History* 83 (1960); see also Chapter 1 at notes 38–39, 52–53.

by repeated rejection of proposals to require "all laws" to operate "impartially and equally," to abolish "any distinctions between citizens."[42]

But, it may be asked, does not the differentiation in §1 between "due process" protection of "life, liberty, and property" and "equal protection of the laws" indicate that "equal protection" was now divorced from the earlier limitation to "life, liberty, and property." Nothing in the debates indicates such a purpose.[42a] "Equal protection of the laws" expressed the central object of the framers: to prevent *statutory* discrimination with respect to the rights enumerated in the Civil Rights Act. That purpose had been loosely expressed in Bingham's earlier formulation: "equal protection in the rights of life, liberty, and property," which he mistakenly identified with the "5th Amendment." Possibly some more perceptive lawyer restored the words "life, liberty, and property" to their Fifth Amendment association with due process, thus insuring access to the courts. At the same time, the established association of due process with judicial procedure made it necessary to block what Stevens denominated "partial and oppressive laws," a purpose succinctly expressed by "equal protection of the laws" to which reference had been made during the debate on the Civil Rights Bill.

FREEDOM FROM DISCRIMINATION VS. ABSOLUTE RIGHTS

The framers sought only to secure to blacks the same specified rights as were enjoyed by whites; if whites did not have them there was no State duty to supply them to anyone, still less a congressional power to fill the gap. So much appears from Shellabarger's explanation that the Civil Rights Bill secures "equality of protection in these enumerated civil rights which

---

42. Supra Chapter 9 at notes 28–35.
42a. Evidence to the contrary is furnished by Farnsworth, infra Chapter 11 at note 98.

the *States may deem proper to confer* upon any race."[43] Before considering further evidence, let us examine tenBroek's argument to the contrary. His was the most sustained effort to give "equal protection" an "absolute" as distinguished from a nondiscriminatory content. The heart of his argument is:

> the basic notion of this phrase is protection; equality is the condition. The equal protection of the laws cannot be supplied unless the protection of the laws is supplied, and the protection of the laws, at least for men's natural rights, being the sole purpose for which governments are instituted, must be supplied. The clause is thus understood to mean: "Every State shall supply to all persons . . . the protection of the laws and the protection shall be equal to all."[44]

Even on the level of verbal analysis the argument is vulnerable. A "condition" is a "restriction or qualification"; it was therefore not "protection unlimited"—the full protection of which laws are capable—that was mandated, but only that such laws as were enacted should be impartial. If the laws supplied no protection, to whites or blacks, there was nothing to which the "equal" condition could attach. To state in this context that "'equal' protection of the laws and the 'full' protection of the laws are virtually synonyms"[45] departs from a decent respect for words—a half-glass given to all is "equal" though it is not "full."

TenBroek's argument is further flawed by the assumption that the "basic idea" of the equal protection clause is that "protection of the laws . . . *must* be supplied." That may be well enough as a jural postulate,[46] but emphatically it was not the premise of the framers. Translating a remark of Hale as "the citizens must rely upon the State for their protection," Bingham

43. Supra at note 18.
44. TenBroek 222.
45. Id. 193.
46. That is likewise Harris' view, supra note 11 at 22, 42.

said, "I admit that such is the rule as it now stands."[47] Later he explained that in his proposed amendment, "the care of the property, the liberty, and the life of the citizen . . . is in the States, and not in the Federal Government. I have sought to effect no change in that respect."[48] Because the rule was dear to the framers, Trumbull reassured the Senate that "if the State of Kentucky makes no discrimination in civil rights between its citizens, this bill has no operation whatever in the State of Kentucky."[49] Protection, if given, must be impartial, but the absence of all protection would afford no ground for federal intervention. It does not advance tenBroek's argument that, in the remarks of the radical extremists Higby-Kelley-Woodbridge, "the qualifying word 'equal' was almost entirely forgotten and

---

47. *Globe* 1093. Hale had stated that the "American people have not yet found their State governments are insufficient to protect the rights and liberties of the citizen." Id. 1064–1065. After concurring, Bingham quoted Federalist No. 45: "The power reserved to the Federal States will extend to all the objects, which, in the ordinary course of affairs, concern the lives, liberties and properties of the people." Id. 1093.

Shellabarger referred to the "rights which the States may deem proper to confer upon any races," supra at note 18. And Senator Fessenden stated, "The power exists now at the present time in all these States to make just such class or caste distinctions as they please. The Constitution does not limit them." Id. 704.

48. Id. 1292.

49. Id. 600. After the Johnson veto of the Civil Rights Bill, Trumbull reiterated that the Bill "in no manner interferes with the municipal regulations of any State which protects all alike in their rights of person or property." Id. 1761.

Contrast this with tenBroek's deduction from Trumbull's statement, "I take it that any statute which is not equal to all, and which deprives any citizen of civil rights *which are secured to other citizens,* is an unjust encroachment" (emphasis added). TenBroek asks, "'secured' how? By the only method by which rights can be secured, namely, by supplying protection . . . Hence, deprivation or denial of laws 'not equal to all' will occur just as much by failure to supply the protection . . . as by the Black Codes imposing special burdens on a selected class"! TenBroek 188.

'protection' treated as if it stood alone.''[50] Against this unrepresentative fringe there is first the fact that a subcommittee of the Joint Committee had proposed that "Congress shall have power to make all laws . . . to secure all persons . . . *full protection* in the enjoyment of life, liberty and property.''[51] Here was a proposal—there were others—that embodied precisely what tenBroek argues for, and its demise demonstrates that the framers had no stomach for "full" protection at the hands of Congress. Their objectives were narrower.

Again and again the framers stated that their purpose was to prevent one law for blacks, another for whites. It was a ban on such discrimination that was expressed in "equality before the law" and "equal protection"—not a mandate that the States must confer rights not theretofore enjoyed by any citizen. In the beginning the Civil Rights Bill had provided:

> There shall be no discrimination in civil rights or immunities . . . but the inhabitants shall have the same right . . . ["as is enjoyed by white citizens"] . . . to full and equal benefit of all laws for the security of person and property, and shall be subject to like punishment . . . and none other.[52]

The word "immunities" carried over into the Amendment, hence Wilson's explanation is germane: "It merely secures to citizens of the United States equality in the exemptions of the law. A colored citizen shall not, because he is colored, be subjected to obligations, duties, pains and penalties from which other citizens are exempted . . . One race shall not be favored

---

50. TenBroek 211. But Woodbridge understood the purpose was to strike at discrimination. Infra note 55. Higby is a poor witness for "absolute" protection, for his "extremely anti-Chinese" views led him to maintain that "the Chinese were 'a pagan race' of no virtue and incapable of citizenship," Harris, supra note 11 at 40, and therefore not entitled to equal protection.

51. January 27, 1866, TenBroek 205 (emphasis added).

52. *Globe* 474, 1366.

in this respect more than another . . . This is the spirit and
scope of the bill, and *it does not go one step beyond.*"[53] Although
the "no discrimination" clause had been deleted at Bingham's
insistence that the words "civil rights" were too broad and "oppressive," the provisions for the "same" rights and immunities
remained untouched. It was understood by the framers that discrimination remained the target as Shellabarger illustrates; the
Bill would require that whatever of these "enumerated rights
and obligations are imposed by State laws shall be for and upon
all citizens alike without distinction based upon race"; such
rights "shall be held by all races in equality."[54]

That persisted as the ground bass of the Amendment; Stevens
explained that it required that a State law "shall operate *equally*
upon all. Whatever law punishes a white man for a crime shall
punish the black man precisely in the same way and to the same
degree."[55] "Equal protection," said Senator Howard, "does
away with the injustice of subjecting one caste of persons to a
code not applicable to another"; the Amendment "establishes
equality before the law."[56] In short, the framers struck at discrimination against the blacks with respect to enumerated privileges and immunities that were accorded to whites; and they
chose a word perfectly suited to the purpose. Among the definitions of "equal" are "uniform in effect or operation; neither less
nor greater; having the same rights or privileges; impartial." A
State provision may be substandard when measured by more enlightened federal or State criteria; but if it is impartial, uni-

---

53. Id. 1117 (emphasis added). The word "immunity," said Bingham,
means "exemption from unequal burdens." Id. 1089.

54. Id. 1293; see supra at note 18.

55. *Globe* 2459, more fully quoted supra at note 30. Woodbridge read the
Bingham prototype amendment to give "to every citizen . . . that protec-
tion to his property which is extended to the other citizens of the State."
Id. 1088.

56. Id. 2766.

formly applied to all within the State, it satisfies the meaning of "equal."[57]

True it is that Bingham and Lawrence of Ohio maintained that the "fundamental," "natural" rights were "absolute," and could not be withheld.[58] But the Republican majority was content to correct discriminations with respect to those rights. Bingham, on whom tenBroek so often relies, is, we have seen, a confused, imprecise, and vacillating witness.[59] Even so, when pressed by Hale whether his proposal "confers upon Congress a *general power* of legislation" in regard to "protection of life, liberty and property," he replied that it was designed "to see to it that the protection *given* by the laws of the State shall be *equal* in respect to life, liberty and property to all persons."[60] Faced with opposition, Bingham once more retreated—Congress was only to correct discrimination.[61] Nevertheless, tenBroek adopts

---

57. In the 1871 debates on the Ku Klux Klan Act, James Garfield, destined before long to become President, "reviewed fully the legislative history of the first section," and stated that "It is not required the laws shall be perfect. They may be unwise, injudicious, even unjust; but they must be equal in their provisions . . . resting upon all with equal weight." *Cong. Globe,* 42d Cong., 1st Sess. App. 153, April 4, 1871.

58. *Globe* 1089–1090, 1832.

59. Supra Chapter 8 at notes 43–56.

60. *Globe* 1094 (emphasis added).

61. "By the Fourteenth Amendment's terms the legal processes (procedures) due equally as protection and remedy to each national citizen were the laws and procedures of a citizen's State. Instead of formulating positively national civil-rights minima, as some Republican Radicals preferred to do, the Amendment forbade unequal deprivation of the broad, uncodified mass of civil rights protections which a state professed to afford equally to the generality of its citizens." H. M. Hyman, *A More Perfect Union* 467–468 (1973).

In 1872 Justice Miller stated, "We doubt very much whether any action of a State not directed by way of discrimination against the negroes as a class . . . will ever be held to come within the purview of this [equal protection] provision." *Slaughter-House Cases,* 83 U.S. (16 Wall.) 36, 81. In 1884, Justice Field stated that the Fourteenth Amendment "only inhibits discriminating and partial enactments, favoring some to the impairment of the rights

Bingham's teetering statement that the States were under an absolute duty to protect those privileges. After remarking on Bingham's "immortal Bill of Rights," he loftily dismisses *Barron v. Baltimore,* wherein Chief Justice Marshall held that the Bill of Rights had no application to the States:

> The "immortal Bill of Rights" not binding on the States! How can one refute an axiom? . . . Chief Justices . . . cannot successfully refute an axiom more than any other mortals . . . [Marshall] could not by any pronouncement of his diminish the obligation of the states to protect men in their natural rights of life, liberty, and property.[62]

What tenBroek regards as axiomatic runs counter to statements in the First Congress that the Bill of Rights was to have no application to the States, and in spite of Madison's urging that freedom of speech and press stood in greater need of protection against the States than against the federal government, to the rejection of his proposal that they be made applicable to the States.[63] In 1789 men were more devoted to their States than to the nascent federal government; they feared the centralized, remote power of the newcomer,[64] hence the limitations imposed on the federal government by the Bill of Rights. There is no inkling that in the intervening 75 years the North had become dissatisfied with the protection they were given by the States. On the contrary, they reaffirmed their attachment to State sovereignty in the 39th Congress.[65] They believed that State governments would be more responsive to their needs, more controllable than the federal regime; and they sought to

---

of others," and does not transfer "to the federal government the protection of all private rights . . ." Butchers' Union Co. v. Crescent City Co., 111 U.S. 746, 759; concurring opinion.

62. TenBroek 214–215; Barron v. Baltimore, 32 U.S. (7 Pet.) 243 (1833).

63. Supra Chapter 8 note 4.

64. Raoul Berger, *Congress v. The Supreme Court* 260–263 (1969).

65. E.g., Hale, supra note 47; Chapter 4 at notes 51–52.

limit federal intrusions to the minimum necessary to protect the personal security of the blacks.

The present generation would read back into the Amendment views that the framers clearly perceived the North would not accept. Much closer to the intention of the framers,[66] the Supreme Court said in 1875, with respect to the First Amendment protection of the right to assemble against "encroachment by Congress": "For their protection in its enjoyment, therefore, the people must look to the States. The power for that purpose was originally placed there, and it has never been surrendered to the United States."[67]

CONGRESSIONAL POWER: CORRECTIVE OR GENERAL

Does the §1 provision "nor shall any State . . . deny to any person within its jurisdiction the equal protection of the laws" empower Congress to enact laws for direct enforcement thereof? Justice Bradley answered, "How can a prohibition, in the nature of things, be enforced until it is violated?"[68] To convert "No State shall deny" into "Congress shall make" does

66. As long ago as 1454, Chief Justice Prisot stated, "the judges who gave these decisions in ancient times were nearer to the making of the statute than we now are, and had more acquaintance with it." Windham v. Felbridge, Y.B. 33 Hen. 4, f.38, 41, pl. 17, quoted in C. K. Allen, *Law in the Making* 193 (6th ed. 1958). For early American statements to the same effect, see Stuart v. Laird, 5 U.S. (1 Cranch) 299, 309 (1803); Ogden v. Saunders, 25 U.S. (12 Wheat.) 213, 290 (1827). Such cases antedate modern access to legislative history, and I would not suggest that such judges can displace the clearly revealed intention of the framers as disclosed by that history, but would point out that their confirmation of that history lends it added weight.

67. United States v. Cruikshank, 92 U.S. 542, 552 (1875). That plainly appears in the history of the Bill of Rights, supra Chapter 8 note 4. Chief Justice Parker declared in Abbott v. Bayley, 6 Pick. 89, 93 (Mass. 1827) that "protection of the persons of those who live under this jurisdiction" was left by the Constitution in the States. See also supra Chapter 8 at notes 86–87.

68. United States v. Cruikshank, 25 F. Cas. (No. 14, 897) 707, 714 (C.C.D. La. 1874).

violence to the text. The distinction between a prohibition of
action and a grant of power was well understood by the 39th
Congress. Even with respect to the prohibitions directed to
Congress by the Bill of Rights, Hale said that the several
amendments "do not contain, from beginning to end, a grant of
power anywhere. On the contrary, they are all restrictions of
power."[69] In addition, there is the fact that "the equality ordained" is, as Dean Phil Neal put it, "a Statewide equality, en-
compassing the persons 'within its jurisdiction' and not a nationwide or external equality."[70] For it is the "laws" of the
State, not of the nation, that are required to afford "equal protection."

Textual analysis is richly confirmed by the legislative history.
Shellabarger, an Ohio Radical, argued on behalf of the Civil
Rights Bill that "if this section did in fact assume to confer or
define or regulate these civil rights which are named . . . then
it would . . . be an assumption of the reserved rights of the
States . . . . Its whole effect is not to confer or regulate rights,
but to require that whatever of these enumerated rights and obligations are imposed by State laws shall . . . be without distinction based on race."[71] Shellabarger's assurance to fellow Republicans that State sovereignty was displaced only insofar as
corrective measures would require was echoed by his colleagues. Speaking to the final form of the Amendment,
Bingham stated: "That great want of the citizen and stranger,

69. *Globe* 1064. Michael C. Kerr of Indiana also rejected the argument that
the first ten amendments "are grants of power to Congress . . . Hitherto
these amendments have been supposed . . . to contain only limitations on
the powers of Congress." *Id.* 1270.

70. Phil C. Neal, "Baker v. Carr: Politics in Search of Law," 1962 S. Ct.
Rev. 252, 293. In Missouri v. Lewis, 101 U.S. 22, 31 (1879), the Court held,
"The Fourteenth Amendment does not profess to secure to all persons in the
United States the benefit of the same laws and the same remedies. Great diver-
sities in these respects may exist in two States separated only by an imaginary
line . . . Each State prescribes its own modes of judicial proceeding."

71. *Globe* 1293.

protection by national law from unconstitutional State enactments, is supplied by the first section of this Amendment. That is the extent it hath; no more."[72] Stevens said of the same draft that the Amendment "allows Congress to correct the unjust legislation of the States, so far that the law which operates upon one man shall operate *equally* upon all."[73] In the Senate, Howard said that "section one is a restriction upon the States, and does not, of itself, confer any power upon Congress";[74] and that §5 "enables Congress, in case the States shall enact laws in conflict with the principles of the amendment, to correct that legislation by a formal congressional amendment."[75]

Powerful confirmation of such expressions is furnished by the jettisoning of the Bingham amendment (H.R. No. 63), cast in terms of a grant to Congress:

72. Id. 2543; see also supra at note 48. Earlier Bingham stated, "The adoption of the proposed amendment will take from the States no rights that belong to the States . . . but in the event they . . . enact laws refusing equal protection to life, liberty or property" Congress can act. *Globe* 1090.

73. *Globe* 2459; see also Trumbull supra at note 49.

74. *Globe* 2766.

75. Id. 2768. Howard also stated, "The great object of the first section of this amendment is, therefore, to *restrain* the power of the States and to *compel them* to respect these great fundamental guarantees." Section 5, he continued, constitutes "a direct affirmative delegation of power to Congress to carry out all the principles of *these* guarantees," i.e., to enforce the "negative" terms of §1. Id. 2766 (emphasis added).

TenBroek would make Howard the exponent of as " 'direct' and 'affirmative' a delegation of power to Congress as could be made" rather than a mere "power to correct state legislation." He argues that if §§ 1 and 5, in Howard's words " 'establish equality before the law' and 'give to the humblest . . . the same protection before the law as . . . to the most powerful' . . . then certainly the power of Congress may be exercised *whenever* there is *not* equality before the law." TenBroek 230 (emphasis added). Here Howard was speaking of the substantive grant, the "discrimination" that would trigger congressional action, not of the time and corrective nature of that action, about which Howard spoke plainly enough, supra, and which statements tenBroek, 230, overlooked.

> The Congress shall have power to make all laws which shall be necessary and proper to secure to the citizens of each State all privileges and immunities . . . and to all persons . . . equal protection in the rights of life, liberty, and property.[76]

Judge Hale justifiably protested that this "is not a mere provision that when the States undertake to give protection which is unequal Congress may equalize it; it is a grant of power in general terms—a grant of the right to legislate for the protection of life, liberty, and property, simply qualified with the condition that it shall be equal legislation."[77] Hale's Republican colleague from New York, Giles W. Hotchkiss, added:

> I desire to secure every privilege and every right to every citizen in the United States that . . . [Bingham] desires to secure. As I understand it, his object . . . is to provide that no State shall discriminate between its citizens and give one class of citizens greater rights than it confers upon another. If this amendment secured that, I should vote for it very cheerfully today . . . I understand the amendment . . . to authorize Congress to establish uniform laws throughout the United States upon the subject named, the protection of life, liberty, and property. I am unwilling that Congress shall have any such power.[78]

76. *Globe* 813, 1034; Bickel 33.

77. *Globe* 1063–1064. When tenBroek, 216, stated that "Bingham and Hale thus completely agree that the equal protection clause was 'a grant of the right to legislate for the protection of life, liberty, and property simply qualified with the condition that it shall be equal legislation,'" he was quoting Hale's criticism of the "positive" grant to Congress of the Bingham amendment, which did not survive. See infra at note 81.

78. *Globe* 1095. Another New York Republican, Davis, who represented "a radical constituency," also opposed the Bingham proposal as an "infringement on the reserved rights of the States" that would "centralize power in the Federal Government," though he was pledged to measures "essential to the protection of their [blacks'] just right." Id. 1086, 1083, 1085. But he rejected the proposal as a "grant of original legislation by Congress." Id. 1087.

Stevens staged a rescue attempt in the form of a rhetorical question addressed to Hale: "is it not simply to provide that where any State makes a distinction in the same law between different classes of individuals, Congress shall have power to correct such discrimination and inequality?"[79] But this put too great a strain on the broader Bingham phraseology, and his approach was abandoned.

That Hale and Hotchkiss voiced the pervasive distrust of a general grant of power to Congress to legislate in the premises may also be gathered from the statement by James F. Wilson of Iowa, chairman of the House Judiciary Committee, that the Bingham proposal was "the embodiment of our greatest danger."[80] Let Henry J. Raymond, an influential New York Republican who voted for the Fourteenth Amendment, sum up: the Bingham amendment "giving to Congress power to secure an absolute equality of civil rights in every State of the Union . . . encountering considerable opposition . . . it was finally postponed"—and never resuscitated.[81] Bingham himself joined ranks when he urged the people, in support of the final draft, to protect "the privileges and immunities of all the citizens of the Republic . . . *whenever* the same shall be abridged or denied by the unconstitutional acts of any State."[82]

Flack comments on this shift from "Congress shall have power" to "no State shall make" that, though the former "was not incorporated into the fundamental law . . . it may properly be asked whether it really did not become a part of it with a

79. Id. 1063.

80. TenBroek 217, notes that when the "Congress shall have formula" was reported out by the Joint Committee, "it was recommitted by a vote of 110 to 37, after a debate in which not only Democrats but also conservative Republicans sharply criticized it as effecting a radical redistribution of powers of the states and the national government."

81. *Globe* 2502.

82. Id. 2542 (emphasis added).

mere change in dress but not in meaning."[83] Such flabby analysis that can translate "no" as "yes" has clogged understanding of the Fourteenth Amendment. TenBroek likewise transforms "no State shall make" into the "obligation of the states to 'make or enforce laws' protecting" men in their "natural rights." There "never would have been any historical question about the revolution in federalism worked or confirmed by the Fourteenth Amendment," he maintained, "were it not for the shift from the positive to what at first glance appears to be a negative form of the amendment."[84] That "first glance," as we have seen, is buttressed by the plainly expressed intention of the framers.

TenBroek attempts to torpedo what he considers the three "mainstays" of the "narrow" construction based on a change-over from grant to prohibition, and begins with Stevens' explanation of the final draft, in which he said that it "fell far short of [his] wishes."[85] This, tenBroek argues, referred solely to Negro suffrage, which was not treated in §1 but only in §2 and §3. The argument grasps at straws. Suffrage was a central concern; it had unmistakably been excluded from the Civil Rights Act, the antecedent of §1, so if Stevens was troubled by the failure to provide for suffrage in §2 inferably he considered it also was unprovided for in §1, thus undermining tenBroek's inference that §1 could "hardly [have been] a source of dissatisfaction to him." Such speculation is beside the point. Stevens had disclaimed a grant of original power to Congress, first, by seeking to save the Bingham amendment by reading it merely to confer "power to correct such discrimination,"[86] and later by

83. Flack 64. Yet he notes that "The Radical leaders were as aware as any one of the attachment of a great majority of the people to the doctrine of State Rights . . . the right of the States to regulate their own internal affairs." Id. 68.

84. TenBroek 223, 216.

85. Id. 217–218.

86. Supra at note 79. TenBroek, 212 note 8, rightly stated that Stevens' rhe-

stating that the final draft "allows Congress to correct the unjust legislation of the States."[87]

The second "mainstay" is that after the shift to the prohibition on States, Andrew J. Rogers, a Democrat and bitter opponent of the several Reconstruction measures, charged that §1 "consolidates everything into one imperial despotism" and "annihilates" States' Rights. TenBroek reinforces this by the testimony of two other Democrats, Aaron Harding and George S. Shanklin of Kentucky, and asks, "Since the amendment was adopted in the teeth of this criticism, might not we as reasonably conclude . . . that the amendment was intended to do the very thing objected to."[88] There is no need to recapitulate the weakness of reliance on opposition obstructiveness designed to inflame the electorate. It is a singular approach to legislative history, shared by other proponents of the tenBroek view, to exalt the opposition and all but ignore the statement of objectives by the Republican leadership who carried the day.

Comes now the third "mainstay":

> "No State shall . . ." at first looks like a negative on state action; and section 5, granting enforcement power would accordingly authorize Congress to impose only such restraints as would prevent States from taking the forbidden action. Section 5 would thus authorize nothing more than a corrective removal of prohibited state acts . . . Does not this interpretation render section 5 altogether nugatory? . . . [S]ince the judges would in any event strike down acts transcending the prohibitions of the amendment, a law by Congress would serve no purpose.[89]

---

torical question to this effect represented his own view: "The latter half of the sentence shows . . . that Stevens has a mind fixed primarily on the narrower interpretation of equal protection," i.e., the "corrective" role of Congress.

87. Supra at note 73.
88. TenBroek 218–219.
89. Id. 220–221.

TenBroek proves too much; on his reasoning a court equally could proceed without waiting for a general (as distinguished from a corrective) congressional law.[90] The "nugatory" test, therefore, does not clarify whether the congressional power is "corrective" or "general."

James A. Garfield's statement in the 1871 debates, made by a framer in the 39th Congress and faithful to the historical record, is entitled to greater respect than present-day speculation: "soon after the ratification of the Amendment," tenBroek states, Garfield explained that Congress had rejected "a clear grant of power to Congress to legislate directly for the protection of life, liberty, and property within the States" in favor of the present form that "limited but did not oust the jurisdiction of the state over the subjects."[91] Justice Bradley's opinion in the *Civil Rights Cases*, therefore, does not betray, but rather responds to, the intention of the framers. The Amendment, he declared,

> does not authorize Congress to create a code of municipal law for the regulation of private rights; but to provide modes of redress against operation of state laws . . . such [congressional] legislation must, necessarily be predicated upon such state laws or state proceedings, and be directed to the correction of their operation and effect . . . [U]ntil some state law has been

90. For discussion of the §5 enforcement power, see infra Chapter 12.

91. TenBroek 216–217. See Hyman, supra note 61. Benedict likewise concludes that the Fourteenth Amendment "in no way challenged the tradition that the states had primary jurisdiction over citizens in matters of police regulation . . . Instead, its first and fifth sections gave Congress power to assure that the police regulations would not discriminate against citizens on account of race . . . where the regulation involved some 'fundamental right' of United States citizens . . . it did not transfer to the national government the power to frame all laws touching on these rights. National jurisdiction could arise only through the states prior wrongdoing." M. L. Benedict, *A Compromise of Principle* 170 (1975).

passed . . . no [federal] legislation . . . can be called into activity.[92]

In sum, the words "equal protection of the laws" were meant to obviate discrimination by laws—that is, statutes—so that with respect to a limited group of privileges the laws would treat a black no differently than a white. If no privilege was accorded to a white, a State was not required to furnish it to anyone. Hence Justice Douglas, in invalidating a State poll tax, was wide of the mark when he based his conclusion, "not on what we think governmental policy should be, but on what the Equal Protection Clause requires." The truth is, as he stated in a preceding sentence, "we have never been confined to historic notions of equality . . . Notions of what constitutes equal treatment for purposes of the Equal Protection Clause *do* change."[93] In plain words, Douglas laid claim to power to revise the historic meaning in accord with his own preferences. For Chief Justice Marshall, on the other hand, the words of the Constitution were not to be "extended to objects not . . . contemplated by the framers"[94]—let alone unmistakably excluded. As Herbert Packer points out, "the new 'substantive equal protection' has under a

92. Civil Rights Cases, 109 U.S. 3, 11, 13 (1883); see also id. 19. Ten years earlier Justice Bradley had stated on circuit that "there can be no constitutional legislation of congress for directly enforcing the privileges and immunities . . . where the State has passed no laws adverse to them . . . " United States v. Cruikshank, 25 F. Cas. at 714.

93. Harper v. Virginia Board of Elections, 383 U.S. 663, 670, 669 (1966), but cf. Hamilton, infra Chapter 17 at note 15.

94. Ogden v. Saunders, 25 U.S. (12 Wheat.) 213, 332 (1827), dissenting opinion. In Church of the Holy Trinity v. United States, 143 U.S. 457, 472 (1891), the Court held that though a rector " is within the letter [he] is not within the intention of the legislature, and therefore cannot be within the statute." For a similar holding by Justice Holmes, see supra note 5; see also Robert Bork, infra, Chapter 11 at note 80; and see infra, Chapter 20.

different label permitted today's justices to impose their prejudices in much the same manner as the Four Horsemen [of the
pre-1937 Court] once did."[95]

95. "The Aim of the Criminal Law Revisited: A Plea for a New Look at
'Substantive Due Process,'" 44 S. Cal. L. Rev. 490, 491–492 (1971). Commenting on Brown v. Board of Education, Professor Lusky stated, "Plainly
the Court was using the term 'unequal' in a new sense. The 'inequality' prohibited by the Constitution was no longer thought limited to unequal distribution of governmental burdens and benefits, but was held to include
measures perpetuating the social isolation of minority groups," Lusky 214,
a subject excluded from the Fourteenth Amendment by its framers.

11

Due Process of Law

nor shall any State deprive any person of life,
liberty, or property, without due process of law

T O this day," Arthur Sutherland wrote in 1965, "no one knows precisely what the words 'due process of law' meant to the draftsmen of the fifth amendment, and no one knows what these words meant to the draftsmen of the fourteenth amendment."[1] True it is that after the 1880s the phrase was transformed by the Court into one of "convenient vagueness";[2] and such "vagueness" has become the reigning orthodoxy.[3] Whether one

---

1. "Privacy in Connecticut," 64 Mich. L. Rev. 283, 286 (1965).

2. Felix Frankfurter, *Mr. Justice Holmes and the Supreme Court* 7 (1938): "phrases like 'due process of law' are, as an able judge [Charles M. Hough] once expressed it, of 'convenient vagueness.' Their ambiguity is such that the Court is compelled to put meaning in the Constitution." Earlier Frankfurter asked, " 'Convenient' for whom or to what end?" Frankfurter, "The Red Terror of Judicial Reform" 40 *New Republic* 110, 113 (1924), reprinted in F. Frankfurter, *Law and Politics* 10, 14 (1938). But as Justice Frankfurter, he declared in 1949 that "Great concepts like . . . 'due process of law' . . . were purposely left to gather meaning from experience. For they relate to the whole domain of social and economic fact." National Ins. Co. v. Tidewater Co., 337 U.S. 582, 646 (1949), dissenting opinion. Compare with Chapter 14 infra at notes 40–43. For the halting, post-Civil War development of substantive due process see Walton H. Hamilton, "The Path of Due Process of Law" in *The Constitution Reconsidered* 167 (C. Read ed. 1938); see also Justice Black, infra note 47.

3. "Due process of law" is among the terms that "doubtless were designed to have the chameleon capacity to change their color with changing moods

can determine "precisely" what due process meant, however, is not nearly so important as the fact that one thing quite plainly *it did not mean,* in either 1789 or 1866; it did not comprehend judicial power to override legislation on substantive or policy grounds. There is first the unmistakable testimony of Alexander Hamilton. Speaking in the New York Assembly in 1787, almost on the eve of the Convention, he stated:

> The words "due process" have a precise technical import, and are only applicable to the process and proceedings of the courts of justice; *they can never be referred to an act of the legislature.*[4]

No statement to the contrary will be found in any of the constitutional conventions, in the First Congress, nor in the 1866 debates.

Hamilton summed up the English and colonial usage, and it is that usage that defines the content of the words "due process of law." It has long been a canon of construction that when the draftsmen employed common law terms, the common law "definitions," as Justice Story stated, "are necessarily included

---

and circumstances." Wallace Mendelson, *Justices Black and Frankfurter: Conflict in the Court* viii (1961). So too, Leonard Levy stated that due process and equal protection are "purposely protean or undefined words." *Against the Law* 27.

4. *The Papers of Alexander Hamilton* 35 (H. C. Syrett and J. E. Cooke eds. 1962) (emphasis added); quoted more fully infra note 11.

When Coke asserted in Dr. Bonham's Case that an Act of Parliament could not make a man judge in his own cause, he did not invoke Magna Charta but "common right and reason," Berger, *Congress v. The Supreme Court* 349, which he had identified with the "law of nature," id. 352, 355 note 31, an identification repeated by Justice Hobart, id. 364. By negative implication, the "law of the land" clause of Magna Charta did not, in Coke's eyes, confer authority to set a statute aside as unreasonable. True, Coke also stated in his *Institutes* that if any statute be made contrary to "Magna Charta it shall be holden for none," id. 358 note 43, but this, in my judgment, merely meant, for example, that a statute which authorized the "imprisonment" of a person without the judgment of his peers would be invalid; for he regarded Magna Charta as "fundamental law," id. 358 note 43.

as much as if they stood in the text" of the Constitution.[5] But when so great a master as Judge Learned Hand concludes that the prohibitions of the Fifth and Fourteenth Amendments are cast "in such sweeping terms that history does not elucidate their contents,"[6] I may be indulged for piling proof on proof to the contrary.

Our conceptions of due process are traceable to the twenty-ninth chapter of Magna Charta, which, roughly speaking, provided that no man should be deprived of his life, liberty, or property, except by the judgment of his peers or the law of the land.[7] Coke stated that "by the law of the land" was meant "by the due course and process of law."[8] Whether due process and "law of the land" were identical in English law[9] need not detain us; for present purposes it may suffice that both related to *judicial procedures* preliminary to the described forfeitures. Prior to 1789 the several State constitutions employed the "law of the land" terminology, usually in the context of other safeguards for those charged with crimes, suggesting that it was viewed in terms of

5. United States v. Smith, 18 U.S. (5 Wheat.) 153, 160 (1820). In his Report on the Virginia Resolutions to the Virginia House of Delegates (Sess. 1799–1800), Madison stated, "It is readily admitted that particular parts of the common law may have a sanction from the Constitution, so far as they are necessarily comprehended in the technical phrases which express the powers delegated to the government." 4 Elliot 563. Chief Justice Marshall gave early expression to this view in Ex parte Bollman, 8 U.S. (4 Cranch) 75, 93–94 (1807): "for the meaning of *habeas corpus* resort may unquestionably be had to the common law." So deeply anchored was this presupposition that when the Framers employed the word "treason," they took pains to define it narrowly in order to obviate some of its harsh common law consequences that otherwise might have attached. Article III, §3(1).

6. *The Bill of Rights* 30 (1962).

7. 4 William Blackstone, *Commentaries on the Laws of England* 424 (1765–1769).

8. 2 Edward Coke's *Institutes* 56, quoted in Hurtado v. California, 110 U.S. 516, 523 (1884).

9. Keith Jurow, "Untimely Thoughts: A Reconsideration of the Origins of Due Process of Law," 19 Am. J. Legal Hist. 265 (1975).

judicial procedure.[10] That the "law of the land" was understood
in Coke's sense is illustrated by Hamilton's 1787 statement.[11]
The members of the First Congress, who employed the words
"due process" in the Fifth Amendment instead of the "law of
the land" contained in the extant State constitutions, presumably intended no departure from prevalent State usage. Given
the great respect Coke enjoyed in the colonies, it is reasonable
to infer that, like Hamilton, they accepted Coke's identification
of the two phrases.[12]

10. Maryland (1776), 1 Poore 818; Massachusetts (1780), id. 958; New
Hampshire (1784), 2 Poore 1282; North Carolina (1776), id. 1410; Pennsylvania (1776), id. 1541–1542; South Carolina (1778), id. 1627; Vermont (1777),
id. 1860; Virginia (1776), id. 1909. See infra at notes 24 and 25.

11. Commenting in the New York Assembly on February 6, 1787, on the
New York Constitution, Hamilton said, "In one article of it, it is said no man
shall be disfranchised or deprived of any right he enjoys under the constitution, but by the *law of the land,* or the judgment of his peers. Some gentlemen
hold that the law of the land will include an act of the legislature. But Lord
Coke . . . in his comment upon a similar clause in Magna Charta, interprets
the law of the land to mean presentment and indictment . . . But if there
were any doubt upon the constitution, the bill of rights enacted in this very
session removes it. It is there declared that, no man shall be disfranchised or
deprived of any right, but by '*due process of law,*' or the judgment of his peers.
The words '*due process*' have a precise technical import, and are only applicable
to the process and proceedings of the courts of justice; they can never be referred to an act of legislature." The Act was that of January 26, 1787, II Laws
of the State of New York 344–345; supra note 4.

Julius Goebel and T. R. Naughton state with respect to seventeenth- and
eighteenth-century due process, "The usual and current employment of the
phrase in English practice was to designate the judicial order appropriate to a
particular procedure and this usage became the rule in eighteenth century
New York." *Law Enforcement in Colonial New York (1664–1776)* 385 (1970). In
his "Letters of Phocion" Hamilton stated, "due process of law" means "by indictment or presentment." 4 *Works of Alexander Hamilton* 230, 232 (Lodge ed.
1904).

12. A persuasive explanation of the shift from "law of the land" to "due
process of law" was advanced by Justice Curtis in Murray's Lessee v. Hoboken Land & Improvement Co., 59 U.S. (18 How.) 272, 276 (1856). He
pointed out that by the sixth and seventh Amendments "special provisions

It has been convincingly shown that due process was conceived in utterly procedural terms, specifically, that a defendant
must be afforded an opportunity to answer by service of process in proper form, that is, in due course. Starting with an
early statute, 28 Edw. III, ch. 3 (1354), which provided that "no
man . . . shall be put out of land or Tenement . . . nor put
to death, without being brought in to answer by due process of
law,"[13] Keith Jurow concluded from a comparison with chapter
10 of the same statute that the due process provision "seems
merely to require that the appropriate writ be used to summon
the accused before the court to answer the complaint against
him."[14] An earlier statute, 25 Edw. III (1352), had provided that
because the "law of the land" required that "none shall be
imprisoned, nor put out of his freehold" and so on, henceforth
"none shall be taken . . . unless it be by indictment or presentment . . . or by process made by writ original at the common
law [and] unless he be duly brought to answer." Jurow concludes that "the word 'process' itself meant writs . . . those
writs which summoned parties to appear in court."[15] His
reading harmonizes with that of Coke, who, referring to a later

---

were separately made for that [jury] mode of trial in civil and criminal cases.
To have followed, as in the state constitutions . . . the words of *Magna
Charta,* and declared that no person shall be deprived of his life, liberty, or
property but by the judgment of his peers or the law of the land, would in part
have been superfluous and inappropriate. To have taken the clause 'law of the
land' without its immediate context, might possibly have given rise to doubts,
which would be effectually dispelled by using those words which the great
commentator on *Magna Charta* had declared to be the true meaning of the
phrase, 'law of the land,' in that instrument, and which was undoubtedly then
received as their true meaning."

Jefferson recorded that there was never "one of profounder learning in the
orthodox doctrines of the British Constitution or what is called British rights"
than Coke. Quoted in E. S. Corwin, *The Doctrine of Judicial Review: Its Legal
and Historical Basis and Other Essays* 31 (1914).

13. Supra note 9 at 266.
14. Id. 267.
15. Id. 268, 272; 25 Edw. III st. 5, ch. 4 (1352).

statute, 37 Edw. III, ch. 3 cap. 8, explains "without due process of the law" thus: "that is by indictment . . . or by writ originall of the common law. Without being brought in to answer but by due process of the common law. No man may be put to answer without presentment . . . or by writ originall, according to the old law of the land."[16] A Massachusetts measure of 1692, duplicated in the colonies of Connecticut and New York, "ordained . . . no person should suffer . . . without being brought to answer by due course and process of law."[17] Blackstone later recurred to 28 Edw. III for the proposition that "no man shall be put to death without being brought to answer by due process of law."[18] Finally, among the Declarations and Resolves of the First Continental Congress, October 14, 1774, was "the respective colonies are entitled to the common law . . . and . . . to the . . . privilege of *being tried* by their peers . . . according to the due course of that law."[19] "Process," accordingly, was by indictment or writ; it was in "due course," that is, in regular course, if the "appropriate" writ was employed.[20] *"Due process" should therefore be regarded as*

16. Quoted in Hurtado v. California, 110 U.S. at 523. Jurow remarks, "The puzzling thing is that Coke cites 3 Edw. III, ch. 8 rather than 28 Edw. III, ch. 3 to support his interpretation, and when he does cite the latter statute he renders it as 'due process of the common law.'" We may assume with Jurow that "Coke was trying to show that only the common law was the law of the land." Jurow, supra note 9 at 277. For present purposes it suffices that due process, by Jurow's own demonstration, was altogether associated with judicial procedure. In English law, he states, "the term 'due process of law' and the word 'process' were always used in the most precise and consistent way," Jurow, id. 279, as Hamilton clearly perceived.

17. 2 James Kent, *Commentaries on American Law* 608–609 (9th ed. 1853).

18. 4 Blackstone, supra note 7 at 318.

19. H. S. Commager, *Documents of American History* 83 (7th ed. 1963; emphasis added).

20. This original meaning of due process as affording a person the opportunity to answer through service of a writ according to established law is incompatible with the "fundamentally fair" procedure structure that the Court has built on the clause. Grey, "Do We Have an Unwritten Constitution?," 27

shorthand for Coke's "by the due course and process of law" in judicial proceedings.[21] These materials demonstrate, parenthetically, that due process was *not* a catchall for all the other safeguards the Bill of Rights provided to a defendant; it had a special and limited function: to insure through service of proper, that is, "due," process that a defendant would be given a chance to answer.[22]

In the interval between 1789 and 1866, the procedural nature of due process received the imprimatur of Kent and Story, who relied on Coke.[23] Because lawyers habitually look to judicial decisions for "constitutional law" they have largely overlooked that in virtually all of the State constitutions extant in 1866 the words "due process of law" and "law of the land" were, as

---

Stan. L. Rev. 703, 711 (1975). As said by Leonard Levy, "fair trial is a principle of such abstraction, complexity and subjectivity that a judge can play on it as if it were an accordion to be squeezed and stretched to render whatever meaning he seeks to express." *Against the Law* 310.

The foregoing materials cast doubt on Justice Frankfurter's generalization: "Due process of law, as a historic and generative principle, precludes defining, and thereby confining, those standards of conduct more precisely than to say that convictions cannot be brought about by methods that offend 'a sense of justice.'" Rochin v. California, 342 U.S. 165, 173 (1952). His history has very shallow roots.

21. Supra at note 8.

22. I must therefore dissent from Levy's statement that "the history of due process shows that it did mean trial by jury and many of the other traditional rights . . . specified separately in the Bill of Rights," and that the Framers "added the due process clause itself, probably as a rhetorical flourish, a reinforced guarantee, and a genuflection towards traditional usage going back to the medieval reenactments of Magna Charta." Levy, *Judgments: Essays in American Constitutional History* 66 (1972). Justice Curtis considered that the Framers carefully avoided surplusage in this respect, supra note 12. And as we have seen, the early statutes identified due process with service of proper process to assure a defendant an opportunity to answer, a guarantee contained in no other provision of the Bill of Rights, and a practice duplicated in early Massachusetts, Connecticut, and New York measures.

23. 2 Kent, supra note 17 at 620–621: "by the law of the land [is] understood to mean due process of law, that is, by indictment . . . and this, says Lord Coke, is the true sense of these words." See also 1 Joseph Story, *Commentaries on the Constitution of the United States* §1789 (5th ed. 1905).

Charles E. Shattuck pointed out more than 85 years ago, almost always found "in a section of the Constitution dealing exclusively with the conduct of criminal trials, with the privileges of the accused, with a process in which the whole question is whether the person concerned shall be deprived of one or another of certain rights; that is of life, or *personal* liberty, or property as a penalty for a crime; and it is declared that he shall not,ˈ without due process of law."[24] The lawyers who framed the Fourteenth Amendment undoubtedly were familiar with this association of due process with judicial procedure,[25] and a departure from this all but universal connotation must be based on more than bare conjecture; the rule is that it must be proved.[26] What Charles P. Curtis, an ardent proponent of judicial "adaptation" of the Constitution, said of the Fifth Amendment could even more truly be said of the Fourteenth. When the Framers put due process "into the Fifth Amendment, its meaning was as fixed and definite as the common law could make a phrase. It had been chiseled into the law so incisively that any lawyer, and a few others, could read and understand. It meant a procedural process, which could be easily ascertained from almost any law book."[27]

24. "The True Meaning of the Term 'Liberty' in Those Clauses in the Federal and State Constitutions Which Protect 'Life, Liberty and Property,'" 4 Harv. L. Rev. 365, 369 (1891).

In 1866 most State constitutions still adhered to the "law of the land" phraseology. A few had adopted the language of due process or due course of law: Alabama (1865), 1 Poore 49; Connecticut (1818), id. 259; Mississippi (1832), 2 Poore 1068; Nevada (1864), id. 1248; New York (1846), id. 1351–1352; South Carolina (1865), id. 1643; Texas (1866), id. 1785. Constitutions fashioned in the Southern States under Northern military occupation in 1865 and 1866 may be taken to reflect Northern opinion.

25. Before 1866, the due process clause "had been looked upon almost universally as only a procedural guarantee." Benjamin R. Twiss, *Lawyers and the Constitution* 26 (1942); see infra note 48; infra at note 42.

26. Supra Chapter 1 note 57.

27. "Review and Majority Rule," in *Supreme Court and Supreme Law* 170, 177 (E. Cahn ed. 1954). As Justice Black stated, "there is no constitutional support whatever for this Court to use the Due Process Clause as though it pro-

THE 39TH CONGRESS

In light of the prominence to which the due process clause has been elevated by the Supreme Court, it is surprising how scanty were the allusions to the clause in the debates of the 39th Congress. It was altogether unmentioned in the Civil Rights Bill; instead the Bill spelled out the concrete rights "to sue, be parties and give evidence"; and it inclusively provided for the "equal benefit of all laws and *proceedings* for the security of person and property." But the debates show plainly enough that by "proceedings" the framers intended to supply judicial protection to Negroes. Senator Daniel Clark of New Hampshire had stated that the Negro "was denied access to the courts, because he had no rights which a white man was bound to respect; he was not permitted to testify because he might tell of the enormities practiced upon him."[28] Samuel McKee of Kentucky asked, "Where is your court of justice in any Southern State where the black man can secure protection?"[29] Senator Henry S. Lane of Indiana stated, "we legislate upon this subject now . . . simply because we fear . . . that the emancipated slaves would not have their rights in the courts of the slave States."[30]

---

vided a blank check to alter the meaning of the Constitution as written so as to add substantive constitutional changes which a majority of the Court at any given time believes are needed to meet present-day problems." Harper v. Virginia Bd. of Elections, 383 U.S. 663, 675–676 (1966), dissenting opinion. See also infra note 47. But as Alexander Bickel noted, under a "very narrow historical meaning of the Due Process Clause, much else in which Justice Black has joined would be relegated to limbo." *The Least Dangerous Branch* 88 (1962). That does not so much prove his reasoning wrong as a failure to live by it.

28. *Globe* 833. A slave was a chattel and could be neither a party to a suit nor a competent witness against a white. Kenneth M. Stampp, *The Peculiar Institution* 197 (1956).

29. *Globe* 653.

30. Id. 602. Sumner stressed "Equality before the law . . . in court room," id. 674. Raymond stated the Negro "will have access to the courts as a citizen of the United States the same as any other citizen has." Id. 1266.

Although due process found no mention in the text of the Bill, its proponents made quite clear that they considered it to be associated with judicial proceedings. John M. Broomall of Pennsylvania explained that blacks were "denied process of law to enforce the right and to avenge the wrong," that is, "denied remedy in the courts."[31] The intention to supply a judicial "remedy" by means of "due process" was more sharply articulated by Chairman Wilson: "the citizen . . . is entitled to a remedy . . . The citizen is entitled to the right of life, liberty and property. Now if a State intervenes, and deprives him without due process of law of those rights [which had been enumerated in the bill] . . . can we not provide a remedy?"[32] Here is the traditional protection afforded by "due process" against the deprivation of life, liberty or property which was later to be expressed in the due process clause of §1. There is no evidence whatsoever that the §1 resort to the due process clause signaled a shift from this intention to furnish a judicial remedy. Evidence to the contrary is furnished by Senator Cowan. Speaking to the Amendment, he said he was opposed to "punishment of any kind upon any body unless by a fair trial where the party himself is summoned and heard in due course of law," the basic conception of due process of law.[33]

The due process clause made its appearance belatedly, almost in a fortuitous manner, deriving from the framers' absorption with equality before the law.[34] At the opening of the session

31. Id. 1263, 1265; see also Logan, supra Chapter 6 at note 66.

32. Id. 1294.

33. Id. 2899.

34. Infra at notes 56–59. Referring to the due process clause, Bingham said, "Thus, in respect to life, liberty, and property the people by their Constitution declared the equality of all men." *Globe* 1292. When Chief Justice Taft held in Truax v. Corrigan, 257 U.S. 312, 332 (1921) that "Our whole system of law is predicated on the general, fundamental principle of equality of application of the law," he overlooked that (1) Article IV, §2 provided for equality with respect to selected rights; (2) Negroes enjoyed no rights whatsoever; and (3) the Fourteenth Amendment again guaranteed them equality only with respect to selected rights, and pointedly excluded suffrage.

Bingham proposed to "secure to all persons . . . equal protection in the rights [of] life, liberty, and property." Later he explained that the Fifth Amendment contained the very words "equal protection in the rights of life, liberty, and property." "Apparently," Joseph B. James comments, "the words 'due process' did not strike him as outstandingly significant"[35]—and, it may be added, they played no great role in the thinking of his contemporaries. Possibly some more acute lawyer in the Joint Committee, perceiving Bingham's mistaken joinder of "life, liberty, or property" in the Fifth Amendment with "equal protection," restored the original conjunction of "due process" with "life, liberty, or property," thus assuring nondiscriminatory protection by the courts, one of the Civil Rights Act's objectives, and went on to articulate the primary objective of the framers—to prevent discriminatory laws, that is, statutes —by the words "equal protection of the laws." Thus were fashioned the complementary "equal protection" and "due process" clauses, which, as we have seen, were foreshadowed by Blackstone if not by Coke.

Bingham left no room for speculation as to what he meant by "due process." When asked by Rogers, "what do you mean by 'due process of law,'" he curtly replied, "the courts have settled that long ago, and the gentleman can go and read their deci-

35. *Globe* 14, 1034; James 83. "In comparison with the concept of equal protection of the laws," tenBroek averred, "the due process clause was of secondary importance to the abolitionists"; there was an "interchangeable" usage tied to protection of "natural rights." TenBroek 119–120, 215. "The basic idea," he stated, "is that of 'equal protection' . . . other elements were later added—privileges and immunities of citizens, due process of law, political rights. These were all either addenda to the basic notion or an elaboration of it." Id. 207. Hence the "due process clause slipped into a subordinate, almost forgotten position, being commonly read and frequently discussed as if it were a part of the equal protection requirement" (id. 232; see also id. 119–120), as Bingham's statement, supra at note 35, illustrates.

Justice Miller noted in 1878 as a "remarkable" fact that in the century since the Fifth Amendment, due process had "rarely been invoked." Davidson v. New Orleans, 96 U.S. 97, 103 (1877).

sions"—a reply that showed he deemed the question frivolous.[36] As James states, Bingham gave due process the "customary meaning recognized by the courts,"[37] and that meaning was all but universally procedural. Because Bingham "appears to have associated 'equal protection' with 'due process of law,'" Graham concludes that he "probably had a substantive conception of due process."[38] That is like arguing that because "equal protection" outlawed discriminatory statutes, "due process" designed for judicial procedure, likewise applied to regulatory statutes. If Bingham entertained that conception, he never expressed it in the debates. According to Graham, "no other member of Congress appears to have used the clause as Bingham [allegedly] did"; and "no other member of the Joint Committee or of Congress . . . manifested his partiality for the due process clause"[39]—a strange inference from his confusion of "equal protection" with the Fifth Amendment! When Stevens explained the Amendment to the House, he made no mention of the clause, but said that the Amendment "allows Congress to correct the unjust legislation of the States, so far that the law which operates upon one shall operate equally upon all," thus exemplifying that freedom from discriminatory laws remained the overriding concern to the end.[40] One of the very few remarks directed to the due process clause, that of Jehu Baker of Illinois, confirms that it was viewed in existing proce-

36. *Globe* 1089. Dred Scott v. Sandford, 60 U.S. (19 How.) 393, 450 (1857), which employed substantive due process, was scarcely among those "decisions" for it was universally execrated by the abolitionists, and also decried by Lincoln.

37. James 86. That is very old learning: "If a statute make use of a word the meaning of which is well known at the common law, the word shall be understood in the same sense it was understood at common law." Matthew Bacon, *A New Abridgement of the Laws of England* at "Statutes" I(4) (3d ed. 1768). See also supra note 5.

38. Graham 52.

39. Id. 58, 32.

40. *Globe* 2459.

dural terms: "The Constitution already declares generally that no person shall 'be deprived of life, liberty, or property without due process of law.' This declares particularly that no *State* shall do it."[41]

Before his conversion,[41a] Graham noted that at this time due process was "merely a limitation upon procedure" and stated that the substantive theory "presupposes what was really an extraordinary viewpoint." He himself wrote, "so long as these were the prevailing usages down to 1866 one is hardly warranted in attributing a more subtle or comprehensive purpose without definite, positive evidence."[42] Graham's discovery of abolitionist ideology led him to mute these views but, as we shall see, he failed to offer "definite, positive evidence" that that ideology was adopted by the framers. The truth is that it was anathema to the centrist-conservative coalition which was in control.[43]

Bingham himself adhered to a procedural view of due process; in mid-August 1866, just two months after passage of the Amendment, he stated in Ohio that §1 "gave 'any citizen' the power to correct wrong by judicial process," thus identifying it with due process.[44] Telling confirmation that "due process" was not conceived in substantive terms is furnished by

41. *Globe App*. 256. Like Bingham's identification of due process with the judicial decisions, Baker's statement furnishes historical footing for Justice Matthews' "irresistible" conclusion that the due process of the Fourteenth Amendment "was used in the same sense and with no greater extent" than that of the Fifth. Hurtado v. California, 110 U.S. at 535. Later Justice Frankfurter stated, "It ought not to require argument to reject the notion that due process of law meant one thing in the Fifth Amendment and another in the Fourteenth." Adamson v. California, 332 U.S. 46, 66 (1947), concurring opinion. We may safely rely on Hamilton, supra at note 4, for its narrow procedural meaning in the Fifth Amendment, there being no evidence whatever to the contrary.

41a. See infra Chapter 13 at note 4.

42. Graham 35, 36; see also infra at note 48.

43. Infra Chapter 13.

44. James 160.

the fact that Senator Reverdy Johnson, probably the foremost lawyer in the 39th Congress and a member of the Joint Committee, "had not used due process, neither Fifth Amendment due process in *Veazie v. Fenno* nor (apparently) Fourteenth Amendment due process after 1868."[45] "[I]s it conceivable," Graham asked, "that *if* Reverdy Johnson, for example, had clearly understood and intended in 1866 that an added due process limitation against the states would constitute a valuable judicial safeguard for business fighting state regulation, that he himself would fail, as he did in 1869 when arguing the hard-fought case of *Veazie v. Fenno,* to employ the due process clause of the *fifth amendment* in behalf of a corporate client fighting against a drastic federal law?"[46] Since the due process of the Fifth and Fourteenth Amendments were regarded as identical, Graham's rhetorical question suggests that no intimation of substantive content had been voiced in the Joint Committee. And after his review of the railroad battles of the mid-sixties, directed by Reverdy Johnson, which moved from the courts to the Pennsylvania legislature and the halls of Congress, Graham observes: "we find no explicit references in the legislative and congressional debates on the repealers [by the legislature] to violation of *due process as such* . . . [T]hese repealers were regarded only as impairing obligations of contracts, and as having been 'passed without any hearing or judicial determination of the fact of misuse or abuse' . . . What we have to remember is that in 1866 the due process tradition was still on the make."[47]

45. Graham 96; Veazie Bank v. Fenno, 75 U.S. (8 Wall.) 533 (1869).
46. Graham 447.
47. Id. 467, 470–471, 487; see also id. 480. If, as is stated by Professor Archibald Cox, "all agree that the [due process] clause calls for some measure of judicial review of legislative enactments," *The Role of the Supreme Court in American Government* 113 (1976), that belief has yet to be rooted in historical fact. The fact is, as Chapter 14 will seek to demonstrate, substantive due process was a judicial construct fashioned in the late nineteenth century to halt the regulation of big business. Justice Black stated that in Chicago, M. & St. P. R. Co. v. Minnesota, 134 U.S. 418 (1890), the Court "gave a new and hitherto undis-

What is the impact of neoabolitionist theorizing on the fore-going facts? The abolitionist theory of racialized substantive due process, Graham tells us, "had gained its original impetus . . . *extra*-judicially, and almost wholly *ante*-judicially . . . *Extra-judicial* due process and *antebellum* equal protection were rankly, frankly heretical."[48] One who maintains that heresy supplanted orthodoxy, and this through the medium of con-genitally conservative lawyers in Congress, carries a heavy bur-den of proof, not at all met by neoabolitionist reliance on Bing-ham as the instrument of change.[49] The abolitionists themselves by no means saw eye to eye on the subject. Two of their re-nowned theorists, Lysander Spooner and Joel Tiffany, "refused to rely upon due process" or "thought of it almost entirely as a formal requirement."[50] In Massachusetts, Graham writes,

---

covered scope for the Court's use of the due process clause to protect property rights under natural law concepts." Adamson v. California, 332 U.S. at 79, dissenting opinion.

48. Graham 242. "Before there could be clear, general insight into the potentialities of . . . due process," Graham remarked, "there had to be pretty explicit judicial use." Substantive due process, he added, "was not yet an obvious or self-evident proposition." Id. 487, 488. Alfred Kelly observed that in 1860 "these doctrines were outside the pale of constitutional ortho-doxy, but the political upheaval incident to the Civil War put a group of old antislavery enthusiasts in a position to control the Thirty-Ninth Congress and to write their radical reformism into the Constitution itself. The debates on the passage of the amendment reveal clearly enough how completely the con-stitutional ideology of the pre-war antislavery movement shaped the objec-tives of the Radical Republicans." Kelly, Fourteenth 1054. Chapter 13 infra will demonstrate that "control [of] the Thirty-Ninth Congress" by radical "enthusiasts" is a figment of the neoabolitionist imagination, and that aboli-tionist ideology fell on stony ground.

49. "The work of Bingham," tenBroek stated, "was the meeting ground, in a sense that the work of no other individual was, of the three concepts and clauses that came to constitute the first section of the amendment." TenBroek 145. Kelly states, "Bingham, principal author of the first section of the amend-ment, had been a leading congressional antislavery constitutional theorist." Kelly, Fourteenth 1054.

50. TenBroek 121.

"even abolitionists remained comparatively earthbound . . .
Charles Sumner . . . the outstanding black-letter scholar of the
movement . . . relied rather on the Republican form of government clause and Equality Before the Law."[51] Such divisions
indicate that substantive due process was not an idea whose time
had come.[52]

Although Graham perceived that evidence of "substantive"
intent is lacking when due process is viewed in the frame of corporate protection, he failed to apply the lesson to employment
of due process for libertarian purposes. To be sure, the Supreme
Court has now dichotomized due process; in the economic
sphere the words have become a "dirty phrase,"[53] whereas certain libertarian claims have been given a "preferred position."[54]
But support for that distinction will not be found in the history
of the Fourteenth Amendment. Rather there was an unmistakable rejection of that most crucial of libertarian rights—the right
to vote—and with it the right to attend unsegregated schools.

The extraordinary transformation of due process by the
Court[55] has turned the Fourteenth Amendment topsy-turvy.
The original design was to make the "privileges or immuni-
ties" clause the pivotal provision in order to shield the "fun-

51. Graham 539.

52. James Garfield, a participant in the 39th Congress debates, said in dis-
cussing a bill for enforcement of the Fourteenth Amendment in 1871, that no
State can "deprive any person of those great fundamental rights . . . of life,
liberty, and property, except by due process of law; that is, by an impartial
trial according to the laws of the land." *Cong. Globe,* 42d Cong., 1st Sess. App.
at 152–153, quoted by Justice Black in Adamson v. California, 332 U.S. at
111, dissenting opinion.

53. Supra, Chapter 1 at note 10.

54. In a footnote to United States v. Carolene Products Co., 304 U.S. 144,
152–153 note 4 (1938), Justice Stone assigned a preferred position to certain
privileges. The genesis and historical footing of that view will hereinafter be
discussed.

55. Before his discovery of abolitionist ideology, Graham, 112, remarked
on the "amazing judicial hybridization of due process of law with the economic tenets of laissez faire [to] which Justice Holmes objected."

damental rights" enumerated in the Civil Rights Act from the Black Codes. Intertwined with that enumeration was repeated emphasis on the enjoyment of the "same rights," and "equal benefit of all laws and proceedings for the security of person and property."[56] Trumbull stated, for example, that the Civil Rights Bill "contains but one single principle . . . to establish equality in the civil rights of citizens,"[57] among them access to the courts. Throughout the "basic idea," as tenBroek stresses, was that of "equal protection."[58] Farnsworth stated that the Amendment "might as well in my opinion read, 'No State shall deny to any person within its jurisdiction the equal protection of the laws'"; the rest he regarded as "surplusage."[59]

For the framers the three clauses of the Amendment were a trinity, three facets of one and the same purpose. This clearly appears from President Johnson's statement, which accompanied his veto of the Civil Rights Act, that he would *cooperate* "to protect [1] the civil rights of the freedmen [2] by judicial process [3] under equal and impartial laws."[60] *Those* objectives were acceptable to him. In lawyers' parlance, the privileges or immunities clause conferred *substantive* rights which were to be secured through the medium of two *adjective* rights:[61] the equal protection clause outlawed statutory, the due process clause judicial, discrimination with respect to those substantive rights. This adjective duality had been expressed in a Massachusetts

56. Supra note 28.

57. *Globe* 600.

58. TenBroek 207.

59. *Globe* 2539. Windom summarized §1 in terms of privileges or immunities and equal protection without any mention of due process. Id. 3171.

60. *Globe* 1681.

61. Alone among the Justices, Justice Harlan perceived that the framers expected the "privileges or immunities" clause to be "the most significant portion of §1," and since it was "expected to be the primary source of substantive protection, the Equal Protection and Due Process Clauses were relegated to a secondary role, as the debates and other contemporary materials make clear." Oregon v. Mitchell, 400 U.S. 112, 163, 164 (1970).

measure of 1692 ordaining that "no person should suffer [1] without express law . . . [2] nor without being brought to answer by due course and process of law," a measure duplicated in the colonies of Connecticut and New York.[62] And it found expression in the Fourteenth Amendment, as may be gathered from Senator Howard's explanation that "without this principle of equal *justice* to all men *and* equal protection under the shield of the *law,* there is no republican government." Senator Clark made the point more clearly: "You admit that the *courts* should be open to the black man, and that he should have the protection of the *laws* as fully as the white man."[63] TenBroek remarks that Bingham "accepted the [abolitionist] amalgamation of natural rights, due process and equal protection."[64] "A common theme of the discussion of the amendment's supporters," Harris comments, "was the mutual interdependence of the privileges and immunities, due process, and equal protection clauses."[65] And in answer to the question "equal protection of what?" he replies: "when the three clauses are read together as they ought to be, it is equal protection by equal laws pertaining to the rights of life, liberty and property, and the privileges and immunities of citizenship. Or, as expressed by Justice Washington, those rights which are in their nature fundamental."[66] But,

62. 2 Kent, supra note 17 at 608–609.

63. *Globe* 2766, 833 (emphasis added). So too, Raymond stated that the Civil Rights Bill "is intended to secure those citizens against injustice that may be done to them in the courts . . . It is intended to prevent unequal legislation . . . affecting them injuriously." *Globe* 1267.

64. TenBroek 145.

65. R. J. Harris, *The Quest for Equality* 35–36 (1960).

66. Id. 44. The triune analysis undercuts that of Chief Justice Warren in Bolling v. Sharpe, 347 U.S. 497, 499 (1954): "The Fifth Amendment . . . does not contain an equal protection clause as does the Fourteenth Amendment . . . But the concepts of equal protection and due process, both stemming from our American ideal of fairness, are not mutually exclusive. The 'equal protection of the law' is a more explicit safeguard of prohibited unfairness than 'due process of law.' " This is sheer fantasy. Equal protection was incorporated in the Fourteenth Amendment to bar discrimination by statutes,

like tenBroek, Harris does not come to grips with *the limited meaning* that "natural," "fundamental" rights, that "life, liberty, or property," had for the framers.[67] Trumbull drew that limited meaning from Justice Washington in drafting the Civil Rights Bill, and it was then embodied in the "privileges or immunities" clause. It is striking evidence of the centrality of the privileges or immunities clause for its contemporaries that hard upon the adoption of the Amendment, in the *Slaughter-House Cases,* equal protection and due process, in the words of Justice Miller, had "not been much pressed,"[68] but that the case was almost entirely pitched on the privileges or immunities clause. For it was that clause that contains the substantive rights the Amendment was designed to protect.

As in the case of the "equal protection" clause, the framers were content to bar discrimination, to assure blacks that they would have judicial protection on the same State terms as whites, no more, no less. It should be apparent from the foregoing that the due process clause was not meant to create a new, federal criterion of justice. Like State *laws* at which "equal pro-

---

due process to secure access to the courts; both were antidiscriminatory, but they were designed to serve quite different purposes. Only eleven years before Warren's statement, the Court held that because of the absence of "equal protection" from the Fifth Amendment, it "provides no guaranty against discriminatory legislation by Congress." Detroit Bank v. United States, 317 U.S. 329, 337 (1943).

67. Thus Harris extracts from the debates the principle "that the equal protection clause means absolute or perfect equality . . . and condemns *every* discrimination perpetuated by unequal laws." Supra note 65 at 55. Although tenBroek discerned that the three clauses represented an amalgam for the "protection of natural rights," tenBroek 145, 239, 120, he did not grasp the limited meaning that "natural," "fundamental" rights had for the framers. Consider only his statement that the "sweeping and comprehensive meaning of the Fourteenth Amendment . . . turns simply upon the nature of the *statutory* plan which was sought to be made constitutionally secure by the amendment." TenBroek 203 (emphasis added). This about an Act that painstakingly specified the limited rights to be protected!

68. 83 U.S. (16 Wall.) 36, 80 (1872); Justice Miller, supra note 35.

tection" was aimed, State *justice* had to be nondiscriminatory. It was "equal justice to all men and equal protection under the shield of law" of which Howard spoke.[69] "[E]quality in the protection of these fundamental rights . . . was the common refrain throughout," as is exemplified by Stevens' "Whatever means of redress *is afforded* to one shall be afforded to all,"[70] by Howard's "equal justice to all," and by Trumbull's assurance that the Civil Rights Bill "will have no operation in any State where the laws are equal, where all persons have the same civil rights."[71] Just as the framers disclaimed an intention to displace nondiscriminatory State laws by a general federal code and were content to "correct" discriminatory State laws, so their parallel aim was to secure impartial access to State judicial proceedings,[72] not to write a judicial code for the nation. All this was summed up by Justice Matthews in *Hurtado v. California*: the due process clause of the 14th Amendment "refers to that law of the land in each State . . . 'Each State prescribes its own mode of judicial proceeding.' "[73]

Even less were the framers minded in requiring nondiscriminatory laws and equal judicial process to create a fresh congeries of rights that ranged beyond those enumerated.[74] Having in mind that the Amendment was designed to constitutionalize the Civil Rights Act, it is clear that the "equal protection" and "due process" clauses were merely a compressed

69. *Globe* 2766.

70. TenBroek 232; *Globe* 2459 (emphasis added). "As Stevens saw it, *discrimination* was the great evil, *equal* protection was the dominant purpose of §1." Fairman, Stanford 44 (emphasis added). Sumner stated that he wanted "Equality before the law, so that there shall be no ban of color in court room." *Globe* 674.

71. *Globe* 476; see also supra Chapter 10 at note 49.

72. See supra at notes 28–30.

73. 110 U.S. at 535; see also Walker v. Sauvinet, 92 U.S. 90, 93 (1875); cf. supra Chapter 10 at note 70.

74. Recall Bingham's objection to the "oppressive" breadth of the term "civil rights," which was deleted at his insistence. Supra Chapter 7 at notes 11–17; *Globe* 1366.

version of the original design. All three clauses, tenBroek states, "refer to the protection or abridgment of natural rights,"[75] rights that had been so carefully spelled out in the Civil Rights Act. There is evidence that these clauses simply echoed the Blackstonian formula that the "fundamental rights" could be *diminished* only by "due course of law" or by the "laws of the land," by which was meant general laws that would apply to all alike. Wilson had quoted Blackstone's pairing of "due process of law" and by the "laws of the land" in commenting on the Civil Rights Bill, exhibiting awareness that Blackstone regarded them as the sole means of curtailing the specified rights. He emphasized that the Bill "does not go one step beyond" protection from discrimination with respect to designated "immunities," that "it is not the object of this bill to establish new rights," but to declare "the equality of all citizens in the enjoyment of civil rights and immunities."[76] For the protection of those enumerated rights, "fundamental rights," the framers fashioned impartial access to judicial process and non-discriminatory legislation. They did not seek to supplant State proceedings and lawmaking, but only to insure, in the words of the Judiciary Committee's interpolation, that an oppressed race should have the "equal benefit of all laws for security of person and property" "*as is enjoyed by white citizens.*"[77] This was the purpose constitutionalized by the Fourteenth Amendment.

It is therefore contrary to historical fact to say, as did Justice Black, that "in view of its historical setting and the wrongs which called it into being, the due process provision of the Fourteenth Amendment—just as that in the Fifth . . . was intended to guarantee procedural standards adequate and appropriate, then and thereafter."[78] And it testifies to the potency of unremitting reiteration that even so perspicacious a judge as Justice Harlan could state that "The Due Process Clause of the

75. TenBroek 239.
76. *Globe* 1117–1118.
77. Id. 1366; see also supra at note 33.
78. Chambers v. Florida, 309 U.S. 227, 235–236 (1940).

Fourteenth Amendment requires that those [State] procedures be fundamentally fair in all respects."[79] That is a judicial construct pure and simple; no such mandate can be drawn from the history of the Amendment.

It has been my purpose in this and the preceding chapter to show that the terms "equal protection of the laws" and "due process of law" grew out of the framers' intention to supply, with respect to a selected group of privileges, protection against discrimination either by legislation or by a bar to judicial succor, that these adjective conceptions were intertwined throughout with the framers' solicitude to guarantee those selected substantive rights. Even if I have failed in that purpose, Robert H. Bork's conclusion seems to me controlling:

> The words are general but surely that would not permit us to escape the framers' intent if it were clear. If the legislative history revealed a consensus about segregation in schools and all the other relations in life, I do not see how the Court could escape the choices revealed and substitute its own, even though the words are general and conditions have changed. It is the fact that history does not reveal detailed choices concerning such matters that permits, indeed requires, resort to other modes of interpretation.[80]

The Court, in short, was not empowered to substitute its policy choices for those of the framers.

---

79. Duncan v. Louisiana, 391 U.S. 145, 172 (1968), dissenting opinion. As late as 1894, the Supreme Court declared that the Fourteenth Amendment "conferred no new and additional rights, but only extended the protection of the Federal Constitution over rights of life, liberty, and property that had previously existed under all state constitutions." Mobile & Ohio Railroad v. Tennessee, 153 U.S. 486, 506 (1894).

80. "Neutral Principles and Some First Amendment Problems," 47 Ind. L. J. 1, 13 (1971); see also infra Chapter 21 at note 28.

PERSON OR CITIZEN

Few, if any, historical reconstructions can tidily accommodate all the unruly facts. The triune analysis does not fit neatly with the fact that the privileges or immunities clause refers exclusively to "citizens," whereas the equal protection and due process clauses refer to "persons." "In constitutionally defining who is a citizen of the United States," Justice Rehnquist stated, "Congress obviously thought it was doing something, and something important . . . The language of that Amendment carefully distinguishes between 'persons' who, whether by birth or naturalization, had achieved a certain status, and 'persons' in general."[81] That distinction, I suggest, was *not* carefully considered, and it raises a number of perplexing problems. Were the rights of "persons" intended to be broader than those of "citizens"? If so, the unremitting labor to make citizens of blacks was superfluous, especially since suffrage was denied them; for they could have enjoyed as "persons" rights withheld from them as "citizens." Or were "persons," like "citizens," only to receive protection for the "fundamental rights" expressed in the due process words "life, liberty, or property," words Bingham originally had coupled with equal protection. This too would render the privileges or immunities clause supererogatory save as an additional cue to the nature of what was sought to be protected. Nor is it reasonable to conclude that the framers were more solicitous for "persons" than for "citizens." To the contrary, they were almost constantly preoccupied with the plight of the former slaves, who were made citizens for their better protection. All in all, it will not do to read the rights of "persons" more broadly than those that were conferred on "citizens."

Little notice has been taken of the relation in this context between "citizens" and "persons,"[82] and it may be useful to pull

81. Sugarman v. Dougall, 413 U.S. 634, 652 (1973), dissenting opinion.

82. Maxwell v. Dow, 176 U.S. 581, 595–596 (1900), presented the question whether a State may provide for criminal trials by a jury of less than twelve.

the historical threads together. So far as regards the Civil Rights Bill it is plain, as Wilson stated, that "the entire structure of this bill rests on the discrimination relative to civil rights and immunities . . . on account of race."[83] Originally §1 of the bill had banned discrimination "in civil rights and immunities among the inhabitants of any State . . . on account of race"; §2 penalized any person who "subjected any inhabitant . . . to the deprivation of any right secured or protected by this act."[84] At the instruction of the Judiciary Committee, Chairman Wilson offered an amendment to §1: "to strike out the words 'but the inhabitants' and insert in lieu the words 'and such citizens,'" so that it would read "no discrimination in civil rights or immunities among the citizens of the United States." He explained that it was "intended to confine the operation of this bill to citizens of the United States, instead of extending it to the inhabitants of the several States, as there seems to be some doubt concerning the power of Congress to extend this protection to such inhabitants as are not citizens."[85] Presumably the doubt was engendered by the fact that the Thirteenth Amend-

---

Justice Peckham stated that the rights secured by the Fifth, Sixth, and Seventh Amendments are not "privileges and immunities granted and belonging to the individual as a citizen of the United States, but they are secured to all persons against the Federal Government, entirely irrespective of such citizenship." Hence, he concluded, the privileges or immunities claim "is not protected by a clause which simply prohibits the abridgment of the privileges or immunities of citizens of the United States."

83. *Globe* 1118. Racial discrimination was the acknowledged concern of the bill: see Trumbull, id. 332, 605; Senator Lane, id. 602; Senator Sumner, id. 674; Senator Sherman, id. 744; Wilson, id. 1117; Senator Howe, *Globe App.* 217. These citations are by no means exhaustive.

But while the "one pervading purpose" as Justice Miller stated was "the freedom of the slave race," supra note 68 at 71, white loyalists who were the victims of discrimination in the South were likewise stated to be "within the intent of the Bingham amendment." See infra at note 91; and see Broomall, *Globe* 1263; Chapter 3 note 40.

84. *Globe* 474–475.

85. Id. 1115.

ment, the chief reliance for the constitutionality of the bill, was restricted to enslaved blacks; but the original "discrimination . . . on account of race" adequately responded to that restriction. Later Bingham, apprised by Wilson that the surviving word "inhabitant" in §2 was "in mistake for 'citizen,'" expostulated against the "terrible enormity of distinguishing here in the laws in respect to life, liberty, and property between the citizen and stranger within your gates." That, he said, "is forbidden by the Constitution," citing the association in the Fifth Amendment of "No person" with "life, liberty, and property" and asserting that "this bill . . . departs from that great law. The alien is not a citizen. You propose to enact this law, you say, in the interests of the freedmen. But do you propose to allow these discriminations to be made . . . against the alien and stranger?"[86] Although the word "inhabitants" was not replaced by "citizens" in §2, Wilson continued to refer to the bill in terms of "citizens," and objected to a proposal to "declare all persons, negroes included, citizens."[87] His understanding that the Bill pertained to "citizens" was shared by William Lawrence and Samuel Shellabarger.[88]

When we turn to the Amendment we find that Bingham pretty consistently sought protection for "persons." In contrast to Stevens, who at the very outset had introduced an amendment requiring all laws to be equally applicable to "citizens," Bingham had proposed to "secure to all persons . . . equal protection in their rights of life, liberty, and property";[89] and this, alongside of a privileges and immunities clause, was later embodied in his prototype amendment.[90] But when challenged, Bingham hedged. Robert S. Hale said, "It is claimed that this

86. Id. 1292.

87. Id. 1295. There was no need to change "inhabitant" in §2 because it was limited to deprivations of rights "protected by this act" which extended to "citizens" only.

88. Id. 1832, 1293.

89. Id. 10, 537; id. 14.

90. Id. 813.

constitutional amendment is aimed simply and purely toward
the protection of 'American citizens of African descent' . . . I
understand that to be the whole intended practical effect of the
amendment." Bingham replied, "It is due to the committee that
I should say that it is proposed as well to protect the thousands . . . of loyal white citizens . . . whose property . . .
has been wrested from them."[91] He recurred, however, to a
broader statement: "all persons, whether citizens or strangers
. . . shall have equal protection . . . in the rights of life,
liberty, and property." Were the word "citizens" used, he
stated, "aliens" who were protected by existing constitutional
guarantees to "persons" would be excluded.[92] On the other
hand, his fellow Republicans—Hiram Price, Thomas T. Davis,
Frederick E. Woodbridge, and Giles W. Hotchkiss—before and
after he spoke, understood his amendment to apply to discrimination between "citizens."[93]

Bingham also described the final version of the Amendment
in terms of the "privileges and immunities of all the citizens . . . and the inborn rights of every person."[94] But once
again his view apparently did not filter into the minds of his colleagues. The Amendment, as we have seen, was understood to
constitutionalize the Civil Rights Bill, which, in the words of
M. Russell Thayer, incorporated the Bill's protection of the
"fundamental rights of citizenship." Ephraim R. Eckley approved it because it secured "life, liberty, and property to all
the citizens."[95] Senator Howard declared, "we desired to
put . . . the rights of citizens and freedmen under the civil
rights bill beyond the legislative power" of those who would
"expose the freedmen again to the oppression of their old
masters," and Broomall also referred to the Amendment in

91. Id. 1065.
92. Id. 1090, 1292.
93. Id. 1066, 1087, 1088, 1095.
94. Id. 2452.
95. Id. 2465, 2535.

terms of "citizens."[96] These references suggest that the minds of most framers were concentrated on the protection of citizens, that they may not have appreciated that the word "persons" was carrying them further. Are so many statements to be viewed as reflecting agreement to use a shorthand version, or do they indicate that Congress did not really grasp that the Amendment applied both to citizens and noncitizens? Bingham never gave thought to the anomalies created by his coupling of the privileges or immunities of "citizens" with the protection of "persons," the fact that he rendered the drive for Negro citizenship and the antecedent specification of the rights epitomized in the privileges or immunities clause superfluous.

Notwithstanding his inept midwifery, the object of the Amendment, whether viewed in the frame of "citizen" or of "person," remains one and the same—the protection of the "fundamental rights" of "life, liberty, or property," which first had been specified in the Civil Rights Bill and then embodied in the privileges or immunities clause.[97] Due process is expressly tied to those rights; the derivation of the equal protection clause shows that it too was designed to shield the same rights against discriminatory laws. As John F. Farnsworth asked, how can a subject "have and enjoy equal rights of 'life, liberty, and the pursuit of happiness' without 'equal protection of the laws'?"[98] Not only is there not the slightest intimation that "persons" were to enjoy broader rights than those that had been so carefully enumerated for "citizens," but those self-same rights of "life, liberty, and property" were repeatedly associated with "persons." One may conclude with tenBroek that "the 'citizen and stranger' are again on the same footing: 'the inborn rights

96. Id. 2896, 2498.

97. Id. 2465; supra Chapter 2. For Wilson, the due process clause served to identify the rights with which the Civil Rights Bill was concerned. Citing the Fifth Amendment, "No person shall be deprived of life, liberty, or property without due process of law," he stated, "these constitute the civil rights belonging to the citizens . . . to which this bill relates." *Globe* 1294.

98. *Globe* 2539.

of every person' and 'the privileges and immunities of citizens' are coupled together [by Bingham] and refer to the same rights."[99] Whether the three clauses of §1 be viewed as a trinity, or whether the equal protection and due process clauses be separated from the privileges or immunities clause by virtue of the differentiation between "citizens" and "persons," the practical effect is the same: protection for the fundamental rights of "life, liberty, and property."

99. TenBroek 228.

12

Section Five:
"Congress Shall Enforce"

SECTION 5 of the Amendment provides that "The Congress shall have power to enforce by appropriate legislation the provisions of this article." In 1879 the Court declared:

> It is *not said* that the *judicial power* of the general government shall extend to enforcing the prohibitions and protecting the rights and immunities guaranteed. It is *not said* that branch of government shall be authorized to *declare void* any action of a State in violation of the prohibitions. It is the power of Congress which has been enlarged. *Congress is authorized to enforce* the prohibitions by appropriate legislation. Some legislation is contemplated to make the amendment fully effective.[1]

One might read this to mean that the courts are without authority to enforce the Fourteenth Amendment except as Congress empowers them to do so. Nevertheless, Justice Brennan stated in 1970, "we have consistently held that the Amendment grants power to the Court" and brushed the issue aside as "of academic interest only."[2] It is a fact that the Court has exercised the power, but it has never grappled with the questions posed by the text of §5 and by the 1879 opinion. It is never "academic" to

---

1. Ex parte Virginia, 100 U.S. 339, 345 (1879) (emphasis partially added).
2. Oregon v. Mitchell, 400 U.S. 112, 264n (1970).

inquire into the constitutional authority for action by any branch of the government. Patently the Court does not derive its power from the text of §5. Whence is it derived? Why did the framers confer the power on Congress rather than the Court?

The preference for Congress over the courts, exhibited by the face of §5, is readily explicable: "Slavery was deeply entrenched in the courts."[3] *Dred Scott* had been so bitterly etched into abolitionist memory that Senator Sumner even sought to bar the customary memorial, placement of Chief Justice Taney's bust in the Supreme Court Chamber, and insisted that his name should be "hooted down in the pages of history."[4] Earlier the fugitive slave decision *Prigg v. Pennsylvania*[5] had incensed the North, and such feelings were exacerbated on the very eve of the Civil War by *Ableman v. Booth,* where an order of the Supreme Court of Wisconsin setting aside a federal commitment of a fugitive slave was reversed.[6] In consequence, Bingham, Stevens, "and others were among the severest critics of the Supreme Court and judicial review . . . [and] viewed it with a profound and ever growing mistrust."[7] James F. Wilson of Iowa rejected "judicial pronouncements" on the "unity of this Republic."[8] Not long after congressional approval of the

---

3. TenBroek 149.

4. Donald, *Sumner II* 193. In the House, Stevens referred to "the infamous sentiment that damned the late Chief Justice to everlasting fame; and I fear, to everlasting fire." *Globe* 75. George Bancroft, the historian, stated in a memorial tribute to Lincoln that "The Chief Justice . . . without any necessity or occasion, volunteered to come to the rescue of the theory of slavery." *Globe* 801. Almost twenty years later Justice Harlan delivered himself of more severe strictures in the Civil Rights Cases, 109 U.S. 3, 57 (1883), dissenting opinion.

5. 41 U.S. (16 Pet.) 539 (1842).

6. 62 U.S. (21 How.) 506 (1858). The pot had been kept boiling by a string of fugitive slave decisions, infra Chapter 14 at notes 25–26.

7. Graham 447–448. Courts "had not normally favored abolitionists before the war. There was consequently little inclination to bestow new powers on the judiciary, but rather to lean on an augmented power of Congress." James 184.

8. *Globe* 2947.

Amendment, Samuel L. Warner, a Connecticut Republican, said he had "learned to place but little reliance upon the dogmas of [the] Court upon any question touching the rights of humanity."[9]

Such statements and sentiments might suggest that the framers intended the §5 grant of enforcement power to be exclusive, an inference apparently drawn by Judge Learned Hand: "Judicial encroachments upon legislative prerogatives in segregation decisions appeared to Hand to be directly contrary to the intent of the Fourteenth Amendment, which gives Congress power to enforce it through appropriate legislation."[10] Hand could draw on the established canon that the express grant to Congress indicates an intention to withhold the enforcement power from the courts.[11]

It needs to be noticed that in 1866 the lower federal courts had no general jurisdiction of cases alleging a deprivation of rights secured by the Constitution. Although Article III confers jurisdiction of "cases arising under this Constitution," it places creation of the "inferior courts" in the discretion of Congress.

9. Fairman, *History* 271. "The Radicals," said R. J. Harris, *The Quest for Equality* 53–54 (1960), "did not trust the judiciary in general and the Supreme Court in particular." "Radical Republicans sought to deny the postwar court the power to review congressional Reconstruction." Morton Keller, *Affairs of State* 73 (1977).

10. Kathryn Griffith, *Judge Learned Hand and the Role of the Federal Judiciary* 138 (1973). Hand stated respecting the desegregation decision, "It is curious that no mention was made of section 5, which offered an escape, from intervening, for it empowers Congress to 'enforce' all the preceding sanctions by 'appropriate legislation.' The court must have regarded this as only a cumulative corrective, not being disposed to divest itself of that power of review that it has so often exercised and as often disclaimed." Hand, *The Bill of Rights* 55 (1962).

11. T.I.M.E. v. United States, 359 U.S. 464, 471 (1959); United States v. Arredondo, 31 U.S. (6 Pet.) 691, 725 (1832). The rule was familiar to the Founders. In the First Congress, Egbert Benson said, "it cannot be rationally intended that all offices should be held during good behaviour, because the Constitution has declared one office to be held by this tenure." 1 *Annals of Congress* 505; and see Alexander White, id. 517.

Consequently, the Supreme Court held, "Congress may withhold from any court of its creation jurisdiction of any of the enumerated controversies."[12] General jurisdiction of such cases, involving so-called "federal questions," was withheld by Congress from the lower courts until the 1870s.[13] Two related factors also require preliminary notice: the existence of the "diversity" jurisdiction of controversies "between citizens of different states," and of appeals to the Supreme Court from State court denials of rights claimed under the Constitution or laws of the United States.[14] But, as the face of the Civil Rights Act discloses, the framers little trusted the State courts to enforce Negro rights;[15] and to have insisted that an impoverished black should pursue his rights in the Supreme Court would have reduced judicial enforcement to an empty promise. The diversity jurisdiction of course was virtually useless to almost all blacks, for their oppressors normally would be residents of the same State.

The framers, however, had made express provision in the Civil Rights Act for federal court jurisdiction to enforce the Act. Section 3 gave (1) the district courts jurisdiction, exclusive of State courts, of all crimes and offenses against the Act; and (2) concurrent jurisdiction with the circuit courts of all causes, civil and criminal, affecting persons who are denied or cannot enforce rights secured by §1 in State courts; plus (3) rights of

12. Sheldon v. Sill, 49 U.S. (8 How.) 441, 449 (1850).

13. "The Civil Rights Act of 1871 (now 28 U.S.C. §1343) created original jurisdiction in the district courts over actions [t]o redress the deprivation, under color of any State law . . . of any right . . . secured by the Constitution . . . And the Act of March 3, 1875 (now 28 U.S.C. §1331), created general federal question jurisdiction in the district courts. The federal courts 'ceased to be restricted tribunals of fair dealing between citizens of different states and became the primary and powerful reliance for vindicating every right given by the Constitution, the laws, and treaties of the United States.' [citing Felix Frankfurter and James M. Landis, *The Business of the Supreme Court* 65 (1928)]." Paul Brest, *Processes of Constitutional Decisionmaking: Cases and Materials* 1297 (1975).

14. Raoul Berger, *Congress v. The Supreme Court* 274 (1969).

15. Infra at note 16.

removal of criminal or civil actions against persons whose rights were secured by the Act.[16] Nothing in the history of the Amendment suggests an intention to repeal this provision. Instead the question arises: did "incorporation" of the Act in the Amendment carry the enforcement provisions with it? It is unreasonable, however, to attribute to the framers an intention to freeze enforcement provisions—the §2 fine of $1,000, for example—into the Constitution. Such provisions are generally subject to change in the light of experience, and the need to preserve flexibility with respect to penalties counsels against such an interpretation. On established canons of construction an unreasonable interpretation is to be avoided. Then too, there is no reason to attribute to Congress an intention to surrender any part of its Article III control of the "inferior courts"[17] by a grant of untouchable jurisdiction in the Fourteenth Amendment, particularly at a time when Congress distrusted the courts. Such a surrender calls for more than references to "incorporation"; in an analogous situation the Court has required a specific provision for the change.[18]

In light of the jurisdiction conferred by §3 of the Act, why was there a need for express congressional "power to enforce"? For it is a puzzling fact that the "necessity" of the §5 authorization was stressed. That §5, said George F. Miller of Pennsylvania, "is requisite to enforce the foregoing sections . . . is not contested."[19] Justice Brennan explained that by "including §5 the

16. *Globe App.* 316. McKee of Kentucky asked, "Where is your court of justice in any southern State where the black man can secure protection." *Globe* 653. See also Senator Lane, supra Chapter 11 at note 30.

17. Supra at note 12.

18. Pierson v. Ray, 386 U.S. 547, 554–555 (1967); see also supra Chapter 1 note 57.

19. *Globe* 2511. Jehu Baker of Illinois declared that §5 "was of course necessary in order to carry the proposed article into practical effect." *Globe App.* 257. See also Senator Poland, *Globe* 2961. Fairman comments, "Poland, like the rest, contemplated action by Congress and ignored direct enforcement by the courts." Fairman, *History* 1296. For a similar comment on Howard, see Fairman, id. 1294.

draftsmen sought to grant to Congress, by a specific provision applicable to the Fourteenth Amendment, the same broad powers expressed in the Necessary and Proper Clause."[20] That leaves the tautology to be accounted for. *Prigg v. Pennsylvania*,[21] a cause célèbre, had decided with respect to the Fugitive Slave Act that Congress has implied power to protect a right derived from the Constitution. Of *Prigg* and the subsequent *Ableman v. Booth*,[22] the abolitionists, we may be sure, were well aware. Practiced lawyers like Senator Reverdy Johnson, Thaddeus Stevens, Judge Robert S. Hale, and Judge William Lawrence would be familiar with those cases, and one hesitates without more to attribute to the framers an intention merely to confirm such judicial interpretations by express constitutional provision. The "necessity" is perhaps better explained by Laurent B. Frantz: *Prigg* and *Ableman* gave Congress implied power to protect constitutional rights from interference by private individuals, whereas *Kentucky v. Dennison* had denied "implied power to exercise any control over a state's officers and agencies."[23] Since

"Senator Howe, a Radical Republican, went back to Wisconsin and made a major address at Madison on August 10 [1866]; '. . . The only effect of the amendment if adopted is to enable the National Legislature . . . to enforce equal justice, when the several States refuse to enforce it.'" Fairman, Stanford 73–74, quoting the *Chicago Tribune,* August 14, 1866.

20. Katzenbach v. Morgan, 384 U.S. 641, 650 (1966).

21. 41 U.S. (16 Pet.) 539, 618–620 (1842). Justice Bradley stated on circuit, "whenever a right is guaranteed by the constitution . . . Congress has the power to provide for its enforcement, either by implication arising from the correlative duty of the government to protect, wherever a right to the citizen is conferred, or under the general power . . . to make all laws necessary and proper for carrying into execution the foregoing powers." United States v. Cruikshank, 25 F. Cas. (No. 14,897) 707, 709 (C.C.D. La. 1874). He instanced Prigg as an example of the former power.

22. Supra note 6.

23. "Congressional Power to Enforce the Fourteenth Amendment Against Private Acts," 73 Yale L.J. 1353, 1357 (1964). Chief Justice Taney held in Kentucky v. Dennison, 65 U.S. (24 How.) 66, 107 (1858), with reference to power to compel a Governor to deliver a fugitive from justice to a sister State, "there is no clause or provision in the Constitution which arms the Government of the United States with this power."

Dennison held, and Bingham considered, that *no* branch of the government enjoyed such power over State officers,[24] a grant of power to the judiciary arguably was equally "necessary." No such grant was made in the Amendment. The 1866 congressional grant to the judiciary in the Civil Rights Act was by the *Dennison* test of dubious constitutionality; it could and can be supplemented by delegation from Congress under its §5 "power to enforce." Derived from Congress, the judicial enforcement power can be withdrawn by it from the "inferior courts."

The debates indicate that the framers meant Congress to play the leading role, that they regarded Congress "as the primary organ for the implementation of the guarantees of privileges and immunities, due process, and equal protection."[25] It was "necessary," said Senator Poland, that Congress "enforce the provision . . . and *compel* its observance."[26] Stevens explained that the Amendment "allows Congress to correct the unjust legislation of the States"; and Charles Fairman observed that "Stevens' thought ran to political rather than judicial action."[27] Other framers also looked to Congress to undertake "corrective" action.[28] The overtones of such expressions were amplified by Senator Howard: section 5

> constitutes a direct affirmative delegation of power to Congress *to carry out* all the principles of these guarantees, a power *not found in the Constitution* . . . It casts upon Congress the *responsibility*

24. Bingham stated that "the continued construction of every department of this Government, legislative, executive and judicial . . . has conceded that no such power [to enforce the rights guaranteed to a citizen "from the beginning"] is vested in the Federal Government," and he therefore proposed a grant to Congress. *Globe 429;* see also Howard, infra at note 29.

25. Harris, supra note 9 at 53–54; James 184.

26. *Globe* 2961 (emphasis added). Woodbridge said the Amendment "is intended to enable Congress by its enactments" to give "protection." Supra Chapter 8 at note 34.

27. *Globe* 2459; Fairman, *History* 1284. In "Stevens' mind, it was Congress that was going to correct unjust State legislation." Fairman, Stanford 44.

28. Supra Chapter 10 at notes 73, 75, 79.

of seeing to it, for the future, that all the sections of the amendment are carried out in good faith, and that no State infringes the
rights of person and property . . . I look upon this clause as
indispensable for the reason that it thus *imposes upon Congress* this
power and *this duty.* It enables *Congress,* in case the States shall
enact laws in conflict with the principles of the amendment, *to
correct* that legislation by a formal congressional amendment.[29]

Some explanation is required why this "responsibility" to
"carry out the principles" of the Amendment did not contem-
plate congressional rather than judicial initiatives. Why did
Hotchkiss protest that §5 "proposes to leave it to the caprice of
Congress" whether or not to enforce antidiscrimination,[30] if it
was assumed that the courts could act in the face of congressional inaction? At the outset Conkling stated that all questions
"arising upon the construction" of the Amendment would go
to the "appropriate forum . . . the forum would be Congress,
and also, perhaps the courts."[31] But §5 made no provision for
enforcement by the courts.

Justice Douglas, apparently unaware of the implications of
his statement for judicial review, stated that "the manner of
enforcement involves discretion; but that discretion is largely
entrusted to Congress, not to the courts."[32] The face of §5 indicates that the "discretion" was *entirely* confided to Congress,
and the debates confirm that the "responsibility" for enforcement was imposed upon Congress, thus confirming the maxim

---

29. *Globe* 2766, 2768 (emphasis added). Justice Brennan cites this passage
for "congressional responsibility for implementing the Amendment." Katzenbach v. Morgan, 384 U.S. at 648.

30. *Globe* 1095.

31. Id. 358.

32. Oregon v. Mitchell, 400 U.S. at 143. Professor Willard Hurst stated, "it
is pretty plain that the actual framers thought they were delegating the rule-
making power to Congress." "The Role of History," in *Supreme Court and
Supreme Law* 60 (E. Cahn ed. 1954).

that a direction to act in one mode excludes another.[33] Judge Learned Hand's inference that the grant to Congress was exclusive is strengthened by the legislative history. So far as I could find that history affords no basis for reading into §5 the judicial power of enforcement it so plainly withheld. Minimally the legislative history indicates that where Congress has spoken, that policy ought to be respected.[34]

A reasoned argument for a judicial power of enforcement of the Fourteenth Amendment—apart from that derived from the grant in the Civil Rights Act of 1866, which Congress is free to withdraw—has yet to be made. Section 5, I would insist, raises questions which go to the heart of judicial enforcement of the Amendment, questions which the Court has never attempted to answer, which have been neglected by scholars, and to which they might well devote further study.

33. Supra note 11.

34. Thus the Equal Educational Opportunities Act of 1974, 20 U.S.C. §§1701 et seq., undertook to "specify appropriate remedies for the orderly removal of the vestiges of the dual school system" and to establish priorities for the employment of such remedies. 20 U.S.C. §1701(b) and §1713. See also Kelly, supra Chapter 6 note 26.

13

Incorporation of Abolitionist Theory in Section One

ENOUGH has been set forth to raise considerable doubt about the Graham-tenBroek theory that §1 of the Fourteenth Amendment embodies the substantive due process–equal protection concepts forged by certain abolitionists in the antislavery crusade of the 1830s–1860s.[1] The abolitionist theorists upon whom Graham and tenBroek relied by no means represented the mainstream of abolitionist theorizing; they were a "handful of relatively unimportant anti-slavery thinkers," overshadowed by the William Lloyd Garrison–Wendell Phillips wing, for whom the natural law of Graham's theologians held no charms.[2] But the fact that a respected historian, Alfred Kelly, considered that Graham and tenBroek "have established quite conclusively that the Fourteenth Amendment both in general ideology and legal phrase was a product of pre-war antislavery theory" and that that view is also taken, albeit less emphatically, by Leonard Levy,[3] calls for further elucidation.

1. Graham 155 et seq.; TenBroek 25, 29, 116, 145, 235.

2. Robert Cover, *Justice Accused: Antislavery and the Judicial Process* 155, 150–153 (1975). Cover justly remarks that Graham and TenBroek discovered in the "visions" of this minority "roots for their own constitutional aspirations." Id. 154.

3. Kelly, Fourteenth 1050–1051. Leonard Levy states, "Graham and ten-

At the outset, it will be recalled, Graham considered that Bingham may have used "due process" in its procedural sense. But on May 4, 1942—he has recorded the date exactly—through a providential "chance Law Library order" for a work by the abolitionist Theodore Weld, a shining new world opened up before him.[4] What Graham found is best summed up in his own words:

> We have been tracing and stressing, not a precise, finished, coherent, consistent body of constitutional doctrine, still less an authoritative one; rather something still inchoate, derivative, opportunist, "sporty and sporting"—hence really a climate of usage, and the sociology and the geography of professional association, influence and knowledge by which due process and equal protection became what they did, when and how they did.[5]

This "inchoate" mass allegedly was incorporated in the Fourteenth Amendment largely through the instrumentality of Bingham, himself an imprecise thinker who exhibited little more understanding of the Bill of Rights than Graham credits the abolitionists with.[6]

The Graham-tenBroek theory was spread before the Supreme Court in *Brown v. Board of Education,* in a brief for which

---

Broek proved that the meaning of Section One must be sought in the pre-1865 period as well as later, and that the evidence of 1866–1868 must be read in the light of a received tradition of abolitionist argument." *Judgments: Essays in American Constitutional History* 70 (1972). See also Thomas Grey, infra Chapter 21 at note 74.

4. Graham 155–156.

5. Id. 543.

6. "That this antislavery constitutional theory was extremely heterodox is clear. It was not primarily the product of minds trained in vigorous case analysis or statutory construction. It confused moral with civil and constitutional rights. It made the Declaration of Independence the basic constitutional document . . . the Federal Bill of Rights a *source* rather than a *limitation* of federal power." Id. 237–238.

Kelly takes responsibility, and in which Graham collaborated.[7] TenBroek plaintively comments that "it is little short of remarkable that the Chief Justice should have cut himself off from these historical origins and purposes, casually announcing, as he did, that 'at best, they are inconclusive.' "[8] It is more than a little remarkable, it is astounding! Here was a Court that had invited briefs on the "original understanding";[9] doubtless it would have rejoiced to base its decision thereon, yet it preferred "political and judicial ethics, social psychology," to their abolitionist history.[10] Such renunciation by a Court eager to believe suggests a large doubt about the soundness of that history.

Let us begin with Bingham, author of §1 and alleged conduit of abolitionist theology.[11] He inflicted a gaping wound on the conduit theory when he stated, in reply to Rogers, that "the courts have settled [the meaning of due process] long ago."[12] Graham himself wrote that due process "at this time, with a few striking [but uninfluential] exceptions [was] merely a limitation upon procedure."[13] To attribute to Bingham an intention to embody substantive due process in §1, in the face of this statement, it is necessary to charge him with a purpose to conceal his real intention; for if he harbored such an intention, he never re-

7. Kelly, Fourteenth 1049; Graham 268–269.

8. TenBroek 25.

9. Bickel 6.

10. Graham 269. Kelly says of the Court's reaction to his brief, "Equipped with an impressive mass of historical evidence [which he himself stated "doctor[ed] all the evidence to the contrary, either by suppressing it . . . or by distorting it . . .] . . . the Court reneged." "As though in embarrassment," the Court "rejected history in favor of sociology." Kelly, "Clio and the Court: An Illicit Love Affair," 1965 S. Ct. Rev. 119, 144. The Court's "embarrassment," I suggest, arose from a hard-headed appraisal of the neo-abolitionist theology. It also had before it Bickel's "impressive" compilation to the contrary. Supra Chapter 7 at note 3.

11. Supra Chapter 11 at note 9.

12. *Globe* 1089.

13. Graham 35, 244; see supra Chapter 11 at notes 4–27. For the "exceptions" see infra Chapter 14 at notes 28–35.

vealed it to the 39th Congress. What boots it that Bingham stated in the House, in January 1857, that "absolute equality of all" is a "principle of our Constitution"[14] when he took a firm stand against Negro suffrage in 1866? What matters it that his Ohio district "had been thoroughly abolitionized by the anti-slavery evangelists in 1835–1837";[15] when Ohio remained a hotbed of Negrophobia; when its Senator Sherman could say in the Senate in 1867, "we do not like Negroes. We do not conceal our dislike";[16] when the Radical George W. Julian of neighboring Indiana could tell the House in 1866, "the real trouble is that *we hate the negro*"?[17] What matters it that "antislavery idealists were backing judicial assault upon segregated schools" when not long before the Civil War they were rebuffed by the Supreme Courts of Massachusetts and Ohio;[18] when Bingham could acknowledge in the 39th Congress that the Ohio Constitution excluded Negroes from voting;[19] when fellow Republican Columbus Delano shrank from the idea of allowing Negroes to serve as jurors;[20] when "many" Northern newspapers, among them the Cincinnati *Commercial*, were opposed to "equality with the Negroes"?[21]

Bingham's early moral fervor had been diluted by political realities. David Donald states that he "was fully aware that his Ohio district could easily go Democratic, since his own average vote in the elections from 1862 through 1870 was only 50.6 per cent of the total. Bitterly he protested against Radical proposals

14. Kelly, Fourteenth 1052.

15. Graham 280.

16. Woodward, "Seeds of Failure in Radical Race Policy," in *New Frontiers of the American Reconstruction* 128 (H. M. Hyman ed. 1966).

17. *Globe* 257. "Negrophobia tended to hold even the sparse Reconstruction institutions that the nation created at low throttle, and played a part in Reconstruction incompleteness." H. M. Hyman, *A More Perfect Union* 447 (1973).

18. Kelly, Fourteenth 1056.

19. *Globe* 1291.

20. Supra Chapter 9 at note 25.

21. Flack 41; see also Donald, *Sumner II* 158.

for 'universal suffrage,' "[22] as is exemplified by his barbed dia-
logue with Boutwell over the admission of Tennessee sans
Negro suffrage.[23] His political instinct did not betray him, for in
the April 1867 elections "Ohio overwhelmed a negro suffrage
amendment by 40,000."[24] Bingham's change of heart illustrates
Russell Nye's pithy summation: after 1865 the "Negro was no
longer a problem in morality, but a problem in politics."[25] The
"chief trouble no doubt," said Senator Sherman, after the 1867
defeat of the Republican forces in Ohio, is the Negro "suffrage
question . . . it will be a burden in every election."[26] To attribute to this selfsame Ohio an intention to embody in §1 through
the medium of Bingham's "vague" phraseology the very suffrage it resoundingly rejected borders on the absurd.

Abolitionist evangelism led Graham and tenBroek to overlook the deep-seated Northern Negrophobia and the fact, noted
by C. Vann Woodward, that during the war years "the great
majority of citizens in the North still abhorred any association

---

22. David Donald, *The Politics of Reconstruction* 46 (1965). Senator Hendricks of Indiana pointed out that "Indiana and Illinois almost continuously
were Democratic States," that in Ohio the Democratic party "for half the time
had maintained an ascendancy," that for many years it controlled Pennsylvania, and was and is a "mighty power" in New York. *Globe* 368.

23. Supra Chapter 5 at notes 43–44.

24. Supra Chapter 4 at note 36. Michael L. Benedict, who made a "scale"
study of voting patterns, concluded that Bingham "led the Republican nonradicals in the House." *A Compromise of Principle* 36 (1975). Bingham's Ohio colleague, Finck, declared on December 21, 1865, that "while I have no ill feeling
toward the negro, I shall ever oppose conferring upon him the right of suffrage in Ohio." *Globe* 118.

25. "Comment on C. V. Woodward's Paper" 148, 152, in Hyman ed.,
supra note 16. Benedict states, "the Republican committee members had eschewed ideology in favor of practicality." Supra note 24 at 182. William Lloyd
Garrison "accurately sensed the new mood when he declared that antislavery
societies served no useful purpose now that slavery was abolished and closed
down the *Liberator*." Donald, *Sumner II* 233.

26. Benedict, supra note 24 at 273.

with abolitionists"[27]—hardly fertile soil for the sowing of abolitionist ideology. Senators Fessenden and Grimes, leading Republicans, held "the extreme radicals" in "abhorrence."[28] Senator Cowan, a Pennsylvania conservative Republican, ridiculed
the notion that the "antipathy that never sleeps, that never dies,
that is inborn, down at the very foundation of our natures," is
"to be swept away by half a dozen debates and the reading of
half a dozen reports from certain abolitionist societies." He bitterly excoriated the Anti-Slavery Society.[29] To the Moderate
leaders the radical leadership was a heavy cross. Many Republicans, reports his biographer, "hated" Stevens. In the Joint
Committee, "his own measures were more voted against than
voted for."[30] Senator Stewart referred to his "destructive senti-

27. *The Burden of Southern History* 73 (1960). Justice Miller, whose "antipa-
thy to slavery" led him to leave Kentucky, wrote in 1854, "An abolitionist has
been my abhorrence all my life." Charles Fairman, *Mr. Justice Miller and the
Supreme Court* 16–17, 27 (1939). Writing to Harold Laski, October 24, 1930,
Justice Holmes stated, "I came to loathe in the abolitionists the conviction that
any one who did not agree with them was a knave or a fool." 2 *Holmes-Laski
Letters: The Correspondence of Mr. Justice Holmes and Harold J. Laski* 1291
(M. Howe ed. 1953). See also supra Chapter 1 note 35a.

28. Kendrick 257. Consider Graham's "the drafters of [§1] . . . Bingham,
Stevens . . . Fessenden . . . were men who in their youth and early man-
hood are known to have been thoroughly exposed to this doctrinal [aboli-
tionist] system," Graham 250, in light of Fessenden's "abhorrence" of
"extreme radicals," Bingham's attack upon "oppressive" invasions of States
rights. For Stevens, see infra at notes 30, 35. Of this aspect of Graham's argument, one may borrow his own criticism of "anachronistic thinking" that
takes "simple patterns of favorable circumstance as evidence of *much more
than that.*" Graham 453 (emphasis added). He himself undercuts the neoabolitionist theory when he states with reference to due process and equal protection, "the early antislavery usage and the racial-humanitarian expansion
and coverage before the Civil War had got forgotten and eclipsed during
Reconstruction." Graham 264.

29. *Globe* 343, 344–345.

30. Fawn Brodie, *Thaddeus Stevens: Scourge of the South* 259, 268 (1959).
Compare this with Kelly's statement, "the Joint Committee was firmly under
the control of the Republican Radicals, several of whom, including John A.

ments."[31] Fessenden gleefully reported a tongue-lashing he gave Sumner on the Senate floor, whom he considered "by far the greatest fool of the lot."[32] Consider Senator Trumbull's scathing comment in 1870: "it has been over the idiosyncracies, over the unreasonable propositions, over the impractical measures of . . . [Sumner] that freedom has been proclaimed and established."[33] "More and more Senators came to distrust," David Donald tells us, "when they did not detest him."[34] Stevens excoriated Sumner for halting the Amendment because it did not give Negroes the vote.[35] Between such men there could be no secret protocols that "vague and amorphous" phrases would leave room for what had been rejected.[36]

The Graham-tenBroek theory requires us to believe that a Negrophobic, anti-abolitionist North was ready to embrace the abolitionist program or that the radicals were in a position to dictate the form of the legislation. Indeed, Kelly stated categorically that after the Civil War "a group of old antislavery enthu-

---

Bingham and Thaddeus Stevens, had been prominently associated with the radical pre-war antislavery movement." Kelly, Fourteenth 1057. "In fact," Donald states, "the Radical wing of the Republican party had rarely exercised effective control." Donald, *Sumner II* 450. TenBroek, 149, states, "Radical control of Congress hung in a precarious and fluctuating balance." See also Benedict, supra note 24.

31. *Globe* 1106.

32. James 74; Eric L. McKitrick, *Andrew Johnson and Reconstruction* 272 (1960).

33. Benedict, supra note 24 at 39.

34. *Sumner II* 248.

35. Id. Brodie, supra note 30 at 269; *Globe* 2459; cf. id. 1224–1231. Sumner, his biographer remarks, "had gravely objected" to the Fourteenth Amendment, Donald, *Sumner II* 9, presumably because it did not accomplish his abolitionist goals.

36. Kelly, Fourteenth 1071. Kelly states, "the principal Radical leaders concerned with the amendment, notably Bingham, Stevens, Morrill, Fessenden and Howard deliberately sought to go far beyond the guarantees of the Civil Rights Act and to place all civil rights, in the expansive Bingham definition, under federal guarantees of equality against state law." Id.

siasts [were] in a position to control the Thirty-Ninth Congress and to write their radical reformism into the Constitution itself."[37] That is at a long remove from the facts. Among the first to discern that underlying political realities called on most Northern Republicans, except for a few Radicals with secure constituencies, to pursue a Moderate course was David Donald: "Moderates had to check extreme Radical proposals or be defeated in the districts they represented"; the "thirty-two Republicans . . . who formed the Moderate faction" were "constantly aware of the need to conciliate the Democrats among their constituents; they were loath to consider imposing . . . Negro suffrage . . . upon the South."[38] Such a one, we have seen, was Bingham. In a recent attempt at more refined "scale" analysis, Michael L. Benedict has classified the Republicans as Conservatives, Moderates (Centrists), and radicals (with a small r). The radicals, he concluded, "did not dominate Congress during the Reconstruction era. More Republican Senators (scaled) consistently conservative than radical"; in the House "consistent nonradicals (Conservatives and Centrists) still outnumbered radicals."[39] One has only to recall that Charles Sumner was not made a member of the Joint Committee and all but excluded from party councils, virtually ostracized,[40] that Stevens regretfully accepted legislation which confessedly fell short of his goals, that Negro suffrage was rejected over Sumner's plea that it was the "Central Guarantee," to realize that Benedict speaks truly. The converse of the fact that the "radicals did not dominate" is that the Conservative-Moderate coalition did.[41] In the

---

37. Id. 1054.

38. Donald, supra note 22 at 51–52, 61; cf. McKitrick, supra note 32 at 300; see also Benedict, supra note 24 at 56–57.

39. Benedict, supra note 24 at 27, 23; see Donald, quoted supra note 30.

40. Donald, *Sumner II* 149–150, 240, 241, 247–248.

41. "Senate Reconstruction policy after 1865 was framed by a non-radical Joint Committee on Reconstruction and a conservative Judiciary Committee." Benedict, supra note 24 at 37; see id. 29, 146–147; cf. Donald, *Sumner II* 149–150. And see Morton Keller, *Affairs of State* 61 (1977).

Senate a handful of radicals opposed the Fourteenth Amendment, evidence that it did not give effect to their wishes.[42] The New York *Herald* remarked that the Amendment "is not the platform of Thaddeus Stevens, Sumner, or any of the noisy radicals in Congress. They can do nothing. It was adopted against all their remonstrances and in spite of their threats."[43] Senator Sherman told a Cincinnati audience in September 1866, while the Amendment was being submitted for ratification, "They talk about radicals; why we defeated every radical proposition in it."[44] Upon the basis of his own studies, Benedict concluded

---

Kelly, Fourteenth 1057, states that "the Joint Committee was firmly under the control of Radical Republicans," but Benedict, on the basis of closer analysis, concluded that the "non-radicals clearly outnumbered the radicals." Supra note 24 at 34, 37. Benedict states that "The centrists' work centered on two committees: Fessenden's Joint Committee on Reconstruction and Trumbull's Senate Judiciary Committee. Between them they fashioned the conservative Reconstruction program of the 39th Congress." Benedict, id. 146–147. Kelly's statement, as well as Graham's, that "Ten members of the Joint Committee . . . are known to have grown up in states which were exposed for years to antislavery theory," Graham 313, is vitiated by the fact that the entire committee signed the report, explaining suffrage was unacceptable. Supra Chapter 5 at note 49.

42. Cf. Donald, *Sumner II* 247–248.

43. *New York Herald,* September 28, 1866, quoted in Benedict, supra note 24 at 198. The *New York Herald,* June 11, 1866, hailed the Amendment as "an ingeniously contrived party platform for the coming fall elections . . . There is nothing here obnoxious to public opinion in the way of negro suffrage." Quoted in Kendrick 352. "The victories Republicans won in 1866," Benedict states, "had demonstrated popular support not for the Radical Republican program but for that of the conservatives and centrists." Benedict, id. at 257; see id. 182, 188. Bingham stated that in the 1866 elections the Amendment was "directly in issue . . . from Maine to California." James 167.

Criticizing the cries of a "white man's government," Stevens said, "I trust the Republican party will not be alarmed at what I am saying. I do not profess to speak their sentiments, nor must they be held responsible for them. I speak for myself." *Globe* 74.

44. James 167. James states it was a "rather consistent practice . . . to disavow all Radical influence in the framing of the congressional proposal." Id. Compare Sherman with Kelly's statement, "The mood of the Radicals was

that "the nonradicals had enacted their program with the sullen acquiescence of some radicals and over the opposition of many."[45] What sustenance does this offer for the embodiment of abolitionist ideology in the Fourteenth Amendment?

To Alfred Kelly, "The debates on the passage of the Amendment reveal clearly enough how completely the constitutional ideology of the pre-war antislavery movement shaped the objectives of the Radical Republicans."[46] To my mind, the debates show that—apart from a handful of extremist radicals and the Democratic opposition, which at every turn sought to besmirch the Republicans with advocacy of all-embracing Negro equality—the Moderate-Conservative coalition steadily adhered to limited objectives: protection of the "person and property" of the Negro against violence and oppression. The means of this protection were carefully specified in the Civil Rights Bill and Congress was repeatedly told that so-called political rights like suffrage, mixed schools, and jury participation were outside the coverage of the Bill. Again and again Congress was told that the Amendment was designed to embody the Civil Rights Act.

A number of questions call for answers by the neoabolitionists. Negro suffrage manifestly was excluded both from the Act and the Amendment. What does this exclusion of Sumner's "Central Guarantee" do to the Graham-tenBroek theory? Why did the Republican majority leave open the door to more abrasive privileges, for example, mixed schools, when they so plainly barred it to suffrage? Why did Chairman Fessenden point out that "existing prejudices" foreclosed "an entire exclusion of all class distinctions"[47] in the Civil Rights Bill, then

not one of caution and restraint; on the contrary it was 'revolutionary' . . . It is important to understand it, for both the Civil Rights Act of 1866 and the Fourteenth Amendment were products of it." Kelly, Fourteenth 1060–1061.

45. Benedict, supra note 24 at 210. Chairman Fessenden "was unwilling to allow the process of reconstruction to be controlled by the radicals." Kendrick 174.

46. Kelly, Fourteenth 1054.

47. *Globe* 705; for a similar remark by Stevens, see id. 537.

abruptly embrace that very exclusion in the neoabolitionist version of §1? What caused the Republican majority, who had so firmly pushed through the restricted Civil Rights Bill, suddenly to abandon it in favor of an unrestricted Amendment? Why did "radical control" of the 39th Congress fail in the former and prevail in the latter? Why did Bingham, who objected to "civil rights" as "oppressive" and an encroachment on States' Rights lend himself to abolitionist ideology in drafting §1? It cannot be attributed to a sudden change in the climate of opinion, because Senator Wilson, the Massachusetts Radical, stated in the Senate in January 1869: "There is not today a square mile in the United States where the advocacy of the equal rights and privileges of those colored men has not been in the past and is not now unpopular."[48]

A word about the allegedly "vague and amorphous" nature of the terms used in §1, and Kelly's summation:

> The intent of certain Radical leaders to go beyond the restrictive enumeration of the Civil Rights Act and to incorporate a series of expansive guarantees in the Constitution is quite clear. In a general sense, the *best evidence* of this is the language of the guarantees which Bingham and the other authors of the Fourteenth Amendment incorporated in the first section. The guarantees they finally adopted—privileges and immunities, due process and equal protection—were not at all derived from the Civil Rights Act, which, with the exception of one vague phrase in its final form, had used the restrictive enumerative device. Instead the authors derived their guarantees deliberately from the prewar Radical antislavery movement.[49]

48. *Cong. Globe,* 40th Cong., 3d Sess. 672. Russell Nye states, "Neither the anti-slavery controversy, nor the Civil War, nor the inconclusive maneuvering of Reconstruction made any basic changes in the prevailing attitudes towards race . . . attributes clearly reflected in the congressional politics of Reconstruction." Nye, supra note 25 at 156.

49. Kelly, Fourteenth 1071 (emphasis added).

It would be more accurate to say, as Bingham in fact indicated in submitting the Amendment, that two of the clauses—"due process" and "privileges or immunities"—were drawn from the Constitution,[50] and under established canons of construction they were to be given their accepted meaning. Bingham himself stated that "due process" was used in its customary decisional, that is, procedural, sense. The meaning of "privileges and immunities" had been drawn to the attention of the framers by Chairman Trumbull, who showed that it paralleled—with the careful exclusion of suffrage—the gloss put upon it by the cases. These meanings are hardly to be overcome by an "inchoate" meaning favored by some abolitionists and which was never explained to the framers. There is also the fact, as Kelly notes, that §1 was presented as "intended merely to constitutionalize the Civil Rights Act." It does not dispose of these representations to say that they were made for strategic political reasons;[51] in the securities field such representations would be branded as deceptive and misleading.

Remains "equal protection of the laws." The central preoccupation of the framers was the oppression of Negroes under Black Codes and similar discriminatory *laws*. "Equal protection of the laws" perfectly expressed their purpose to halt such discrimination; and the "laws" were such as gave rise to the evils the framers meant to prevent. They did *not* mean to prevent exclusion from suffrage, segregated schools, or miscegenation laws. For this there is evidence in the debates on the Civil Rights Bill. Where is the evidence of a change of purpose? In the case of suffrage, the intention to leave State control of suffrage untouched is plain. It will not do in the face of such facts to infer

50. Id. 1072.

51. Id. 1071. Kelly states that had the Radicals pressed home the proposition that "their amendment would undoubtedly consummate the destruction of caste and class legislation in the states, an important element of moderate Republican support might be alienated . . . Political strategy called for ambiguity, not clarity." Id. 1084. For discussion of this remarkable interpretive approach, see supra Chapter 6.

a "clear intent . . . to go beyond the restrictive enumeration of the Civil Rights Act."

In justice to Kelly, it should be noted that a decade after publication of his article on the Fourteenth Amendment, and under the impact of an "extraordinary revolution in the historiography of Civil War Reconstruction," he tacitly abandoned his earlier analysis.[52] Now he adverted to

> the limitation imposed by the essentially federal character of the American constitutional system, which at last made it *impossible* to set up a comprehensive and *unlimited* program for the integration of the negro into the southern social order. Such a program could have been effected only by a revolutionary destruction of the states and the substitution of a unitary constitutional system . . . [T]he commitment to traditional state-federal relations meant that the radical *Negro reform* program could be *only a very limited one.*[53]

Even less than integration in the South were whites prepared for reconstruction of their institutions to accommodate total Negro integration in the North. It needed no revolution in historiography to learn that the framers were strongly attached to State sovereignty, that they had "a very limited" program in mind, as was heavily stressed during the debates on the Civil Rights Bill. Fessenden made that plain when he stated that "existing prejudices" barred "an entire exclusion of all class dis-

52. Kelly, "Comment on Harold M. Hyman's Paper" 40, in Hyman ed., supra note 16. That tacit recantation, published in a sheaf of Reconstruction essays by others, would escape the notice of legal scholars accustomed to search for criticism of the earlier law review article in legal indices.

53. Id. 55 (emphasis added). Benedict comments that "the proposed amendment again demonstrated Republicans' reluctance to expand the national government's jurisdiction over its citizens." Supra note 24 at 170. See also Hyman, supra note 17 at 304, 425, 426, 439, 440, 522–523. The idealistic Graham revealingly states, "The flaws and loopholes . . . were products of a Reconstruction society still willing and able to sacrifice the slave race, to defer protection during the Reconstruction crisis." Graham 297.

tinctions.''[54] A lawyer not committed to the revisionist or any other school, and who holds no brief for "lawyer's history," may be permitted to say that all that was needed was some familiarity with established rules for the interpretation of legislative history, among them to discount heavily oppositionist obstructionism, to read the terms "natural rights" and "fundamental rights" as they had been understood from Blackstone through Kent, as they, so explained Trumbull, were embodied in the Civil Rights Bill, to indulge in something like a presumption that the powers reserved to the States are not diminished by a subsequent amendment in the absence of a clear intention to do so. And above all, to substitute undiluted realism in the appraisal of what happened in 1866 for twentieth-century idealistic fervor, which all too often leads to wishful thinking.[55]

Against this background it is now possible to measure Chief Justice Warren's statement in *Brown v. Board of Education* that the historical evidence is "inconclusive":[56]

The *most avid* proponents of the post-War amendments undoubtedly intended them to remove all legal distinctions

54. Supra at note 47. Senator Doolittle of Wisconsin, who favored Negro suffrage, recognized that it could not "be imposed upon the [Northern] States." *Globe* 2143; see supra Chapter 4 at notes 28–33. Desegregation of schools was even more unpalatable.

55. In a tacit reference to the neoabolitionist writings, Fairman stated, "some of the studies go to historical origins and through their reinterpretation, report the discovery of high moral purposes which, though lost awhile, are now offered as authentic. In some of these works of great good will it seems as though the fervor to hasten justice now has, however unwittingly, been given ascendancy over devotion to cold truth." *History* 1117.

56. Miller and Howell consider it "rather doubtful that the historical record is so 'inconclusive' as Chief Justice Warren asserted in Brown v. Board of Education . . . , insofar as the framers of the fourteenth amendment had any intent regarding racially segregated schools." "The Myth of Neutrality in Constitutional Adjudication," 27 U. Chi. L. Rev. 661, 674 note 48 (1960). See also Thomas Grey, "Do We Have An Unwritten Constitution?," 27 Stan. L. Rev. 703, 712 (1975).

among "all persons born or naturalized in the United States."
Their opponents just as certainly were antagonistic to both the
letter and spirit of the Amendments and wished them to have the
most limited effect. What others in Congress and in the state
legislatures had in mind cannot be determined with any degree
of certainty.[57]

This sets up an irrelevant antithesis—between the Democrats
and "the most avid proponents," the extremist radicals—neither
of whom really influenced the outcome. In fact, Democrats often
voted with a leading extremist, Sumner, in order "to kill moderate reconstruction proposals."[58] What "others," the decisive
Conservative-Moderate coalition, "had in mind" can be determined with considerable "certainty." Chairman Wilson, for example, stated that the terms "civil rights and immunities" in
the Civil Rights Bill did not mean that all "children shall attend
the same schools," and the evidence demonstrates that he spoke
for the framers.[59] On the score of Negro suffrage, the proof that
it was deliberately left to the States is indeed "overwhelming."
Warren's summation, therefore, hardly does justice to the facts;
but it was merely window-dressing for the rationale of his
opinion:

> we cannot turn back the clock to 1868 when the Amendment
> was adopted . . . We must consider public education in the

57. 347 U.S. 483, 489 (1954) (emphasis added).

58. Donald, *Sumner II* 248. As Senator Yates of Illinois observed, "If we do
not meet the views of the Radicals on the one hand, nor the views of the
pro-slavery Democracy upon the other, we at all events have the medium, the
moderation which has been agreed upon." *Globe* 3038. See supra at note 42.

59. Supra Chapter 2 at note 26; Chapter 6. One of the distinguished lawyers
of our generation, Dean Acheson, testified before the Senate in 1971 that "The
most complicated thing in the world, race relations, came out of the judges,
who took over this problem and found in a phrase, the equal protection of the
laws, the way to deal with this complicated question, which didn't deal with
it." *Hearings on Executive Privilege before the Senate Subcommittee on the Separation of Powers* 266, 92d Cong., 1st Sess. (July 1971).

light of its full development and its present place in American life throughout the Nation. Only in this way can it be determined if segregation in public schools deprives plaintiffs of the equal protection of the laws.[60]

Stated baldly, what the framers meant by the words they employed is not binding on the Court; the Court lays claim to power to revise the Constitution to meet present needs. A celebrant of the Warren Court, Paul Murphy, commented that *Brown* disclosed Chief Justice Warren's "unabashed and primary commitment to justice and his willingness to shape the law to achieve it."[61] He did not merely "shape" the law, he upended it; he revised the Fourteenth Amendment to mean exactly the opposite of what its framers designed it to mean, namely, to leave suffrage and segregation beyond federal control, to leave it with the States, where control over internal, domestic matters resided from the beginning.

60. 347 U.S. at 492–493. See infra Chapter 15 note 11.
61. *The Constitution in Crisis Times* 312 (1972).

Part II

14

From Natural Law to Libertarian Due Process

SUBSTANTIVE ECONOMIC DUE PROCESS

THE development of substantive due process was described by Robert G. McCloskey, a friend of the Court, as "the classic example of 'government by judiciary.'"[1] So accustomed are we grown to this development—whereby courts substitute their own views of policy for those of legislative bodies—that one recalls with a start that the doctrine was only launched in the late nineteenth century.[2]

The shift from judicial supervision of procedure *in the courts* to control of *legislative* policymaking constitutes a truly extraordinary transformation. For judicial review was conceived in narrow terms—as a means of policing the constitutional boundaries, the "limits" of a given power. Little did the Framers dream that the judicial power would be construed as a li-

---

1. *The American Supreme Court* 132 (1960). "'Government by Judiciary,' is no idle phrase." A. T. Mason and W. M. Beaney, *American Constitutional Law* 21 (1954).

2. See Walton Hamilton, "The Path of Due Process of Law" in *The Constitution Reconsidered* 167 (C. Read ed. 1938); Charles G. Haines, *The Revival of Natural Law Concepts* 104–165 (1930). In Adamson v. California, 332 U.S. 46, 79 (1947), Justice Black said of an 1890 case that it "gave a new and hitherto undiscovered scope for the Court's use of the due process clause to protect property rights under natural law concepts."

cense to supersede the exercise of power by the other branches within those boundaries.[3] In fact, judicial participation in legislative policymaking was unmistakably excluded.[4] Under the guise of substantive due process, therefore, the Court has invaded the exclusive jurisdiction of a sister branch; it has violated the injunction of the separation of powers, made explicit in the 1780 Massachusetts Constitution, that "the judiciary shall never exercise the legislative power."[5] And it has encroached on the sovereignty reserved to the States by the Tenth Amendment. It has done this in the name of a self-created doctrine to legitimate the exercise of power once rationalized under the garb of natural law.[6] But neither the Framers of the Constitution nor of the Fourteenth Amendment entertained such notions.

It is axiomatic that all wielders of power, judges included, ever thirst for more.[7] This appetite for extraconstitutional

3. Judicial review "should be confined to occasions when the statute or order was outside the grant of power to the grantee, and should not include a review of how the power has been exercised." Learned Hand, *The Bill of Rights* 66 (1962); for confirmatory materials, see infra Chapter 16 at notes 20–26. Madison stated that none of the departments "ought to possess, directly or indirectly, an overruling influence over the others in the administration of their respective powers." Federalist No. 48 at 321. See infra note 5. "The judicial cannot prescribe to the legislative department of the government limitations upon the exercise of its acknowledged powers." Veazie Bank v. Fenno, 75 U.S. (8 Wall.) 533, 548 (1869).

4. Infra Chapter 16.

5. Article XXX provided that "the legislative department shall never exercise the executive and judicial powers . . . the executive shall never exercise the legislative and judicial powers . . . the judicial shall never exercise the legislative and executive powers." 1 Poore 960. For the same utterance by Madison, see 1 *Annals of Congress* 435–436.

6. The "modern definition of 'due process' is merely the 'natural justice' . . . under a new name." J. A. C. Grant, "The Natural Law Background of Due Process," 31 Colum. L. Rev. 56, 65 (1931); Haines, supra note 2 at 305, 101, 103; Graham 239. Justice Black referred to the "'natural law due process notion' by which this Court frees itself from the limits of a written Constitution." In re Winship, 397 U.S. 358, 381 (1970).

7. Madison stated,' "It will not be denied, that power is of an encroaching

power found classical expression in Justice Samuel Chase's opinion in *Calder v. Bull* (1798). Taking off from an hypothetical horrible—"a law that takes property from *A* and gives it to *B*"—Chase declared that even in the absence of express restraint by the Constitution, "it is against all reason and justice, for a people to entrust a Legislature with such powers . . . the general principles of law and reason" forbid such acts.[8] His appeal to extraconstitutional power was flatly rejected by Justice James Iredell, whose cogent advocacy of judicial review had anticipated that of Hamilton.[9] True, "some speculative jurists," Iredell noted, had stated that "a legislative act against natural justice must, in itself, be void"; but, given a "constitution which imposed no limits on the legislative power . . . whatever the legislative power chose to enact would be lawfully enacted, and the judicial power would never interpose to declare it void."[10] Reflecting David Hume,[11] he said that "the ideas of natural justice are regulated by no fixed standard: the ablest and purest men have differed upon the subject."[12] Natural law therefore differed little from the "mandate from heaven" of a Chinese emperor, which was "so vague that emperors could readily

---

nature, and that it ought to be effectually restrained from passing the limits assigned to it." Federalist No. 48 at 321. One of the ablest of Justices, William Johnson, remarked on "the necessity of watching the advancement of judicial power, in common with all power." Ramsay v. Allegre, 25 U.S. (12 Wheat.) 611, 616 (1827), concurring opinion. Justice Frankfurter commented that "Judicial power is not immune against this human weakness." Trop v. Dulles, 356 U.S. 86, 119 (1958), dissenting opinion. See also infra Chapter 15 at note 37.

8. 3 U.S. (3 Dall.) 386, 388 (1798).

9. Raoul Berger, *Congress v. The Supreme Court* 82–83 (1969).

10. 3 U.S. at 398.

11. "The word natural is commonly taken in so many senses, and is of so loose a signification, that it seems vain to dispute whether justice be natural or not." Quoted in Robert M. Cover, *Justice Accused: Antislavery and the Judicial Process* 23 (1975).

12. 3 U.S. at 398.

identify their own will with the will of heaven."[13] Dean Pound
justly characterized it as "purely personal and arbitrary."[14]

Iredell, not Chase, represented the received opinion. The
Founders were deeply committed to positivism, as is attested by
their resort to written constitutions—positive law. Adams, Jefferson, Wilson, Madison, and Hamilton, states Robert Cover,
"were seldom, if ever, guilty of confusing law with natural
right." For them a constitution represented the will of the people "that would determine explicit . . . allocations of power
and its corresponding limits." Chase's notion, to borrow from
Cover, "that out beyond [a constitution] lay a higher law,"[15]
departed from the Founders' commitment to written limits on
all power. That commitment sprang from an omnipresent
dread of the greedy expansiveness of power, graphically expressed by Jefferson: "It is jealousy and not confidence which
prescribes limited constitutions to bind down those whom we
are obliged to trust with power . . . In questions of power,
then, let no more be heard of confidence in man, but bind him
down from mischief by the chains of the Constitution."[16]

13. Herbert Muller, *Uses of the Past* 350 (1952).

14. Roscoe Pound, "Common Law and Legislation," 21 Harv. L. Rev. 383,
393 (1908).

15. Cover, supra note 11 at 29. Cover comments that this "was never a part
of the mainstream of American jurisprudence." Id. John Adams and his
compeers "used nature to take the measure of law [e.g. "fundamental
rights"] . . . but not as a source for rules of decision." Id. 27. But see Haines,
supra note 2 at 52–55. Morton Horwitz states that post-Revolution Americans
regarded written constitutions as embodying the " 'will' of the people," and
"tended to assert the ultimate primacy of the legislature and of statute law,"
with the result "that the original natural law foundation of common law rules
began to disintegrate." There was a vigorous demand for codification because
" 'the very nature of the constitution requires the judge to follow the letter of
the law.' " "The Emergence of an Instrumental Conception of American Law,
1780–1820," in 5 *Perspectives in American History* 287, 309–310 (1971). My
reasons for concluding that the Founders clung to a "fixed Constitution," to
positive, not natural, law, are set forth infra Chapter 21 at note 88 to the end.

16. 4 Elliot 543. In the Virginia Ratification Convention, Francis Corbin
stated, "Liberty is secured, sir, by the limitation of its [the government's]

Cover's view may seem to be contradicted by Chief Justice Marshall's reference to natural law in *Fletcher v. Peck*,[17] but Marshall's allegiance to the doctrine is debatable. Justice Frankfurter considered his occasional references to natural law "not much more than mere literary garniture . . . and not a guiding means for adjudication."[18] Let the contrary be assumed,[19] and the Marshall view must yet yield to the Founders' ceaseless emphasis on a federal government of "limited" powers,[20] to the deep distrust of a federal judicial system.[21] Incorporation of natural law as a basic presupposition would set at naught the Framers' efforts to temper federal judicial control over the States. And the ongoing debate about the legitimacy of judicial review itself[22] counsels against adoption of the most extreme view of the power—one infinitely expansible by calling on "higher law"; for, as Lord Camden stated, "One should naturally expect that the law to warrant it should be clear in proportion as the power is exorbitant."[23] On this score, finally, when *M'Culloch v. Maryland* came under attack nine years later, Marshall

---

powers, which are clearly and unequivocally defined." 3 Elliot 110. In the First Congress, James Jackson said: "we must confine ourselves to the powers described in the constitution, and the moment we pass it, we take an arbitrary stride towards a despotic Government." 1 *Annals of Congress* 489. See also infra Chapter 15 note 19. For additional citations to the Founders, see Berger, supra note 9 at 13–14.

17. 10 U.S. (6 Cranch) 87, 135–136 (1810). This was echoed by Chancellor Kent in Gardner v. Newburgh, 2 Johns. Ch. 162, 166–167 (N.Y. 1816). But as H. S. Commager remarked, "the impressive thing is the paucity of such occasions in the first half a century of our history." "Constitutional History and the Higher Law," in *The Constitution Reconsidered* 225 (C. Read ed. 1938).

18. "John Marshall and the Judicial Function," 69 Harv. L. Rev. 217, 225 (1955); see also infra Chapter 21 at notes 12–28.

19. See G. E. White, *The American Judicial Tradition* 18, 26 (1976).

20. Berger, supra note 9 at 13–16.

21. National Ins. Co. v. Tidewater Co., 337 U.S. 582, 647 (1949), Frankfurter, J., dissenting opinion; see also Berger, supra note 9 at 260–264.

22. See infra Chapter 19 at note 16.

23. Entick v. Carrington, 19 How. St. Tr. 1029, 1065–1066 (1765).

repeatedly and emphatically disclaimed any intimation that constitutional powers could be expanded by construction,[24] assurances that were meaningless if the result could be achieved through the medium of natural law.

The Founders' commitment to written limits on all power received powerful endorsement when a succession of judges, including Shaw, Story, and McLean, put the commands of the Fugitive Slave Act above the agonizing demands of conscience and the higher law. In a typical fugitive slave case, *Miller v. McQuerry*, Justice John McLean stated, "It is for the people . . . in making constitutions and in the enactment of laws, to consider the laws of nature . . . This is a field which judges cannot explore . . . They look to the law, and to the law only."[25] Such were also the views of Justice Story and Chief Justice Lemuel Shaw.[26]

Against this background, judges in whom Chase's yearning for extraconstitutional power survived understandably would be more comfortable with a constitutional catchphrase that "disguised individual opinions and gave them the sanction and prestige of a supreme fundamental law."[27] They found it in *Wynehamer v. The People* (1856),[28] the *locus classicus* of substan-

---

24. *John Marshall's Defense of McCulloch v. Maryland* 185, 182, 184 (G. Gunther ed. 1969), discussed infra Chapter 21 at notes 10–19.

25. 17 F. Cas. (No. 9583) 332, 339 (C.C.D. Ohio, 1853).

26. Shaw stated, "an appeal to natural rights . . . was not pertinent! It was to be decided by the Constitution . . . and by the Law of Congress . . . These were to be obeyed, however disagreeable to our natural sympathies." Account in *The Liberator*, Nov. 4, 1842, at 3, quoted in Cover, supra note 11 at 169. For Story, see Cover, id. at 171, 193. Still other cases were collected and analyzed by Cover, and he concludes that "The judiciary was superbly consistent in a wide variety of contexts in that positivist approach." Id. at 116.

Horwitz considers that "Story's theory in the *Commentaries* is a pure will theory of law, anticipating the most advanced forms of modern, secular, amoral, legal positivism." "The Conservative Tradition in the Writing of American Legal History," 17 Am. J. Legal Hist. 275, 288 (1973).

27. Graham 117.

28. 13 N.Y. 378 (1856).

tive due process. But first they too dismissed the doctrine of natural law. Justice Selden declared, "the doctrine that there exists in the judiciary some vague, loose and undefined power to annul a law, because in its judgment it is 'contrary to natural equity and justice,' is in conflict with the first principles of government and can never, I think, be maintained."[29] His associates were equally plainspoken.[30] This, however, did not exemplify a triumph of judicial self-restraint. While barring abolitionist reliance upon natural law, Corwin said, the Court fashioned substantive due process as a means of *confining* protection to vested property rights.[31] But Justice A. S. Johnson cited much the same type of horrible example that had been adduced for resort to natural law, without explaining the leap from procedural due process in a criminal trial to invalidation of a statute, content to appeal to the ostensibly discarded natural law reasoning under a new label.[32]

Wynehamer, it needs to be underscored, was a sport; it "found no place in the constitutional law that was generally recog-

---

29. Id. 430.

30. Justice Hubbard stated, "I am opposed to the judiciary . . . declaring a statute invalid upon any fanciful theory of higher law or first principles of natural rights outside the constitution." Id. 453; see also id. 390–391, 476.

31. Edward Corwin, "The Decline of Due Process Before the Civil War," 24 Harv. L. Rev. 460, 471 (1911). He stated that the court was "dismayed by the abolitionists quoting the same [natural rights] scripture to their purposes." Id. Justice Comstock referred to the "great danger in attempting to define the limits" of legislative power, and said that "danger was less apparent" in Marshall's time "than it is now, when theories, alleged to be founded in natural reason or inalienable rights but otherwise subversive of the just and necessary powers of government, attract the belief of considerable classes of men." 13 N.Y. at 391.

32. "For instance, a law that any man who, after the age of fifty years, shall continue to live, shall be punished by imprisonment or fine would be beyond the power of the legislature. It would be so, upon the ground that he cannot be deprived of life, liberty, or property without due process of law." 13 N.Y. at 420.

nized" in 1856; nor did it thereafter find acceptance.[33] When its argument was pressed on Chief Justice Ames of the Rhode Island Supreme Court in 1858, he held that the due process clause of the State constitution was not "designed to inhibit the legislature from regulating the vendibility of property" but was the "shield of *one accused of crime*,"[34] as almost all State constitutions made quite plain. Shortly thereafter, in 1866, the New York Court itself repudiated "the inconsiderate dicta of some of the judges" in *Wynehamer*.[35] Nevertheless, Justice Miller, recurring to typical natural law examples in 1874, averred, "It must be conceded that there are such rights in every free government beyond the control of the State."[36] Yet Miller himself had categorically rejected such concepts in 1869:

33. Corwin, supra note 31 at 474–475; Charles Warren, "The New 'Liberty' Under the Fourteenth Amendment," 39 Harv. L. Rev. 431, 442–445 (1926). The Supreme Court dwelled on the procedural aspect of due process in Murray's Lessee v. Hoboken Land & Improvement Co., 59 U.S. (18 How.) 272, 276–277 (1856). Although Dred Scott v. Sandford, 60 U.S. (19 How.) 393 (1857), employed substantive due process for protection of property in a slave, over a vigorous dissent by Justice Curtis, that case outraged abolitionist opinion and was roundly condemned in the 39th Congress.

34. State v. Kieran, 5 R.I. 497, 506, 507 (1858) (emphasis added). Chief Justice Ames stated, "Surely, if any clause in the constitution has a definite meaning, which should exclude all vagaries which would render courts the tyrants of the constitution, this clause . . . can claim to have, both from its history and its long received interpretation. It is no vague declaration concerning the rights of property, which can be made to mean anything and everything; but an intensely practical, and somewhat minute provision, guarding the rights of persons *accused of crime*." Id. 505. See also Charles Curtis, supra Chapter 11 at note 27.

35. Metropolitan Board of Excise v. Barrie, 34 N.Y. 657, 668 (1866).

36. Loan Association v. Topeka, 87 U.S. (20 Wall.) 655, 662 (1874). Following in the path of Iredell, Justice Clifford dissented: "Where the constitution of the State contains no prohibition upon the subject . . . neither the State nor Federal courts can declare a statute of the State void as unwise, unjust, or inexpedient . . . unless it be repugnant to the Constitution," quoting Chief Justice Marshall: "The interest, wisdom, and justice of the representative body furnish the only security in a large class of cases not regulated by any constitutional provision. [Bank v. Billings, 4 Peters 563]." 87 U.S. at 668–669.

This whole argument of the *injustice* of the law . . . and of its opposition to the spirit of the Constitution, is too abstract and intangible for application to courts of justice, and is, above all, dangerous as a ground on which to declare the legislation of Congress void by the decisions of a court. It would authorize this court to enforce theoretical views of the genius of government, or vague notions of the spirit of the Constitution and of abstract justice, by declaring void laws which did not square with those views. It substitutes our views of policy for judicial construction, an undefined code of ethics for the Constitution, and a court of justice for the natural legislature.[37]

That substitution persists now that "due process has come to be the main provision through which natural law theories were made a part of current constitutional law."[38] And it bears

37. Hepburn v. Griswold, 75 U.S. (8 Wall.) 603, 638 (1869), dissenting opinion. Compare Hamilton, infra Chapter 15 at note 43. "Justice Iredell's scorn of natural law as a limitation on state legislative power might be applied equally well to due process. Since this concept provided no 'fixed standard' all the Court could properly say in raising it as a constitutional bar was that the legislature had passed an act that in the opinions of the judges was inconsistent with abstract principles of justice." Mason and Beaney, supra note 1 at 412.

38. Haines, supra note 2 at 112; see also supra at notes 28–32. Professor Archibald Cox considers "the very persistence of such evocative, rather than sharply definitive, phrases, attests the strength of our natural law inheritance *as authority for legal change.*" *The Role of the Supreme Court in American Government* 113 (1976). He adds, "The Court's persistent resort to notions of substantive due process for almost a century attests the strength of our natural law inheritance in constitutional adjudication." Id. 113. To my mind it merely evidences unquenchable judicial thirst for extraconstitutional power, power that plainly was withheld. For recurrent criticism, see supra notes 6, 36, 37 and infra note 89; see also supra at notes 25–26; infra Chapter 21 at notes 60–63, 87–94. Cox himself has noted that the pre-1937 era "was marked by a vigorous reaction against natural law . . . There was a sense that the Justices made a mess of things when they attempted to enlarge their orbit." Cox, id. 34. That era has been repudiated in the field of economic-substantive due process by the Court itself. Infra at notes 77–78. And proponents of "natural law" must explain why the Founders, who manifestly excluded the judiciary from policymaking, who distrusted judicial discretion, even denied its exercise, could leave the barn door wide to unlimited discretion under natural law.

emphasis that until deep into the twentieth century the Court did not employ due process to succor the Negro for whose benefit the Fourteenth Amendment was framed, but rather as "a judicial weapon to strike down social legislation."[39]

The "convenient vagueness"[40] of due process is of the Court's own making. After noting the "fixed" procedural character of due process, Charles P. Curtis, who rejoiced in judicial "adaptation" of the Constitution, asked: "But who made it a large generality? Not they [the Framers]. We [the Court] did."[41] Justly did Justice Black state that "any broad unlimited power to hold laws unconstitutional because they offend what this Court conceives to be the 'conscience of our people' . . . was not given by the Framers, but rather has been bestowed on the Court by the Court."[42] It is the Court that made due process an obscurantist phrase.[43]

39. Wallace Mendelson, *Justices Black and Frankfurter: Conflict in the Court* 64 (1961); Wallace Mendelson, *The Supreme Court: Law and Discretion* 21 (1967). In 1917, a Negro leader "insisted on the powerful influence of Supreme Court decisions in snatching liberty from the hands of his race." Paludan, *A Covenant with Death* 5 (1975). See also infra Chapter 17 at notes 67–69.

"For years," Justice Douglas stated, "the Court struck down social legislation when a particular law did not fit the notions of a majority of Justices as to legislation appropriate for a free enterprise system." Poe v. Ullman, 367 U.S. 497, 517 (1961), dissenting opinion. In Ferguson v. Skrupa, 372 U.S. 726, 731 (1963), the Court itself referred to "our abandonment of the use of the 'vague contours' of the Due Process Clause to nullify laws which a majority of the Court believed to be economically unwise . . . We refuse to sit as a 'super-legislature to weigh the wisdom of legislation.'"

40. Supra Chapter 11 at note 2.

41. Curtis, supra Chapter 11 at note 27.

42. Griswold v. Connecticut, 381 U.S. 479, 520 (1965), dissenting opinion. Thereby the Court, as Robert G. McCloskey stated, was enabled "to invalidate any law that struck a majority of the members as 'arbitrary' or 'capricious.' Those wonderfully ambiguous definitions . . . permitted the judiciary to exercise or withhold [their judicial] veto in any given case, subject to no guiding principle except the judges' own sense of discretion." McCloskey, supra note 1 at 152.

43. Charles Fairman refers to "such obscurantist phrases as 'the spirit of our free institutions' [repudiated by Hamilton, infra Chapter 15 at note 46], 'funda-

Among the remarkable aspects of this transformation is that Justice Frankfurter, the apostle of "self-restraint," should so warmly have embraced its end-product:[44] "once we go beyond its strictly procedural aspects . . . [it is] precisely defined by neither history nor in terms."[45] How could it be when the Court drew substantive due process out of thin air? His revered predecessors, Justices Holmes and Brandeis, understood this full well.[46] His frequent references to the "vagueness" of due process ill fits his deference to the common law meaning of words which have a "deposit of history."[47] Whatever the scope of procedural

---

mental conceptions lying at the basis of our social compact.'" *Mr. Justice Miller and the Supreme Court 1862–1890* 3 (1939). It is a tribute to the power of ceaseless repetition that even a judge so critical of judicial activism as Justice Harlan should have stated: "the very breadth and generality of the Amendment's provision suggest that its authors did not suppose that the nation would always be limited to mid-19th century conceptions of 'liberty' and 'due process of law' but that the increasing experience and evolving conscience of the American people would add new [meanings]." Duncan v. Louisiana, 391 U.S. 145, 174–175 (1968). I find some difficulty in reconciling this with his condemnation of the "reapportionment" decisions for arguably they responded to an "evolving conscience." Compare infra Chapter 17 at note 62.

44. "The course of history," he remarked, cast responsibilities upon the Court which it would be "stultification" to evade. Rochin v. California, 342 U.S. 165, 173 (1952). See also infra at note 141.

45. Frankfurter, supra note 18 at 228–229.

46. Arguments contrary to the application of due process to "matters of substantive law" had seemed "persuasive" to Justice Brandeis. Whitney v. California, 274 U.S. 357, 373 (1927), concurring opinion. Shortly thereafter, Justice Holmes stated, "Of course the words 'due process of law,' if taken in their literal meaning have no application to this case; and while it is too late to deny that they have been given a much more extended artificial signification." Baldwin v. Missouri, 281 U.S. 586, 595 (1930). Like Brandeis, Judge Learned Hand "considered the whole concept of [substantive] due process a judicial fabrication." Kathryn Griffith, *Judge Learned Hand and the Role of the Federal Judiciary* 129 (1973).

47. Frankfurter justly stated that "a term gains technical content" by "the deposit of history"; "No changes or chances can alter the content of the verbal symbol of 'jury.'" Rochin v. California, 342 U.S. at 169–170. Indisputably the "technical content" of "due process" was purely procedural, without a trace

due process, the "deposit of history" incontrovertibly shows
that it did not comprehend a judicial veto of legislation on policy
grounds. Frankfurter acknowledged that the "vagueness" of due
process "readily lends itself to make of the Court a third chamber
with drastic veto power."[48] He wrote in 1926 that, "through its
steady expansion of the meaningless meaning of the 'due
process' clause of the Fourteenth Amendment, the Supreme
Court is putting constitutional compulsion behind the private
judgment of its members upon disputed and difficult questions
of social policy."[49] Now that he had donned the robe he apparently was satisfied that such power was safe in his hands—a
familiar and very human reaction. But he disclaimed enforcement of his own "private view rather than the consensus of
society's opinion which, for purposes of due process, is the
standard enjoined by the Constitution."[50] "What is this consensus?" George Braden asked, and showed that it bristles with
complexities in both definition and ascertainment.[51] "Essentially," Frankfurter explained, what is involved is a "judgment

---

of "substantive" historical "content," for which we need go no further than
Hamilton. See also infra Chapter 21 at note 48.

48. Supra note 18 at 229.

49. *New Republic* (1926), quoted in Philip Kurland, *Politics, the Constitution
and the Warren Court* xiv (1970).

50. Louisiana ex rel. Francis v. Resweber, 329 U.S. 459, 471 (1947), concurring opinion. But compare with Hamilton, infra Chapter 17 at note 15.

51. "The Search for Objectivity in Constitutional Law," 57 Yale L. J. 571,
584–585 (1948). Among other things, given that a Justice "knows what he is
looking for," how does he "find it? By a Gallup poll? By editorials in leading
newspapers . . . By the number of states which follow a given course?" Id.
A Frankfurter disciple, Professor Louis Jaffe, stated, "There is no sure way to
discover the conscience of the people . . . it is seldom that there is not a great
contrariety of representative voices." "Was Brandeis an Activist? The Search
for Intermediate Premises," 80 Harv. L. Rev. 986, 998 (1967). In fact, the
Court "has demanded a number of social changes which do not command
majoritarian support . . . [it] is now often declaring a rule that is unpopular." Lusky 277.

that reflects deep, even if inarticulate, feelings of our society. Judges must divine that feeling as best they can."[52] Does not repudiation of the Court's strictures against the death penalty by legislation in some thirty-odd States demonstrate that the Court is not in possession of a divining rod?[53] The overwhelmingly negative public reaction to Frankfurter's flag-salute opinion indicates that his own powers of divination were unreliable.[54] It furnished proof for his statement that "As history amply proves, the judiciary is prone to misconceive the public good by confounding private notions with constitutional requirements,"[55] and confirmed Learned Hand's belief that the judge "has no right to divination of public opinion which runs counter to its last formal expression."[56]

52. Haley v. Ohio, 332 U.S. 596, 603 (1948), concurring opinion. This is squarely opposed to Hamilton's assurance in Federalist No. 78. See infra Chapter 17 at note 15. Frankfurter also stated that a judge should "have antennae registering feeling and judgment beyond logical, let alone quantitative, proof." *Of Law and Men* 39 (Philip Elman ed. 1956), introducing a psychic quality that is itself beyond measurement, and not a little resembles the Chinese emperor's "mandate from heaven" of which he was the sole repository.

53. Furman v. Georgia, 408 U.S. 238 (1972). For a scathing critique of the decision, see Levy, *Against the Law* 389 et seq. In Gregg v. Georgia, 96 S. Ct. 2909, 2928 (1976), Justice Stewart acknowledged that "it is now evident that a large proportion of American society continues to regard [capital punishment] as an appropriate and necessary sanction," pointing to legislative enactments in "at least 35 states" in the wake of Furman "that provide for the death penalty."

54. Minersville School District v. Gobitis, 310 U.S. 586 (1940). Frankfurter utterly misconceived public opinion with respect to a compulsory flag salute in a public school. A. T. Mason, *The Supreme Court: Palladium of Freedom* 165 (1962). Even his close friend Harold Laski thought he was "wrong." J. P. Lash, *From the Diaries of Felix Frankfurter* 69–70 (1975).

55. A. F. of L. v. American Sash Co., 335 U.S. 538, 556 (1949), concurring opinion. Experience has shown, said Professor Lusky, "that the Justices are not endowed with divine insight into the needs of a society." Lusky 107.

56. L. Hand, *The Spirit of Liberty* 14 (1952).

Frankfurter's "canons of decency and fairness which express the notions of justice of English-speaking people"[57] were scornfully dismissed—paradox of paradoxes—by Justices Black and Douglas, whose record of writing *their* predilections into the Constitution will long be unsurpassed.[58] Justice Black labeled such tests the "catchwords and catchphrases invoked by judges who would strike down under the Fourteenth Amendment laws which offend their notions of natural justice."[59] To him such tests represented a claim of "unlimited power to invalidate laws";[60] for Douglas, judgment would then turn on "the idiosyncracies of the judges."[61] Lest this stamp me as a Black partisan in his running debate with Frankfurter, let me avouch Arthur Sutherland, a Frankfurter friend. He concludes that though Justice Frankfurter was "dissatisfied" with Black's position on incorporation of the Bill of Rights in the Fourteenth Amendment, he "could find no substitute adequate to explain the revisory function of the Supreme Court," that one of his formulas "left us as much at large as we were with mere 'due

57. Rochin v. California, 342 U.S. at 169. Dissenting from the majority's condemnation of use of a stomach pump to obtain evidence of narcotic traffic, Justice Douglas, seeing that the outlawed practice "would be admissible in the majority of states where the question has been raised," refused to hold that it violates the " 'decencies of civilized conduct' when formulated by responsible courts with judges as sensitive as we are." Id. 177–178.

58. Black was an "overpowering advocate" who believed that he "had a mission to impose his convictions on the nation," Levy, *Against the Law* 36, a conviction shared by Chief Justice Warren and Justice Douglas. Lusky stated that Black "did his full share of judicial constitution-making, stoutly maintaining all the while that he was merely following directions set forth in the text of the Constitution and its Amendments . . . [finding] meanings . . . which none of his colleagues (or any one else) could find there." Lusky 74. See also Kurland, supra note 49 at 4.

59. Griswold v. Connecticut, 381 U.S. at 511 note 4. He rang the changes on this view from Adamson v. California, 332 U.S. 46, 69 (1947), through Sniadach v. Family Finance Corp., 395 U.S. 337, 350, 351 (1969).

60. Rochin v. California, 342 U.S. at 176.

61. Id. 179; see supra note 57.

process of law.' " Is "outraging the Supreme Court's sense of justice," Sutherland asked, "any more definite . . . ?"[62]

Not that Justice Black's insistence on his "impersonal" standard was free of self-delusion. To accomplish control over the States he jumped off from the untenable assumption that the Fourteenth Amendment incorporates the Bill of Rights; upon closer examination it appears that the "specifics" of the Bill of Rights also exhibit "subjective" open spaces.[63] It would take us far afield once more to compare the Black and Frankfurter philosophies.[64] Let it suffice, as George Braden concludes, that both "put into the Fourteenth Amendment what they want to"; [e]ach theory collapses, on analysis, into little more than a front for policy-making."[65] "How can a strict constructionist, so-called, like Black," Philip Kurland rightly asks, "have acquiesced in the reapportionment cases?"[66] Those decisions, in the words of Justice Stewart, "mark a long step backward into that unhappy era when a majority of the members of the Court were thought by many to have convinced themselves and each other that the demands of the Constitution were to be measured not by what it says, but by their own notions of wise political

62. "Privacy in Connecticut," 64 Mich. L. Rev. 283, 285, 287 (1965). Another Frankfurter disciple, Professor Louis Jaffe, wrote, "it must be admitted that the Frankfurterian formulation is somewhat deceptive . . . In a number of cases it is the essence of the problem that the public has been unable to clarify its conscience or formulate a position." "The Court Debated—Another View" (1960), *The New York Times Magazine,* June 5, 1960, in Levy, *Warren* 199, 205. Justice Brennan also charged Frankfurter with subjective standards, unaware, as Leonard Levy stated, that his own "were no less imprecise . . . and subjective." Levy, *Against the Law* 398.

63. See Braden, supra note 51 at 590–591; Mendelson, *Supreme Court,* supra note 39 at 25–26; Mendelson, *Black and Frankfurter,* supra note 39 at 69; Alexander Bickel, *The Least Dangerous Branch* 87–88 (1962).

64. Mendelson, *Black and Frankfurter,* id. at 69; Braden, supra note 51 at 582–594.

65. Braden, id. 591, 593–594.

66. Kurland, supra note 49 at 180.

theory."[67] Black it was who declared, "there is no constitutional support whatever for this Court to use the Due Process Clause as though it provided a blank check to alter the meaning of the Constitution as written so as to add substantive constitutional changes which a majority of the Court at any given time believes are *needed to meet present day problems.*"[68] What were the "one man, one vote" decisions in which Black concurred but exactly such instances? For the Fourteenth Amendment, by virtue of its unmistakable history, as good as provides that control of suffrage was left to the States.[69] And what happened, Miller and Howell justly ask, to Frankfurter's "vaunted sense of self-restraint" in the desegregation case,[70] which, to quote his condemnation of a reapportionment decision, was also "a massive repudiation of the experience of our whole past in asserting destructively novel power."[71] That case also interfered with matters that had been a matter of State concern from the beginning, and which the framers of the Fourteenth Amendment plainly intended to leave with the States. Yet Frankfurter "was wary of judicial efforts to impose Justice on the people—to force upon them 'better' government than they were able at the moment to give themselves. It was his deepest conviction that no five men, or nine, are wise enough or good enough to wield

67. Lucas v. Colorado Gen. Assembly, 377 U.S. 713, 747–748 (1964), dissenting opinion.

68. Harper v. Va. Board of Elections, 383 U.S. 663, 675–676 (1966), dissenting opinion (emphasis added).

69. In Oregon v. Mitchell, 400 U.S. 112, 124–125 (1970), Justice Black stated, "My Brother Harlan has persuasively demonstrated that the Framers . . . intended the States to keep for themselves, as provided in the Tenth Amendment, the power to regulate elections . . . I agree as to the States' power to regulate the elections of their own officials."

70. "The Myth of Neutrality in Constitutional Adjudication," 27 U. Chi. L. Rev. 661, 699 note 108 (1960). Compare supra Chapter 7 at notes 47–53. Justice Frankfurter observed that "The Court is not saved from being oligarchic because it professes to act in the service of humane ends." A. F. of L. v. American Sash Co., 335 U.S. at 555–556.

71. Baker v. Carr, 369 U.S. 186, 267 (1962), dissenting opinion.

such power over an entire nation."[72] The lesson to be drawn from the cross-recriminations of the Justices is that the cry for self-restraint is directed to the other fellow, to decry identification of *his* predilections with constitutional mandates.[73] Each Justice has a blind spot for the identification of his own predilections with constitutional dogma. A beautiful illustration is furnished by Justice Douglas in the contraceptive case *Griswold v. Connecticut:* "We do not sit as a super-legislature to determine the wisdom, need, and propriety of laws that touch economic problems . . . or social conditions. This law, however, operated directly on an intimate relation of husband and wife."[74] The inarticulate premise, as Alpheus Thomas Mason points out, is that "the Court does sit as a super-legislature in safeguarding the penumbral rights of privacy."[75] To justify the differentiation Douglas relies on the cobwebby "penumbras formed by emanations,"[76] but in essence he exemplifies the readiness of the Justices to act as a "super-legislature" when their own emotions are engaged.

In the economic realm the Court itself has confessed error. In 1970 it recalled the "era when the Court thought the Fourteenth Amendment gave it power to strike down state laws 'because they may be unwise, improvident, or out of harmony with a particular school of thought' . . . That era has long ago passed into history."[77] "We have returned," it said on another occasion, "to the original constitutional proposition that courts do not substitute their social and economic beliefs for the judgment

72. Mendelson, *Supreme Court,* supra note 39 at 14.

73. Mendelson refers to the "ancient tradition of restraint which all American judges have professed—when their particular 'preferred place' values were not at stake." Id. 13.

74. 381 U.S. at 482; A. T. Mason, "The Burger Court in Historical Perspective," 47 N.Y. State Bar J. 87, 89 (1975). Compare with Justice White, infra note 121.

75. Mason, supra note 74 at 89.

76. 381 U.S. at 484.

77. Dandridge v. Williams, 397 U.S. 471, 485 (1970); see supra note 39.

of legislative bodies who are elected to pass laws,"[78] as had earlier been stated by Justice Holmes.[79] These statements, however, are only accurate in part. At the same time it engaged in
this overdue renunciation of usurped power in the economic
sphere, the Court expanded the application of substantive due
process to libertarian categories to which at length it assigned a
"preferred position." To the uninitiated it might seem that if
the Fourteenth Amendment, in Justice Holmes' famous phrase,
"does not enact Herbert Spencer's Social Statics,"[80] no more
does it incorporate Kenneth Clark's social psychology.[81] In this
Black and Frankfurter professedly were in accord. Justice
Frankfurter stated: "The Constitution does not give us greater
veto power when dealing with one phase of liberty than another . . . Our power does not vary according to the particular provision of the Bill of Rights which is invoked."[82] Justice
Black affirmed that "The Due Process Clause with an 'arbitrary
and capricious' or 'shocking to the conscience' formula was liberally used by this Court to strike down economic legislation
. . . That formula, based on subjective considerations of 'natural justice,' is no less dangerous when used to enforce this
Court's views about personal rights than those about economic
rights."[83] The logic that bars the one equally bars the other.

History reveals that property actually was more highly
prized by the Founders than "civil liberties." "The great and
chief end . . . of men," Locke wrote, in "putting themselves

78. Ferguson v. Skrupa, 372 U.S. at 730.

79. "I cannot believe that the Amendment was intended to give us *carte
blanche* to embody our economic or moral beliefs in its prohibitions." Baldwin
v. Missouri, 281 U.S. 586, 595 (1930), dissenting opinion.

80. Lochner v. New York, 198 U.S. 45, 75 (1905), dissenting opinion.

81. Clark's psychology was invoked by Chief Justice Warren in Brown v.
Board of Education, 347 U.S. 483, 494 note 11 (1954).

82. Board of Education v. Barnette, 319 U.S. 624, 648 (1943), dissenting
opinion.

83. Griswold v. Connecticut, 381 U.S. at 522, dissenting opinion.

under government, is the preservation of their property."[84] For
the Founders property "was the basic liberty, because until a
man was secure in his property, until it was protected from arbitrary seizure, life and liberty could mean little."[85] Hence they
"warmly endorsed John Adams' deep-seated conviction that
'property is as sacred as the laws of God' ";[86] and such views
were expressed in the Convention by Madison: "The primary
objects of civil society are in the security of property and the
public safety."[87] Neither the Fifth nor the Fourteenth Amendment drew a distinction between "liberty" and "property,"
and, as Learned Hand remarked, the Framers would have
regarded the current reading of the Fifth Amendment as "constituting severer restrictions as to Liberty than Property" as a
"strange anomaly." "There is no constitutional basis," he
averred, "for asserting a larger measure of judicial supervision
over" liberty than property.[88] There is no escape, to my mind,
from Stanley Morrison's summation that the difference merely

84. 2 John Locke, *Treatise on Government,* chapter 2, quoted in J. R. Randall,
The Making of the Modern Mind 343, 342 (1940).

85. 1 Page Smith, *John Adams* 272 (1962). Anatole France made the point
ironically: the poor are as free as the rich to sleep under a bridge.

86. Mason, supra note 74 at 91.

87. 1 Farrand 147. Justice William Paterson, a leading Framer, declared in
1795 that "The preservation of property, then, is the primary object of the social compact." Van Horne's Lessee v. Dorrance, 2 U.S. (2 Dall.) 304, 309 (1795).
Quoting Lord Camden in Entick v. Carrington, 19 How. St. Tr. 1029, 1066
(1765), the Supreme Court declared, "The great end for which men entered
into society was to secure their property. That right is preserved sacred."
Boyd v. United States, 116 U.S. 616, 627 (1886).

88. Hand, supra note 3 at 50, 51. Commenting on the theory that "'personal liberties' deserve more stringent protection than 'property rights'
because society should assign them greater value," Archibald Cox justly
observes that "The rationale merely asserts the conclusion." "The New
Dimensions of Constitutional Adjudication," 51 Wash. L. Rev. 791, 797–798
(1976).

represents "the subjective preferences or convictions of the individual judge."[89]

To this Fred Rodell replies that "regardless of syllogistic consistency about judicial review—this nation puts, or should put, a higher premium on individual dignities and freedoms than on material matters like the getting and keeping of money, and that the Court should honor that preference under the Constitution." Patently what this nation "should put" merely reflects Rodell's own preferences; whether the "nation puts" raises the question: at what point in time? Not from 1788 to the mid-twentieth century of a certainty. If it be the nation today, we have only Rodell's conjecture, a very insecure footing for constitutional doctrine. Leonard Levy correctly points out that such views merely reject the Court's earlier economic predilections because they were "illiberal," not because the Court "made policy," often arbitrarily. And he comments that this view "loses nothing of its monstrous character when the Court

---

89. "What Mr. Justice Black has voted to do [in Adamson] is to abolish substantive due process in the economic field and preserve it in the field of civil liberties. This, however, represents a logical difficulty which is nearly insuperable. If substantive due process is a natural-law gloss in the economic field, it is just as much so in the field of civil liberties. There is no basis for rejecting the doctrine in the one case and adopting it in the other except the subjective preferences of the individual judge. History affords no justification for the choice made. Thus the judge who resorts to natural law to protect civil liberty is using the same techniques as the judges who resorted to natural law to protect economic liberty." Stanley Morrison, "Does the Fourteenth Amendment Include the Bill of Rights?," 2 Stan. L. Rev. 140, 167 (1949). Chief Justice Stone said as much in 1945, see infra at note 137. As late as 1956 the Court held that "as no constitutional guarantee enjoys preference, so none should suffer subordination." Ullman v. Poe, 350 U.S. 422, 428 (1956). Professor Herbert Packer stated, "I find it extraordinarily difficult to draw a distinction between 'economic' legislation and legislation that affects 'fundamental rights.' " "The Aim of the Criminal Law Revisited: A Plea for a New Look at 'Substantive Due Process,' " 44 S. Cal. L. Rev. 490, 493 (1971). See also Levy, *Against the Law* 239; Justices Black and Frankfurter, supra at notes 82 and 83.

is praised simply for reaching the right or just result."[90] Let us now briefly consider the means whereby the distinction was judicially fashioned.

From Economic Due Process to the "Preferred Position"

The "preferred position" assigned by the Court to "civil liberties" may be traced back to the brief vogue of "liberty of contract." To preserve it, the Court struck down a statute in *Lochner v. New York* (1905)[91] that limited working hours to 10 hours daily and 60 weekly as an interference with a bakery worker's right to work longer hours. Casuistry seldom rose to greater heights. "There is grim irony," Justice Stone later wrote, "in speaking of the freedom of contract of those who, because of their economic necessities, give their services for less than is needful to keep body and soul together."[92] First adopted in *Allgeyer v. Louisiana* (1897),[93] "liberty of contract" flourished so lustily that by 1923 Justice McReynolds could say in *Meyer v.*

90. Rodell, "The Crux of the Court Hullabaloo," *The New York Times Magazine,* May 29, 1960, quoted in Levy, *Warren* 192, 195; Levy, id. 186; compare Cox, supra note 88.

91. 198 U.S. 45 (1905).

92. Morehead v. Tipaldo, 298 U.S. 587, 632 (1936), dissenting opinion. A revealing glimpse of the callousness of the class to which Lochner catered is afforded by the remark of Joseph Choate, the most eminent lawyer of his day, that he saw no reason why "a big husky Irish washerwoman should not work more than ten hours a day in a laundry if she and her employer so desired." Quoted in Ernest Samuels, *Henry Adams: The Major Phase* 412 (1964).

93. 165 U.S. 578 (1897); C. Warren, supra note 33 at 448. But Justice Holmes wrote, "The earlier decisions . . . began within our memory and went no farther than an unpretentious assertion of the liberty to follow the ordinary callings. Later that innocuous generality was expanded into the dogma, Liberty of Contract . . . It is merely an example of doing what you want to do, embodied in the word liberty." Adkins v. Children's Hospital, 261 U.S. 525, 568 (1923), dissenting opinion.

Nebraska, "without doubt, it denotes not merely freedom from bodily restraint."[94] History disproves the claim. The learning was assembled in two landmark articles by Charles E. Shattuck (1891)[95] and Charles Warren (1926).[96] After collating the earlier history, Shattuck noted Blackstone's summation, defining personal liberty as the "power of locomotion, of changing situation . . . without imprisonment or restraint of the person."[97] When Warren reviewed the materials some twenty-five years later, he concluded, "there seems to be little question that, under the common law, 'liberty' meant simply 'liberty of the person,' or in other words, 'the right to have one's person free from physical restraint.'"[98] This was the established connotation of "liberty" when the Thirteen State constitutions adopted the "life, liberty, or property" phrase.

Before "liberty of contract" was abandoned, the Justices had timidly extended the concept of "liberty" to freedom of speech. As late as 1922 the Court had held that the Constitution "imposes upon the States no obligation to confer upon those within their jurisdiction . . . the right of free speech."[99] Three years later, in *Gitlow v. New York,* the Court "assume[d] that freedom of speech and of the press are among the fundamental personal rights and 'liberties' protected by the due process clause of the Fourteenth Amendment from impairment by the States."[100] Justice Holmes furnished the clue in his dissenting opinion: free speech "must be taken to be included in the Fourteenth Amendment *in view of the scope that has been given* to the

94. 262 U.S. 390, 399 (1923).

95. "The True Meaning of the Term 'Liberty' in Those Clauses in the Federal and State Constitutions Which Protect 'Life, Liberty and Property,'" 4 Harv. L. Rev. 365.

96. Supra note 33.

97. Shattuck, supra note 95 at 377; for Blackstone, see supra Chapter 2 at note 3.

98. Warren, supra note 33 at 440.

99. Prudential Ins. Co. v. Cheek, 259 U.S. 530, 538 (1922).

100. 268 U.S. 652, 666 (1925).

word 'liberty.'"[101] But this was precarious footing; Justice Brandeis averred that free speech and press are protected "from invasion by the States" because they are "fundamental rights comprised within the term 'liberty.'" In one of his finest perorations he attributed it to those "who won our independence," who believed "that this should be a fundamental principle of the American government."[102] Brandeis' attribution to the Founders, as will appear, falls afoul of historical fact. On the eve of *Gitlow*, his foremost disciple, Professor Frankfurter, wrote: "Even the most rampant worshipper of judicial supremacy admits that wisdom and justice are not the tests of constitutionality . . . Particularly in legislation affecting freedom of thought and freedom of speech much that is illiberal would be clearly constitutional."[103] In the post-Warren Court euphoria, when the test of constitutionality is assumed to be that the result is socially desirable, we are apt to overlook Chief Justice Marshall's caution that "The peculiar circumstances of the moment may render a measure more or less wise, but cannot render it more or less constitutional."[104]

Charles Warren tellingly argues that the "free speech" of the First Amendment could not have been comprehended in the due process of the Fifth Amendment because, "having already provided in the First Amendment an *absolute prohibition* on Congress to take away certain rights," it is "hardly conceivable that the framers" would, in the Fifth, provide that "*Congress might take away* the same rights by due process of law."[105]

---

101. Id. 672 (emphasis added). But compare supra note 93.

102. Whitney v. California, 274 U.S. 357, 373, 375 (1927), concurring opinion.

103. "Can the Supreme Court Guarantee Toleration?" 43 *New Republic* 85, 87 (1925), quoted in Mendelson, *Black and Frankfurter,* supra note 39 at 54.

104. *John Marshall's Defense of McCulloch v. Maryland* 190–191 (G. Gunther ed. 1969). "The criterion of constitutionality," said Justice Holmes, "is not whether we believe the law to be for the public good." Adkins v. Children's Hospital, 261 U.S. at 570, dissenting opinion.

105. Warren, supra note 33 at 441.

"The right of free speech," Warren points out, "was not included as one of a person's fundamental . . . rights in any Bill
of Rights adopted by any of the States prior to the Federal Constitution."[106] More important, when the First Amendment was
proposed, Madison urged the First Congress that "it was
equally necessary that [free speech] be secured against the State
Governments," but his plea was fruitless.[107] Jefferson, the great
champion of free speech and free press, wrote in 1804 to Abigail
Adams; "While we deny that Congress have a right to controul
the freedom of the press, we have ever asserted the rights of the
states, and their exclusive right to do so."[108] This was the premise on which the First Congress had acted. One may agree
with Justice Cardozo that free speech is "the matrix, the indispensable condition, of nearly every other form of freedom,"[109]
but the fact remains that the one time the American people had
the opportunity to express themselves on whether free speech
was "so rooted in the tradition and conscience of our people as
to be ranked as fundamental"[110] was in the First Congress,
which drafted the Bill of Rights in response to popular demand.
There they voted down interference with State control. Justice
Byron White brushed the 1789 history aside as of "little relevance in interpreting the Due Process Clause of the Fourteenth
Amendment, adopted specifically to place limitations upon the

---

106. Id. 461. I have checked the constitutions of the original thirteen States
and would add a qualification. Article XII of the 1776 Pennsylvania Constitution provided, "the people have a right to freedom of speech, and of writing,
and publishing their sentiments; therefore the freedom of the press ought not
to be restrained." A similar provision was contained in the 1786 Constitution
of Vermont. 2 Poore 1542, 1869. The prohibition, however, is confined to the
press. Most of the other States mention only free press.

107. Warren, supra note 33 at 434, 435; 1 *Annals of Congress* 435, 755.

108. September 11, 1804, quoted in Frankfurter, supra note 18 at 226; see
also Bork, "Neutral Principles and Some First Amendment Problems," 47
Ind. L. J. 1, 22 (1971).

109. Palko v. Connecticut, 302 U.S. 319, 327 (1937).

110. Id. at 325.

States."[111] That begs the question. Where is the evidence that in 1866 the framers meant to advance beyond the limited goals of the Civil Rights Act? Where is the evidence that they meant to enlarge the meaning due process had for the Founders in 1789? Instead, the record establishes that the framers had limited objectives; that they carefully avoided encroaching on the States beyond those limits; that they chose technical words apt for their purpose, which, in the case of due process, meant to them access to the courts according to due course of law, not a roving commission to revise State institutions.[112] On the heels of the Fourteenth Amendment Thomas Cooley concluded that "Obstacles stood in the way of an unconditional commitment to human freedom. Innovations, he believed, required historical basis, and American history was singularly lacking in precedents for national power used in behalf of individual freedom."[113]

Charles Warren had prophesied in 1926 that by enlarging the Fourteenth Amendment to protect free speech, the Court had opened the door to adoption of the rest of the Bill of Rights.[114] Faced with mounting pressure to do so, Justice Cardozo, in *Palko v. Connecticut* (1937), fashioned a confining doctrine—"ordered liberty": some "immunities that are valid as against

111. Duncan v. Louisiana, 391 U.S. 145, 153 note 20 (1968).

112. My search of the debates in the 39th Congress turned up two expressions (there may be others) respecting freedom of speech. Price remarked that "for the last thirty years a citizen of a free State dared not express his opinion on the subject of slavery in a slave State," but at the same time he construed "privileges or immunities" to afford to a Northern visitor "the same protection" that a Southern State accorded to its own citizens. *Globe* 1066; see also the remarks of Broomall, id. 1263. Southern citizens, however, enjoyed no greater right to attack the sacred institution—the subject was taboo, Edmund Wilson, *Patriotic Gore* 4, 228, 365 (1962); Kenneth M. Stampp, *The Peculiar Institution* 211–212, 28 (1956). The free speech sought by Price, as in the case of other privileges, was that accorded by the States, provided that it was nondiscriminatory.

113. Paludan, supra note 39 at 263.

114. Warren, supra note 33 at 458–460.

the federal government by force of the specific pledges of particular amendments have been found to be implicit in the concept of ordered liberty, and thus, through the Fourteenth Amendment, become valid as against the States."[115] Such portions of the Bill of Rights as had been "absorbed" in the Amendment rested on "the belief that neither liberty nor justice would exist if they were sacrificed." "Absorption" proceeded from those "principle[s] of justice so rooted in the tradition and conscience of our people as to be ranked as fundamental."[116] As in the case of the Chinese "mandate from heaven," we learn a right is "fundamental" only after the Court attaches that label.[117] Cardozo, it needs to be borne in mind, took due process as it was handed to him and therefore could say, "Out of the vague precepts of the Fourteenth Amendment a court frames a rule which is general in form."[118] "Ordered liberty," as Louis Lusky states, "is too vague to describe a national objective. It says that order and liberty are both to be sought, but provides no standard for reconciling the eternal conflict between them." "It is a vehicle," he justly comments, "for whatever meaning the Court gives it, and thus enables the Court to apply its own conceptions of public policy."[119] Several Justices concur in this view. In a book written by Justice Owen Roberts after his retirement, he stated, in a passage quoted by Justice Douglas, that the cases will fall "on the one side of the line or the other as a majority of nine justices appraise conduct as either implicit in the concept of ordered liberty or as lying without the confines

115. 302 U.S. at 324–325.

116. Id. 326, 325, quoted more fully supra at note 110.

117. See infra at note 139. "[W]hether a particular right is denominated as 'fundamental,'" Lusky comments, "depends upon a value judgment so broad" as to be unverifiable "by reference to any known standard." Lusky 264. "[T]here is no authoritative schedule of fundamental rights." Jaffe, supra note 51 at 998.

118. Snyder v. Massachusetts, 291 U.S. 97, 114 (1934).

119. Lusky 107, 105; see also Jaffe, supra note 51 at 997.

of that vague concept."[120] Justice Byron White likewise regards the concept as no more than a means whereby a majority of the Court can impose "its own philosophical predilections upon State legislatures or Congress."[121] And Justice Black maintained that the concept merely embodied " 'natural law due process' notion[s] by which this Court frees itself from the limits of a written Constitution."[122] Like that of Brandeis, Cardozo's reliance on the "traditions and conscience of our people" is rebutted by the refusal of the First Congress to proscribe *State* interference with free speech and free press. That, to borrow from Learned Hand, was the "last formal expression" of the will of the people. No departure from that will can be found in the history of the Fourteenth Amendment; instead, but for the narrow enclave of the Civil Rights Act, the framers plainly withheld from the Court power to intrude into State regulation of domestic affairs.

About four months after *Palko,* Lusky tells us, Justice Stone, in a footnote to *United States v. Carolene Products Co.,*[123] "under-

---

120. *The Court and the Constitution* 80 (1951), quoted in Poe v. Ullman, 367 U.S. at 518–519, dissenting opinion. "Of course," Roberts added, ". . . in this view, the due process clause of the Fifth Amendment . . . may be repetitious of many of the other guaranties of the first eight amendments and may render many of their provisions superfluous," a result that argues against the "absorption" view.

121. Dissenting in Robinson v. California, 370 U.S. 660, 689 (1962), Justice White stated, "I suspect the Court was hard put to find a way to ascribe to the Framers of the Constitution the result reached today rather than to its own notion of ordered liberty. If this case involved economic regulation, the present Court's allergy to substantive due process would surely save the statute and prevent the Court from imposing its own philosophical predilections upon State legislatures or Congress. I fail to see why the Court deems it more appropriate to write into the Constitution its own abstract notions of how best to handle the narcotics problem, for it obviously cannot match either the States or Congress in expert understanding."

122. In re Winship, 397 U.S. 358, 381–382 (1970), dissenting opinion.

123. 304 U.S. 144 (1938).

took to articulate a more satisfactory justification."[124] At that time Lusky was Justice Stone's law clerk, and he submitted a draft of what eventuated as the second and third paragraphs of the footnote.[125] "It is unnecessary to consider," reads paragraph two, "whether legislation which restricts those political processes which can ordinarily be expected to bring about repeal of undesirable legislation is to be subjected to more exacting scrutiny . . . than are most other types of legislation." "Nor need we enquire," paragraph three states, whether statutes that impinge upon religious or racial minorities that were objects of prejudice which might hamper relief through political processes should also be subjected to "more searching judicial scrutiny."[126] Thus, by a disclaimer of the need to decide, in a case that had "curiously not involved liberties in any way,"[127] the Court, as it has so often done, launched a major constitutional doctrine. Notwithstanding that it was tucked away in a footnote, it "disturbed" Chief Justice Hughes; consequently, the present first paragraph was added, stating that "there may be a narrower scope" for operation of the presumption of constitutionality when legislation "appears on its face to be within a specific prohibition of the Constitution, such as those of the first ten amendments . . . when held to be embraced within the Fourteenth."[128] Paragraph one was designed to qualify the second and third paragraphs in order to still Hughes' doubts, as the exchanges between him and Stone make plain.

Lusky explains that paragraphs two and three "make no reference to the words or intentions of the Constitutors. They speak, rather of the dynamics of government," that is, they as-

124. Lusky 108.

125. A. T. Mason, *Harlan Fiske Stone: Pillar of the Law* 513 (1956); Mason, *The Supreme Court,* supra note 54 at 151–159.

126. 304 U.S. at 152–153 note 4.

127. Paul Murphy, *The Constitution in Crisis Times, 1918–1969* at 182.

128. Mason, *The Supreme Court,* supra note 54 at 155. In his reply to Hughes, Stone stated that the footnote was a caveat, "without, however, committing the Court to any notion contained in it." Id.

sume that "government by the people, and government for the whole people" are "fairly ascribable to the Constitutors," and that the Court has a "special ability to effectuate them" by acting in the two described situations.[129] And it is the Court itself which is to decide for which purposes it has "special aptitude."[130] Once more the "genius of government" is to override the sovereignty in domestic matters that the Framers reserved to the States; once more their rejection of judicial participation in policymaking[131] and the reservation in 1866 of suffrage and other local matters to the States is ignored. Although the Hughes' first paragraph seems narrower, Lusky considers that by it "the Court is left entirely at large. There is virtually no limit to its ability to attribute new meaning to the 'specific prohibitions,' once it is liberated from the need to interpret them as the Constitutors expected." This has "come to be known as the 'preferred position' theory, which affirms that certain rights are . . . so important that the Court should protect them . . . and that the Court's power to select them is limited only by its ability to manipulate words contained in the Constitution. It . . . assumes that any meaning the Court chooses to ascribe to the sacred text will be accepted as authentic revelation."[132] These strictures, it seems to me, are no less applicable to a theory divorced from "the words or intentions of the Constitutors" and founded on "the dynamics of government."

Lusky's pronounced preference for the Stone-Lusky second and third paragraphs of the *Carolene* footnote derives from the belief that it fits in with his newly fashioned theory of the Court's "implied power" to revise the Constitution, his answer to the anguished question, "*By what right* does it revise the Constitution?"[133] His search for a new theory to undergird judicial

129. Lusky 109.
130. "The Court must take the responsibility for proclaiming its own superior fitness to attain the objective." Lusky 112.
131. Infra Chapter 16.
132. Lusky 111–112.
133. Id. 19.

revision testifies that the footnote is without constitutional roots, that as George Braden says, "it is simply a part of one man's set of values for his society which he holds strongly enough to be willing to enforce when the opportunity arises."[134]

Stone himself, according to Lusky, "seems to have underestimated" the importance of the distinction Lusky draws,[135] illustrating anew the tendency to read into an utterance meaning never contemplated by the author. And before long he was disenchanted with the course pursued by the Court. Long before the Warren Court worked its revolution,[136] Chief Justice Stone wrote (1945): "My more conservative brethren in the old days [read their preferences] into the Constitution . . . [H]istory is repeating itself. The Court is now in as much danger of becoming a legislative and Constitution making body, enacting into law its own predilections, as it was then."[137] His forebodings

---

134. Braden, supra note 51 at 581.

135. Lusky 312.

136. Infra Chapter 15 note 1. Levy observes that to the eyes of "both the Court's admirers and critics . . . the Justices seemed to consider themselves as movers and shakers of the country's destiny rather than as impersonal spokesmen for the law." Levy, *Warren* 5. Compare infra Chapter 17 note 55.

Professor Abram Chayes remarks that judicial action in the last two decades "adds up to a radical transformation of the role and function of the judiciary in American life . . . Its chief function now is as a catalyst of social change with judges acting as planners of large scale." "The New Judiciary," 28 Harv. L. Sch. Bull. 23, 24 (1976). To accomplish the reform, Archibald Cox states, the courts have been required "to formulate controversial programmes of affirmative action requiring detailed administration for protracted periods under constant judicial supervision." Cox, supra note 38 at 77, a remarkable departure from the nay-saying role of the laissez faire Court. "The decrees thus directly regulate the lives of millions of people without a voice in the decision." Id. 87. See infra Appendix II.

137. A. T. Mason, *Security Through Freedom: American Political Thought and Practice* 145–146 (1955). "Justice Stone was no rabid proponent of expanded judicial power." Lusky 83. Justice Frankfurter was "vehemently opposed to

were overfulfilled; "the Warren Court," Archibald Cox stated, "behaved even more like a Council of Wise Men and less like a Court than the *laissez faire* Justices."[138] Once again Stone exemplifies that the measure of tolerance is effectuation of one's own predilections; when they are exceeded at the hands of other Justices, they are anathematized.

This drastically telescoped survey of divers judicial rationalizations of expanded judicial revision for the benefit of libertarian ideals underlines the wisdom of Judge Learned Hand's conclusion that judges

> wrap up their veto in a protective veil of adjectives such as . . . "reasonable," "inherent," "fundamental" . . . whose office usually, though quite innocently, is to disguise what they are doing and impute to it a derivation far more impressive than their personal preferences, which are all that in fact lie behind the decision.[139]

Because Frankfurter overlooked the fact that "due process" was not a provision "without a fixed technical meaning"—minimally it excluded control over legislation, both in 1789 and 1866—he could allude to "the evolution of social policy by way of judicial application of Delphic provisions of the Constitu-

---

the preferred freedom concept." Mason, *The Supreme Court*, supra note 54 at 173. Judge Learned Hand likewise stated, "I do not think that the interests mentioned in the First Amendment are entitled in point of constitutional interpretation to a measure of protection different from other interests." Hand, supra note 3 at 56. "As several of the Justices have noted in dissent, there is only a verbal difference between the 'fundamental rights' branch of the compelling governmental interest test and the now discredited due process of such cases as Lochner v. New York (1905). Both of them leave the Court entirely at large, with full freedom to enact its own natural law conceptions. The only difference is in the type of interests that are protected." Lusky 266.

138. Cox, supra note 38 at 50.

139. Hand, supra note 3 at 70; see also Justice Holmes, supra note 93.

tion."[140] And struggling to arrive at an adequate rationalization of the "desegregation" decision, Frankfurter, we are told, stated in the Conference of the Justices: "It was too bad history had conspired to make the Court the trustee of that incorrigible changeling, the due process clause, and therefore impose upon the Justices a policy-making function unlike that borne by any other court in any other nation."[141] The burden, however, was self-assumed—not unlike the "white man's burden" once employed to justify imperialism. On the most charitable view, Justice Frankfurter had induced a state of self-hypnosis by his frequent incantations to the "convenient vagueness" of due process. Justice Harlan was content, in a case that outraged his sympathies, to state that the historical arguments, among others the limitation of due process to "procedural fairness," "have not been accepted by this Court as delineating its scope."[142] Yet he later insisted, with respect to suffrage, that the Court was bound by the framers' intention to exclude it from the scope of the Fourteenth Amendment.

With vision unclouded by claims to power, there is no reason why students of the judicial process should be caught in such toils. It is their duty to discern and proclaim that it is the judges, not the Constitution, that speak, as Frankfurter himself advised President Franklin Roosevelt on the eve of the Court-packing

140. Frankfurter, supra note 18 at 229, 231. In 1930, however, Professor Frankfurter wrote, "let us face the fact that five Justices of the Supreme Court *are* molders of policy, rather than impersonal vehicles of revealed truth." "The Supreme Court and the Public," 83 Forum 329, 334 (1930), quoted in A. T. Mason, "Myth and Reality in Supreme Court Drama," 48 Va. L. Rev. 1385, 1397 (1962).

141. Richard Kluger, *Simple Justice* 681 (1976). Apparently this is based on a reconstruction of Justice Burton's notes, id. 680. Compare with Frankfurter's views supra at notes 49 and 72.

142. Poe v. Ullman, 367 U.S. at 540, dissenting opinion: "I believe that a statute, making it a criminal offense for *married* couples to use contraceptives" invades privacy "in the most intimate concerns of an individual's personal life." Id. 539.

plan,[143] just as in a simpler age the words which fell from the lips of the Delphic Oracle were spoken into a speaking tube by priests secreted below.

Those who consider that judgment is inescapably subjective will chortle that thus far I have merely proved the obvious. But even in their magisterial survey of such inescapability, Arthur S. Miller and Ronald F. Howell state: "It is, of course, only those constitutional provisions of inherent ambiguity that pose problems of interpretation. Where the intention is clear . . . no interpretation is necessary."[144] Even less is 180-degree *revision* "necessary"; the "ambiguity" of substantive due process was not "inherent" but judicially contrived. Miller and Howell, however, suggest a constrictive criterion, instancing "clear" provisions for the number of Senators, for a President and a Vice-President, and dismissing as a "filo-pietistic notion" something "called the intention of the framers."[145] Nevertheless, they do not suggest that "the judge is wholly free" to sit "kadi-like under a tree dispensing 'justice' by whim or caprice," calling attention to one limitation on such freedom—"adherence to precedent."[146] Why should "adherence to precedent" rise above effectuation of the framers' clearly expressed intention, which expresses the value choices of the sovereign people, not merely of judicial predecessors? The Justices themselves are by no means in accord with the now widely shared Miller-

143. "People have been taught to believe that when the Supreme Court speaks it is not they who speak but the Constitution, whereas, of course, in so many vital cases, it is *they* who speak and *not* the Constitution. And I verily believe that that is what the country needs most to understand." *Roosevelt and Frankfurter: Their Correspondence, 1928–1945* 383 (M. Freedman ed. 1967). Shortly before Solicitor General Robert H. Jackson became a Justice he wrote, "This political role ["continuous constitutional convention"] of the Court has been obscure to laymen—even to most lawyers." *The Struggle for Judicial Supremacy* xi (1941).

144. Miller and Howell, supra note 70 at 683.

145. Id.

146. Id. 676.

Howell view that it is the function of the Court to "update the Constitution."[147] The powerful and repeated dissents across the judicial spectrum, condemning or disclaiming subjective judgment, evidence ongoing soul-searching by members of the Court whether the broad policymaking role academe strenuously defends[148] comports with constitutional limits and the demands of a democratic society.

But this in turn compels us to face the naked question wrung from the lips of Graham. Confronted with the framers' imperfect "understanding of equal protection as applied to educational matters," their acceptance of "segregation in schools," he stated:

> To argue that this means we today are bound by that understanding and practice is to transform the mores and laws of slave code days into constitutional sanctions impossible to be cast off or even moderated . . . Does it follow—dare it follow . . . [that] we *today* are bound by that imperfect understanding of *equal protection* of the laws?[149]

Graham's inarticulate premise was that change could not be accomplished by amendment as the Constitution provides—desegregation could not win assent of two-thirds of the Congress and three-fourths of the States. Accordingly, it fell to the Court to strike the shackles of the past. Whence does the Court derive the power to free the American people from the "chains of the Constitution," from the "tyranny of the dead," that is, the Founders? Such questions will be considered in subsequent chapters.

147. Id. 684; see also Levy, *Against the Law* 29, 30.

148. Levy id; Miller and Howell, supra note 70 at 689–693. "As dissenting Justices complain ever more often that the Court has revised rather than followed the Constitution, one's readiness to discount their charges as disgruntled polemic becomes gradually less confident." Lusky 75.

149. Graham 290 note 70, 291.

15

"The Rule of Law"

FOR a generation the constitutional basis for the "revolutionary" changes wrought by the Warren Court has gone virtually unchallenged.[1] Justice Black, to be sure, unremittingly attacked decisions which to his mind rested on supraconstitutional authority, but his views could be heavily discounted because he himself was guilty of wholesale importation and participated in some of the Court's most debatable constitutional revisions. In a perceptive essay, Thomas C. Grey noticed a turning of the tide, the joinder of distinguished commentators in Black's criticisms; although he dissents, he called for a clear statement and adequate defense of the position.[2] With Grey, I

1. "The 15 years since [Warren] became Chief Justice have been years of legal revolution. In that time the Supreme Court has brought about more social change than most Congresses and most Presidents." Anthony Lewis, "A Man Born to Act, Not to Muse," *The New York Times Magazine,* June 30, 1968, in Levy, *Warren* 151. Justice Douglas complained that one decision entailed a "vast restructuring of American law." Johnson v. Louisiana, 406 U.S. 356, 394 (1972), dissenting opinion. Professor Lusky refers to "a revolutionary change in the criminal process." Lusky 161. A. T. Mason, *The Supreme Court: Palladium of Freedom* 170 (1962): "On May 17, 1954, the Court initiated the greatest social revolution of this generation." See also supra Chapter 14 note 136.

2. "Do We Have an Unwritten Constitution?," 27 Stan. L. Rev. 703–705 (1975).

consider the question whether the Court may "enforce principles of liberty and justice" when they are "not to be found
within the four corners" of the Constitution as "perhaps the
most fundamental question we can ask about our fundamental
law," excluding only "the question of the legitimacy of judicial
review itself."[3] The issue may for present purposes be stated
more concretely: given that the Fourteenth Amendment plainly
left suffrage and segregation to the States, may the Court "interpret" it in exact contradiction of the framers' design—to take
control away from the States? Where is the constitutional
authority for a power so awesome?

It is important to make clear at this point what Part II of this
study is not about. It does not deal with the interpretation of
amorphous constitutional provisions such as "commerce,"[4]
which, unlike "due process," have no historical content; nor
with the weight to be accorded "enigmatic" history. As Part I
demonstrated, the framers of the Fourteenth Amendment made
their intention abundantly plain: to exclude suffrage and segregation from the ambit of its terms. For me those terms, "equal
protection" and "due process," illuminated by clear history, are
neither "vague" nor "ambiguous." Nor will I deal with whether
or not judicial review is antidemocritarian,[5] for if judicial re-

---

3. Id. 703.

4. Professor Frankfurter commented on Marshall's "use of the commerce
clause" to subject state authority "to such limitations as the Court finds it necessary to apply for the protection of the national community" as an "audacious doctrine, which, one may be sure, would hardly have been publicly
avowed in support of the Constitution. Indeed The Federalist in effect denied
it." *The Commerce Clause Under Marshall, Taney and Waite* 18–19 (1937). Had it
been avowed it would have wrecked adoption of the Constitution. For the
Founders' jealous attachment to State sovereignty, see Raoul Berger, *Congress
v. The Supreme Court* 260–264 (1969). That attachment was made explicit by
the Tenth Amendment. That Marshall's views have carried the day is of no
moment in a discussion that seeks to build on first principles. See infra at note
15, infra at notes 29–30, 56–57.

5. I consider that Eugene V. Rostow failed to meet Henry Steele Commager's attack on the antidemocratic administration of judicial review up

view of the Warrenite scope was authorized by the Constitution, its antidemocratic nature has constitutional sanction. Nor will the craftsmanship of the Court, about which rivers of ink have been spilled, come into question.[6] If judicial intervention with respect to suffrage, for example, is without constitutional warrant, it cannot be excused by the most elegant craftsmanship. Nor will consideration be given to the extensive debate about "neutral principles," because I concur with John Ely that if a "neutral principle" "lacks connection with any value the Constitution marks as special," that is, if it is not rooted in the Constitution, "it is not a constitutional principle and the Court has no business imposing it." What is of paramount importance, as Ely stresses, is that the Court "is under obligation to trace its premises to the charter from which it derives its authority."[7] Finally, the "subjectivity" involved in making value choices[8] plays no role in my view of the meaning of the Fourteenth Amendment, for it was not given to the courts to prefer federal judicial control of suffrage to the State control the Amendment deliberately left untouched. The Justices' value

---

to 1937. Rostow, "The Democratic Character of Judicial Review," 56 Harv. L. Rev. 193 (1952); Commager, "Judicial Review and Democracy," 19 Va. Quarterly Rev. 417 (1943). See infra Chapter 17 at note 69.

Leonard Levy finds the Rostow argument unconvincing and comments, it is "of comparatively recent vintage, raising the suspicion that the arguments have been concocted to rationalize a growing satisfaction with judicial review among liberal intellectuals and scholars." L. Levy ed., *Judicial Review and the Supreme Court* 24 (1967).

6. "Assessment of the Nixon Court's craftsmanship is as subjective as the art of judging, and experts will doubtless disagree, as they have about the Warren Court's craftsmanship." Levy, *Against the Law* 438.

7. "The Wages of Crying Wolf: A Comment on Roe v. Wade," 82 Yale L. J. 920, 949 (1973). Bruce M. Claggett suggests a "neutral principle," the "intent of the framers which, where knowable, surely should be conclusive." "Book Review," 27 Harv. L. Sch. Bull. 3, 4 (1976).

8. A. S. Miller and R. F. Howell, "The Myth of Neutrality in Constitutional Adjudication," 27 U. Chi. L. Rev. 661 (1960).

choices may not displace those of the Framers;[9] or, as Chief Justice Marshall stated, the words of the Constitution are not to be "extended to objects not . . . contemplated by its framers"[10] —let alone to those which unmistakably were excluded.

Intoxicated by the Warren Court's libertarian breakthrough, academicians have dismissed such restrictions. Fred Rodell exulted that Chief Justice Warren "brush[ed] off pedantic impedimenta to the results he felt were right," that he was not a "look-it-up-in-the-library" intellectual, and that he was "almost unique" in his "off-hand dismissal of legal and historical research from both sides and in [his] pragmatic dependence on the present day results of separate schools."[11] On this view the Constitution itself is a superfluous, even obstructive, "scrap of paper." Leonard Levy labeled this approach as "anti-intellectual,"[12] but Rodell merely expressed in pungent terms what is more decorously phrased by his fellow "instrumentalists."[13] The underlying reality, as another Warren enthusiast,

9. See infra Chapter 17 at notes 34–35, 62.

10. Ogden v. Saunders, 25 U.S. (12 Wheat.) 213, 332 (1827), dissenting opinion.

11. Fred Rodell, "It is the Warren Court," *The New York Times Magazine,* March 13, 1966, in Levy, *Warren* 137, 142, 138–139. In both Brown v. Board of Education (desegregation) and Reynolds v. Sims (reapportionment), Rodell takes pleasure in recounting, "Warren was quite unworried that legislative history, dug from a library, might not support his reading." Id. 142.

12. Levy, *Warren* 188.

13. E.g., "judicial decisions should be gauged by their results and not by . . . their coincidence with a set of allegedly consistent doctrinal principles." Miller and Howell, supra note 8 at 690–691. Warren, said Paul Murphy, "had utilized the judiciary as a constructive policy-making instrument . . . Intent more upon social ends than upon legal subtleties and refinements, and candidly prepared to say so, he had pushed the nation, through his Court's legal rulings, to take public actions that Congress was unprepared to recommend and the executive was incapable, unilaterally, of effectively securing." Murphy, *The Constitution in Crisis Times, 1918–1969* 457 (1972). Apparently this meets with his approval, id. 466 et seq. He states that McCune (*Nine Young Men* 83 (1947)), praises the Black-Douglas-Murphy bloc because it " 'would seldom let red tape [!] stand in its way of arriving at an end it felt desirable.' " Id. at 194.

Edmond Cahn, stated, was that "as a practical matter it would have been impossible to secure adoption of a constitutional amendment to abolish 'separate but equal,' only the Court possessed effective power to relieve American education of this incubus," thereby assuming that it had constitutional warrant.[14]

Inquiry into the source of power to set aside Article V of the Constitution, "which prescribes the Amendment process,"[15] and to impose a solution on the people that confessedly could not have obtained their assent is hardly a sheerly antiquarian exercise.[16] Given a Constitution designed to "limit" the exercise of all delegated power,[17] it is a response to the admonition contained in the Massachusetts Constitution of 1780, drafted by John Adams and paralleled in a number of early State constitutions, that "A frequent recurrence to the fundamental principles of the constitution . . . [is] absolutely necessary to preserve the advantages of liberty and to maintain a free government. . . . The people . . . have a right to require of their law givers and magistrates an exact and constant observance of them."[18] Such provisions evidence what Willard Hurst considers to be "a very basic principle of our constitutionalism . . . a

14. Edmond Cahn, "Jurisprudence," 30 N.Y.U.L. Rev. 150, 156–157 (1955). In the same way, Martin Shapiro assumed the existence of such power when he adverted to "Learned Hand's eloquent plea for judicial abdication of most of the power of judicial review," *Law and Politics in the Supreme Court* 24 (1964), when in fact Hand entertained grave doubts about its legitimacy and therefore would confine it to a narrow compass.

15. Lusky 79; see infra Chapter 17 at notes 15–22.

16. Although poles removed from Rodell's uncritical subjectivity, Leonard Levy lends credibility to such views by his reference to "an antiquarian historicism that would freeze [the Constitution's] original meaning . . . and was not intended to." Levy, *Judgments: Essays in American Constitutional History* 17 (1972). The remarks of Jefferson and Madison plainly look the other way. See infra Chapter 20, at notes 5 and 18.

17. Supra Chapter 1 note 4; Berger, supra note 4 at 13–16.

18. Article XVIII, 1 Poore 959; New Hampshire (1784), Article 38, 2 Poore 1283; North Carolina (1776), Article XXI, 2 Poore 1410; Pennsylvania (1776), Article XIV, 2 Poore 1542; Vermont (1777), Article XVI, 2 Poore 1860.

distrust of official power,"[19] as Jefferson's insistence on binding officials "with the chains of the Constitution" attests.[20]

CONSTITUTIONALISM AND THE RULE OF LAW

When Howard Jay Graham acknowledged that the framers excluded segregation from the compass of "equal protection," but concluded that we dare not be bound by their "imperfect understanding,"[21] he premised that the Court, as it had done in *Brown v. Board of Education* (1954), should strike the "chains of the Constitution." The demands of justice, in short, must rise above the law, or, as libertarians put it, humanitarian goals must override what they regard as arid legalism. To dismiss adherence to "the rule of law," observance of the limitations imposed by a written Constitution, is to strike at the very root of our democratic system.[22] History confirms Justice Black's state-

19. "Discussion" in *Supreme Court and Supreme Law* 75 (E. Cahn ed. 1954). James Iredell, who fought against great odds in North Carolina for adoption of the Constitution, stated, "The only real security of liberty . . . is the jealousy and circumspection of the people themselves. Let them be watchful over their rulers." 4 Elliot 130. In Virginia, Randolph said, "I hope that my countrymen will keep guard against every arrogation of power." 3 Elliot 207. Iredell stated that "unlimited power . . . was not to be trusted without the most imminent danger, to any man or body of men on earth." 2 G. J. McRee, *Life and Correspondence of James Iredell* 145–146 (1857–1858). See also Corbin, supra Chapter 14 note 16. The Supreme Court adverted to "Fear of unchecked power, so typical of our State and Federal Governments." Duncan v. Louisiana, 391 U.S. 145, 156 (1968).

20. Supra Chapter 14 at note 16.

21. Supra Chapter 14 at note 9.

22. Supra at note 11. Miller and Howell, supra note 8 at 683, label regard for the "intention of the framers" as a "filiopietistic notion." Cf. Levy, *Judgments* supra note 16. Earlier McDougal and Lans gave vent to a string of spluttering expletives: "absolute artifacts of verbal archeology," "strictly, a matter of concern only to rhetoricians," "the idiosyncratic purposes of the Framers." "Treaties and Congressional-Executive or Presidential Agreements: Interchangeable Instruments of National Policy," 54 Yale L. J. 181, 239 note 104, 291, 212 (1945). If laws were "scorned," John Adams wrote, "in God's name

ment that the struggle for a written constitution was "to make
certain that men in power would be governed by *law*, not the
arbitrary fiat of the man or men in power," "according to the
'law of the land,'" not by the "law of judges."[23] The Framers,
as will appear, had no stomach for the dispensation of "justice"
by a kadi under a tree. Justice, to be sure, is the aim of a democratic state, but there can be no justice without a government of
laws, least of all when power is uncurbed. It is for this reason, I
suggest, that judges are not required by Article VI, §3, to take
an oath to do justice but rather "to support this Constitution."
Our system is committed to "Equal Justice *Under* Law," not to
"Justices Above the Law."[24] They were not authorized to revise
the Constitution in the interests of "justice."

---

what is ever to be respected? What is there worth living for?" 2 Page Smith,
John Adams 690 (1962).

23. In re Winship, 397 U.S. 358, 384 (1970), dissenting opinion. Chief Justice Waite declared in 1874 that "Our province is to decide what the law is, not
to declare what it should be." Minor v. Happersett, 88 U.S. (21 Wall.) 162, 178
(1874). In Houston v. Moore, 18 U.S. (5 Wheat.) 1, 48 (1820), Justice Story declared that the Court was "not at liberty to add one jot of power to the national government, beyond what the people have granted by the constitution," dissenting opinion. For similar expressions by Chief Justice Marshall,
see infra Chapter 21 at notes 12–19.

24. Cardozo wrote that judges do not have "the right to ignore the mandate of a statute, and render judgment in despite of it." Benjamin N. Cardozo,
The Nature of the Judicial Process 129 (1921). It is said that when Holmes left the
Massachusetts Court for the Supreme Court, "he was admonished to do justice. He responded thoughtfully that his job was merely to enforce the law."
Wallace Mendelson, *Justices Black and Frankfurter: Conflict in the Court* 116
(1961). Holmes wrote, "I have said to my brethren many times that I hate justice, which means that I know that if a man begins to talk about that, for one
reason or another he is shirking thinking in legal terms." *The Mind and Faith of
Justice Holmes* 435 (M. Lerner ed. 1943). See also supra Chapter 14 at
notes 37 and 103.

Writing of self-conscious judicial activism, Dean Acheson stated that a
judge "may conscientiously be seeking to administer justice, but it is personal
justice—the justice of Louis IX or Harun-al-Rashid—not that described on
the lintel of the Supreme Court Building, 'Equal Justice Under Law.'" *Morn-*

Mechanical repetition over the years—like a child's unthinking daily pledge of allegiance—has dulled the significance of the rule of law; it has been called a "useful fiction."[25] For the Framers, however, it was the essence of constitutional government. "The government of the United States," said Chief Justice Marshall in one of his earliest decisions, "has been emphatically termed a government of laws and not of men."[26] That the judiciary, too, was meant to stay within bounds was spelled out in the 1780 Massachusetts Constitution, which ordained that the legislature should never exercise judicial power, and never should the judiciary exercise legislative power, so that this may be a "government of laws and not of men."[27] Even more plainly, judges were not left free to exercise the supreme "legislative power" of the people, to revise the Constitution in accordance with their own predilections. As the Massachusetts House wrote to the Earl of Shelburne in 1768, "There are, my Lord, fundamental rules of the Constitution . . . which neither the supreme Legislative nor the supreme executive can alter. In all free states, the *constitution is fixed;* it is from thence,

---

ing and Noon 69 (1965). Lusky suggests that some of the Court's decisions may be inexplicable "except on the premise that the Justices *consider themselves to be above the law*—to be wholly unconstrained by pre-existing principle." Lusky 101. Precisely this won praise from admirers of the Warren Court. Supra at note 11, and notes 11 and 13. See also Levy, supra Chapter 14 at note 136.

In defense of President Ford's pardon of Richard Nixon, Assistant Secretary of Transportation Roger W. Hooker, Jr., stated, "I have never been entirely comfortable with the shibboleth [!] that ours is a nation of laws, not of men. It is true that for the most part it is and should be, but in times of extreme moral crisis throughout history, strong leadership has emerged to supersede the letter of the law and deliver us from the evils of vindictiveness." Hooker, "A 'Quiet, Undramatic' Leader," *The New York Times,* August 19, 1976, at 39. In short, Ford acted above the law to save us from an "extreme moral crisis"!

25. Miller and Howell, supra note 8 at 695.

26. Marbury v. Madison, 5 U.S. (1 Cranch) 137, 163 (1803).

27. Massachusetts Constitution of 1780, Article XXX, 1 Poore 960, more fully quoted supra Chapter 14 note 5. The Framers made plain that the judiciary was not to exercise legislative power. Infra Chapter 16 at notes 8–12.

that the legislative derives its authority; therefore it cannot change the constitution without destroying its own foundation."[28] This was addressed to an "omnipotent" Parliament and the Crown under an unwritten Constitution; it was an article of faith among the colonists and Founders.[29] In substituting a written Constitution and expressly providing for change by amendment, they evidenced that they had created a "fixed" Constitution, subject to change by that process alone.[30] That "fixity" was meant to serve as a bulwark for cherished liberties, not a mere parchment. "Our peculiar security," Jefferson declared, "is the possession of a written Constitution. Let us not make it a blank paper by construction."[31] The written Constitution was thus the highest expression of the "rule of law," designed to limit the exercise of power and to make the agents of the people accountable. Once limits are prescribed, Chief Justice Marshall stated, they may not "be passed at pleasure." It was because constitutions were bulwarks against oppression that, in his words, "written constitutions have been regarded with so much reverence."[32]

The Constitution represents fundamental choices that have been made by the people, and the task of the Courts is to effec-

28. H. S. Commager, *Documents of American History* 65 (7th ed. 1963).

29. "The colonials shared Bolingbroke's belief in the fixity of the constitution." Julius Goebel, *Antecedents and Beginnings to 1801, History of the Supreme Court of the United States,* vol. 1, p. 89 (1971). "The principle that government must be conducted in conformity with the terms of the constitution became a fundamental political conception." Id. 95.

In 1785 Madison stated that rulers "who overleap the great barrier which defends the rights of the people . . . are tyrants." 2 James Madison, *Writings of James Madison* 185 (G. Hunt ed. 1900–1910). In the Connecticut Convention Oliver Ellsworth stated, Congress may not "overleap their limits." 2 Elliot 196. For other citations, see Berger, supra note 4 at 13–14.

30. Madison stated in the Convention that "it would be a novel and dangerous doctrine that a legislature could change the constitution under which it held its existence." 2 Farrand 92. See infra Chapter 17 at notes 15–22.

31. 8 *Writings of Thomas Jefferson* 247 (P. L. Ford ed. 1892–1899).

32. Marbury v. Madison, 5 U.S. (1 Cranch) 137, 178 (1803).

tuate them, "not [to] construct new rights."[33] When the judiciary substitutes its own value choices for those of the people it subverts the Constitution by usurpation of power. No dispensation was given to the Court to step outside its powers; it is no less bound by constitutional limits than are the other branches, as the historical evidence makes plain. First, it was clearly excluded from participation in the making of policy, the function of the legislature.[34] No agent, said Hamilton, "can new-model his commission,"[35] and the most benign purpose does not authorize the judiciary to remodel its powers. Indeed, we need to be rid of "the illusion that personal power can be benevolently exercised."[36] The Founders knew, in Jacob Burckhardt's phrase, that "Power is of its nature evil, whoever wields it."[37] They knew, as Madison stated, that all "power is of an encroaching nature, and that it ought to be effectually restrained from passing the limits assigned to it."[38] "Judicial power," Justice Frankfurter remarked, "is not immune against this human weakness";[39] and the Court's progressive intrusion over the years into the domain of policymaking, from which it was plainly excluded, points the moral. Second, as Chief Justice Warren recognized, "We are oath-bound to defend the Constitution. This obligation requires that congressional enactments

33. R. J. Bork, "Neutral Principles and Some First Amendment Problems," 47 Ind. L.J. 1, 8 (1971); see infra Chapter 17 at notes 34–35.

34. See infra Chapter 16 at notes 8–13.

35. "Letters of Camillus," 6 Alexander Hamilton, *Works of Hamilton* 166 (Lodge ed. 1904). This was said of the President by the foremost advocate of a "strong" presidency. See also supra note 30.

36. Thurman Arnold, "Professor Hart's Theology," 73 Harv. L. Rev. 1298, 1311 (1960).

37. Quoted in Gertrude Himmelfarb, *Victorian Minds* 185 (1968).

38. Federalist No. 48 at 321, quoted more fully supra Chapter 14 note 7.

39. Trop v. Dulles, 356 U.S. 86, 119 (1958), dissenting opinion. Justice Black stated, "The history of governments proves that it is dangerous to freedom to repose such [law-making] powers in courts." Katz v. United States, 389 U.S. 347, 374 (1967), dissenting opinion. See also supra Chapter 14 note 7, and John Dickinson, infra Chapter 16 at note 12.

be judged by the standards of the Constitution."[40] Substituted judicial made-to-order "standards" are not really the "standards of the Constitution,[41] as the State "reapportionment" cases plainly evidence. The significance of the judicial oath is illuminated by that of the President, who does not swear to defend the nation, but to "preserve and defend the Constitution,"[42] on the inarticulate premise that the life of the nation hangs on the preservation of the Constitution. Third, conclusive evidence that the judiciary was designed only to police constitutional boundaries, not to exercise supraconstitutional policymaking functions, was furnished by Hamilton. In Federalist No. 78 he stressed that the courts were to serve as "bulwarks of a limited Constitution against legislative encroachments"—a note repeatedly sounded in the subsequent Ratification Conventions.[43] The word "encroachments" posits prior legislative action; it excludes judicial policymaking initiatives on ground of legislative inaction. This is confirmed by Hamilton's statement that the judiciary "can take no active resolution whatever. It may truly be said to have neither FORCE nor WILL, but merely judgment."[44] Chief Justice Marshall rephrased this in unmistakable terms: the Court was only to give "effect to the

40. Trop v. Dulles, 356 U.S. at 103.

41. "[T]he choice was made by the Framers," Justice Douglas declared, "a choice which sets a standard . . . The Framers made it a standard." Rochin v. California, 342 U.S. 165, 178–179 (1952), concurring opinion. Justice Black stated that "when a 'political theory' embodied in our Constitution becomes outdated . . . a majority of the nine members of this Court are not only without constitutional power but are far less qualified to choose a new constitutional theory than the people of this country proceeding in the manner provided by Article V." Harper v. Virginia Bd. of Elections, 383 U.S. 663, 678 (1966), dissenting opinion. Yet both Black and Douglas joined in the "reapportionment" decisions.

42. Article II, §1(8). Note John Adams' insistence on "exact" observance of the "fundamental principles of the constitution," supra at note 18, by which he surely included the text and the Framers' explanations.

43. Federalist at 508; Berger, supra note 4 at 12–16.

44. Federalist No. 78 at 504.

will of the legislature."[45] Hamilton rejected the argument that the courts were empowered "to construe the laws according to the *spirit* of the Constitution";[46] "penumbras formed by emanations"[47] were not for him. What he meant is made quite clear by his rejection of the notion "that the courts on the pretence of a repugnancy, may substitute their own pleasure to the constitutional intentions of the legislature,"[48] a statement, Louis Lusky notes, that "is hard to square with anticipation of judicial constitution-making power."[49] Finally, well aware that there existed considerable distrust of the proposal for judicial review, Hamilton sought to allay it in Federalist No. 81 by calling attention to the

> important constitutional check which the power of instituting impeachments . . . would give to that body [Congress] upon the members of the judicial department. This is alone a complete security. There can never be danger that the judges, by a series of deliberate usurpations on the authority of the legislature, would hazard the united resentment of the body intrusted with it.[50]

45. Infra Chapter 16 at note 41.

46. Federalist No. 81 at 524.

47. Griswold v. Connecticut, 381 U.S. 479, 484 (1965). Justice Douglas held that "specific guarantees of the Bill of Rights have penumbras, formed by emanations from those guarantees, that give them life and substance." Webster, as A. T. Mason points out, "defines *penumbra* as a 'marginal region or borderland of partial obscurity.'" "The Burger Court in Historical Perspective," 47 N.Y. State Bar J. 87, 89 (1975). It is an odd conceit that "obscure borderland regions" lend "life and substance" to explicit guarantees. Nor does a region of "partial obscurity" offer the solid footing required for a novel intrusion into the relations of a State with its citizens that the Tenth Amendment protects.

48. Federalist No. 78 at 507. Justice Frankfurter explained that "The reason why from the beginning even the narrow judicial authority to nullify legislation has been viewed with a jealous eye is that it serves to prevent the full play of the democratic process." Board of Education v. Barnette, 319 U.S. 624, 650 (1943), dissenting opinion.

49. Lusky 72.

50. Federalist at 526–527. When I first considered this provision in 1969, it was in the context of the congressional power to make "exceptions" to the

These were no idle words, for both the English and the Founders regarded "usurpation" or subversion of the Constitution as the most heinous of impeachable offenses.[51]

Today there is a tendency to reduce the Constitution to the status of a "symbol" of continuity and unity,[52] but for the Founders it was a living reality. They swore the President to "preserve and defend the Constitution" because it represented a "bulwark" of their liberties, not a mere symbol. They indited a charter which delegates power to the "servants and agents of the people,"[53] with "limits," "checks and balances" to guard against its abuse. It bears witness to the creation of a *government by consent* of the sovereign people; "just government," stated the Declaration of Independence, "is founded on the consent of the governed." The terms of that consent are spelled out in the Constitution. "The people," averred James Iredell, one of the ablest of the Founders, "have chosen to be governed under such

---

Supreme Court's appellate jurisdiction, while arguing that that power could not have been designed to curb judicial "excesses," citing Hamilton's statement that the impeachment provision "is the only provision on the point which is consistent with the necessary independence of the judicial character." Federalist No. 79 at 514. When I went on to quote James Wilson's statement that judges were not to be "impeached, because they decide an act null and void, that was made in defiance of the Constitution," Berger, supra note 4 at 290–291, I did not, because the point was not involved, draw the distinction between an exercise by the Court of its jurisdiction to police constitutional boundaries (infra Chapter 16 at notes 5–6, 26–27), which neither the impeachment nor the "exceptions" power can correct, and the usurpation of "legislative power," which is an impeachable offense. The meaning of usurpation was made clear by Iredell: "If Congress, under pretense of executing one power, should in fact usurp another, they will violate the Constitution." 4 Elliot 179. A congressional usurpation can be set aside by the Court; a judicial usurpation, as Hamilton stated, can be met by impeachment.

51. Raoul Berger, *Impeachment: The Constitutional Problems* 33, 39, 86 (1973).

52. A. Bickel, *The Least Dangerous Branch* 31 (1962).

53. "Those in power," said Iredell, are "servants and agents of the people." 4 Elliot 9. Archibald Maclaine stated in the North Carolina Convention that the people can "delegate power to agents." Id. 161. See Hamilton, supra at note 35.

and such principles. They have not chosen to be governed or promised to submit upon any other."[54] Substitution by the Court of its own value choices for those embodied in the Constitution violates the basic principle of government by consent of the governed. We must therefore reject, I submit, Charles Evans Hughes' dictum that "the Constitution is what the Supreme Court says it is."[55] No power to revise the Constitution under the guise of "interpretation" was conferred on the Court; it does so only because the people have not grasped the reality—an unsafe foundation for power in a government by consent.

Too much discussion of constitutional law is centered on the Court's decisions, with not enough regard for the text and history of the Constitution itself. We need to recall Justice Gibson's great statement in 1825:

> in questions of this sort, precedents ought to go for absolutely nothing. The Constitution is a collection of fundamental laws, not to be departed from in practice nor altered by judicial decision, and in the construction of it, nothing would be so alarming as the doctrine of *communis error,* which offers a ready justifica-

54. 2 McRee, supra note 19 at 146. This was powerfully stated in the First Congress by Alexander White of Virginia: "This is a Government constituted for particular purposes only; and the powers granted to carry it into effect are specifically enumerated . . . If these powers are insufficient . . . it is not . . . within our power to remedy. The people who bestowed them must grant further powers . . . This was the ground on which the friends of the Government supported the Constitution . . . [otherwise] the Constitution would never have been ratified" in Virginia. 1 *Annals of Congress* 514–515.

55. Embarrassed by this incautious remark, Hughes explained that he was not picturing interpretation "as a matter of judicial caprice." *The Autobiographical Notes of Charles Evans Hughes* 143 (D. J. Danielski and J. S. Tulchin eds. 1973). One need not charge Justices Field and Pierce Butler with "caprice"; it suffices that they sincerely identified their own predilections with constitutional dogma. Professor Frankfurter wrote to President Franklin Roosevelt that it is the Justices "who speak and not the Constitution." *Roosevelt and Frankfurter: Their Correspondence 1928–1945* 383 (M. Freedman ed. 1967).

tion for every usurpation that has not been resisted *in limine* . . . the judge who asserts [the right of judicial review] ought to be prepared to maintain it on the principles of the Constitution.[56]

Like Chief Justice Burger and Justices Douglas and Frankfurter, I assert the right to look at the Constitution itself, stripped of judicial incrustations,[57] as the index of constitutional law and to affirm that the Supreme Court has no authority to substitute

56. Eakin v. Raub, 12 S. & R. 330 (Pa. 1825), dissenting opinion. That view was expressed by Justice Holmes and quoted by Justice Brandeis in Erie Ry. Co. v. Tompkins, 304 U.S. 64, 79 (1938) when the doctrine of Swift v. Tyson, 40 U.S. (16 Pet.) 1 (1842), was branded "an unconstitutional assumption of power by courts of the United States which no lapse of time or respectable array of opinion should make us hesitate to correct."

Justice Gibson's opinion is often regarded as impugning judicial review in the federal courts; but Gibson was careful to distinguish between the Pennsylvania Constitution (of 1790, 2 Poore 1548), which contained neither a "supremacy clause" (Article VI, §2), nor an "arising under" clause (Article III, §2), and the federal Constitution, which does. 12 S. & R. at 345, 346, 347, 356, 357. Although Gibson spoke in the context of state powers and duties, federal judges too are "bound" only by "laws" of Congress that are "consistent with the Constitution." Infra Chapter 19 at notes 18–21. Moreover, Gibson made no reference to expressions by the Founders in both the Federal and State Conventions that judicial review was contemplated, infra Chapter 19 at notes 25–28, presumably because they were not germane to the Pennsylvania Constitution under adjudication, and because they had not yet been published.

57. Chief Justice Burger "categorically" rejected the "thesis that what the Court said lately controls over the Constitution . . . By placing a premium on 'recent cases' rather than the language of the Constitution, the Court makes it dangerously simple for future Courts using the technique of interpretation to operate as a 'continuing Constitutional Convention.'" Coleman v. Alabama, 399 U.S. 1, 22–23 (1970). Justice Douglas wrote, a judge "remembers above all else that it is the Constitution which he swore to support and defend, not the gloss which his predecessors may have put upon it." "Stare Decisis," 49 Colum. L. Rev. 735, 736 (1949). Justice Frankfurter stated that "the ultimate touchstone of constitutionality is the Constitution itself and not what we have said about it." Graves v. O'Keefe, 306 U.S. 466, 491–492 (1939), concurring opinion.

an "unwritten Constitution" for the written Constitution the Founders gave us and the people ratified.

Constitutionalism—limited government under the rule of law—was a paramount aim, not to be warped in order to achieve some predilection of any given bench. Solicitor General, later Justice, Robert H. Jackson, perceived, as Chief Justice Warren did not, that "the rule of law is in unsafe hands when courts cease to function as courts and become organs for control of policy."[58] Even a celebrant of the Warren era, Thurman Arnold, stated that without a continuing pursuit of "the ideal of the rule of law we would not have a civilized government." But although he labeled it as of "tremendous importance," he viewed it as "unattainable."[59] That is a romantic view which can be invoked to shirk the attainable. Effectuation of the Fourteenth Amendment's decision to leave suffrage to the States, for example, was not "unattainable"; attainment was balked only by the Court's drive to restructure the Constitution. For the Founders "the rule of law" was no "unattainable" ideal, but a basic imperative. And so it must remain. As Charles McIlwain wrote, "The two fundamental correlative elements of constitutionalism for which all lovers of liberty must yet fight are the

58. Jackson, *The Struggle for Judicial Supremacy* 322 (1941). And as Justice, one of the most gifted that served on the Court, Jackson "took the notion of a rule of law seriously," G. E. White, *The American Judicial Tradition* 248 (1976); he deemed it inappropriate for judges "to seize the initiative in shaping the policy of the law." And he "attacked the 'cult of libertarian judicial activists' on the Court whose attitude, he felt, 'encourage[d] a belief that judges may be left to correct the results of public indifference to the issues of liberty.'" White, id. 246.

To "engage in result-oriented jurisprudence," Leonard Levy wrote, is to leave "far behind the idea of the rule of law enforced by impersonal and impartial judges." Levy, *Against the Law* 438. Wallace Mendelson stated, "we must begin again the unending struggle for the Rule of Law, for government by something more respectable than the will of those who for the moment hold high office." *The Supreme Court: Law and Discretion* 40 (1967).

59. Arnold, supra note 36 at 1311.

legal limits to arbitrary power and a complete responsibility of government to the governed."[60]

If this be arid legalism, it was shared by Washington, who stated in his Farewell Address:

> If in the opinion of the People, the distribution or modification of the Constitutional powers be in any particular wrong, let it be corrected by an amendment in the way in which the Constitution designates. But let there be no change by usurpation; for though this, in one instance, may be the instrument of good, it is the customary weapon by which free governments are destroyed. The precedent must always greatly overbalance in permanent evil any partial or transient benefit which the use can at any time yield.[61]

It is because Americans continue to regard the Constitution as the bulwark of their liberties that they hold it in reverence. "[E]very breach of the fundamental laws, though dictated by necessity," said Hamilton, "impairs the sacred reverence which ought to be maintained in the breasts of the rulers towards the constitution."[62]

60. *Constitutionalism: Ancient and Modern* 146 (rev. ed. 1947).
61. 35 G. Washington, *Writings* 228–229 (J. Fitzpatrick ed. 1940).
62. Federalist No. 25 at 158.

16

The Judiciary Was Excluded from Policymaking

THE COUNCIL OF REVISION

I T is a singular fact that the most significant single piece of evidence that the Framers excluded the judiciary from policymaking —rejection of their participation in a Council of Revision of legislation—went unnoticed by bench and bar until it was called to their attention by a political scientist, Benjamin F. Wright.[1] Not the least remarkable aspect of judicial neglect of this history is that it should finally be invoked by Justices Black (1965)[2] and Douglas (1968),[3] oblivious to the shattering effect that it has on their own sweeping policymaking decisions.

Edmund Randolph proposed in the Convention that the President, "and a convenient number of the National Judiciary, ought to compose a council of revision" to examine every act of Congress and by its dissent to constitute a veto.[4] When his

1. Benjamin F. Wright, *The Growth of American Constitutional Law* 18-20 (1942); see also A. T. Mason, *The Supreme Court: Palladium of Freedom* 67–70 (1962).

2. Griswold v. Connecticut, 381 U.S. 479, 514 note 6 (1965).

3. Flast v. Cohen, 392 U.S. 83, 107 (1968); Justice Frankfurter had cited it in Board of Education v. Barnette, 319 U.S. 624, 650 (1943): the Framers "denied such legislative powers to the federal judiciary [and] chose instead to insulate the judiciary from the legislative function."

4. 1 Farrand 21.

fellow Virginian George Mason argued for judicial participation in the presidential veto, he recognized that judges already

> could declare an unconstitutional law void. But with regard to every law *however unjust oppressive* or pernicious, which did not come plainly under this description, they would be under the necessity as Judges to give it a free course. He wished further use to be made of the Judges, of giving aid in *preventing every improper law*.[5]

A similar differentiation was drawn by James Wilson:

> Laws may be *unjust, may be unwise, may be dangerous,* may be destructive; and yet be *not so unconstitutional* as to justify the Judges in refusing to give them effect. Let them have a share in the Revisionary power [in order to "counteract"] the improper views of the Legislature.[6]

Despite the fact that the proposal had the support of Madison, and, therefore, of perhaps the most influential trio in the Convention, it was rejected for reasons that unmistakably spell out the exclusion of the judiciary from even a share in policymaking. Nathaniel Gorham saw no "advantage of employing the Judges in this way. As Judges they are not to be presumed to possess any peculiar knowledge of the mere policy of public measures."[7] Elbridge Gerry, one of the most vigorous advocates of judicial review, opposed judicial participation in the Council:

> It was *quite foreign* from the nature of ye office to make them *judges of the policy* of public measures . . . It was making Statesmen of the Judges; and setting them up as the guardians of the Rights of the people. He relied for his part on the Representatives

5. 2 Farrand 78 (emphasis added).
6. 2 id. 73 (emphasis added).
7. Id.

of the people as the guardians of their Rights and Interests. It was making the Expositors of the Laws, the Legislators which ought never to be done.[8]

Charles Pinckney also "opposed the interference of the Judges in the Legislative business."[9] Rufus King joined in the opposition on the ground that as "the judges must interpret the Laws they ought not to be legislators."[10] Roger Sherman "disapproved of Judges meddling in politics and parties."[11] It is reasonable to infer that John Dickinson expressed a widely shared view in cautioning that "The Judiciary of Aragon . . . became by degrees the law-givers."[12] Plainly the Framers refused to make the judiciary "law-givers," even to the extent of allowing them to share in the legislative making of law, let alone *finally* to decide on policy, an exclusive legislative function.[13] They drew a line between the judicial reviewing function, that is, *policing* grants of power to insure that there were no encroachments beyond the grants, and legislative policymaking *within* those bounds. "Dangerous" and "destructive" as such policies might be, they were yet to be the exclusive province of the legislature. That is the inescapable inference from the facts, and, as will appear, it is fortified by still other historical facts.

Justice Douglas therefore stood on solid ground in stating that "when the Court used substantive due process to deter-

8. 1 Farrand 97–98; 2 Farrand 75 (emphasis added). Wright stated, "Gerry is not alone in this, for the same point of view is expressed by almost every man who says anything at all on this subject in the Convention and in the ratification controversy." "The judiciary," Wright concluded, "would not be concerned with the policy, the reasonableness or arbitrariness, the wisdom of legislation." Supra note 1 at 18, 244; see also id. 19–20.

9. 2 Farrand 298.

10. 1 Farrand 108; cf. id. 98.

11. 2 Farrand 300.

12. Id. 299.

13. Mason, *The Supreme Court,* supra note 1 at 70, 94, 117; Julius Goebel, *Antecedents and Beginnings to 1801, History of the Supreme Court of the United States,* vol. 1, p. 238 (1971).

mine the wisdom or reasonableness of legislation, it was indeed transforming itself into the Council of Revision which was rejected by the Constitutional Convention."[14] In a remarkable example of compartmentalized thinking he went on to say, "we no longer exercise that kind of power," just as he had earlier stated in *Griswold v. Connecticut* that the Court no longer acts as a "super legislature"—except in a case touching the "right of privacy."[15]

The history of the Council of Revision also serves to refute the view that judicial review is an expression of "distrust in popular government,"[16] or, in Corwin's oft-quoted phrase, having bet on democracy, the Framers then "covered their bet."[17] The "cover," however, went no further than to prevent the legislature from "overleaping its bounds." In fact the judiciary was *excluded* from halting "dangerous . . . destructive" legislation that was within those bounds. If the Framers "covered their bet," they gave the last trump to Congress: judges who usurped power, for example, exercised a power withheld, said Hamilton, could be impeached. The Founders unequivocally rejected the judiciary as "guardians of the people"; they preferred, in Gerry's words, to put their trust in "the Representatives of the people." For judicial review was an innovation by no means universally admired; it was a departure from Blackstone's

14. Flast v. Cohen, 392 U.S. at 107. Through the due process clauses, A. T. Mason stated, the Court "became the final arbiter of public policy . . . the very authority the framers deliberately refused to confer under the proposed council of revision." Mason, *The Supreme Court,* supra note 1 at 117. Yet Rodell could write that those who complain talk in "abstract phrases"—"judicial usurpation of legislative functions." "The 'Warren Court' Stands Its Ground," *The New York Times Magazine,* September 27, 1964, in Levy, *Warren* 208, 211.

15. Supra Chapter 14 at note 74.

16. Wallace Mendelson, *Justices Black and Frankfurter: Conflict in the Court* 126 (1961).

17. Quoted in Mason, *The Supreme Court,* supra note 1 at 63: "Judicial review represents an attempt by American Democracy to cover its bet."

"omnipotent parliament."[18] Having "smarted" under the "omnipotent power of the British parliament," said James Iredell, we should "have been guilty of . . . the grossest folly" had we "established a *despotic* power among ourselves."[19] If this could be said of a legislature that could be turned out of office periodically, constitution-makers were even less ready to entrust unlimited power to an untried, unelected judiciary appointed for life.

The judicial role, it cannôt be unduly emphasized, was limited to policing constitutional boundaries. James Wilson said it is necessary that Congress be "kept within prescribed bounds, by the interposition of the judicial department."[20] The courts, said Oliver Ellsworth, were a "check" if Congress should "overleap their limits," "make a law which the Constitution does not authorize."[21] Judges, John Marshall stated in the Virginia Convention, could declare void "a law not warranted by any of the powers enumerated."[22] Hamilton stressed that the courts were to serve as "bulwarks of a limited Constitution against legislative encroachments."[23] But "within those limits," Madison said, there were "discretionary powers."[24] The exercise of that discretion, as we have seen, is for the branch to whom it has been confided. No one, so far as my search of the several convention records uncovered, looked to the Court for "leadership" in resolving problems that Congress, the Pres-

18. Raoul Berger, *Congress v. The Supreme Court* 38–42, 29 (1969).

19. 2 G. J. McRee, *Life and Correspondence of James Iredell* 145–146 (1857–1858).

20. 2 Elliot 445.

21. Id. 196.

22. 3 Elliot 553. For additional citations, see Berger, supra note 18 at 13–16.

23. Federalist No. 78 at 508. At another point he stated that the courts were an "excellent barrier to encroachments and oppressions of the representative body." Id. 503.

24. 1 *Annals of Congress* 438 (1789). "The Legislative powers," Madison stated, "are vested in Congress, and are to be exercised by them uncontrolled by any of the Departments, except the Constitution has qualified it otherwise." Id. 463.

ident, or the States failed to solve. That view is a product of post-Warren euphoria. The courts were expected to "negative" or set aside unauthorized action, to "check" legislative excesses, to "restrain" Congress within its prescribed "limits," to prevent the "usurpation" of power. The Court, in other words, was to act as *nay-sayer,* not as initiator of policy. Justice Stephen Field, supreme activist of his time, stated upon his retirement in 1897 that "This negative power, the power of resistance, is the only safety of a popular government."[25]

When, therefore, James Bradley Thayer and Learned Hand insisted that the role of the Court was to police the boundaries of constitutional grants, not to interfere with the exercise of legislative or executive discretion *within* those boundaries,[26] they rested firmly on the authority of Hamilton and the preponderant view of the Founders. For 150 years the Court was content with this policing function;[27] even the headstrong laissez-faire Court merely acted as a nay-sayer. It fell to the Warren Court to *initiate* policy when the legislative and executive failed

25. Letter to the Court, October 12, 1897, 168 U.S. 713, 717 (1897). Gouverneur Morris stated that it was the judicial function to reject a "direct violation of the Constitution." 2 Farrand 299. The Court "gained its power as an agency trusted to establish and enforce constitutional limitations on the excessive use of governmental authority," i.e., in excess of granted authority. Paul Murphy, *The Constitution in Crisis Times, 1918–1969* 154 (1972).

26. J. B. Thayer, "The Origin and Scope of the American Doctrine of Constitutional Law," 7 Harv. L. Rev. 129, 135 (1893); L. Hand, *The Bill of Rights* 66, 31 (1962). That control of executive discretion lies beyond the judicial function was held in Marbury v. Madison, 5 U.S. (1 Cranch) 137, 169–170 (1803), and in Decatur v. Paulding, 39 U.S. (14 Pet.) 497, 515 (1840).

27. Cf. Murphy, supra note 25 at 154. Professor Kurland stated, "the Court would remain true to its function of preserving the original meaning of the Constitution if it were to act more aggressively to prevent the executive from overreaching his constitutionally limited function." *Politics, the Constitution and the Warren Court* 17 (1970). "Throughout most of our history the form of the Supreme Court's contributions to public policy was negative." Archibald Cox, "The New Dimensions of Constitutional Adjudication," 51 Wash. L. Rev. 791, 813 (1976).

to act, to take the lead in deciding what national policy ought to be.[28] But the failure of Congress to exercise legislative power does not vest it in the Court.

JUDICIAL "DISCRETION" IN 1787

A common historicist fallacy is to import our twentieth-century conceptions into the minds of the Founders. At the adoption of the Constitution the notion that judges, for example, could *make law* as an instrument of social change was altogether alien to colonial thinking. "Instrumentalism" was yet to come. In a valuable essay Morton J. Horwitz observed that "fear of judicial discretion had long been part of colonial political rhetoric" and described the prevalent jural conceptions that combined to circumscribe the judicial function in the eighteenth century.[29] There was first the fact that the common law rules—that is, judicially enunciated rules in the field of contracts and the like—"were conceived of as *'founded in principles, that are permanent,* uniform and universal.'" Consequently, judges "conceived their role as merely that of discovering and applying preexisting legal rules" and derived "the rule of strict precedent" from such "preexisting standards discoverable by judges." It followed that "judicial innovation itself was

28. "[T]here *were* outrages in American life . . . no other arm of government was doing anything about them." Anthony Lewis, "A Man Born to Act, Not to Muse," *The New York Times Magazine,* June 30, 1968, in Levy, *Warren* 151, 159 (1968). See also Martin Shapiro, *Law and Politics in the Supreme Court* 247–248 (1964). In the words of Professor Lusky, the Court is "acting as a prime mover rather than a modulator of efforts at change initiated elsewhere . . . As a prime mover . . . it has demanded a number of changes which do not command majoritarian support." Lusky 227. See also supra Chapter 14 note 136. For the transformation of the judicial function this has entailed, see Appendix II. See also infra Chapter 20 note 8.

29. "The Emergence of an Instrumental Conception of American Law, 1780–1820," in 5 *Perspectives in American History* 287, 303 (1971).

regarded as an impermissible exercise of will."[30] Horwitz cites the statement of Chief Justice Hutchinson of Massachusetts in 1767: "the *Judge* should never be the *Legislator:* Because then the Will of the Judge would be the Law: and this tends to a State of Slavery."[31] Not long afterward Edward Gibbon wrote, "the discretion of the judge is the first engine of tyranny."[32] Horwitz concluded that "In eighteenth century America, common law rules were not regarded as instruments of social change; whatever legal change took place generally was brought about through legislation . . . American judges . . . almost never self-consciously employed the common law as a creative instrument for directing men's energies towards social change."[33] Those who would rest an implied power of judges to act as such instruments of social change in the field of constitutional law

30. Id. 296, 297, 298. Zephaniah Smith, Chief Justice of Connecticut, stated, "Judges have no power to frame laws — they can only expound them." 1 Z. Smith, *A System of Laws of the State of Connecticut* 93–94 (1795–1796). Lord Mansfield's reforming work "convinced Thomas Jefferson that a check need be established on the common law powers of judges." Horwitz, supra note 29 at 310. This in the field of commercial, not constitutional, law.

31. Horwitz, id. at 292. For additional materials illustrating the Founders' aversion to judicial discretion, see Gordon Wood, *The Creation of the American Republic 1776–1789* 301–302 (1969). As one writer put it, if the judges "put such a construction on matters as they think most agreeable to the spirit and reason of the law . . . they assume what is in fact the prerogative of the legislature." Wood, id. 302.

32. 4 Edward Gibbon, *The History of the Decline and Fall of the Roman Empire* 518 (Nottingham Soc. undated). Blackstone had written, "law, without equity, though hard and disagreeable, is much more desirable for the public good than equity without law; which would make every judge a legislator, and introduce most infinite confusion." 1 Blackstone, *Commentaries on the Laws of England* 62 (1765–1769). Wendell Phillips quoted Lord Camden: "The discretion of a Judge is the law of tyrants . . . In the best of times it is often times caprice — in the worst, it is every vice, folly and passion, to which human nature is liable." Quoted in Robert Cover, *Justice Accused: Antislavery and the Judicial Process* 152 (1975).

33. Supra note 29 at 287.

have the burden of producing evidence that the Framers intended to depart from these norms. The exclusion of judges
from the Council of Revision alone points to the contrary.

"Instrumentalism," Horwitz shows, largely began to develop
in the early nineteenth century—after the adoption of the Constitution; the examples he cites are all drawn from application of
common law; not once is a judicial claim of power to alter a
statute, let alone a constitution, asserted. To such negative implications may be added Hamilton's statement in the very context of judicial review (Federalist No. 78), that the judicial role
is one of "judgment" not "will," that "to avoid arbitrary discretion in the courts, it is indispensable that they should be
bound down by strict rules and precedents, which serve to define and point out their duty in every particular case that comes
before them."[34] What could be further from the current free-
wheeling conception of judicial review than these words by the
foremost apologist for judicial review, designed to reassure
opponents of ratification? Courts were not merely to be "bound
down" by the "chains of the Constitution," but by "strict rules
and precedents" as well. Even when the tide began to turn
toward instrumentalism, Judge William Cranch of the Circuit
Court for the District of Columbia stated in his preface to 1
Cranch of the Supreme Court's decisions (1803): "In a government which is emphatically stiled a government of laws, the
least possible range ought to be left for the discretion of the
judge."[35]

---

34. Horwitz, supra note 29 at 309–326; Federalist No. 78 at 504, 510. Kent
stated that without the common law, i.e., the precedents, "the courts would
be left to a dangerous discretion to roam at large in the trackless field of their
own imaginations." 1 James Kent, *Commentaries on American Law* 373 (9th ed.
1858).

35. 5 U.S. (1 Cranch) iii (1803). Cranch was a nephew of, and appointed by,
President John Adams, and a classmate and esteemed friend of his cousin John
Quincy Adams. *Life in a New England Town: 1787, 1788. Diary of John Quincy
Adams* 21 note 2 (1903). Horwitz quotes an unpublished opinion on circuit by
Justice William Johnson (1813) that to invite "judicial discretion" would "in-

There are also contemporary judicial statements that display the circumspection with which the judges approached the novel task of judicial review. In one of the earliest State cases, *Commonwealth v. Caton* (1782) Edmund Pendleton, president of the highest Virginia court, stated: "how far this court . . . can go in declaring an act of the Legislature void, because it is repugnant to the Constitution, without exercising the Power of Legislation, from which they are restrained by the same Constitution? is a deep, important, and I will add, an awful question"[36]— which, he rejoiced, he had no occasion to decide. Subsequently, Pendleton served as the presiding officer of the Virginia Ratification Convention, and it is unlikely that he translated the examples furnished by his colleagues, all addressed to checking encroachments on reserved powers, into unlimited power of review. No one remotely intimated that there would be judicial power to rewrite the Constitution.[37] Nothing could have been better calculated to defeat ratification than a claim of judicial power that would leave the States altogether at the mercy of the federal courts;[38] and such State jealousy was met by the Judiciary Act of 1789 which withheld from the inferior federal courts jurisdiction of cases "arising under" the Constitution.

Even with respect to the policing function, Justice James Iredell, who had been one of the most cogent advocates of judicial review, stated in 1798 that the power to declare a legislative act "void is of a delicate and awful nature, [hence] the Court will never resort to that authority but in a clear and urgent case."[39]

---

crease the oddity of the state of things" in that the judiciary "would be left at large to be governed by their own views on the Fitness of things." Supra note 29 at 306–307.

36. Commonwealth v. Caton, published in 2 *Letters and Papers of Edmund Pendleton* 416, 422 (D. J. Mays ed. 1967).

37. For citations to Madison, Marshall, and Nicholas, see Berger, supra note 18 at 77, 140, 15.

38. Cf. id. 263.

39. Calder v. Bull, 3 U.S. (3 Dall.) 386, 399 (1798); Justice Chase said, "a very clear case." Id. 395. Earlier, Iredell, rebutting criticism of judicial review

In *M'Culloch v. Maryland* Chief Justice Marshall indicated that
something like a "bold and plain usurpation to which the constitution gave no countenance" was required "to invoke the judicial power of annulment."[40] And in 1824 he averred that "judicial power is never exercised for the purpose of giving effect
to the will of the judge; always for the purpose of giving effect
to the will of the legislature."[41] For Chief Judge Cardozo, Marshall's statement was the expression "of an ideal," which "Marshall's own career" illustrates "is beyond the reach of human
faculties to attain."[42] It would be more accurate to say, as
Charles L. Black pointed out, that it reflected the colonists' conception that "*Law is a body of existing and determinate rules,*"
which "*is to be ascertained*" by the judge by consulting "statutes,
precedents and the rest," and that "the function of the judge
was thus placed in sharpest antithesis to that of the legislator,"
who alone was concerned "with what the law ought to be."[43]
So Marshall understood the judicial role: "Courts are mere instruments of the law and can will nothing. When they are said
to exercise a discretion, it is a mere legal discretion, a discretion to be exercised in discerning the course *prescribed by*

---

by Richard Spaight (then a delegate to the Convention), had stressed that an
Act "should be unconstitutional beyond dispute before it is pronounced
such." 2 McRee, supra note 19 at 175.

40. 17 U.S. (4 Wheat.) 316, 402 (1819).

41. Osborn v. Bank of the United States, 22 U.S. (9 Wheat.) 738, 866
(1824).

42. B. N. Cardozo, *The Nature of the Judicial Process* 169–170 (1921). It is not
merely an "ideal" but a requirement of the separation of powers, supra
Chapter 15 at notes 27, 43–49. Marshall recognized judicial limits in his
pseudonymous defense of M'Culloch v. Maryland, to meet stormy charges
of judicial usurpation. See infra Chapter 21 at notes 12–19. Least of all can
the judiciary say one thing and do another; it cannot afford conflicts between
word and deed. Nor does Marshall's disregard of constitutional bounds
legitimize his displacement of the Framers' "will" by his own.

43. Black, *The People and the Court* 160 (1960).

law"[44]—that is, by the legislators or the people gathered in Convention.

Marshall, it needs always to be remembered, had fought on behalf of judicial review in the Virginia Ratification Convention and was well aware of the views entertained by the Founders. His 1824 statement confirms that among the presuppositions the Founders brought to the several conventions was a bias against judicial discretion and policymaking. There is no evidence whatsoever that these presuppositions were thrown overboard in the creation of the judiciary. To the contrary, the established presumption is that the Founders created a judiciary in familiar terms, except insofar as they envisaged its "policing" function. Judicial alteration of the fundamental law ran counter to their belief in a "fixed Constitution"; it was altogether outside their contemplation, as Hamilton made plain.[45] Justice Frankfurter, therefore, was close to the mark in stating that the Framers were on guard "against the self-will of the courts."[46]

44. Osborn v. Bank, 22 U.S. at 866, emphasis added.

45. The foregoing materials, to my mind, refute Bickel's view that the Framers "certainly had no specific intent relating to the nature and range of the power" of judicial review. *The Least Dangerous Branch* 104 (1962).

46. National Ins. Co. v. Tidewater Co., 337 U.S. 582, 647 (1949), dissenting opinion.

17

The Turnabout of
the Libertarians

WHY did the libertarians, after decades of berating the Court for reading its laissez-faire predilections into
the Constitution and imposing its own economic policy on the
nation,[1] turn around and defend it for pursuing the same course
with respect to libertarian values? One may view the turnabout
merely as another illustration of "whose ox is gored";[2] but
perhaps the explanation lies deeper. Arthur Sutherland explained that between 1920 and 1940 academe "viewed the federal judiciary with dismay" and was "deeply imbued with faith
in majorities." A "change of political theory developed"
between 1938 and 1948, deriving from "Hitler's popularity

1. In the pre-1937 era, Archibald Cox states, "Historians and politicians
were 'proving' that judicial review was a usurpation of power defeating the
original intent. There was a sense that the Justices made a mess of things when
they attempted to enlarge their orbit, as they did in resisting government regulation of the economy." *The Role of the Supreme Court in American Government*
34 (1976).

2. An unconscious example is Rodell's statement in 1964: "Not since the
Nine Old Men of unhallowed memory struck down the first New Deal almost 30 years ago . . . has any Supreme Court used its politico-legal power
so broadly and boldly as did Earl Warren's," a performance that gave him
joy, whereas the predecessors were "unhallowed." Fred Rodell, "The Warren
Court Stands Its Ground," *The New York Times Magazine,* September 27,
1964, in Levy, *Warren* 208, 209.

among the German people, public support of the Un-American Activities Committee and McCarthy Hearings" and so on, for "votaries of unreviewed majoritarianism" suddenly realized that "unrestricted majorities could be as tyrannical as wicked oligarchs . . . We could not say in plain terms that occasionally we have to select wise and able people and give them the constitutional function of countering the democratic process."[3] Looking back in 1976 and writing with equally praiseworthy candor, Archibald Cox, who had played a major role as Solicitor General in persuading the Supreme Court to adopt some of the epochal decisions of the 1960s,[4] stated:

> By the 1950s the political atmosphere had changed. The legislative process, even at its best, became resistant to libertarian, humanitarian, and egalitarian impulses. At worst, the legislatures became repressive, in the libertarian view, because of the Cold War, increased crime, the fear of social disorder, and perhaps, the strength of established economic and political power . . . [I]n the new era these impulses were not shared so strongly and widely as to realize themselves through legislation. They came to be felt after the early 1950s by a majority of the Supreme Court Justices, perhaps by the fate which puts one man upon the Court rather than another, perhaps because the impulses were felt more strongly in the world of the highly educated.[5]

Mark that these "impulses" were "not shared so strongly and widely as to realize themselves through legislation," that they "were felt more strongly in the world of the highly educated," and were realized through the "fate which puts one man upon the Court rather than another." Because for the nonce the majority of the Court shared the predilections of the "highly educated," the latter looked kindly upon the Court's imposition

3. "Privacy in Connecticut," 64 Mich. L. Rev. 283–284 (1965).
4. See Ward Elliot, *The Rise of a Guardian Democracy* (1974).
5. Cox, supra note 1 at 35.

of its will upon the people.[6] But, as Myres McDougal wrote some years ago, "Government by a self-designated elite—like that of benevolent despotism or Plato's philosopher kings— may be a good form of government for some, but it is not the American way."[7] No intellectual but can from time to time be disappointed by the vox populi, whether it be by the choices it makes—Richard Nixon, for example—or its imperviousness to the cultural values intellectuals cherish. In some it leads to a sense of alienation from the commonality; but, as Winston Churchill observed, the alternatives to democracy are even worse. With Lincoln, I cling to faith in the ultimate good sense of the people;[8] I cannot subscribe to the theory that America needs a savior, whether in the shape of a President or of nine— oftimes only five—Platonic Guardians.

It does not dispose of the uncomfortable historical facts to be told that "the dead hand of the past need not and should not be binding," that the Founders "should not rule us from their graves."[9] To thrust aside the dead hand of the Framers is to thrust aside the Constitution. The argument that new meanings

---

6. Writing in September 1976, Professor Joseph W. Bishop, Jr., stated, "Those who favor abortion, busing . . . and oppose capital punishment, call themselves and are generally regarded as liberals. But they obviously have no faith whatever in the wisdom or the will of the great majority of the people, who are opposed to them. They are doing everything possible to have these problems resolved by a small minority in the courts or the bureaucracy." Bishop, "What is a Liberal—Who is a Conservative?," 62 *Commentary* 47.

7. McDougal and Lans, "Treaties and Congressional-Executive or Presidential Agreements: Interchangeable Instruments of National Policy," 54 Yale L. J. 181, 577–578 (1945).

8. President Charles W. Eliot of Harvard University wrote, "I should like to be saved from loss of faith in democracy as I grow old and foolish." Ernest A. Samuels, *Henry Adams: The Major Phase* 359 (1964).

9. Leonard Levy ed., *Judicial Review and the Supreme Court* 143 (1967); Arthur S. Miller, "An Inquiry into the Relevance of the Intentions of the Founding Fathers, With Special Emphasis upon the Doctrine of Separation of Powers," 27 Ark. L. Rev. 584, 601 (1973).

may be given to words employed by the Framers[10] aborts their design; it reduces the Constitution to an empty shell into which each shifting judicial majority pours its own preferences. It is no answer to argue, as did Charles Curtis, "we cannot have our government run as if it were stuck in the end of the eighteenth century when we are in the middle of the twentieth,"[11] because, as Willard Hurst replied, "the real issue is *who is to make the policy choices* in the twentieth century: judges or the combination of legislature and electorate that makes constitutional amendments."[12] Since, for example, it would have been impossible to secure a desegregation amendment,[13] the libertarians premise that submission of such an issue to the people by amendment is at all costs to be avoided. McDougal and Lans genteelly explained that because "the process of amendment is politically difficult, other modes of change have emerged."[14] In less opaque terms, the cumbersomeness of the process authorizes

10. Infra Chapter 20 at notes 28–39.

11. "The Role of the Constitutional Text," in *Supreme Court and Supreme Law* 64, 68 (E. Cahn ed. 1954).

12. Willard Hurst, "Discussion," in *Supreme Court and Supreme Law,* id. 75, emphasis added. Hurst also disposed thereby of the citation to Holmes' "The present has a right to govern itself." Leonard Levy, *Judgments: Essays in American Constitutional History* 17 (1972). For Holmes' views see infra Chapter 21 at notes 33–42.

13. Supra Chapter 15 at note 14.

14. McDougal and Lans, supra note 7 at 293. Chief Justice Burger stated, "however cumbersome or glacial, this is the procedure the Constitution contemplated." Wheeler v. Montgomery, 397 U.S. 280, 284 (1970), dissenting opinion.

It is ironical that libertarians who argue for judicial "adaptation" of the Constitution because amendment is cumbersome should, like Eugene V. Rostow, state, "Given the possibility of constitutional amendment, there is nothing undemocratic in having responsible and independent judges act as important constitutional mediators." "The Democratic Character of Judicial Review," 66 Harv. L. Rev. 193, 197 (1952). Judges, in short, may alter the Constitution because resort to the people is onerous, but that very cumbersome process is recommended to the people to curb judicial infractions. Compare infra note 31.

the servants of the people informally to amend the Constitution
without consulting them! That, however, collides head-on with
Hamilton's assurance in the midst of his defense of judicial review in Federalist No. 78:

> Until the people have, by some solemn and authoritative act, an-
> nulled or changed the established form, it is binding upon them-
> selves collectively, as well as individually; and no presumption,
> or even knowledge of their sentiments, can warrant their repre-
> sentatives in a departure from it, prior to such an act.[15]

Neither Frankfurter's finely tuned antennae for ascertaining the
inarticulate sentiments of the people, nor "even knowledge of
their sentiments, can warrant" a "departure from" the Constitution by the Justices. Change, thus laid down the leading expositor of judicial review, must come via amendment. The reason
was put in a nutshell by Bruce Claggett: the Constitution requires that:

> changes in our fundamental law be made only when and if they
> have been subjected to the degree of deliberation and com-

---

15. Federalist No. 78 at 509. For a similar comment by Jefferson see infra at
note 90. Compare this with Alexander Bickel's view that "The Framers
knew . . . that nothing but disaster could result for government under a
written constitution if it were generally accepted that the specific intent of the
framers of a constitutional provision is ascertainable and is forever and specifically binding, subject only to the cumbersome process of amendment." *The
Least Dangerous Branch* 106 (1962). See also Madison, 1 *Annals of Congress* 739.
Elias Boudinot, erstwhile President of the Continental Congress, referred in
the First Congress to "the great danger" in "modifying the principles of the
Constitution." We "may begin with the alpha and go to the omega, changing,
reversing, and subverting every principle contained in it . . . [T]his never
was the intention of our constituents; they never sent us here for the purpose
of altering the system of Government; they reserved that power to themselves." 1 *Annals of Congress* 530. See also Alexander White, supra Chapter 15
note 54.

manded the preponderance of assent, involved in adoption and
ratification of a constitutional amendment . . . [T]he requirement was agreed upon (what legitimacy has our scheme of government had except as a compact?) and unilateral change involves usurpation, at least as much when effected by a court as
by a majority in Congress. If one thinks the more-than-simple
majorities required for constitutional change are too onerous,
one disagrees with the Constitution itself.[16]

It is not as if the difficulties of amendment were unperceived
by the Founders. Patrick Henry argued in the Virginia Ratification Convention that "four of the smallest states, that do not
collectively contain one tenth part of the population . . . may
obstruct the most salutary . . . amendments."[17] But James
Iredell expressed the prevailing view: the Constitution "can be
altered with as much regularity, and as little confusion, as any
Act of Assembly; not, indeed, quite so easily, which would be
extremely impolitic . . . so that alterations can without difficulty be made, agreeable to the general sense of the people."[18] In
Massachusetts, Charles Jarvis said, "we shall have in this article
an adequate provision for all purposes of political reforma-
tion."[19] In the First Congress, Elbridge Gerry, one of the im-

16. "Book Review," 27 Harv. L. Sch. Bull. 3, 4–5 (1976). See also supra
Chapter 15 at note 61. For what consent meant to the Founders, see supra
Chapter 15 at note 54.

17. 3 Elliot 49.

18. 4 Elliot 177.

19. 2 Elliot 116. In the Virginia Convention, Judge Edmund Pendleton
stated, "remote possible errors may be eradicated by the amendatory clause in
the Constitution . . . the system itself points out an easy mode of removing
errors which shall have been experienced." 3 Elliot 303. This was a judge who
had faced up to the issue of judicial review, supra Chapter 16 at note 36, and it
speaks volumes that it never occurred to him that there might be an even eas-
ier judicial way of revision than the "easy mode" provided by Article V.

portant Framers and erstwhile President of the Continental Congress, stated: "The people have" directed a "particular mode of making amendments, which we are not at liberty to depart from . . . Such a power [to alter] would render the most important clause of the Constitution nugatory."[20] In other words, Article V constitutes the *exclusive* medium of change, under the long-standing maxim that to name a particular mode is to exclude all others.[21] And, as Gerry stated, "an attempt to amend" the Constitution in "any other way" but by Article V "may be a high crime and misdemeanor," that is, an impeachable offense for subversion of the Constitution.[22] Because arguments to the contrary are couched obliquely—for example, "each generation of citizens must in a very real sense interpret the words of the Framers to create its own Constitution"[23] —one is apt to overlook that these are arguments for "change" outside Article V, by the judicial "interpreters" rather than the people. Libertarians, in short, would read the exclusivity of Article V out of the Constitution and cede to the Court a power that is to be exercised only by the people, and then only in accordance with its terms. The "shackles" from which libertarians would free us had the sanction of the people expressed through their State conventions, whereas judicial revision represents only the will of judges who would circumvent submission of a change to the people.

The Court itself, however, has not been overeager to acknowledge the crown academe would press upon its brow; it has never in terms asserted a right to strike the shackles of the past. Though it has often repudiated the design of the Framers,

20. 1 *Annals of Congress* 503 (1789).

21. See supra Chapter 12 note 11.

22. 1 *Annals of Congress* 503 (1789); see Hamilton, supra Chapter 15 at note 50.

23. McDougal and Lans, supra note 7 at 215.

it has done so by indirection, by resort to "lawyer's history,"[24] to far-fetched theorizing in search of an anchor in the Constitution. Robert Bork justly comments that "The Supreme Court regularly insists that its results . . . do not spring from the mere will of the Justices in the majority but are supported, indeed compelled, by a proper understanding of the Constitution . . . Value choices are attributed to the Founding Fathers, not to the Court."[25] Let Chief Justice Warren himself furnish an example: "The provisions of the Constitution are not time-worn adages or hollow shibboleths. They are vital living principles that authorize and limit governmental power in our Nation. They are the rules of government."[26] As Bork observes, "The way an institution advertises tells you what it thinks its customers demand."[27] Were the issue put squarely to the American people whether they would elect to have the Court strike the "shackles" of the past or to live under the constraints of the Constitution, I doubt not that they would resoundingly prefer

24. "The present use of history by the Court is a Marxist-type perversion of the relation between truth and utility. It assumes that history can be written to serve the interests of libertarian idealism. The whole process calls to mind the manipulation of scientific truth by the Soviet Government in the Lysenko controversy. The Court's purposes may be more laudable . . . but the assumptions about the nature of reality are the same." Kelly, "Clio and the Court: An Illicit Love Affair," 1965 S. Ct. Rev. 119, 157. Nevertheless Kelly applauded the decision in the desegregation case. Thomas Grey comments on the Court's "resort to bad legislative history and strained reading of constitutional language to support results that would be better justified by explication of contemporary moral and political ideals not drawn from the constitutional text." "Do We Have an Unwritten Constitution?," 27 Stan. L. Rev. 703, 706 (1975). See also Charles A. Miller, *The Supreme Court and the Uses of History* (1969).

25. "Neutral Principles and Some First Amendment Problems," 47 Ind. L. J. 1, 3–4 (1971); see Grey, supra note 24.

26. Trop v. Dulles, 356 U.S. 86, 103 (1958).

27. Bork, supra note 25 at 4.

the "idiosyncratic purposes of the Framers"[28] to those of the Justices.[29]

Some have sought a rationale in common law affirmations. Alexander Bickel referred to Holmes' statement that it is "revolting" to adhere to a rule of law, the grounds of which "have vanished long since."[30] Holmes wrote in the frame of the common law, where the courts have long been entrusted with the task of shaping the law of contracts and the like. If the results were at times displeasing to Parliament, they could be overruled in easy fashion by an act of Parliament. Decisions of constitutional question cannot, however, be overruled by the

28. McDougal and Lans, supra note 7 at 291. Professor Lusky also prefers "misgovernment by law" to "enlightened government by decree." Lusky 271. Hans Linde remarks that the "whole enterprise of constitutional law rests, after all, on the premise that the nation cares about its Constitution, not about its courts." "Judges, Critics and the Realist Tradition," 82 Yale L. J. 227, 256 (1972).

"In Professor [David] Truman's terms, large numbers of, and perhaps most, Americans entertain certain expectations or values about the Court's neutrality—values that have been called the 'judicial myth' [D. Truman, *The Governmental Process* 498 (1948)]." Martin Shapiro, *Law and Politics in the Supreme Court* 29 (1964). From childhood on the American expectation that the umpire will not espouse the cause of the opposing side is no "myth." If judicial umpires alone are not impartial arbiters let that fact be made known. See infra Chapter 23 at notes 30–35.

29. Judicial idiosyncrasy finds ready illustration in Justice Douglas. For example, he joined in the decision in Williams v. Florida, 399 U.S. 78 (1970), holding that the phrase "trial by jury" did not require a jury of twelve. But he dissented when the Court held in Johnson v. Louisiana, 406 U.S. 356 (1972), that these words did not require a unanimous verdict, condemning "this radical departure from American traditions"—"two centuries of American history are shunted aside." Id. at 381, 383. For centuries both a 12-man jury *and* a unanimous verdict had been indissoluble components of trial by jury. See infra Chapter 22. Douglas weakly sought to distinguish the 12-man jury decisions because "neither evidence nor theory suggested the 12-man jury decision was more favorable to the accused than six." Id. 382 note 1. On that analysis his appeal to history was superfluous. See also supra Chapter 14 at note 74.

30. Bickel, supra note 15 at 16. For a similar view, see Levy, *Judgments,* supra note 12 at 17. But compare Justice Holmes, infra note 32.

legislature; resort must be had to the "cumbersome" amendment process—it took eighteen years to overrule the income
tax decision![31] Then, too, if the common law is to serve as a
model, it needs to be remembered that at the adoption of the
Constitution judicial discretion was feared and confined by
strict adherence to precedent as a curb on the "impermissible
exercise of will,"[32] a course far removed from the present
Court's habit of leaving "precedents in a shambles."[33] Nevertheless, a free and easy judicial approach to constitutional
"adaptation" derived in no small part from the freedom American courts assumed in the early nineteenth century to reshape the
common law for the benefit of an emerging entrepenurial
system. Witting or unwitting, it was a carryover from a practice
so plainly described by Chancellor Kent in extolling his own
role in the shaping of American equity jurisdiction: "I might
once & a while be embarrassed by a technical rule, *but I most
always found principles suited to my views of the case.*"[33a] This

31. P. B. Kurland, *Politics, the Constitution and the Warren Court* 176–177
(1970); Raoul Berger, *Congress v. The Supreme Court* 207 (1969); Pollock v.
Farmers Loan & Trust Co., 157 U.S. 429 (1895). Justice Brandeis stated, "In
only two instances—the Eleventh and the Sixteenth Amendments—has the
process of constitutional amendment been successfully resorted to, to nullify
decisions of this Court." Burnet v. Coronada Oil & Gas Co., 285 U.S. 393,
409 note 5 (1932), dissenting opinion.

32. Supra Chapter 16 at notes 30–35, 44. Even in the adjudication of
common law cases, the norm was to leave "novel and unique" changes to the
legislature, not "to replace a durable impersonal body of common law principles with intuitive individual notions of justice in a given case." G. E. White,
The American Judicial Tradition 277 (1976). Or, as Justice Holmes stated,
"judges do and must legislate, but they can do so interstitially; they are confined from molar to molecular motions. A common law judge could not say I
think the doctrine of consideration a bit of historical nonsense and shall not
enforce it." Southern Pacific Co. v. Jensen, 244 U.S. 205, 221 (1917), dissenting opinion.

33. Levy, *Against the Law* 260.

33a. Quoted in Morton J. Horwitz, *The Transformation of American Law* 125
(1977). This "transformation," Horwitz justly concludes, "enabled emergent
entreprenurial and commercial groups to win a disproportionate share of

remarkable confession that law was to be manipulated to achieve a desired result—"my views of the case"—might perhaps be extenuated in an area where courts had been left to make the initial choices. But no such authority was conferred in the policing of constitutional boundaries. For, as Judge J. Skelly Wright observed (in an article devoted to castigating the "self-appointed scholastic mandarans" who criticized the Warren Court): "Constitutional choices are in fact different from ordinary decisions . . . the most important value choices have already been made by the framers of the Constitution." Judicial "value choices," he continued, "are to be made only within the parameters" of those choices.[34] If, as Judge Wright declared, even "imprecise" constitutional guarantees "provide a direction, a goal," and "rule out many alternative directions, goals,"[35] all the more does the exclusion of suffrage from the Fourteenth Amendment, for example, leave no room for judicial choices such as "one man, one vote."

"Instrumentalism" describes the approach derived from early-nineteenth-century common law practice, a view, Hans Linde points out, later expressed in the "realist canon" that new decisions are to "be measured by instrumental success in effecting a socially desirable outcome."[36] But at the adoption of the Constitution judges were considered to be without discretion to alter the law. And "desired" by whom? Oft-times the "sense of the community" has turned on the opinion of a swing man, for example, Justice Owen Roberts, whose change of position in 1937 on minimum wages was perhaps not entirely

---

wealth and power in American society." More crudely stated, the courts loaded the costs of an expanding industrial society on those least able to bear it—"forced subsidies to growth coerced from victims of the process." Id. xvi.

34. "Professor Bickel, The Scholarly Tradition, and the Supreme Court," 84 Harv. L. Rev. 769, 777, 784, 785 (1971). See also Hamilton, infra Chapter 21 at note 93; Linde, supra note 28 at 254; Justices Black and Douglas, supra Chapter 15 note 41; Cardozo, supra Chapter 15 note 24.

35. Wright, supra note 34 at 785; see supra at note 15.

36. Supra note 28 at 228–229.

coincidental.[37] When the Court splits 5 to 4 it evidences a deep cleavage as to the "desired" result. Frequently an "outcome" that is stubbornly resisted by a dominant majority of the Court is quickly adopted upon the retirement of one or more Justices when their replacements transform the dissenting minority into a new majority. On the heels of a decision that declared the greenback law unconstitutional, President Grant "carefully chose men who he had reason to believe would uphold the Legal Tender Acts." His hopes were gratified by a 5-to-4 reversal.[38] Such swings of the pendulum are a commonplace of

37. White, supra note 32 at 193. Of the overruled decision, Adkins v. Children's Hospital, 261 U.S. 525 (1923), T. R. Powell said that 5 Justices invalidated the minimum wage law that 35 judges (including 4 Justices) held valid. Powell, *Vagaries and Varieties in Constitutional Interpretation* 40 (1956). Roberts, as Fred Rodell remarked, was "the perfect personification of the chanciness of government by judges. It was he who . . . changed his mind and his major votes three separate times . . . on the bed-rock issue of governmental power to regulate business; it was he who, by holding the decisive Court vote . . . was for years the most powerful person in the United States." And he owed his appointment to the accident that Judge John Parker was turned down by the Senate. Rodell, *Nine Men* 221–222 (1955). Alexander Bickel observed that 5 to 4 opinions highlight "the fact that one man had the decision . . . It just makes unavoidable for everybody the awareness of the authoritarian nature of the institution, and of how narrowly that authority resides in one individual perhaps." *Hearings on the Supreme Court before the Senate Subcomittee on the Separation of Powers* 108, 90th Cong., 2d Sess. (June 1968).

38. R. H. Jackson, *The Struggle for Judicial Supremacy* 42 (1941). The overruled decision had been procured by Lincoln in the same fashion. He "confided that he chose Salmon Chase as Chief Justice . . . chiefly because ' . . . we wish for a Chief Justice who will sustain what has been done in regard to . . . legal tenders.' Chase had been Lincoln's Secretary of the Treasury . . . and had supported the Legal Tender Acts." Jackson, id. at 32–33. Chase performed as expected and then came Grant's turn.

In the same way, Richard Nixon selected men who would give effect to his desires. "That the Nixon Court favored law-enforcement values is no surprise. Burger, Blackmun, Powell and Rehnquist got their seats on the bench because of their supposed or known lack of sympathy for the rights of the criminally accused." Levy, *Against the Law* 422. Dissenting in Boys Market v. Clerks' Union, 398 U.S. 235, 256 (1970), from the discard of a 1962 precedent,

Supreme Court history: constitutional law is given a "new look" when a Warren succeeds a Vinson, a Goldberg succeeds a Frankfurter. The changes can be fateful. Vinson "held fast to the position that the judiciary should not be an aggressive instrument for invalidating school segregation."[39] He was succeeded in the midst of the desegregation case by Warren,[40] and Rodell tells us he learned from law clerks that "in conference at least three Justices came close to dissenting until their new Chief put on all the pressure he could wield."[41] A similar "major turning point" marked the succession of Frankfurter by Goldberg.[42] Citations can be multiplied. Should what is "socially desirable"

Justice Black stated, "Nothing at all has changed, in fact, except the membership of the Court and the personal opinion of one Justice." It has been said that American constitutional history may be viewed as a "series of minor court-packing plans." White, supra note 32 at 197.

39. Paul Murphy, *The Constitution in Crisis Times, 1918–1969* 309 (1972). "The Chief Justice [Vinson] found it 'Hard to get away' from the contemporary view by its framers that the Fourteenth Amendment did not prohibit segregation." Richard Kluger, *Simple Justice* 590, 589 (1976).

40. Cf. Cox, supra at note 5.

41. Fred Rodell, "It Is the Warren Court," *The New York Times Magazine,* March 13, 1966, in Levy, *Warren* 136, 139. Rodell adds, "I tell this tale—and let him who can prove it wrong deny it—to illustrate the result-minded pragmatism and power of Earl Warren." Id. After the first argument before Chief Justice Vinson, "Frankfurter . . . listed Clark—along with Vinson, Reed and Jackson—as probable dissenters if the Court had voted to overturn Plessy in the spring of 1953." Kluger, supra note 39 at 612. Bickel, who had served as a law clerk to Justice Frankfurter when the desegregation case first was argued before the Vinson Court, stated, "there is reason to believe that had Chief Justice Vinson lived, something very different from the opinion read by Earl Warren . . . would have come down." A. Bickel, "Is the Warren Court Too 'Political?,'" *The New York Times Magazine,* September 25, 1966, in Levy, *Warren* 216, 217.

42. "Today [1964] the close civil liberties cases (as opposed, in legal parlance, to those involving Negroes' civil *rights*), which used to come down predictably while Frankfurter sat, five to four against the liberty claimed, have for the past two terms come down just as predictably five to four the other way." Fred Rodell, supra note 2 at 208, 211.

for a nation of 200 million people turn on such accidents?[43] Should grave national policy be the sport of circumstance? Justices themselves have inveighed against the creation of novel constitutional doctrine on so fortuitous a base.[44] These shifts in opinion underscore Justice Jackson's aphorism: "we are not final because we are infallible, but we are infallible only because we are final."[45] Just as "perception of community standards varies" from Justice to Justice, so no agreement on such matters is to be found in academe, for law professors also are not agreed upon what results are "good."[46] Were there such agreement, the judgment of cloistered scholars is no substitute for the will of the people.

Even when the Court is unanimous it is not peculiarly fitted to be a thermometer of community feeling, as the Framers emphasized during their discussion of judicial participation in the Council of Revision. The Sixteenth Amendment attests that the Court did not represent the sense of the community when it declared the income tax unconstitutional.[47] Its recent decision that the age-old death penalty for murder constitutes "cruel and unusual punishment" quite plainly is opposed to popular senti-

---

43. Murphy, supra note 39 at 428.

44. Such shifts, Justice Frankfurter stated, afford "fair ground for the belief that Law is the expression of chance . . . of unexpected changes in the Court's composition and the contingencies in the choice of successors." United States v. Rabinowitz, 339 U.S. 56, 86 (1950), dissenting opinion. Yet he regarded Vinson's demise as providential. Supra Chapter 7 at note 47. To the same effect, Justice Black, supra note 38; Justice Stewart, Mitchell v. W. T. Grant Co., 416 U.S. 600, 636 (1974).

45. Brown v. Allen, 344 U.S. 443, 540 (1953), concurring opinion.

46. Levy, supra note 9 at 199—200; J. H. Ely, "The Wages of Crying Wolf: A Comment on Roe v. Wade," 82 Yale L. J. 920, 944 (1973).

47. So too, Justice Holmes pointed out in Lochner v. New York, 198 U.S. 45, 75 (1905), that the majority was deciding the case "upon an economic theory which a large part of the country does not entertain." Dissenting opinion.

ment.[48] So, too, the procedural safeguards required of States for criminals run counter to public opinion.[49] Some consider that the Court's rulings on obscenity do not reflect popular opinion;[50] and in the result the nation is deluged by a flood of blatant pornography and filth that the people are powerless to

48. Furman v. Georgia, 408 U.S. 238 (1972); see supra Chapter 14 note 53.

Justice Black's invocation to history in 1971 deserves notice: "These words cannot be read to outlaw capital punishment because that penalty was in common use and authorized by law . . . at the time the Constitution was adopted. It is inconceivable to me that the framers intended to end capital punishment by the [Eighth] Amendment." McGautha v. California, 402 U.S. 183, 226 (1971), concurring opinion. See infra Chapter 21 note 39. The case for rejection of judicial policymaking and for a restricted judicial function is even stronger. Supra Chapter 16.

Like politics, adjudication makes strange bedfellows. Chief Justice Burger, dissenting in Furman v. Georgia, stated, "a punishment clearly permissible under the Constitution at the time of its adoption and accepted as such by every member of the Court until today, is suddenly so cruel as to be incompatible with the Eighth Amendment." 408 U.S. at 381–382. And in Trop v. Dulles, 356 U.S. at 99, Chief Justice Warren stated that "the death penalty has been employed throughout our history, and, in a day when it is still widely accepted, it cannot be said to violate the constitutional concept of cruelty."

49. In 1968, "a Gallup poll revealed that the majority believed that the Court was 'too soft' on criminals, protected their rights at the expense of society." Levy, *Against the Law* 3. Richard Nixon rode into office in no small part because of his appeal to "law and order." The "people think that the Court has contributed to the crime wave." Kurland, supra note 31 at 95. Levy states that Congress regarded one such decision as "'a harmful blow at the nationwide effort to control crime'" and enacted a countermeasure. Levy, *Against the Law* 252.

50. Professor Louis Jaffe stated it is overwhelmingly the case that "the 'public conscience' does not support the claim" of constitutional protection for "obscenity," commenting that "the Legislatures, Federal and State, had openly and universally for upwards of 100 years seen fit to condemn obscenity." L. Jaffe, "The Court Debated—Another View," *The New York Times Magazine,* June 5, 1960, in Levy, *Warren* 199, 205; cf. Kurland, supra note 31 at 31, and J. W. Bishop, "The Warren Court is Not Likely to be Overruled," *The New York Times Magazine,* September 7, 1969, in Levy, *Warren* 93, 103.

deal with.[51] Even desegregation, an undeniably noble goal, did not have[52] and does not have the consent of the nation. The Report of the National Advisory Commission on Civil Disorders found "pervasive racism" across the country,[53] as is evidenced by continued resistance in the North to busing. An admirer of *Brown v. Board of Education*, Anthony Lewis, ruefully wrote in May 1974 that the issues of race and poverty are "much more complicated, more intractable than we imagined."[54] Soberly appraising the situation in the Fall of 1975 Derrick Bell, a black scholar, stated that "Today, opposition to desegregation is, if anything, greater than it was in 1954." He referred to "nationwide opposition to meaningful implementation of school desegregation," saying, "it should now be clear that Brown can [not] integrate our schools." The "real sickness is that our society in all its manifestations is geared to the manifestations of white

51. Archibald Cox adds, "One wonders, too, whether the Supreme Court, in extending the protection of the First Amendment to sheer vulgarity, useful only in its ability to shock, does not give the vulgarities an imprimatur which contributes to the lowering of public discourse." Cox, supra note 1 at 47–48.

52. Supra Chapter 15 at note 14.

53. Lewis M. Steel, "Nine Men in Black Who Think White," *The New York Times Magazine,* October 13, 1968, in Levy, *Warren* 83, 91.

54. "A Time to Celebrate," *The New York Times,* May 13, 1974, at 29. He added, "we seem unlikely to solve [the problems] soon, to the general satisfaction, in terms of either law or politics." On October 16, 1976, Professor Charles Black stated, "To the *victims* of inequality, inequality is often perceived as a denial of liberty . . . The poor are indeed unfree . . . [But] reliance on the judiciary to correct this kind of unfreedom is tragically misplaced . . . [W]hat will be wanted, and indispensably needed, is that major shift of resources, and that systematic reorganization, which cannot succeed without very weighty action by the political branches. The most serious single mistake possible at this time would in my judgment be to write Congress off, and to try to tackle poverty by invoking the judicial power." Black, Address, "The Judicial Power as Guardian of Liberties," before a Symposium on "The Supreme Court and Constitutional Liberties in Modern America," Wayne State University, Detroit, Mich.

superiority."[55] Bell's careful bill of particulars raises large doubts whether the disease is curable by judicial fiat. This is not to deny that the side-effects of *Brown* in other areas of desegregation have been beneficial in the extreme. Here our focus is on the absence of a national consensus, the fact that the desegregation decree did not and still does not represent the "sense of the community," but is rather a prime example of how the Justices imposed their will upon the people. Justice Black, who was ready enough to impose his own will, rightly declared that there is no "gadget which the Court can use to determine what traditions are rooted in the conscience of the people."[56]

If the argument of necessity can be made for desegregation because segregation is a reproach to our society, what need was there for the Court's decision that the centuries-old requirement of trial by a jury of 12 was not binding on the present? No social

---

55. D. Bell, "The Burden of Brown on Blacks: History Based on Observations on a Landmark Decision," 7 N.C. Cent. L. J. 25, 26, 36 (1975). See also Thomas Sowell, "A Black 'Conservative' Dissents," *The New York Times Magazine,* August 8, 1976, at 14. The issue of racial discrimination "has been fanned into the most protracted, rancorous, and divisive domestic blaze of the post-war era." Chester E. Finn, Jr., "Book Review," *Commentary* 78 (April 1976). Philip Kurland had written in 1970 that the segregation "cases demonstrate, I think, that rapid movement toward equality of the race is not attainable through the judicial process. The Court has moved faster than society is prepared to go." Kurland, supra note 31 at 113.

56. Griswold v. Connecticut, 381 U.S. 479, 519 (1965). Levy numbers Black, Douglas, and Warren among the Justices who believed that "they have a mission to impose their convictions upon the nation," to "mold its public policy," Levy, *Warren* 110. "Earl Warren is the closest thing the United States has had to a Platonic Guardian, dispensing law from a throne without any sensed limits of power except what is seen [by him] as the good of society." Anthony Lewis, "A Man Born to Act, Not to Muse," *The New York Times Magazine,* June 30, 1968, in Levy, *Warren* 151, 161. Professor Louis Henkin stated, there is "a preference by some Justices for results which fit an image of the nation not projected by the Constitution and which the Justices cannot prove to be justified by history, need, the philosophy of the people, or anything better than the Justices' faith or inclination." Henkin, "Some Reflections on Current Constitutional Controversies," 109 U. Pa. L. Rev. 637, 660 (1961).

urgency called for judicial tampering with what had been a central concern of the Founders.[57] What urgent necessity dictated overthrow of the death penalty to which more than half of the States are attached? Such decisions confirm Hamilton's prescient caution in Federalist No. 25: "every breach of the fundamental laws, though dictated by necessity, . . . forms a precedent for other breaches where the same plea of necessity does not exist at all."[58]

For a realistic and unusually candid disclosure of the uses of instrumentalism we are indebted to a member of the Nixon administration, Donald E. Santarelli, an Associate Deputy Attorney General, who described himself in April 1973 as in charge of "an idea shop," which "work[s] on concepts" and "plans" for the President. He considered that the "separation of powers is obsolete," that the

> Constitution is flexible . . . Your point of view depends on whether you're winning. The constitution isn't the real issue in this; it is how you want to *run the country,* and achieve national goals. The language of the Constitution is not at issue. It is what you can interpret it to mean in the light of modern needs. In talking about a "Constitutional crisis" we are not grappling with the real needs of running the country but are using the issues for the self-serving purpose of striking a new balance of power . . . Today, the whole Constitution is up for grabs.[59]

To my knowledge, the Nixon administration did not repudiate this interview, and it was tacitly confirmed by Richard Nixon himself. As said by Leonard Levy, "Nixon's search for conservative strict constructionists has been more than a candid attempt to alter the trend of decisions, it is an acknowledgment that at

---

57. For a powerful critique of the 6-man jury decision see Levy, *Against the Law* 259 et seq. My own studies have convinced me that the Founders unfailingly identified trial by jury with a jury of twelve. See infra Chapter 22.

58. Federalist No. 25 at 158.

59. *The New Yorker,* April 28, 1973, at 32–34.

the very apex of our government of laws and not of men, the men who interpret the laws, rather than the laws themselves, are the decisive factors.[60] It is difficult to deny that "a result-oriented adjudication . . . is a corruption of the judicial process, that leaves too far behind the rule of law enforced by impersonal and objective judges."[61]

Instrumentalism, in short, substitutes the will of the Justices for that of the people. That requires more than jurisprudential justification, more than a response to the needs of a changing world; it calls for the informed "consent of the governed." Although Justice Harlan, in measuring the impact of the Fourteenth Amendment on voting, stated that "the amending process is not the only way in which constitutional understanding alters with time . . . as conditions change the Constitution changes as well," he went on to say:

> when the Court gives the language of the Constitution an unforeseen application, it does so, whether explicitly or implicitly, in the name of some underlying purpose of the Framers . . . [T]he federal judiciary . . . has no inherent general authority to establish the norms for the rest of society . . . When the Court *disregards the express intent* and understanding of the Framers, it has invaded the realm of the political process to which the amending power was committed, and it has violated the constitutional structure which it is its highest duty to protect.[62]

In terms of this discussion, the limited goals of the Fourteenth Amendment were explained to the people; they gave their consent in conformity with Article V, and if their decision needs to

60. Levy, *Warren* 9.

61. Levy, *Against the Law* 438; cf. Kathryn Griffith, *Judge Learned Hand and the Role of the Federal Judiciary* 192 (1973). An admirer of judicial policymaking averred that the Court "has ceased to be a student of law . . . It has become the crusading political philosopher of populism." Shapiro, supra note 23 at 252.

62. Oregon v. Mitchell, 400 U.S. 112, 202–203 (1970) (emphasis added).

be changed, let it be, as President Washington counseled, by action in the same constitutional manner: let the people decide.

Instead of searching for the "sense of community," some would have the Court serve as a "national conscience," as "an educational body . . . teachers in a vital national seminar."[63] That notion, Wallace Mendelson stated, "sounds strange in the mouths of its liberal sponsors. By their standards, most of the Court's teaching in this area has been erroneous"[64]—let alone that the Court has not been content merely to teach but has imposed its teachings on the nation. There is no need to dwell on the fact that judges of high stature—Black, Frankfurter, Learned Hand, and Robert Patterson—have rejected the roles of preacher, teacher, crusader;[65] instead, let us examine how this "conscience" has served the nation. Careful scholars confirm Robert H. Jackson's stricture: "time has proved that [the Court's] judgment was wrong on most of the outstanding issues upon which it has chosen to challenge the popular branches."[66] Consider first the Japanese relocation case, which stands as a dreadful precedent for racial concentration camps; the Court failed 70,000 Japanese at the very moment they stood

63. A. S. Miller and R. F. Howell, "The Myth of Neutrality in Constitutional Adjudication," 27 U. Chi. L. Rev. 661, 689 (1960). Rostow, supra note 14 at 208. See also infra at note 81.

64. Wallace Mendelson, "Mr. Justice Frankfurter: Law and Choice," 10 Vand. L. Rev. 333, 341 (1957).

65. Black: Jaffe, supra note 50 at 204–205; Frankfurter: "From the Wisdom of Felix Frankfurter," 3 *Wisdom* 25 (1959), quoted in Griffith, supra note 61 at 209; Hand: *The Bill of Rights* 71 (1962); Patterson: Griffith, id. at 88.

Miller and Howell, supra note 63 at 678, noted a "lack of consensus on the Court as to the appropriate role of the judiciary."

66. Jackson, supra note 38 at x, 37; Robert Dahl, "Decision-Making in a Democracy: The Supreme Court as a National Policy-Maker," 6 J. Pub. Law 279, 292–293 (1957). The "Supreme Court, mainly during history, though not in recent decades, work[ed] as a buttress against the expansion of individual liberty and civil rights." James McGregor Burns, "Dictatorship—Could It Happen Here?," in *Has the Court Too Much Power?* 234, 236 (C. Roberts ed. 1974).

most in need of protection against West Coast hysteria.[67] From
the very outset the Court gutted the minimal protection afforded the Negro by the Fourteenth Amendment. By a series of
decisions, Leonard Levy said, "the Court crippled and voided
most of the comprehensive program for protecting the civil
rights of Negroes after the Civil War. These decisions paralyzed
or supplanted legislative and community action and played a
crucial role in destroying public opinion that favored meeting
the challenge of the Negro problem."[68] The record, said Henry
Steele Commager, with respect to the pre-1937 Court,

> discloses not a single case, in a century and a half, where the
> Supreme Court has protected freedom of speech, press . . .
> against Congressional attack. It reveals no instance . . . where
> the Court has intervened on behalf of the underprivileged—
> the Negro, the alien, women, children, workers, tenant
> farmers. It reveals, on the contrary, that the Court has effectively
> intervened, again and again, to defeat Congressional attempts to
> free the slave, to guarantee civil rights to Negroes, to protect
> workingmen, to outlaw child labor, to assist hard-pressed
> farmers, and to democratize the tax system.[69]

So wretched a performance, I suggest, inspires little confidence
in the Court as the "national conscience." In their rapture over
the Warren Court's adoption of *their* predilections, the libertarians tend to overlook that "A single generation's experience
with judicial review . . . does not wipe out the experience of a
century and a half."[70] Already there are anguished outcries that

67. E. V. Rostow, "The Japanese-American Cases—A Disaster," 54 Yale
L. J. 489 (1945); Levy, supra note 9 at 20.

68. Levy, supra note 9 at 33–34. "Meanwhile," Levy states, "millions of
Negroes suffered lives of humiliation for five or more decades . . . because
the Court betrayed the intent of the Reconstruction Amendments." Id. 35.

69. H. S. Commager, "Judicial Review and Democracy," 19 Va. Quarterly Rev. 417, 428 (1943). See also John Frank, "Review and Basic Liberties,"
in *Supreme Court and Supreme Law* 109, 114 (E. Cahn ed. 1954).

70. Levy, supra note 9 at 23.

the Burger Court is acting "against the law."[71] But the name of the game is "Two Can Play";[72] once the legitimacy of judicial policymaking is recognized, new appointees may properly carry out the policies which they were appointed to effectuate.[73]

What the "national conscience" is at any given moment depends on shifting personnel and the nature of the appointees. The replacement of one or two Justices may result in a complete reversal of the prevailing conscience, as when Chief Justice Warren succeeded Chief Justice Vinson. How can we put our trust in a conscience that changes color with every judicial succession, itself subject to shifting political winds?

The conscience of the nation is a tender thing, and one may well shrink from entrusting it to some of the incumbents who have served over the years. Shall we prefer the Four Horsemen to Brandeis and Stone as keepers of the conscience? Learned Hand believed that judges "must be expected to express the points of view of the class to which they belong rather than that of the whole community."[74] Justice Field's close ties with the railroad barons of the West Coast furnishes one example,[75]

71. Levy, *Against the Law,* some aspects of which are discussed infra Chapter 18.

72. In 1942 I pointed out that the "reconstructed" Court was sanctifying the deplorable example of the "Four Horsemen" and that that stamp of approval might yet come back to haunt the libertarians. Raoul Berger, "Constructive Contempt: A Post-Mortem," 9 U. Chi. L. Rev. 602, 604–605 (1942). For a similar expression, see Richard Goodwin, "The Shape of American Politics," *Commentary* 25, 26–27 (June 1967), quoted in Kurland, supra note 31 at 18.

73. See supra at note 60.

74. Griffith, supra note 61 at 90; Hand, *The Spirit of Liberty* 203 (I. Dillard ed. 1952).

75. Graham 14, 102–103. For other Justices with similar ties, see Fred Rodell, *Nine Men* 30–31 (1955). Justice Samuel Miller wrote, "It is vain to contend with judges who have been at the bar the advocates for forty years of railroad companies . . . when they are called upon to decide cases where such interests are in contest." Quoted in Charles Fairman, *Mr. Justice Miller and the Supreme Court* 374 (1939).

Chief Justice Taft another. Although Taft confessed to feeling "less acute and more confused" as he grew older, he felt duty-bound "to stay on the Court in order to prevent the Bolsheviki from getting control."[76] Presumably Brandeis was one of the "Bolsheviki";[77] and Taft opposed the appointments of Cardozo and Learned Hand because they might "herd" with Brandeis.[78] Justice Brewer's overheated warnings against the "black flag of anarchism . . . and the red flag of socialism"[79] long furnished the rallying cry of the embattled Court, which felt duty-bound to save "society from itself."[80]

Now it was the turn of the libertarians to look to the Court as the savior of democracy. Edmond Cahn considered that it was incumbent upon a judge to shoulder his moral responsibility rather than to defer to community standards, preferring the "wisdom" of such a judge as Learned Hand.[81] But Learned Hand in his wisdom wanted Platonic Guardians no more than did Elbridge Gerry 173 years earlier.[82] It is disheartening to go

76. Levy, *Judgments,* supra note 12 at 98.

77. In 1920 W. H. Taft referred to "the new school of constitutional construction" led by Brandeis and Clarke, which tended to encourage "Socialist raids on property." Taft, "Mr. Wilson and the Campaign," 10 Yale Rev. (N.S.) 1 (October 1920), quoted in 1 *Holmes-Laski Letters: The Correspondence of Mr. Justice Holmes and Harold J. Laski* 347 note 1 (M. Howe ed. 1953).

78. A. T. Mason, *The Supreme Court: Palladium of Freedom* 122 (1962). Taft considered "Hand had proved his poor judgment in 1912, when he 'turned out to be a wild Roosevelt man, a progressive.'" Id. See also White, supra note 32 at 179–180.

79. See supra Chapter 1 note 8.

80. Robert McCloskey, *The American Supreme Court* 165 (1960). Justice Field was convinced "that the salvation of democracy lay in a judicial trusteeship." Graham 149.

81. Edmond Cahn, *The Moral Decision: Right and Wrong in the Light of American Law* 310, quoted in Griffith, supra note 61 at 158.

82. Hand, supra note 65 at 73; Gerry, supra Chapter 16 at note 8. Hand considered that the law "must be content to lag behind the best inspiration of its time until it feels behind it the weight of such general acceptance." Supra note 74 at 15–16. See also supra at note 65. And always there is the question

over the roster of "wise and able men" to whom Arthur Sutherland would confide "the constitutional function of countering
the democratic process." Rodell justly refers to Truman's
"inept cronies";[83] the revulsion not long since against some
proposed Nixon appointments, including an ineffable trio who
shall here be nameless,[84] illustrates that the nation's salvation is
dependent upon the "luck of the draw." Anthony Lewis observed that "the run of Supreme Court appointments in our history has not been particularly distinguished."[85] Levy more
bluntly stated that they have run from "mediocre to competent"[86]—with a few distinguished exceptions such as Holmes

---

whether even "general acceptance" can dispense with amendment under Article V. See Hamilton, supra at note 15.

83. "It Is the Warren Court," supra note 41 at 145.

84. Levy, *Against the Law* 44, 48.

85. "What Qualities for the Court?," *The New York Times Magazine*, October 6, 1957, in Levy, *Warren* 114, 119. Writing of the Associate Justices, many
of whom he knew personally, John Quincy Adams said, "Not one of them,
except Story, has been a man of great ability. Several of them have been men
of strong prejudices, warm passions, and contracted minds." Quoted in Samuel F. Bemis, *John Quincy Adams and the Union* 406 note 79 (1956).

86. *Judgments,* supra note 12 at 105. He adds, "the politics of appointment . . . are surely not calculated to bring the ablest men to our supreme
tribunal." For a scathing critique of the run of appointments over the years,
see Rodell, *Nine Men.* Robert G. McCloskey, a searching student of the Court,
said that at any given time "You are not likely to find more than a handful
who are capable of performing the rather awesome intellectual task that these
ventures of [the Justices] involve. We have had on the Court in modern times,
I would say offhand maybe three . . . Frankfurter, Jackson, and probably
Harlan, but they in general, were swimming against the tide." *Hearings,* supra
note 37 at 109. Philip Kurland likewise testified that "the personnel of the
Court is not up to the task that has been assigned to it." Id. at 149. Paul Freund,
who as chief aide to the Solicitor General was in a position to observe the
Court at close quarters, is quoted as saying that Justice George Sutherland
"did not have a very 'searching mind.' McReynolds was a very 'idiosyncratic' man and was often 'childish and peevish.'" Tim Cooper, "Freund:
40 Years of Supreme Court History Recalled." 64 Harv. L.S. Rec. 1, 9 (1977).

and Brandeis, who often were relegated to dissent.[87] Learned Hand, one of the wisest and most profound jurists, disclaimed any knowledge of how to choose Platonic Guardians.[88] A succession of presidents have demonstrated that they know still less.

One who studies the course of events since the advent of the Warren era is struck by how short is the memory of man. One hundred years of judicial misrule have been wiped out by a fifteen-year interlude during which libertarian aspirations at length were gratified. Now the intellectuals eagerly embraced the Court as a "law-giver," forgetful of Tocqueville's comment on the then prevailing respect for the judiciary that imprudent appointments might bring forth evil fruit.[89] Do we need Hitler or Indira Gandhi to remind us that the lesson of history is: put not your trust in saviors? The enduring strength of our institutions is not a little due to our veneration of the Constitution as the bulwark of our liberties. We need to take to heart a statement made by Jefferson when he was President and had been urged to take a dubiously broad view of his own powers:

> I had rather ask for an enlargement of power from the nation, where it is found necessary, than to assume it by a construction which would make our powers boundless. Our peculiar security is in possession of a written Constitution. Let us not make it a blank paper by construction. If [power is boundless] then we

87. Morris R. Cohen wrote to Frankfurter in January 1936, "you think in terms of Holmes, Brandeis and Cardozo, and you think more men of that type would make the Supreme Court a good institution. In this you ignore the fact that it is only by accident that men of that type can get on the Supreme Court and that when they do they are more likely to be on the minority side." L. C. Rosenfield, *Portrait of a Philosopher: Morris Raphael Cohen in Life and Letters* 270 (1962), quoted in Joseph P. Lash, *From the Diaries of Felix Frankfurter* 55 (1975).

88. Hand, supra note 65 at 73.

89. "[I]f the Supreme Court is ever composed of imprudent men or bad citizens, the Union may be plunged into anarchy or civil war." 1 Alexis de Tocqueville, *Democracy in America* 150 (1900).

have no Constitution. If it has bounds, they can be no other than the definition of the powers which that instrument gives.[90]

For him those definitions were to be read in light of the explanations made to those who ratified the Constitution.[91]

90. Letter to Wilson Cary Nicholas, September 7, 1803, 8 *The Writings of Thomas Jefferson* 247 (P. L. Ford ed. 1897).
91. See infra Chapter 19 at note 42.

18

Liberals and the Burger Court

LAMENTATIONS over the "regressive" course of the Burger Court in the field of civil liberties fill the air. *The New York Times,* for example, stated: "There was a time not so far distant when the United States Supreme Court was the staunch and ultimate defender of civil rights and liberties . . . [T]he Court seems clearly to be beating a path of retreat from its once proud forward position in this delicate and difficult area of the relationship between citizen and state."[1] Undoubtedly the Court is tilting the scales from what many regarded as excessive tenderness toward criminals;[2] it is haltingly attempting to return some criminal administration to the States.[3] But, as

1. *The New York Times,* March 31, 1976, p. 36; see also Nathan Lewin, "Avoiding the Supreme Court," *The New York Times Magazine,* October 17, 1976, at 31.

2. Edward R. Korman, "Book Review," 4 Hofstra L. Rev. 549, 556 (1976), refers to "the near hysterical response in certain quarters that accompanies every opinion of the 'Nixon Court' affirming the conviction of a murderer, rapist or robber." Professor Louis Jaffe stated that judges "have been insensitive to the public's need for a sense of security." "Was Brandeis an Activist? The Search for Intermediate Premises," 80 Harv. L. Rev. 986, 1002 (1967).

3. Cf. Stone v. Powell, 96 S. Ct. 3037 (1976), limiting the use of habeas corpus for review of state court convictions on the basis of illegally obtained evidence.

Leonard Levy points out, "That the Nixon Court favored law-enforcement values" should come as "no surprise. Burger, Blackmun, Powell and Rehnquist got their seats on the bench because of their supposed or known lack of sympathy for the rights of the criminally accused."[4] This, however, is only the latest of what G. E. White felicitously described as a "series of minor court-packing plans."[5] Now that a new set of predilections is displacing their own, libertarians who rejoiced in the "creative" role of the "wise and able men" are despondent. But the "revolutionary" changes in the criminal process[6] by the Warren Court had not won the assent of the people.[7] And it cannot be gainsaid that the Burger Court rulings in this area are closer to the original design than were those of the Warren Court. For, as we have seen, the Bill of Rights was not made applicable to the States, either by its framers or in the 39th Congress.

"Between 1937 and 1961 the Court's constitutional rulings in criminal cases had rarely touched law enforcement and trial practices that were generally permitted by state law and were in widespread use." Lusky 159. Justice Harlan, dissenting in Chapman v. Alabama, 386 U.S. 18, 46–47 (1967), stated, "I regard the Court's assumption of what amounts to a general supervisory power over the trial of federal constitutional issues in state courts as a startling constitutional development that is wholly out of keeping with our federal system and completely unsupported by the Fourteenth Amendment where the source of such power must be found." A swing of the pendulum was acknowledged by Justice Lewis F. Powell in an address on August 11, 1976, before the American Bar Association convention. The changes were due to a "'leveling off' in activism by the Court"; "a more traditional, and in my view, a sounder balance is evolving between the rights of accused persons and the right of a civilized society to have a criminal justice system that is effective as well as fair." *The New York Times*, August 12, 1976, at 18.

4. Levy, *Against the Law* 422 (1974).

5. G. E. White, *The American Judicial Tradition* 197 (1976).

6. Lusky 161.

7. See supra Chapter 17 note 49. "The Court's 'coddling' of criminals became a major issue in the 1968 elections; [after the election] new appointees were selected in part on their commitment to law enforcement and their hostility to 'criminal forces.'" White, supra note 5 at 364–365.

Not that the Burger Court is abjuring lawmaking; its "six-man jury" decision furnished evidence to the contrary.[8] It has not held that the Court has no business regulating State death penalties because the "cruel and unusual punishment" phrase of the Bill of Rights has no application to the States, or because, as Chief Justices Warren and Burger and Justice Black stated, it did not encompass a death penalty for murder.[9] Instead, in *Gregg v. Georgia* and companion cases it has weighed whether a death penalty is or is not a "cruel and unusual punishment" on an apothecary's scale.[10] It would be inopportune to show in detail that the "strict constructionist" Burger Court clings as firmly to judicial governance as its predecessor.[11] Archibald Cox observed that "the new Justices seem not to shrink from using constitutional law as an instrument of reform when an existing rule offends their preferences."[12]

It is more to the purpose to examine how the Burger Court has thrown "liberal" analysis into disarray, as Leonard Levy's recent book *Against the Law: The Nixon Court* illustrates. Levy's earlier studies give evidence of incisive analysis and a richly stocked mind; but *Against the Law* leaves one with a baffling sense of ambivalence, of seeming unawareness that his views are often incongruent. In what follows I am not to be taken as a partisan of the Burger Court, but rather as seeking to test Levy's theories by his criticism of that Court. By way of background let us begin with his sympathetic introduction to a group of articles on the Warren Court. The phrases of the Constitution are "Delphic"; the Court

---

8. Infra Chapter 22.

9. Supra Chapter 17 note 48.

10. Gregg v. Georgia, 96 S. Ct. 2909 (1976).

11. See infra Chapter 22.

12. "The New Dimensions of Constitutional Adjudication," 51 Wash. L. Rev. 791, 803 (1976). Cf. Justice White, Roberts v. Louisiana, 96 S. Ct. 3001, 3020 (1976); see also Cox, *The Role of the Supreme Court in American Government* 34 (1976).

is indeed, and cannot help but be [a superlegislature]. The reason is simply that the Constitution, as Jefferson said in exasperation, is "merely a thing of wax" which the Court "may twist and shape into any form they please . . . " Judge Learned Hand observed that . . . "The words [a judge] must construe are empty vessels into which he can pour nearly anything he will." Legal erudition, legal rules, legal logic, legal precedents do not decide cases involving the ambiguous clauses of the Constitution . . . Inevitably, then, our constitutional law is subjective in character and to a great degree result oriented.[13]

Levy continues in this strain in his commentary on the Burger Court: "From the beginning . . . the Court . . . read the Constitution to mean whatever it wanted. Despite pretenses to the contrary, the Court could do no other, for . . . American constitutional law exists in the collective eye of those who happen at any moment in time to dominate the Court."[14] If this be so, how can the decisions of the "Nixon Court" be "Against the Law"? And "why," to borrow Levy's adoption of Justice Black's rhetorical question, "have a written Constitution at all if its interpreters are left only to the admonitions of their own consciences?"[15] Is this reconcilable with Levy's view that the

13. Levy, *Warren* 7, 9, 10. Why then criticize Justice Rehnquist's approach as "that of an ideologue advocating the embodiment of his political choices in constitutional law"? Levy, *Against the Law* 58. And if "legal rules, legal precedents" and the like "do not decide cases" then Rodell was not "anti-intellectual" in dismissing the "look-it-up-in-the-library" intellectual. Supra Chapter 15 at notes 11–12.

Jefferson was lamenting that the Court had *made* of the Constitution "a thing of wax," letter to Spencer Roane, September 6, 1819, 12 *Works of Thomas Jefferson* 135, 137 (Fed. ed. 1905). He had hoped that officials would be bound "from mischief by the chains of the Constitution." See also infra Chapter 20 at note 6. So too, Learned Hand's reference to words as "empty vessels" must be balanced against his confession of failure to understand the Court's function as a "third legislative chamber" except as a *coup de main*. *The Bill of Rights* 55 (1962).

14. Levy, *Against the Law* 25.

15. Levy, *Warren* 186.

Court "is and must be for all practical purposes a 'continuous
constitutional convention' in the sense that it must keep updating the original charter . . . it simply cannot decide cases
on the basis of what the Constitution says"?[16]

Given that constitutional law is "inevitably . . . result-
oriented," one can understand Levy's view that any decision
other than *Brown v. Board of Education* "would have been
unthinkable, unbearable, unspeakable"[17] (though not to Chief
Justice Vinson and Justices Reed and Jackson),[18] that "strict con-
structionism means reversing the decision of Appomatox . . . a
return to . . . Jim Crow."[19] That is not a return that I should
recommend, but is this not the very "reasoning backwards"
so vigorously condemned by Levy: "In constitutional cases
. . . the judge who first chooses what the outcome should
be and then reasons backwards to apply a rationalization replete with rules and precedents has betrayed his calling; he has
decided on the basis of prejudice and prejudgment, and has
made constitutional law little more than the embodiment of his
policy preferences, reflecting his subjective predilections."[20]
That, however, is "inevitable" once it is postulated that "our
constitutional law is subjective in character and to a great degree result-oriented."[21] Nevertheless Levy states that "result-
oriented constitutional adjudication . . . is a corruption of the
judicial process that leaves too far behind the rule of law enforced by impersonal or objective judges."[22] He himself avers,
however, "We may not want judges who start with the answer
rather than the problem . . . but as long as mere mortals sit on

16. Levy, *Against the Law* 29–30. "Burger was quite accurate when he accused the Court of operating as a 'continuing constitutional convention.' It
cannot operate in any other way." Id. 230.

17. Levy, *Warren* 10, 20.

18. Supra Chapter 7 at notes 43–44, 54–55.

19. Levy, *Against the Law* 30–31.

20. Levy, *Warren* 186.

21. Levy, *Against the Law* 35.

22. Levy, *Against the Law* 438.

the Court and must construe that majestic but muddy Constitution, we will rarely get any other kind."[23] Yet he emphasizes in *Against the Law* that "result-oriented jurisprudence . . . [is a] judicial monstrosity that gains nothing when the Court reaches a just result merely because of its identification with underdog litigants."[24]

Now unless I am sadly at sea, it seems to me that Levy is riding off in opposite directions. He cannot at one and the same time maintain that the words of the Constitution "are empty vessels into which [a judge] can pour nearly anything he will" and then insist that the "*purpose* of the Sixth Amendment was to *bind* the federal government to the system of trial by jury that was traditional and familiar."[25] On that analysis the words "trial by jury" are not "empty vessels" but have a fixed content. So, too, he has been unable to decide whether a result-oriented jurisprudence is "inevitable" or a "monstrosity." It may be one or the other, but it cannot be both.[26] The core of Levy's complaint, unless I grossly misconceive his concluding remarks, seems to be against the Burger Court's craftsmanship, its failure "to weigh criticism," "to develop carefully reasoned judgments," "to make bad law in the sense of being badly crafted."[27] But, as he recognizes, "experts will doubtless dis-

23. Levy, *Against the Law* 35.
24. Id. xiii.
25. Id. 289 (emphasis added).
26. So, too, affirmation that "inevitably . . . constitutional law is subjective," supra at note 13, is incompatible with Levy's statement that the Brennan-Marshall explanations "were like Band-Aids covering their very personal and humanitarian reading of present-day values," Levy, *Against the Law* 398, as well they might do in "updating" the Constitution. For similar criticism see Robert H. Horn, "Book Review," 88 Harv. L. Rev. 1924, 1925 (1975).
27. Levy, *Against the Law* 438–439. "His alarm arises more from the style, manners and rationale with which the decisions have been rendered than from the decisions themselves . . . he concentrates his detailed analytical criticism on the *how* instead of the *what*." D. G. Stephenson, "Book Review," 61 Va. L. Rev. 1338, 1341 (1975).

agree" about "the Nixon Court's craftsmanship" as "they have
about the Warren Court's craftsmanship."[28] Whether it be good
or bad, however, is of no moment in a jurisprudence that is
"inevitably . . . result-oriented." The result, not the reasoning, is what counts.[29]

Some of Levy's severest strictures are reserved for the Burger
Court's treatment of precedents: one new reading "left its precedents in shambles"; the Court "obliterates them."[30] Yet, he
considers that "precedents do not decide cases."[31] And in disregard of precedents the Burger Court yields the palm to its
predecessor. "The list of opinions destroyed by the Warren
Court," Philip Kurland observed, "reads like a table of contents
from an old constitutional law casebook."[32] It is difficult to
agree that Chief Justice Burger "displayed an egregious contempt for precedents" when he rejected the "thesis that what
the Court said lately controls over the Constitution."[33] He may

28. Levy, *Against the Law* 438.

29. Stephenson, supra note 27 at 1344, justly remarks, "*what* the Court does
has a greater and more lasting effect on its place in the political system than
how it reaches its judgment." One has only to compare the impact of the "desegregation case" with its inadequate reasoning. Levy, finding a decline in Justice Douglas' analytical powers, remarks that "Douglas's opinions provoked
some of his liberal admirers to take the cynical position that if constitutional
adjudication is basically result-oriented, Douglas voting for the 'right' side
was better than any Nixon appointee voting the other way." Levy, *Against
the Law* 38. See Rodell, supra Chapter 15 at note 11, Chapter 17 note 41.

30. Levy, *Against the Law* 260, 423.

31. Id. 34.

32. *Politics, the Constitution and the Warren Court* 90 (1970). An ardent
admirer of the Warren Court stated that "in a whole series of precedent-
shattering decisions, the Court extended the protection of parts of the Bill of
Rights well beyond old-established limits and set aside several past Court
rulings to do so . . . [a] well-nigh unprecedented display of judicial power."
Fred Rodell, "The 'Warren Court' Stands Its Ground," *The New York Times
Magazine,* September 27, 1964, in Levy, *Warren* 209, 210.

33. Levy, *Against the Law* 28–29. Like Chief Justice Burger, Justices
Douglas and Frankfurter claimed the right to look at the Constitution rather
than what the Court had said about it. Supra Chapter 15 note 57.

be indulged in returning to older precedents that the Warren Court had only recently discarded,[34] particularly since, as Justice Henry Baldwin early observed, "There is no more certainty that a last opinion is more correct than the first."[35] Let Levy sum up:

> In all these cases . . . the Burger Court no less than the Warren Court displayed an audacious disregard for and circumvention of precedents, clearly revealing its own values and policy choices. Despite pretenses to the contrary, it could do no other for as beauty exists in the eye of the beholder, so American constitutional law exists in the collective eye of those who happen at any moment to dominate the Supreme Court.[36]

Burger spoke in a "right to counsel" case, Coleman v. Alabama, 399 U.S. 1, 22 (1970), dissenting opinion. Levy notes that at the adoption of the Constitution, "the counsel clause . . . meant no more than the right to retain counsel of one's choice at one's own expense," that it was only in 1938 that the Court held counsel must be supplied, and "that rule was not extended to state crime proceedings until 1963." Levy, *Against the Law* 197. Similarly Levy complains that Kirby v. Illinois, 406 U.S. 682 (1972), "emasculated" United States v. Wade, 388 U.S. 218 (1967) (right to counsel at police lineup). Why should the Burger Court feel bound by a "precedent" first created only five years earlier? Levy notices that "Congress viewed Wade as a 'harmful blow at the nation-wide effort to control crime.'" Levy, id. 252.

34. Consider Justice Brennan's dissent in United States v. Ash, 413 U.S. 300, 326 (1973): "today's decision marks simply another step towards the complete evisceration of the fundamental constitutional principles *established* by this Court *only six years* ago" (emphasis added).

Horn, supra note 26 at 1926–1927 comments, "In large part these decisions were less than a decade old when the Burger era opened. Professor Levy is entitled to regard them as 'settled meanings of the Constitution' (p. 422) regardless of how greatly these Warren Court decisions unsettled what in some instances had been an apparently settled meaning since the Bill of Rights itself had been adopted," i.e., for 150 years.

35. Livingston's Executor v. Story, 36 U.S. (11 Pet.) 351, 400 (1837), dissenting opinion. See also Justice Jackson's comment on judicial infallibility, supra Chapter 17 at note 45.

36. Levy, *Warren* 251.

Such are the fruits of a value-oriented system which make of "constitutional [case] law" a veritable whirligig. No rhetoric can disguise that this is but the kadi administering justice under a tree.

Where Levy entertained misgivings about judicial review but swallowed them,[37] Charles Black was an uncurbed partisan of the Warren Court, a panegyrist of Justice Black who sought to justify the policymaking ways of the Court to man.[38] Now Black has come forth with a semi-recantation, taking on himself some of the blame for encouraging a result-focused jurisprudence.[39] The "fresh raw wound" caused by the Burger Court's death penalty cases of July 2, 1976, set him to "wondering whether we liberals . . . may not be in part to blame for a . . . quite evident trend toward the point of view that reason doesn't matter much, and can be brushed aside, if only the result is thought desirable."[40] One should not be captious with a repentant sinner, but Black's semi-recantation contains the seeds of further error; and, as one who wrote in 1942 that the test of constitutionality cannot be the embodiment of predilections which I share,[41] I may be forgiven for seeking to lay those errors bare.

37. "If there must be an answer, the most satisfying is the most equivocal or gingerly balanced, that of the mugwump caught in the classic stance with his mug on one side of the fence and his wump on the other." Leonard Levy ed., *Judicial Review and the Supreme Court* 42 (1967).

38. C. L. Black, *The People and the Court* (1960); *Hugo Black and the Supreme Court: A Symposium,* "Foreword" by C. L. Black (S. P. Strickland ed. 1967). As Levy observed, "the defense of judicial review has come mainly from those who have welcomed the trend of judicial decision in recent years and have rushed to the Court's protection." Supra note 37 at 24.

39. Address, "The Judicial Power as Guardian of Liberties," before a Symposium on "The Supreme Court and Constitutional Liberties in Modern America," Wayne State University, Detroit, Mich., Oct. 16, 1976 (not yet published); hereinafter cited as Black, Wayne.

40. Id. 2.

41. Supra Chapter 1 at note 13.

There is first Black's repeated appeal to "reason."[42] The recent death-penalty cases moved him to ask "whether we do well to entrust this Court with the job of a rational defense of ordered liberty—and even whether we did well to refrain from talking too loud about it when the same [Burger] Court without adequate reason given, decided the abortion case as it did."[43] Like Professor Black, I too am a devotee of reason and well recall the richly deserved criticisms of the Warren Court, couched in terms of deplorable "craftsmanship"[44]—without a peep from Black.[45] He himself recognizes that "painstaking reason often leads to different results in different minds" and that "no important result is dictated wholly by reason; there must lie at its heart a normative judgment not reachable by reason alone."[46] In other words, "reason" starts from premises that another may reject. Chief Justice Warren proceeded in

42. The death-penalty "cases represented as definite an abandonment of the responsibility to justify a result by coherent reason as has ever occurred in the history of the Court." Black, Wayne 4. He urges that the bar "never cease to call the Court to account, and to urge reason upon it," id. 9, lest a "miasma of illegitimacy . . . hang about all judicial work." Id. 10. Even more vital is it that the Court must act within the bounds of its authority for, as he states, it is "a prime political postulate that the government is not to travel outside its allocated sphere," supra note 38 at 41, and that also goes for the judiciary.

43. Black, Wayne 7.

44. Black's Yale colleagues, Alexander Bickel and Harry Wellington, wrote in 1957, "The Court's product has shown an increasing incidence of the . . . formulation of results accompanied by little or no effort to support them in reason." "Legislative Purpose and the Judicial Process: The Lincoln Mills Case," 71 Harv. L. Rev. 1, 3 (1957). Dissenting Justices complained that the Warren majority failed to "confront complicated constitutional issues with professional expertise and consistency." Levy, *Warren* 17. Kurland observed that "the defenders of the [Warren] Court do not tend to argue that the opinions are well reasoned." Supra note 32 at 183. See also supra at note 28.

45. He considered protests against the "reasoning" in the Brown case as "wrong." Black, Wayne 3. In other contexts he now bemoans his own silence, infra at note 51.

46. Black, Wayne 11.

Reynolds v. Sims (reapportionment) from the Declaration of Independence and the Gettysburg Address, notwithstanding that the framers of the Fourteenth Amendment found that the Declaration had not deprived the States of control over suffrage, and that Lincoln saw no prospect of Negro "equality." And he totally ignored the incontestable evidence that Justice Harlan spread before the Court that the framers excluded suffrage from the scope of the Amendment. Even now Black does not ask whether the Justices may displace the framers' value-choices with their own "normative judgments."

The frailty of "reason" is further illustrated by Black himself; he regards *Brown v. Board of Education* "as nearly syllogistic as a real law case can be. The Fourteenth Amendment, in *the clear light of its history* . . . forbade *all* discrimination against black people."[47] He may be indulged for his inability to abandon a view to which he was committed as a member of the NAACP legal counsel in that case; he "threw all his passionate brilliance into the NAACP effort."[48] But, to the astonishment of Kelly, Graham, and others, the "clear" neoabolitionist history they pressed on the court was branded by Chief Justice Warren— anxious though he was to rule in favor of desegregation—as "inconclusive." How can we rely on "reason" that converts the very limited and "clear" purposes of the framers into a ban on "all" discrimination?

Black recalls that he "expressed some doubt about the application of the equal protection clause to legislative apportionment, in *Baker v. Carr,* but, looking back, I know that I muted that doubt." Came *Oregon v. Mitchell,* and Professor Black perceived "that the plurality opinion of four was plainly wrong,

47. Id. 2 (emphasis added). In 1959 he wrote that the case "was a debatable one." Supra note 38 at 137. His Yale colleague, Bickel, wrote what Justice Frankfurter considered an "impressive" memorandum, and advised that "it is impossible to conclude that the 39th Congress intended that segregation be abolished." Supra Chapter 7 at note 8.

48. Kluger 645.

and the deciding concurrence of Mr. Justice Black so egregiously wrong as to be . . . all but incredible."[49] In justice to Justice Black, it deserves to be repeated that he recanted (though without so stating) with respect to apportionment for State offices, saying that he "agreed" with Justice Harlan's demonstration that control over suffrage was deliberately left by the framers with the States.[50] Of this Professor Black says not a word. One of the remarkable aspects of his address in fact is that not once does he advert to the historical limitations on judicial policymaking with respect to the Bill of Rights, segregation, and reapportionment set forth by Fairman, Bickel, and Harlan; he puts his trust in "reason." Because reason can lead in different directions, however, the all-but-incontestable proof that suffrage was left by the framers to the States, offers a safer, surer mooring.

But to resume Professor Black's threnody; looking back to the Warren Court's extension of the school desegregation case "to other forms of segregation, involving neither schools nor children" in cases "decided *per curiam* and without opinion," Black now wishes that he "had fullthroatedly joined Herbert Wechsler in his protest against this procedure, which was so self-evidently wrong that one is ashamed to have glossed it over just because the result was what one wanted and thought right."[51] This was more than a departure from a lawyer's "commitment . . . to reason";[52] it represents a departure from standards that led the people to place their trust in scholars. Like scientists, constitutional scholars, as Thomas Huxley said upwards of a century ago, should "respect nothing but evidence,

49. Black, Wayne 3–4.

50. "My Brother HARLAN has persuasively demonstrated that the Framers . . . intended to keep for themselves . . . the power to regulate elections . . . I agree as to the State's power to regulate the elections of their own officials." Oregon v. Mitchell, 400 U.S. 112, 124–125 (1970), concurring and dissenting in part.

51. Black, Wayne 8–9.

52. Id. 9.

and . . . believe that their highest duty lies in submitting to it, however it may jar against their inclinations."[53] That duty carries with it, I submit, publication, not suppression, of scholarly findings.

Oregon v. Mitchell induced some soul-searching in Black: "What if all this *is turned on us?* If real reason goes out of fashion, can we be sure it will not happen? . . . Have we not, after all, asked for it?"[54] It is not unfair to conclude, I trust, that Black's jeremiad illustrates once more the "whose ox is gored" adage. He held his peace when "the result was what one wanted and thought right," but now protests against a departure from "reason" when he is "heartbroken that the legal killing of people is to be resumed."[55] Not a word about the manifest preference of the people to the contrary, about the formidable evidence that the Fourteenth Amendment did not make the Bill of Rights applicable to the States, that the death penalty was not deemed a "cruel and unusual punishment" by the Framers—a view to which the Supreme Court adhered until 1972.[56] Instead Black apparently remains faithful to a judicial power to revise the Constitution—if only it be clothed in "reason."

---

53. Supra Chapter 1 epigraph.
54. Black, Wayne 4 (emphasis added).
55. Id. 2.
56. Supra Chapter 17 note 48.

19

The Legitimacy
of Judicial Review

THE most fundamental question of all, as Thomas Grey rightly stated, is "the legitimacy of judicial review itself,"[1] a question that goes beyond the scope of the power to its very existence, however limited. After remarking, "Whether this enormous power can fairly be deduced from the language of the Constitution, and whether the framers of that instrument intended to confer it on the Justices, has been the subject of vast learned controversy . . . unlikely ever to be resolved," Joseph Bishop reassuringly stated, "No matter; the power exists."[2] It is true that the power has long been exercised, but whether it "exists"—has constitutional warrant—is something else again. Edmond Cahn, however, opined that "it is too late to reopen the question of whether the Court ought to determine constitutional issues."[3] On the contrary, it is never too late to chal-

---

1. "Do We Have an Unwritten Constitution?," 27 Stan. L. Rev. 703 (1975).

2. "The Warren Court is Not Likely to Be Overruled," *The New York Times Magazine,* September 7, 1969, in Levy, *Warren* 93–94. See also E. V. Rostow, "The Democratic Character of Judicial Review," 66 Harv. L. Rev. 193, 196 (1952). But see infra Chapter 21 at note 44.

3. E. Cahn, "Brief for the Supreme Court," *The New York Times Magazine,* October 7, 1956, in Levy, *Warren* 28, 29; cf. Robert G. McCloskey, *The American Supreme Court* 17–18 (1960). But see infra Chapter 23 at note 2.

lenge the usurpation of power; one gains no title by prescription against the government,[4] still less against the sovereign people. Power reserved to the people by the Tenth Amendment can not be taken over by "squatter sovereignty." "It will not be denied," Chief Justice Marshall stated, "that a bold and daring usurpation might be resisted, after an acquiescence still longer and more complete than this."[5] In *Erie Ry. Co. v. Tompkins* the Court, per Justice Brandeis, branded its own course of conduct stretching over one hundred years as "unconstitutional,"[6] in a situation not nearly as important as the "enormous power" to impose the judicial will upon the nation. Usurpation—the exercise of power not granted—is not legitimated by repetition.[7] The people, as John Adams inscribed in the Massachusetts Constitution of 1780, are ever entitled to demand of their magistrates an "exact and constant observance" of the principles of the Constitution,[8] above all, to exercise no powers not granted. We may not, therefore, shut our eyes to the issue of legitimacy.

In the course of a penetrating summary of the issues posed by judicial review, Leonard Levy states: "The charges of usurpa-

4. United States v. 1,629.6 Acres of Land, County of Sussex, Del., 503 F.2d 764, 767 (3d Cir. 1974); United States v. Oglesby, 163 F. Supp. 203, 204 (W.D. Ark. 1958); Blask v. Sowl, 309 F. Supp. 909, 914 (W.D. Wis. 1967).

5. M'Culloch v. Maryland, 17 U.S. (4 Wheat.) 316, 401 (1819). Hamilton stated that judicial "usurpations on the authority of the legislature" would be impeachable. Supra Chapter 15 at note 50.

6. 304 U.S. 64, 77–78 (1938): referring to Swift v. Tyson, 40 U.S. (16 Pet.) 1 (1842), the Court held, "the unconstitutionality of the course pursued [by the courts] has now been made clear, and compels us" to "abandon" the "doctrine so widely applied throughout nearly a century." For Justice Brandeis' quotation from Justice Holmes, see supra Chapter 15 note 56.

7. Powell v. McCormack, 395 U.S. 486, 546–547 (1969): "That an unconstitutional action has been taken before surely does not render the same action any less unconstitutional at a later date." See also Ogden v. Saunders, 25 U.S. (12 Wheat.) 213, 290 (1827).

8. Massachusetts Constitution, 1780, Part the First, Article XVIII, 1 Poore 959, quoted more fully supra Chapter 15 at note 18. See also supra Chapter 15 note 19.

tion most certainly cannot be proved; it is without merit. The difficulty is that the legitimacy of judicial review in terms of the original intent cannot be proved either."[9] This attempt at even-handed analysis overlooks the fact that under a Constitution which delegates and limits power, the burden is on a claimant to point to the source of his power—failing which, it is a usurpation.[9a] After dwelling on the materials which led him to conclude that the framers left a "very incomplete and extraordinarily ambiguous record,"[10] Levy comments on Charles Black's argument that judicial review has been "legitimized by popular acquiescence, and therefore popular approval, over the course of American history." In Black's own words, "the people have, precisely through the political process, given the stamp of approval in the only way they could give approval to an institution in being—by leaving it alone." To this Levy retorts: "The simple fact is that at no time in our history have the American people passed judgment, pro or con, on the merits of judicial review over Congress. Consent freely given, by referendum, by legislation, or by amendment is simply not the same as failure to abolish or impair."[11] If in fact no provision for judicial review was made by the Constitution, Black's argument would substitute for the constitutional machinery for change by amendment revision by tacit acquiescence. Neglect or inaction would excuse noncompliance with the amendment provision; usurpation would be legitimized by inertia. But, as Hamilton stated in Federalist No. 78, the Constitution is "binding"— "until the people have, by some *solemn and authoritative act,*

---

9. *Judicial Review and the Supreme Court* 2 (1967); cf. McCloskey, supra note 3 at 8–9.

9a. See infra Chapter 23 at note 2.

10. Levy, supra note 9 at 3.

11. Id. 30–31. In the same essay, however, Levy earlier stated, "Long acquiescence by the people and their representatives has legitimated judicial review. . . . Judicial review, in fact exists by the tacit consent of the governed." Id. 12.

annulled or changed the established form."[12] The Black argument, which takes little or no account of historical roadblocks, is, as Willard Hurst said in an analogous context, "a way of practically reading Article V out of the Constitution."[13]

To read popular acquiescence in judicial vetoes as ratification of a judicial power to change the Constitution offends against still another requirement: complete disclosure. The people could rely on Hamilton's rejection in Federalist No. 78 of the possibility that "the courts on the pretense of repugnancy, may substitute their own pleasure to the constitutional intention of the legislature," on his representation that the judges had no warrant to depart from the Constitution. As Lusky put it, the people expect the Justices to view the Constitution as expressing "the will of those who made" it and "to ascertain their will."[14] Until the Court candidly discloses—as Justice Jackson vainly urged—that it is "making new law for a new day," the people can hardly be held to acquiesce in what they have not been told. They have been told that the Court speaks with the voice of the Constitution;[15] they are constantly told that "the

12. Quoted in full, supra Chapter 17 at note 15 (emphasis added).

13. Willard Hurst, "Discussion" in *Supreme Court and Supreme Law* 74 (E. Cahn ed. 1954). Learned Hand also adhered to amendment as the proper means of change. Kathryn Griffith, *Judge Learned Hand and the Role of the Federal Judiciary* 83 (1973). Justice Black rang the changes on this theme, e.g., in Griswold v. Connecticut, 381 U.S. 479, 522 (1965).

The issue has generally been ignored by the instrumentalists. Yet it is central, for as Lusky asks, "does establishment of new constitutional rules by the Court offend Article V . . . which prescribes the amendment process? Does it outrage the principle of separation of powers? . . . In short, is the Court guilty of plain usurpation?" Lusky 79. Elbridge Gerry, as we have seen, regarded change outside Article V as a subversion of the Constitution and impeachable. Supra Chapter 17 at notes 20–22.

14. Federalist 507; Lusky 31–32.

15. Professor Felix Frankfurter wrote President Franklin Roosevelt, "People have been taught to believe that when the Supreme Court speaks it is not they who speak but the Constitution, whereas, of course . . . it is *they* who speak and *not* the Constitution. And I verily believe that that is what the country needs most to understand." *Roosevelt and Frankfurter: Their Corre-*

Constitution (not the Justices) requires." And that cannot be converted into ratification of progressive judicial violation of its limits.

On Levy's view that judicial review has no sure constitutional basis[16] and that it has not been "approved" by the American people, it is, like Mahomet's coffin, suspended in midair. Thus, the awesome power of judicial review is left altogether without footing. My own studies, set forth in *Congress v. The Supreme Court* (1969), convinced me that judicial review *was* contemplated and provided for by the Framers, albeit limited to policing constitutional boundaries and divorced from participation in policymaking. The fundamental importance of legitimacy impels me to comment briefly on Levy's objections to the evidence avouched for it.

Levy begins by asking, if the Framers "intended the Court to have the power, why did they not provide for it?"[17] In my view they did. Article III, §2, extends the judicial power to cases "arising under this Constitution"; one who claims that a constitutional right was invaded presents such a case. Article VI, §2, provides that "This Constitution and the Laws . . . which shall be made in Pursuance thereof . . . shall be the supreme Law of the Land; and the Judges in every State shall be bound thereby." Federal judges and all federal and State officials were no less "bound" than State judges by the "supreme Law."[18] If a judge is "bound" *only* by a law "in pursuance" of the Constitu-

---

spondence 1928–1945 383 (M. Freedman ed. 1967). But as a Justice, sitting on the desegregation case, he could not bring himself to tell the people, as Justice Jackson urged, that the Justices were "declaring new law for a new day." Supra Chapter 7 at notes 52, 55. See also supra Chapter 17 at notes 25–26.

16. Levy, supra note 9 at 2. After examining the arguments pro and con, Archibald Cox likewise concludes that the argument for judicial review "hardly adds up to conclusive proof that the basic charter, as originally adopted, conferred supremacy upon constitutional questions to the Judicial Branch." *The Role of the Supreme Court in American Government* 16 (1976).

17. Levy, supra note 9 at 2.

18. Raoul Berger, *Congress v. The Supreme Court* 236–344 (1969).

tion, that is, consistent therewith, by necessary implication he is *not bound* by an inconsistent law.[19] Obviously a judge would be required to make a preliminary decision whether or not he was "bound" by the law, exercising the judicial power to decide lodged in a federal judge by Article III.[20] As said by Herbert Wechsler, federal judges "enforce the Constitution" because "they must decide a litigated issue that is otherwise within their [Article III] jurisdiction and in doing so must give effect to the supreme law of the land."[21] In other words, a judicial issue is presented by the question whether a statute is the "supreme Law of the Land" and the Article III "judicial power" embraces such questions. Read together, Articles III and VI therefore confer the power of judicial review. Those who find it difficult to draw these deductions should bear in mind that *the Framers so understood* the two provisions, the evidence for which I have supplied in 86 heavily documented pages.[22]

19. To the Founders "in pursuance thereof" meant "consistent with." Id. 228–236.

20. Id.

21. Quoted in id. 245 note 101.

22. Id. 198–284. Levy asserts that "Articles III and VI . . . established . . . judicial review . . . over the acts of the states, the subordinate agencies within the federal system, but not over the President and Congress." Levy, supra note 9 at 7. But Article VI refers to "laws of the United States which shall be made in pursuance" of the Constitution; only congressional laws consistent with the Constitution are made the "supreme law of the land." The companion argument—that only state judges are "bound" by the Constitution—would free every other official, state or federal, from constitutional bonds, an absurd result, and one incompatible with the Founders' design. Berger, supra note 18 at 236–242. Levy's inarticulate premise, that the Framers were more solicitous to protect Congress than the States from review, runs counter to historical fact. The Founders cherished the States as the bastion of their rights and *feared* the remote and new federal government; they sought to protect the States against federal incursions, and to do so initially confided judicial review to the State courts. Id. 258–278. They repeatedly referred to judicial review as a curb on *congressional* encroachments. Id. 13–14; Hamilton, supra Chapter 15 at note 50. See Hamilton, infra note 33.

Next Levy turns to "Corwin's vacillations" which allegedly testify "to the confusing and inconclusive nature of the evidence."[23] Undeniably Corwin swung like a pendulum, but the important question is not what he thought but what are the facts. Now the facts, set forth by Charles Beard, criticized by Corwin in 1913, but richly confirmed by Corwin in 1914,[24] are in the words of his 1914 summary:

> That the members of the Convention of 1787 thought the Constitution secured to the courts . . . the right to pass on the validity of acts of Congress under it cannot reasonably be doubted. Confining ourselves simply to the available evidence that is strictly contemporaneous with the framing and ratifying of the Constitution, as I think it only proper to do, we find the following members of the Convention that framed the Constitution definitely asserting that this would be the case . . . True these were only seventeen names out of a possible fifty-five, but let it be considered whose names they are. They designate fully three-fourths of the leaders of the Convention.[25]

Only two men, Gunning Bedford and John Mercer, who carried little weight, expressed a contrary view.[26] As Corwin stated, "on no other feature of the Constitution with reference to which there has been any considerable debate is the view of the Convention itself better attested."[27] To these seventeen are added a number of prominent Founders, such as Oliver Ellsworth of Connecticut and John Marshall of Virginia, who spoke in the Ratification Conventions. After painstakingly

23. Levy, supra note 9 at 3.

24. For a critique of Corwin's 1913 review, see Berger, supra note 18 at 106–114. His reversion in 1937 to his 1913 view was colored by his espousal of the Court-packing plan as a means of halting the Court's assault on the New Deal. For comment on some of his 1937 views, see Berger, id. at 114 note 312.

25. More fully quoted in Berger, id. at 104–105.

26. Id. 69 note 109, 63.

27. Id. 105.

sifting all the evidence I concluded that Beard and the 1914 Corwin evaluation were fully supported.[28]

A few comments seriatim on the selected items Levy would discredit will suffice. When the Convention discussed the "arising under" clause, Madison "expressed doubt about 'going too far' and advocated that jurisdiction over such cases be 'limited to cases of a Judiciary Nature.' "[29] This merely sought to obviate a roving commission to declare legislation unconstitutional and to confine that function to properly litigated cases. Levy himself explains that the Court "cannot strike down an act at will, however unconstitutional, it must wait passively for a zealous litigant to raise a real case or controversy over which it has jurisdiction."[30] The Convention did not see need to act on Madison's suggestion because of the general belief that "the jurisdiction given was constructively limited to cases of a Judiciary Nature"[31]—to "cases or controversies." Levy also stresses Madison's inconsistent positions.[32] Undoubtedly Madison was inconsistent over the years. Who is not? But if we look to what he said in the Federal and State Conventions—the proper frame, as Corwin noted, because those utterances were meant to influence fellow delegates—there is actually little or no inconsistency. On July 23, 1787, Madison declared that "A Law violating a constitution established by the people themselves, would be considered by the judges as null and void,"[33] a view

---

28. Id. 47–141.
29. Levy, supra note 9 at 5.
30. Id. 27–28.
31. 2 Farrand 430.
32. Levy, supra note 9 at 4–6.
33. Berger, supra note 18 at 73. Following William Crosskey, Levy states this was "wrenched out of context to give the misleading impression that Madison supported judicial review over Congress," whereas Madison referred "to the possibility that state judges would declare unconstitutional a state act in violation of the federal constitution." Levy, supra note 9 at 4. But Levy himself calls attention to Hamilton's explanation "that the Court's power was intended to hold Congress in check, thereby safeguarding the States against national aggrandizement." Levy, id. at 6. The Founders were far more con-

often expressed by other Founders, including Marshall in the Virginia Convention.[34] On August 27 Madison stated: "The right of expounding the Constitution in cases not of this [Judiciary] nature ought not to be given to that Department."[35] By plain implication, if the right *was* of a Judiciary Nature, "the right of expounding" was given, and "expounding" had been employed by the Members to include decisions on constitutionality, which embraced "laws of the United States [congressional acts] . . . in pursuance" of the Constitution.[36]

Then Levy turns to Hamilton: "it is not irrelevant" that Hamilton's own plan made no provision "for any sort of judicial review."[37] I suggest that it is utterly irrelevant. Hamilton did not propose to submit a complete scheme of government, but merely "to suggest the amendments which he should probably propose to the plan of Mr. R[andolph] in the proper stages of its future discussion." The Randolph plan provided for a judiciary as a "check" on the legislature.[38] Levy also depreciates Hamilton's exposition of judicial review in Federalist No. 78 because it adopted Robert Yates' demonstration (in opposition to adoption of the Constitution) that it provided for judicial review.[39] Adoption of an opponent's argument generally is a tacit tribute to its force. Levy explains that

cerned about checking Congress than the States. Supra note 22. See also Madison's statement that the Bill of Rights, aimed at Congress, would enable the courts to act as a bulwark. Infra Chapter 21 at note 65.

34. Berger, supra note 18 at 15–16.

35. Id. 74.

36. Id., Index under "Expounding."

37. Levy, supra note 9 at 6; but see Hamilton, supra note 33.

38. 1 Farrand 291, 28; Berger, supra note 18 at 19 note 53.

39. Levy, supra note 9 at 6. For Yates, see Berger, supra note 18 at 201–202. Yates had been anticipated by James Iredell, an advocate of the Constitution and judicial review, in a reply to Richard Spaight, who had written him from the Convention. Berger, id. at 82–83.

Levy also argues, supra note 9 at 7, that Hamilton argued in Federalist No. 78 "from general principles" rather than from the words of the Framers. Since he was defending their handiwork, he had to appeal to outside authority—the argument from principle.

Hamilton tried to convince his readers that the Court's power was intended to hold Congress in check, thereby safeguarding the states against national aggrandizement. A few [?] advocates of the Constitution, like Oliver Ellsworth and John Marshall, sought in the same manner to allay popular apprehensions that Congress might exceed its power . . . Their remarks, like Hamilton's in #78, are evidence of shrewd political tactics, not of the framers' intention to vest judicial review in the Supreme Court over acts of Congress.[40]

If they did not mean what they were saying (as to which there is no evidence whatever),[41] they were guilty of false representations to "allay" fears on which votes depended. Those who voted for adoption of the Constitution were entitled to rely on such representations; consequently, the Constitution is to be construed, in Jefferson's words, in accordance with the "meaning contemplated by the plain understanding of the people at the time of its adoption—a meaning to be found in the explanation of those who advocated it."[42] Let it be assumed that the remarks of Madison and Hamilton are open to Levy's doubts, they cannot tip the scales against the clear recognition of judicial review by 15 members who spoke to the issue in the Convention, plus 6 or 7 delegates who spoke thereafter.[43]

Finally, Levy finds it "striking . . . that there were so few State precedents prior to the Convention."[44] That is not surprising in view of the short span between 1776 and 1787, during most of which the States were fighting for survival. If some "precedents" are "spurious" in light of present-day research, the important fact is that they were thought to exemplify judi-

40. Levy, supra note 9 at 6.
41. Laurent Frantz observed of a similar argument, "the issue is not what Madison really thought but how the First Amendment was presented to those who voted for its enactment." "Is the First Amendment Law?—A Reply to Professor Mendelson," 51 Calif. L. Rev. 729, 739 (1963).
42. Berger, supra note 18 at 120.
43. Id. 112–113.
44. Levy, supra note 9 at 8.

cial review.[45] What men think the facts are is more influential than the actual facts.[46] Levy himself says, "The idea of judicial review was, nevertheless, rapidly emerging, a fact which adds retrospective significance to the few precedents."[47] The decade preceding adoption of the Constitution was one of great intellectual ferment in which, Gordon Wood has shown, a revolution in political thinking was taking place.[48] The postulate, for example, that sovereignty was in the people, that rights need not flow from the Crown, was far more revolutionary than judicial review.[49] The Founders, as Corwin emphasized, took "Federalism, checks and balances, judicial review . . . not in the form of institutions tested and hammered into shape by practice, but as raw ideas."[50] What has since become obscure to this generation was clear enough to a great contemporary, James Wilson, second only to Madison as an architect of the Constitution and chief advocate in Pennsylvania of its adoption. In 1790–91 he was a Justice of the Supreme Court as well as a professor of law in Philadelphia. In the course of a series of Lectures on Law he declared that under the Constitution the effect of legislative "extravagancies may be prevented . . . by the judicial authority." "Every transgression" of the constitutional "bounds of legislative power" shall thus be "adjudged and rendered vain and fruitless."[51]

45. Berger, supra note 18 at 38–39.
46. Charles Evans Hughes said of the colonists' reliance on Magna Charta, "It matters not whether they were accurate in their understanding of the Great Charter, for the point is . . . what the colonists thought it meant" in framing their own constitutional provisions. C. E. Hughes, *The Supreme Court of the United States* 186 (1928).
47. Levy, supra note 9 at 11.
48. *The Creation of the American Republic 1776–1787* 389, 524, 555, 564, 589 (1969); the changes proceeded at a rapidly accelerating pace, id. at 92, 259, 300, 318.
49. Id. at 344–389.
50. Berger, supra note 18 at 46.
51. Id. 150–151.

Were the evidence that judicial review was contemplated and provided for by the Framers far less weighty, it should yet be preferred to a theory which rests judicial review on no evidence at all, for that represents a naked usurpation of power nowhere granted. If, however, judicial review is in fact derived from the text and history of the Constitution, it must be within the compass envisaged by the Framers—policing of boundaries and exclusion of policymaking reserved to the legislature. History cannot be invoked to establish the power, then discarded when seen to limit its scope.

20

Why the "Original Intention"?

C URRENT indifference to the "original intention"—shorthand for the meaning attached by the framers to the words they employed in the Constitution and its Amendments —is a relatively recent phenomenon. Those who would adhere to it are scornfully charged with "filio-pietism," "verbal archeology,"[1] "antiquarian historicism that would freeze [the] original meaning" of the Constitution.[2] We are told that the Framers intended to leave it "to succeeding generations [meaning judges] . . . to rewrite the 'living' constitution anew,"[3] an argument opposed to historical fact. The sole and exclusive vehicle of change the Framers provided was the amendment

---

1. Myres McDougal and Asher Lans, "Treaties and Congressional-Executive or Presidential Agreements: Interchangeable Instruments of National Policy" 54 Yale L.J. 181, 212, 214, 291 (1945).

2. L. Levy, *Judgments: Essays in American Constitutional History* 17 (1972).

3. A. S. Miller, "An Inquiry into the Relevance of the Intentions of the Founding Fathers, With Special Emphasis upon the Doctrine of the Separation of Powers," 27 Ark. L. Rev. 584, 595 (1973). The Constitution was "not intended to" "freeze its original meaning." Levy, supra note 2. Professor Miller might have cited Edward Corwin, who, in 1925, dismissed "speculative ideas about what the framers of the constitution . . . intended it should mean" because "the main business of constitutional interpretation . . . is to keep the constitution adjusted to the advancing needs of time." *American Constitutional History* 108 (Mason and Garvey eds. 1964).

process; judicial discretion and policymaking were in high disfavor; all "agents and servants of the people" were to be "bound by the chains" of a "fixed Constitution." Certainly Justice Story did not regard himself as holding a commission "to rewrite the 'living' constitution anew":

> Nor should it ever be lost sight of that the government of the United States is one of limited and enumerated powers; and that a departure from the true import and sense of its powers is pro tanto, the establishment of a new Constitution. It is doing for the people, what they have not chosen to do for themselves. It is usurping the functions of a legislator.[4]

Why is the "original intention" so important? The answer was long since given by Madison: if "the sense in which the Constitution was accepted and ratified by the Nation . . . be not the guide in expounding it, there can be no security for a consistent and stable government, more than for a faithful exercise of its powers."[5] A judicial power to revise the Constitution transforms the bulwark of our liberties into a parchment barrier. This it was that caused Jefferson to say, "Our peculiar security is in the possession of a written constitution. Let us not make it a blank paper by construction."[6] Given a system founded on a dread of power, with "limits" to fence it about, those who demand compliance with those limits (pursuant to the counsel of four or five early State constitutions) are not to be charged with invoking the shades of the Framers in order to satisfy "the need for certainty . . . If we pretend that the framers had a special sort of wisdom, then perhaps we do not have to

---

4. 1 Story, *Commentaries on the Constitution of the United States* §426 at 325–326 (5th ed. 1905). "It is not the function of the courts or legislative bodies . . . to alter the method [for change] which the Constitution has fixed." Hawke v. Smith, 253 U.S. 221, 227 (1920). See also supra Chapter 17 at notes 15–22.

5. Supra Chapter 1 note 7; see infra note 38.

6. See supra, Chapter 17 at note 90.

think too hard about how to solve pressing social problems."[7] The issue rather is whether solution of those "pressing social problems" was confided to the judiciary.[8]

Effectuation of the draftsman's intention is a long-standing rule of interpretation in the construction of all documents— wills, contracts, statutes—and although today such rules are downgraded as "mechanical" aids, they played a vastly more important role for the Founders. Hamilton, it will be recalled, averred: "To avoid arbitrary discretion in the courts, it is indispensable that they should be bound down by *strict rules* and precedents, which serve to define and point out their duty in every particular case that comes before them."[9] That Hamilton was constrained thus to reassure the ratifiers testifies to prevailing distrust of unbounded judicial interpretive discretion.[10] Some fifty years later, Justice Joseph Story, perhaps the greatest scholar who sat on the Supreme Court, emphasized that such

7. Miller, supra, note 3 at 595–596.

8. "[S]ince the mid-1950's the Supreme Court also has become the principal agent of change within our political order. Tackling political issues that the 'political' branches could not, would not, or dared not touch, the Court assumed the responsibility for political innovation, forcing changes long blocked by a Congress or by state legislatures dominated by minority elements." Rondel G. Downing, "Judicial Ethics and the Political Role of the Courts," 35 L. & Contemp. Prob. 94, 102 (1970). See also supra Chapter 16 note 28.

9. Supra, Chapter 16 at note 34 (emphasis added). This conception was deeply rooted in the common law. Chief Justice Fortescue, Corwin tells us, was guided by maxims which "constituted the very substance of the peculiar science of the judges"; and Coke paid reverence to such "fundamental points of the common law," among them, borrowed from Coke by "early American judges and lawyers," are "the numerous rules for the construction of written instruments which were originally adapted from the same sources to the business of constitutional construction." E. S. Corwin, "The 'Higher Law' Background of American Constitutional Law," 42 Harv. L. Rev. 149, 365, 370, 371 (1928).

10. Jefferson expressed confidence in the judiciary if "kept strictly to their own department." 5 *The Writings of Thomas Jefferson* 81 (P. L. Ford ed. 1892–1899).

rules provided a "fixed standard" for interpretation,[11] without which a "fixed Constitution" would be forever unfixed. The Constitution, in short, was written against a background of interpretive presuppositions that assured the Framers their design would be effectuated.

The rules governing "intention" reach far back in legal history; but for our purposes it suffices that English case-law emphasis on effectuation of the "original intention" was summarized in Bacon's *Abridgment* (1736)[12] and restated in 1756 by Thomas Rutherforth,[13] in a "work well known to the colonists."[14] Rutherforth assimilated the interpretation of statutes to that of contracts and wills and stated that "The end, which interpretation aims at, is to find out what was the intention of the writer, to clear up the meaning of his words."[15] And he concluded that "the intention of the legislator is the natural measure of the extent of the law."[16] The influence of these presuppositions on the Founders is no matter of conjecture. On the heels of the Convention, Justice James Wilson, a leading participant, said: "The first and governing maxim in the interpretation of a statute is to discover the meaning of those who made it."[17] Not long thereafter Jefferson pledged as President to administer the Constitution "according to the safe and honest meaning con-

11. 1 Story, supra note 4, §400 at 305. The object of such standards is to avoid "the passions and prejudices of the day." Id.

12. Matthew Bacon, *A New Abridgment of the Laws of England,* "Statute" I (5) (1736). Citations herein are to the 3d ed. 1768. Justice Story stated that "Bacon's Abridg. title Statute I contains an excellent summary of the rules for construing statutes." 1 Story §400 at 305 note 2.

13. *Institutes of Natural Law* (1754–1756).

14. Robert M. Cover, *Justice Accused: Antislavery and the Judicial Process* 12 (1975). Some of Rutherforth's criteria are quoted in 1 Story §402.

15. 2 Rutherforth, supra note 13 at 307, 309. Story likewise stated, "The first and fundamental rule in the interpretation of all instruments is, to construe them according to the sense of the terms and the intention of the parties." 1 Story §400.

16. 2 Rutherforth, supra note 13 at 364.

17. 1 *The Works of James Wilson* 75 (McCloskey ed. 1967).

templated by the plain understanding of the people at the time of its adoption—a meaning to be found in the explanations of those who advocated . . . it."[18] That view was echoed by Chief Justice Marshall, himself a participant in the Virginia Ratification Convention: if a word "was so understood . . . when the Constitution was framed . . . [t]he convention must have used it in that sense."[19] It was reaffirmed by Justice Holmes: an amendment should be read in a "sense most obvious to the common understanding at the time of its adoption."[20]

Enchanted by judicial fulfillment of libertarian hopes, academe, on one ground or another, has endeavored to discredit "original intention," to rid us of the "dead hand of the past."[21] But neither has openly been repudiated by the Court. To the contrary, it has been the Court's practice over the years to consult the intention of the Framers; the Court's concern, as Louis Pollak remarked, "for the original intent of the framers of the Constitution remains high."[22] An arresting example is furnished by the exchange between two "activists," Justices Black and Goldberg, aligned on opposing sides. To Black's condemnation of judicial "amendment," Goldberg responded: "Of course our constitutional duty is to construe, not to rewrite or amend the Constitution! . . . Our sworn duty to construe the Constitution requires, however, that we read it to effectuate the

18. 4 Elliot 446.

19. Gibbons v. Ogden, 22 U.S. (9 Wheat.) 1, 190 (1824). See also infra note 39.

20. Eisner v. Macomber, 252 U.S. 189, 220 (1920), dissenting opinion.

21. Supra Chapter 17 at note 9. McDougal and Lans, supra note 1 at 545: the "dead cannot bind the living."

22. Louis Pollak, "The Supreme Court Under Fire," 6 J. Pub. L. 428, 441 (1957). "[A]ll questions of constitutional construction," Justice Horace Gray stated, are "largely a historical question." Sparf v. United States, 156 U.S. 51, 169 (1895), dissenting opinion. Bickel brushed aside "the proposition that the original understanding is simply not relevant. For arguments based on that understanding . . . have been relied on by judges well aware that it is a *constitution* they were expounding." A. Bickel, "The Original Understanding and the Segregation Decision," 69 Harv. L. Rev. 1, 3–4 (1955).

intent and the purposes of the Framers."[23] So, too, both Justices Black and Frankfurter, on opposite sides of the fence in *Adamson v. California,* invoked the original intention.[24]

To impeach the "original intention," academicians sought to discredit resort to "legislative history" in general on the ground that the records are incomplete,[25] that they are inconclusive because strewn with conflicting claims. Such charges are irrelevant to the records of the 39th Congress, a "complete" verbatim record of the entire debates. Insofar as there were conflicting opinions, the views of racist Democrats who sought to kill both the Civil Rights Bill and the Fourteenth Amendment carry no weight; those of a handful of radical dissentients for whom neither Bill nor Amendment went far enough are overborne by the will of the great Republican majority—for example, to leave control of suffrage to the States. That will is implicitly stated in the §2 curtailment of representation when a State denies or abridges suffrage—recognition of power to do so; it is unequivocally confirmed by the Report of the Joint Committee on Reconstruction, by those in charge of the Bill and the Amendment, and by many others in the course of the debates. On a centuries-old canon of interpretation, that intention is as good written into the text.[26] When a legislature "has

23. Bell v. Maryland, 378 U.S. 226 (1964). Black: "changes in the Constitution . . . are to be proposed by Congress or conventions and ratified by the States. The Founders gave no such amending power to this Court." Id. 342, dissenting opinion; Goldberg, id. 288, concurring opinion.

24. 332 U.S. 46, 63–64, 72–73 (1947). For Frankfurter, see also supra Chapter 14 note 44.

25. John Wofford, "The Blinding Light: The Uses of History in Constitutional Interpretation," 31 U. Chi. L. Rev. 502, 504–506 (1964). The intentions of the Framers "are clothed in mystery." Miller, supra note 3 at 596. Miller goes further: "even if that history is clear, it is really not relevant." Id. 598. Compare with Bickel, supra note 22, and with Miller and Howell supra Chapter 1 note 25.

26. Bacon's *Abridgment,* "Statute" I(5): "A thing which is within the intention of the makers of a statute, is as much within the statute as if it were within the letter." The principle has often been applied by the Supreme Court. See supra Chapter 1 note 24.

intimated its will, however indirectly," Justice Holmes held, "that will should be recognized and obeyed . . . it is not an adequate discharge of duty for courts to say: 'We see what you are driving at, but you have not said it.' "[27] The intention of the sovereign people, whether expressed in convention or through the amendment process, demands even greater obedience.

Another attempt to dissolve traditional bonds was by way of semantics. To demonstrate that "only present current meanings are pertinent,"[28] Charles Curtis delivered himself of a "profound discourse on the meaning of meaning,"[29] liberally sprinkled with Aristotelian essences and linguistics.[30] But four years earlier, in an article giving some sage counsel to draftsmen, Curtis advised, "What the author of a legal document is trying to control is the future . . . to control this person's conduct in the future"[31]—more graphically expressed in Jefferson's "bind him down . . . by the chains of the Constitution." If that be the purpose of drafting, as seems indisputable, it is aborted by a theory that leaves another person free to read his own meaning into the draftsman's words. Commenting on Curtis' "meaning of meaning," Willard Hurst matter-of-factly pierced to the heart of the matter: "When you are talking about constitutional law, you are talking about the balance of power in the community and the question of how you find meaning boils down concretely here to who finds the meaning."[32] May the Justices supplant the value-choices of the Framers with their own? An officeholder like Santarelli appreciated such realistic implications.[33]

27. Johnson v. United States, 163 F. 30, 32 (1st Cir. 1908); quoted in Keifer & Keifer v. R.F.C., 306 U.S. 381, 391 note 4 (1939).

28. "The Role of the Constitutional Text" in *Supreme Court and Supreme Law* 64, 68 (E. Cahn ed. 1954).

29. Paul A. Freund, "Discussion," in id. at 71.

30. Curtis, id. at 68–70.

31. C. P. Curtis, "A Better Theory of Legal Interpretation," 3 Vand. L. Rev. 407, 423 (1950).

32. Willard Hurst, "Discussion," in *Supreme Court and Supreme Law* 74 (E. Cahn ed. 1954).

33. Supra, Chapter 17 at note 59.

If the Court may substitute its own meaning for that of the Framers it may, as Story cautioned, rewrite the Constitution without limit. But, Leonard Levy maintains: "Whatever the framers of the Fourteenth intended, there is no reason to believe that they possessed the best insights or ultimate wisdom *as to the meaning of their words* for subsequent generations . . . Words do not have fixed meanings. As Justice Holmes once remarked, a word is 'the skin of living thought and may vary greatly in color and content according to the circumstances and time in which it is used.' "[34] Of course, were Holmes *drafting* he would use words in their present meaning, but that is a far cry from the view that he would feel free to substitute his own meaning in a subsisting document for that of bygone draftsmen. As we have seen, he felt bound to give effect to the intention of the legislators, and it will hereafter appear that he held that words must be given the meaning they had at the time they were set down.[35] There is, moreover, a serious flaw in the Levy analysis, which appears more plainly in John Wofford's statement that if "the meaning of a word is its use, and if its use can never be found apart from its context, then we need only add that an inseparable constituent of context is the time at which the use occurs to show that a past meaning can not bind the present."[36] Now one who reads what another has written or seeks to interpret it does not in common usage really "use" the word. It is the writer who "used" it, and the traditional function of interpretation, as Rutherforth stated above 200 years ago, is to ascertain "what was the intention of the *writer?*"[37] On the Levy-Wofford analysis we are free to read Hamlet's statement that he "can tell a hawk from a handsaw," then meaning a heron, as if he referred to our pointed-tooth cutting tool because the meaning of "handsaw" has changed, reducing Shakespeare to nonsense.[38]

34. Levy, supra note 2 at 71 (emphasis added).
35. Infra Chapter 21 at notes 38–42.
36. Wofford, supra note 25 at 523.
37. Supra at note 15 (emphasis added).
38. Paul Brest states, "suppose that the Constitution provided that some acts were to be performed 'bi-weekly.' At the time of the framing of the Con-

Even Humpty-Dumpty did not carry it so far as to insist that when Alice "used" a word *he* could dictate what *she* meant. With Willard Hurst, I would underscore that "if the idea of a document of superior authority"—the "fixed Constitution" to which the Founders were attached—"is to have meaning, terms which have a precise history filled content to those who draft and adopt the document [such as "due process"] or to which they attach a clear meaning [such as "equal protection"] must be held to that precise meaning."[39] To hold otherwise is to convert the "chains of the Constitution" to ropes of sand.

Like the Constitution, the Fourteenth Amendment was written against the Bacon-Rutherforth background, clearly re-

---

stitution, this meant only 'once every two weeks'; but modern dictionaries, bowing to pervasive misuse, now report 'twice a week' (i.e. semi-weekly) as an acceptable definition. To construe the definition now to mean 'semi-weekly' would certainly be a change of meaning (and an improper one at that)." P. Brest, *Processes of Constitutional Decisionmaking: Cases and Materials* 146 note 38 (1975).

That has been the accepted view: "The Constitution is a written instrument. As such its meaning does not alter. That which it meant when adopted it means now . . . 'Any other rule of construction would abrogate the judicial character of this court, and make it the mere reflex of the popular opinion or passion of the day.'" South Carolina v. United States, 199 U.S. 437, 448, 449 (1905). See also Hawke v. Smith, 253 U.S. at 227. On the opposite view constitutional limitations are writ on water.

39. W. Hurst, "The Process of Constitutional Construction," in *Supreme Court and Supreme Law* 55, 57 (E. Cahn ed. 1954). From the beginning the courts looked to the common law for the meaning of constitutional terms. Chief Justice Marshall declared with respect to the word "treason," "It is scarcely conceivable that the term was not employed by the framers of our constitution in the sense which had been affixed to it by those from whom we borrowed it. So far as the meaning of any terms, particularly terms of art, is completely ascertained, those by whom they are employed must be considered as employing them in that ascertained meaning." United States v. Burr, 25 F. Cas (No. 14,693) 55, 159 (C.C. Va. 1807). See also Ex parte Grossman, 267 U.S. 87, 108–109 (1925); United States v. Wong Kim Ark, 169 U.S. 649, 654 (1898). In the Convention, John Dickinson cited Blackstone to show that ex post facto means retroactivity in criminal cases. 2 Farrand 448. See also supra Chapter 11 note 5; infra Chapter 22 notes 6 and 42.

stated in 1860.[40] Even Charles Sumner, archradical of the 39th Congress, was well aware that

> Every Constitution embodies the principles of its framers. It is a transcript of their minds. If its meaning in any place is open to doubt, or if words are used which seem to have no fixed signification, we cannot err of we turn to the framers; and their authority increases in proportion to the evidence which they left on the question.[41]

A "transcript of their minds" was left by the framers in the debates of the 39th Congress, and they left abundant evidence that, for example, in employing "equal protection of the laws" they had in mind only a ban on discrimination with respect to a limited category of "enumerated" rights. Disregard of that intention starkly poses the issue whether the Court may "interpret" black to mean white, to convert the framers' intention to leave suffrage to the States into a transfer of such control to the Supreme Court.

---

40. Vaughan Hawkins, "On the Principles of Legal Interpretation, With Reference Especially to the Interpretation of Wills," 2 Jur. Socy. Papers 298 (1860):

> in the interpretation of written language . . . the object is a single one—to ascertain the meaning or intention of the writer—to discover what were the ideas existing in his mind, which he desired and endeavored to convey to us . . . we desire . . . to know what the writer meant by the language he used.

Quoted in Curtis, supra note 31 at 407.

41. *Globe* 677.

21

Arguments for Judicial Power of Revision

CHIEF JUSTICE MARSHALL

WHERE early claims to extraconstitutional power were made in the name of "natural law," the present fashion is to invoke the "living Constitution" when it is sought to engraft or amputate a limb.[1] Commentators at a loss to justify judicial arrogations fall back on Marshall's sonorous reference to a "constitution intended to endure for ages to come."[2] In an oft-quoted apostrophe, Justice Frankfurter declared that it "expressed the core of [Marshall's] constitutional philosophy . . . the single most important utterance in the literature of

---

1. The "doctrine of the living Constitution amounts to little more than willful disregard of the express or implied intent of the framers." James McClellan, *Joseph Story and the American Constitution* 116–117 (1971). Thomas Grey more diplomatically states that "Our characteristic contemporary metaphor is 'the living Constitution' . . . sufficiently unspecific to permit the judiciary to elucidate the development and change in the content of those rights over time." "Do We Have an Unwritten Constitution?," 27 Stan. L. Rev. 703, 711 (1975).

2. Auerbach, "The Reapportionment Cases: One Person, One Vote—One Vote, One Value," 1964 S. Ct. Rev. 1, 75; cf. Louis Pollak, "The Supreme Court Under Fire," 6 J. Pub. L. 428, 441 (1957).

constitutional law."[3] It has become a mythic incantation.[4] Chief Justice Hughes, when confronted by the "mortgage moratorium"—"impairment of contract" problem, declared:

> If by the statement that what the Constitution meant at the time of its adoption it means today, it is intended to say that the great clauses of the Constitution must be confined to the interpretation which the framers, with the conditions and outlook of their time would have placed upon them,[5] the statement carries its own refutation. It was to guard against such a narrow conception that Chief Justice Marshall uttered a memorable warning—"We must never forget that it is a *Constitution* we are expounding . . . a constitution intended to endure for ages to come, and consequently to be adapted to the various *crises* of human affairs."[6]

3. Frankfurter, "John Marshall, and the Judicial Function," 69 Harv. L. Rev. 217, 218–219 (1955). That utterance, Frankfurter said, requires "a spacious view in applying an instrument of government 'made for an undefined and expanding future.'" Youngstown Sheet & Tube Co. v. Sawyer, 343 U.S. 579, 596 (1952). Compare the severely restricted gloss Marshall put upon his words, infra at notes 12–18. And compare the Founders' views as to change by amendment. Supra Chapter 17 at notes 15–22.

4. "It is important," said Justice Frankfurter, "not to make untouchable dogmas of the fallible reasoning of even our greatest judge." Frankfurter, supra note 3 at 219.

5. Many are the instances in which the Framers *did* place an interpretation upon their words, or used words of known common law meaning. To phrase the issue in terms of what meaning they "*would* have placed upon them" beclouds it.

6. Home Building & Loan Assn. v. Blaisdell, 290 U.S. 398, 442, 443 (1934). Small as is my esteem of Justice Sutherland, I consider nevertheless that his dissent has a firmer historical base. My friends inquire whether I am not troubled to find myself in such company. Edmund Wilson called this "the 'bedfellow' line of argument, which relies on producing the illusion of having put you irremediably in the wrong by associating you with some odious person who holds a similar opinion." E. Wilson, *Europe Without a Baedeker* 154 (1966). To which I would add, "I would rather be right with my enemy than wrong with my friend."

At best Marshall's dictum represents a self-serving claim of power to amend the Constitution. In Justice Black's words, "in recalling that it is a Constitution 'intended to endure for ages to come,' we also remember that the Founders wisely provided for the means of that endurance: changes in the Constitution are to be proposed by Congress or conventions and ratified by the States."[7] Claims to the contrary need to be measured by Lord Chief Justice Denman's observation that "The practice of a ruling power in the State is but a feeble proof of its legality."[8] Such judicial claims stand no better than the bootstrap "precedents" created by a number of presidents for reallocation to themselves of the warmaking power confided to Congress, in justification of single-handed commitments of the nation to war, as in Vietnam.[9] But the fact is, as I shall show, that Marshall's words have been removed from context, that he flatly repudiated the revisory power Hughes attributed to him, and that other Marshall utterances also show that the conventional view of *M'Culloch* does not represent the "core of his constitutional philosophy."

Marshall's dictum was uttered in *M'Culloch v. Maryland;* the issue was whether the Constitution empowered Congress to establish the Bank of the United States, and that turned on whether a bank was a proper *means* for execution of other expressly granted powers. Marshall reasoned that a government "intrusted with such ample powers" as "the great powers, to lay and collect taxes; to borrow money; to regulate commerce,"

> must also be intrusted with *ample means* for their execution. The power being given, it is in the interest of the nation to facilitate its execution . . . This could not be done, by confining the *choice of means* to such narrow limits as not to leave it in the

7. Bell v. Maryland, 378 U.S. 226, 342 (1964); cf. supra Chapter 15 at note 61; Chapter 17 at notes 15–22.

8. Stockdale v. Hansard, 112 E. R. 1112, 1171 (Q. B. 1839).

9. See Raoul Berger, *Executive Privilege: A Constitutional Myth* 75–88 (1974) for citations.

power of congress to adopt any which might be appropriate
. . . To have prescribed the means by which government
should, in all future time execute its powers, would have
been . . . [to give the Constitution] the properties of a legal
code.[10]

Manifestly, this was merely a plea for some freedom in the
"choice of means" to execute an existing power, not for license
to create a fresh power at each new crisis. Marshall himself
flatly denied such license-claims in a pseudonymous debate
with Judges Spencer Roane and William Brockenbrough of
Virginia.

M'Culloch immediately had come under attack. To Madison
the Court's ruling seemed

to break down the landmarks intended by a specification of the
powers of Congress, and to substitute, for a definite connection
between means and ends, a legislative discretion as to the
former, to which no practical limits can be assigned . . . [A]
regular mode of making proper alteration has been providently
provided in the Constitution itself. It is anxiously to be
wished . . . that no innovation may take place in other modes,
one of which would be a constructive assumption of powers
never meant to be granted.[11]

Thus, the chief architect of the Constitution rejected the replacement of the amendment process by judicial revision as an
"assumption of powers never meant to be granted." Even more
severe strictures were published by Roane and Brockenbrough.
Marshall leapt to the defense under a pseudonym; speaking to
the "intended to endure for ages" phrase, he said:

10. 17 U.S. (4 Wheat.) 316, 407, 408, 415 (1819) (emphasis added).
11. H. C. Hockett, *The Constitutional History of the United States 1826–1876*
4 (1939); see supra Chapter 15 at note 61; Chapter 17 at notes 15–22; for the
explanation of Madison's anxiety see infra at note 20 and note 22.

it does not contain the most distant allusion to *any extension by construction of the powers* of congress. Its sole object is to remind us that a constitution cannot possibly enumerate *the means* by which the powers of government are to be carried into execution.[12]

Again and again he repudiated any intention to lay the predicate for such "extension by construction." There is "not a syllable uttered by the court," that "applies to an enlargement of the powers of congress."[13] He rejected any imputation that "those powers ought to be enlarged by construction or otherwise."[14] He emphasized that "in all the reasoning on the word 'necessary' the court does not, in a single instance, claim the aid of a 'latitudinous' or 'liberal' construction."[15] He branded as a "palpable misrepresentation" attribution to the Court of the view of the "necessary and proper clause" "as augmenting those powers, and as one which is to be construed 'latitudinously' or even 'liberally.'"[16] "It is not pretended," he said of the "choice of means," "that this right of selection may be fraudulently used to the destruction of the fair landmarks [Madison's term] of the constitution."[17] Finally, the exercise of the judicial power to decide all questions "arising under the constitution and laws" of the United States *"cannot be the assertion of a right to change that instrument."*[18] Slender as was the justification for invocation of Marshall's dictum prior to Gerald Gunther's discovery of Marshall's Defense, it has been shattered altogether by Marshall's

12. *John Marshall's Defense of McCulloch v. Maryland* 185 (G. Gunther ed. 1969) (emphasis added).
13. Id. 182.
14. Id. 184.
15. Id. 92.
16. Id. 97.
17. Id. 173.
18. Id. 209 (emphasis added).

categorical disclaimer of judicial "right to change that instrument."[19]

Before leaving *M'Culloch,* account should be taken of a proposal in the Federal Convention to authorize Congress "to grant charters of incorporation." Rufus King pointed out that it "will be referred to the establishment of a Bank, which has been a subject of contention" in Philadelphia and New York. Modified to apply only to canals, it was voted down 8 to 3.[20] Louis Pollak points out that "This legislative history was known at the time *M'Culloch v. Maryland* was decided, for Jefferson had utilized it in his 1791 memorandum to Washington opposing the Bank Bill."[21] As a successor to Jefferson as Secretary of State, Marshall had more reason than most to know. His omission to notice it is the more puzzling in light of his allusion to the heated debate on the subject in 1789.[22] For the moment discussion of a possible clash between word and deed may be deferred to examination of other Marshall opinions—strangely never mentioned in the "living Constitution" incantations—which adhere to the "constitutional philosophy" he proclaimed in the Roane-Brockenbrough debates.

In *Ogden v. Saunders,* Marshall stated that the words of the Constitution are not to be "extended to objects not . . . contemplated by its framers."[23] In *Gibbons v. Ogden* he stated that if a word was understood in a certain sense "when the Constitution was framed . . . [T]he convention must have used it in

19. Commenting on the impact of that Defense, Professor Gunther observes that "If virtually unlimited congressional [or judicial] discretion is required to meet twentieth century needs, candid argument to that effect, rather than ritual invoking of Marshall's authority, would seem to me more clearly in accord with the Chief Justice's stance." Supra note 12 at 20–21.

20. 2 Farrand 321, 325, 615–616.

21. Pollak, supra note 2 at 441 note 87.

22. Supra note 10 at 401. In the February 1791 debate Madison "well recollected that a power to grant charters of incorporation had been proposed in the General Convention and rejected." 2 *Annals of Congress* 1896 (1791).

23. 25 U.S. (12 Wheat.) 213, 332 (1827), dissenting opinion.

that sense," and it is that sense that is to be given judicial effect.[24] In *Osborn v. Bank of the United States,* he stated: "Judicial power is never exercised for the purpose of giving effect to the will of the judge; always for the purpose of giving effect to the will of the legislature"[25]—that is, of the "original intention." In *Providence Bank v. Billings,* he stated: "The constitution . . . was not intended to furnish the corrective for every abuse of power which may be committed by the State governments. The interest, wisdom, and justice of the representative body and its relation with its constituents furnish the only security . . . against unwise legislation generally," echoing Gerry's rejection of judicial "guardians."[26] These statements are irreconcilable with the interpretation Hughes put on the *M'Culloch* dictum. Their significance was summed up by Marshall's associate, Justice Henry Baldwin, who, after noting Marshall's "a constitution we are expounding," went on to say, "no commentator ever followed the text more faithfully, or ever made a commentary more accordant with its strict intention and language."[27]

The evidence, I submit, calls for an end to the incantatory reliance on Marshall's "a Constitution . . . to be adapted to the various crises of human affairs." If the Constitution is to be altered by judicial fiat, let it not be under seal of a reading Marshall himself repudiated.[28]

MR. JUSTICE HOLMES

Another lofty dictum canonized by proponents of judicial lawmaking is that of Justice Holmes in *Missouri v. Holland:*

24. 22 U.S. (9 Wheat.) 1, 190 (1824); see supra Chapter 20 note 38; infra Chapter 22 note 6.

25. 22 U.S. (9 Wheat.) 738, 866 (1824).

26. 29 U.S. (4 Pet.) 514, 563 (1830).

27. H. Baldwin, *A General View of the Origin and Nature of the Constitution and Government of the United States* 100 (1837).

28. See supra note 19.

when we are dealing with words that also are a constituent act,
like the Constitution . . . we must realize that they have called
into life a being the development of which could not have been
foreseen completely by the most gifted of its begetters. It was
enough for them to realize or to hope that they had created an
organism; it has taken a century and cost their successors much
sweat and blood to prove that they created a nation. The case before us must be considered in the light of our whole experience
and not merely in what was said a hundred years ago.[29]

The magic spell of the superb literary artist must not blind us to
the narrow issue actually decided; for it is a fundamental tenet
of case law that all statements in a case are to be confined to that
decision.[30] At issue was whether the treatymaking power extended to an agreement with Great Britain for the protection of
migratory birds which annually traversed parts of the United
States and of Canada. Addressing the argument that the treaty
infringed powers reserved to the States by the Tenth Amendment, Holmes held, "Wild birds are not in the possession of any
one; and possession is the beginning of ownership. The whole
foundation of the State's rights is the presence within their jurisdiction of birds that yesterday had not arrived, tomorrow may
be in another State, and in a week a thousand miles away." He
therefore found that the "States are individually incompetent to
act," that the national interest in such migratory birds was of
the "first magnitude" and "can be protected only by national
action in concert with that of another power,"[31] and concluded
that "it is not lightly to be assumed that in matters requiring national action, 'a power which must belong to and somewhere

29. 252 U.S. 416, 433 (1920).

30. Marshall dismissed his own dicta in Marbury v. Madison when they
were pressed upon him in Cohens v. Virginia, 19 U.S. (6 Wheat.) 264, 399
(1821), saying that dicta do not receive the careful consideration accorded to
the "question actually before the court."

31. 252 U.S. at 434, 433.

reside in every civilized government' is not to be found."[32]
Holmes might have cited Hamilton's explanation that the treaty
power was to have "the most ample latitude—to render it competent to all the stipulations which the exigencies of national
affairs might require."[33] Instead he rose to one of his great rhetorical flights:

> The case before us must be considered in the light of our whole
> experience and not merely in that of what was said a hundred
> years ago. The treaty . . . does not contravene any prohibitory
> words to be found in the Constitution [nor in its history]. The
> whole question is whether it is forbidden by some invisible radi-
> ation from the general terms of the Tenth Amendment. We
> must consider what this country has become in deciding what
> the Amendment has reserved.[34]

The reader will indulge an attempt at more pedestrian analysis. The Tenth Amendment, on which *Missouri* relied, provides
that "The powers not delegated to the United States by the
Constitution, nor prohibited by it to the States, are reserved to
the States respectively, or to the people." Given that in this area
a State is "incompetent" to act, it could hardly lay claim to a
"reserved" power to do so. According to Hamilton, a power to
enter into "*all* the stipulations which the exigencies of national
affairs might require" *had* been delegated to the United States. It
follows that a plenary treaty power did not invade a nonexistent
State power.[35] Consequently *Missouri v. Holland* furnishes no

32. Id. 433. But Madison stated, "Had the power of making treaties, for example, been omitted, however necessary it might have been, the defect could
only have been lamented, or supplied by an amendment of the Constitution."
2 *Annals of Congress* 1900–1901 (February 2, 1791).

33. "Letters of Camillus," 6 Hamilton, *Works* 183 (Lodge ed. 1904).

34. 252 U.S. at 433–434.

35. Willard Hurst, who served as law clerk to Justice Holmes and wrote a
valuable monograph on Holmes' view of constitutional history, states that in
Missouri v. Holland Holmes "in effect . . . says that *when all other evidence* of
the Constitution-makers' intent *fails,* we must yet be guided by what we

warrant for encroachment upon actual, reserved State powers, nor for revision of express or implicit constitutional provisions because a new day has dawned.

The cases which confirm that Holmes respected and adhered to the intention of the draftsmen may for the moment be deferred while we consider Holmes' dicta in *Gompers v. United States:* "[the] provisions of the Constitution . . . are organic living institutions transplanted from English soil. Their significance is to be gathered not simply by taking the words and a dictionary but by considering their origin and the line of their growth."[36] Like "living constitution" the words "the line of their growth" have become a shibboleth of judicial lawmaking, for a Constitution, be it remembered, "grows" only by judicial accretions. *Gompers* merely involved the meaning of a common law term, "contempts" of court, and the legal meaning of that term could no more be ascertained by resort to a dictionary than could that of "trial by jury" or "habeas corpus." For that purpose resort to the common law was essential, and in traditional fashion Holmes looked to the common law for the "origin" and "line of growth" of contempts. The issue was whether a criminal contempt lies for violation of an injunction. Justice Holmes held: "So truly are they crimes that . . . in the early law they were punishable only by the usual criminal procedure" and in England still "are tried that way."[37] By this "origin" and "line of growth" he was not remotely claiming judicial power to "change" the Constitution, but was giving a common law term its traditional meaning.

Other Holmes opinions confirm that such a claim was far removed from his thinking. In *Johnson v. United States* he held that

---

know to be their most general objective . . . to provide a structure within which the future may settle its own problems." "The Process of Constitutional Construction," in *Supreme Court and Supreme Law* 55, 57–58, (E. Cahn ed. 1954) (emphasis added). This is no license to ignore "evidence of the Constitution-makers' intent."

36. 233 U.S. 604, 610 (1914).

37. Id. 610–611.

when a legislature "has intimated its will . . . that will should be recognized and obeyed."[38] Although this referred to a statute, Holmes scarcely attached more importance to the will of a legislature than to that of the people met in convention. Indeed, he applied the parallel rule to an Amendment in the subsequent case of *Eisner v. Macomber:* "I think that the word 'incomes' in the Sixteenth Amendment should be read in 'a sense most obvious to the common understanding at the time of its adoption.'"[39] Earlier, in *Lochner v. New York,* he had protested against the majority's identification of its economic predilections with the Fourteenth Amendment;[40] and a few years after *Gompers,* in *Baldwin v. Missouri,* he stated;

> I have not yet adequately expressed the more than anxiety that I feel at the ever increasing scope given to the Fourteenth Amendment in cutting down what I believe to be the constitutional rights of the States. As the decisions now stand, I see hardly any limit but the sky to the invalidating of those rights if they happen to strike a majority of this Court as for any reason undesirable. I cannot believe that the Amendment was intended to give us *carte blanche* to embody our economic or *moral beliefs* in its prohibitions. . . . Of course the words "due process of law," if taken in their literal meaning, have no application to this case; and while it is too late to deny that they have been given a much more extended and artificial signification, still we ought to remember the great caution shown by the Constitution in limiting the power of the States, and should be slow to construe the clause in the Fourteenth Amendment as committing to the Court, with no guide but the Court's own discretion, the validity of whatever laws the States may pass.[41]

38. 163 F. 30, 32 (1st Cir. 1908).

39. 252 U.S. 189, 219–220 (1920). In Weems v. United States, 217 U.S. 349, 389, 397 (1910), Justice Holmes joined in a dissent by Justice Edward White stating that the meaning of "cruel and unusual punishment" was to be derived from English and pre-1787 State practices.

40. 198 U.S. 45, 75 (1905).

41. 281 U.S. 586, 695 (1930) (emphasis partially added).

In short, Holmes deplored judicial invasion of rights reserved to the States, condemned uncurbed judicial discretion to identify personal predilections with constitutional mandates, and recognized the perversion of due process that made such practices possible—all of which is diametrically opposed to the current reading of the *Gompers* and *Holland* dicta. Those who march under the pennons of those dicta have overlooked Holmes' statement that "I do not expect or think it desirable that the judges should undertake to renovate the law. That is not their province."[42]

MR. JUSTICE FRANKFURTER

Proponents of a power to "adapt" the Constitution to current needs also quote a dictum of Justice Frankfurter in *Youngstown Sheet & Tube Co. v. Sawyer:* "It is an inadmissibly narrow conception of American constitutional law to confine it to the words of the Constitution and to disregard the gloss that life has' written about them."[43] Once again this is a statement lifted from its context. Frankfurter had in mind the rule that a long-standing executive interpretation illuminates an ambiguous provision: "In short, a systematic, unbroken executive practice, long pursued to the knowledge of Congress and never before questioned . . . may be treated as a gloss on 'Executive Power' vested in the President." To avert a too-sweeping implication he explained that "Deeply embedded traditional ways of conducting a government *cannot supplant the Constitution* or legislation; but they give meaning to the words of the text or supply them,"[44] that is, if the meaning is otherwise obscure.

That Frankfurter did not refer by such a "gloss" to judicial encrustations is inferable from his assertion on another occasion

42. O. W. Holmes, Jr., *Collected Legal Papers* 239 (1920); see also supra Chapter 17 note 32.

43. 343 U.S. at 610–611, concurring opinion.

44. Id. 610, emphasis added.

of a right to look to the Constitution itself rather than to what his predecessors had said about it.[45] Then, too, in *United States v. Lovett* he had distinguished "broad standards," which "allow a relatively wide play for individual legal judgments," from "very specific provisions" such as the prohibition of "bills of attainder," which must be read as "defined by history. Their meaning was so settled by history that definition was superfluous."[46] To be sure, he placed "due process of law" among the "broad standards"; in this, however, he was mistaken, for history leaves no doubt that there was no "substantive" due process, that due process did not apply to legislative action but was confined to procedure in the courts, as was unmistakably expressed by Hamilton in 1787. The purely "procedural" content of due process was, in the words of Charles Curtis, "as fixed and definite as the common law could make a phrase."[47] Frankfurter himself adverted to the "fundamental principles that inhere in 'due process of law' as understood at the time of the adoption of the Constitution."[48] Under his own criterion respecting common law terms—they must be read as "defined by history"—we cannot, to borrow from one of his opinions, "extend the definitions . . . Precisely because 'it is *a constitution* we are expounding' . . . we ought not to take liberties with it."[49] And precisely because, in Frankfurter's own words, "there was a deep distrust of a federal judicial system"[50] in 1787, and of the courts in 1866 as well, we should not read "due process" to confer untrammeled lawmaking power on the judiciary. Although the "deepest conviction" he cherished was that

45. Supra Chapter 15 note 57.
46. 328 U.S. 303, 321 (1946), concurring opinion.
47. Supra Chapter 11 at note 27.
48. Anti-Fascist Refugee Committee v. McGrath, 341 U.S. 123, 161–162 (1951), concurring opinion.
49. National Ins. Co. v. Tidewater Co., 337 U.S. 582, 646 (1949), dissenting opinion.
50. Id. 647.

"no five men, or nine, are wise enough or good enough to wield such power over an entire nation,"[51] it was not deep enough to overcome his confidence in his own wisdom when he ascended to the bench.[52]

To convert the Marshall-Holmes-Frankfurter statements into constitutional dogma is both to disregard how narrow were their actual decisions and their reaffirmations that judges are under a duty to effectuate the original understanding and to respect the historical meaning of common law terms. Reliance on those statements for a doctrine of judicial power to "change" the Constitution only exposes the hollowness of the case for judicial revisionism.

Proponents of a "living Constitution" often twit me with the discrepancy between Marshall's deeds and his words. It is true that some of his decisions may be regarded as judicial lawmaking. Willard Hurst observed that "To rule that a corporation charter enjoyed the protection of a 'contract' under the constitutional provision [impairment of contracts clause] was a clear-cut act of judicial law-making."[53] And if knowledge can be brought home to Marshall that the Convention had specifically rejected a proposal for incorporation of banks, his disclaimers respecting *M'Culloch* might be regarded as "fraudulent."[54] But such examples afford a sad triumph for revisionists. To do what one disclaims as he acts is a reproach to any man, all the more when it is done by the oracles of the law whom we are urged to regard as the "national conscience." Of no one should more fastidious morality be required than of the Supreme Court.

51. Supra Chapter 14 at note 72.

52. See supra Chapter 7 at notes 48–53, 63–65, and Chapter 14 at notes 140–141.

53. *The Legitimacy of the Business Corporation in the Law of the United States* 63 (1970).

54. See supra at note 17.

PROFESSORS THOMAS C. GREY AND LOUIS LUSKY

Sensible of the deficiences of conventional arguments for judicial lawmaking, Thomas Grey and Louis Lusky have proffered new theories on which the function should be based. Grey would invoke a continuing "natural law" tradition, while Lusky finds that the Founders conferred an "implied right" of judicial revision.

Grey espouses the Court's "role as the expounder of basic national ideals of individual liberty and fair treatment, even when the content of these ideals is not expressed as a matter of positive law in the written Constitution."[55] He concedes, however, that "such a role . . . is more difficult to justify than is the role assigned by the pure interpretive model," his label for Justice Black's restrictive view of judicial review.[56] That view, he states, "is one of great power and compelling simplicity . . . deeply rooted in our history and in our shared principles of political legitimacy. It has equally deep roots in our formal constitutional law."[57] The "grave difficulties" that attend the lawmaking model explain the judicial tendency, he continues, "to resort to bad legislative history" to support desired results. If "judges resort to bad interpretations in preference to honest exposition of deeply held but unwritten ideals, it must be because they perceive the latter mode of decision-making to be of suspect legitimacy."[58]

To answer the "question whether in our Constitution we have actually granted this large power to our judges" he briefly sketches an argument that he hopes to expand and document later.[59] His posits that the generation that framed the Constitution was attached to "the concept of a 'higher law' protecting

55. Grey, supra note 1 at 706.
56. Id. 706, 705.
57. Id. 705.
58. Id. 706; cf. supra Chapter 7 at notes 54–59.
59. Grey, supra note 1 at 715 note 49.

'natural rights,' and taking precedence over ordinary positive law . . . Thus in the framing of the original American constitutions it was widely accepted that there remained unwritten but still binding principles of higher law. The Ninth amendment is the textual expression of this idea in the Federal Constitution." It was "widely assumed," he states, "that judges would enforce as constitutional restraints the unwritten natural rights."[60] Since Grey postponed documentation for these propositions, detailed commentary is not possible. Robert Cover concluded, however, that the Founders were attached to positive rather than to natural law.[61] Judicial review was an innovation that had excited the animosity of several State legislatures;[62] its proponents advocated it in restricted terms: the policing of constitutional "limits."[63] My own study of the records of the Federal Convention uncovered no intimations that natural law would empower judges to rise above the positive limitations of the Constitutions; evidence to the contrary may be postponed to examination of the Lusky thesis, for that evidence, I consider, refutes both the Grey and Lusky theories.

Here it may suffice to inquire in what way the "Ninth amendment is the textual expression" of the "idea" that "there remained unwritten but still binding principles of higher law." Were they binding on the courts? The Amendment provides: "The enumeration in the Constitution, of certain rights, shall not be construed to deny or disparage others retained by the people." Because certain nonenumerated rights are "retained by the people," it does not follow that federal judges are empowered to enforce them. Apart from "diversity" suits between

60. Id. 715–716. For the settled scope of "natural rights," see Kelly, supra Chapter 2 note 55.

61. Chapter 14 at note 15. Professor Cox alludes to "a deep and continuing American belief in natural law." *The Role of the Supreme Court in American Government* 16 (1976). For additional quotations from Cox, see supra Chapter 14 note 38.

62. Raoul Berger, *Congress v. The Supreme Court* 38, 40, 42 (1969).

63. Id. 13–14.

citizens of different States, fashioned to "insure fair dealing between citizens of different States,"[64] federal jurisdiction is limited to cases "arising under this Constitution," for example, one invoking Fourth Amendment guarantees. It needs at least to be asked whether federal courts are authorized to enforce extraconstitutional "rights" that have neither State nor federal sanction. An implication to the contrary may be drawn from Madison's explanation in the First Congress immediately following his reference to the Ninth Amendment. If the guarantees of the Bill of Rights, he said, would be incorporated in the Constitution, the "independent tribunals of justice . . . will be naturally led to resist every encroachment upon rights *expressly stipulated* for in the Constitution by the Declaration of Rights."[65] The appeal to the Ninth Amendment was made by Justice Goldberg in *Griswold v. Connecticut*,[66] but the cases he cited lend no support for invocation of the Ninth Amendment; they involve either Bill of Rights guarantees that the Court has embodied in the Fourteenth Amendment, or rights like those of the right to travel or to associate which the Court found protected by the "liberty" of the Fifth and Fourteenth Amendment due process clauses.[67] In short, when the Court deemed a right

64. See supra Chapter 12 note 13.

65. 1 *Annals of Congress* 439 (emphasis added).

66. 381 U.S. 479, 492 (1965), concurring opinion. Compare with Chief Justice Marshall, supra at note 26. Dissenting, Justice Black replied, "the Ninth Amendment was intended to protect against the idea that 'by enumerating particular exceptions to the grant of power to the Federal Government,' those rights which were not singled out were intended to be assigned" to it. 381 U.S. at 519, quoting 1 *Annals of Congress* 439.

67. Cantwell v. Connecticut, 310 U.S. 296 (1940): First Amendment—freedom of religion; New York Times Co. v. Sullivan, 376 U.S. 254 (1964): First Amendment—freedom of speech; Kent v. Dulles, 357 U.S. 116 (1958) and Aptheker v. Secretary of State, 378 U.S. 500 (1964): Fifth Amendment "liberty"—right to travel; Gideon v. Wainright, 372 U.S. 335 (1963): Sixth Amendment—right to counsel; N.A.A.C.P. v. Alabama, 357 U.S. 449 (1958): Fourteenth Amendment "liberty"—freedom of association; Bolling v. Sharpe, 347 U.S. 497 (1954): Fifth Amendment "liberty"—desegregated schools in District of Columbia.

worthy of protection it grounded intervention on the Bill of
Rights or the Fourteenth Amendment, rendering resort to the
Ninth Amendment superfluous. For me, as for Justice Black,
the Amendment "was passed not to broaden the powers of this
Court . . . but . . . to limit the Federal Government to the
powers granted."[68]

Grey considers that the Fourteenth Amendment likewise was
influenced by "natural rights"·

> Natural rights reasoning in constitutional adjudication persisted
> up to the Civil War, particularly with respect to property and
> contract rights, and increasingly involving "due process" and
> "law of the land" clauses in constitutional texts. At the same
> time, an important wing of the anti-slavery movement devel-
> oped a natural-rights constitutional theory, built around the con-
> cepts of due process, of national citizenship and its rights, and of
> the human equality proclaimed in the Declaration of Independ-
> ence.
>
>   Though this latter movement had little direct effect on pre-
> Civil War decisions, it was the formative theory underlying the
> due process, equal protection and privileges and immunities
> clauses of the 14th amendment. Section 1 of the 14th amendment
> is thus properly seen as a reaffirmation and reenactment in posi-
> tive law of the principle that fundamental human rights have
> constitutional status.[69]

Prior to the Civil War the courts were most inhospitable to
"natural rights" as Robert Cover convincingly shows in his review of the fugitive slave cases.[70] Even in a "property" case,

---

  Instead of employing the language of "natural rights" the Court has enjoyed equal freedom by resort to "fundamental rights"; we learn that some
right is "fundamental" only after the Court attaches the label. Supra Chapter
14 note 117. But that judicial practice cannot draw on the embodiment of
"natural law" in the Constitution.

  68. Griswold v. Connecticut, 381 U.S. at 520.
  69. Supra note 1 at 716.
  70. Supra Chapter 14 at notes 25–26.

Wynehamer v. The People, the court dismissed claims based on "natural law" and fabricated a novel theory of "substantive due process." But that theory found no favor with other courts[71] until the Supreme Court, under ceaseless prodding by Justice Field, embraced it in the 1890s. It is true that the framers embodied "fundamental human rights" in the Civil Rights Act and thence in the Fourteenth Amendment, but those were regarded as restricted in scope and enumerated, for example, the right to own property, to contract; "political and social" rights were unmistakably excluded.[72] The equality (only partially) envisaged in the Declaration of Independence plainly found no place in the thinking of the framers of the Fourteenth Amendment.[73] Gray's reference to the "constitutional theory" of a "wing of the anti-slavery party" that allegedly "was the formative theory" underlying §1 invokes the Graham-tenBroek-Kelly theory, which simply cannot stand up against the historical facts.[74] In the history of the Fourteenth Amendment, it may confidently be stated, there is not a glimmering of intention to authorize judges to enforce rights beyond those enumerated in the Civil Rights Act. Far from endowing the judiciary with a broad power to enforce "natural rights" going beyond those so enumerated, the courts were pointedly omitted from the §5 power to enforce even the rights granted by §1.[75]

Lusky, who sought an improved rationale for judicial intervention in behalf of libertarian ideals as long ago as 1938, when he aided Justice Stone in fashioning the *Carolene Products* footnote,[76] was at last driven to ask: "*By what right* does [the Court] revise the Constitution?"[77] His attempt to supply an answer by

71. Id. at notes 28–35.
72. Supra Chapter 2 at notes 26–30, 35–36, 39.
73. Supra Chapter 4 at notes 57–66, Chapter 2 at notes 26, 30, Chapter 10 at note 6.
74. Supra Chapter 13.
75. Supra Chapter 12.
76. Supra Chapter 14 at notes 123–125.
77. Lusky, 19.

way of a theory of "implied power" to do so is set forth in his book *By What Right?* Many of his comments on the cases are rewarding, but strange is his line of demarcation. Down to 1961 or 1962 "the Court maintained its traditional passive posture,"[78] but after 1962 it engaged in "a dazzling display of seemingly freehand constitution-making without apparent concern for the intention of the Constitutors."[79] Few would regard *Brown v. Board of Education* (1954) as exemplifying the Court's "passive posture"; the evidence set forth in Chapter 6 hereof demonstrates that it was "making new law for a new day." In fact, Lusky praises "the tremendously valuable work it has done in the past third of a century." It "has performed splendidly" as the "citadel of the republic—the main instrument for societal self-perfection,"[80] a performance far removed from a "passive posture."

Lusky's anxiety was aroused by the "neoprivacy" (contraceptive and abortion) cases, where the discredited "substantive due process began to reappear . . . under a different banner bearing the watchword privacy."[81] These are the cases he regards as "usurpation of power."[82] Yet neither the constitutional text nor its history forbid judicial interference with State regulation of the right of privacy, whereas the history of the Fourteenth Amendment plainly does preclude such interference with State control of suffrage and segregation. We may therefore with Justice Harlan view the State reapportionment cases "as a much more audacious and far-reaching judicial interference with the state legislative process . . . then the comparatively innocuous use of judicial power in the contraceptive case."[83] Presumably Lusky considers that the desegregation and

78. Id. 274.
79. Id. 263–264.
80. Id. 6.
81. Id. 337; see also id. 336, 339–341.
82. Id. 6.
83. The quotation is in the paraphrase of Professor Paul Kauper, "Penumbras, Peripheries, Emanations, Things Fundamental and Things Forgotten: The Griswold Case," 64 Mich. L. Rev. 235, 256 (1965).

reapportionment cases meet the criteria he suggests for employment of the "implied power" to revise the Constitution, but he
himself recognizes that whether those tests are "so vague as to
be illusory" poses a question "on which the validity of the [im-
plied power] must stand or fall."[84] Examination of that question
may be dispensed with because, as will appear, his argument for
existence of the "implied power" is fundamentally defective, and
because the materials I shall set out to demonstrate that defect
equally dispose of Grey's resort to "natural law."

Lusky bases his "implied power" to "revise the Constitution . . . exercising the prerogatives of a continuing constitutional convention," upon a sweeping assumption:

> One perpetrates no violence upon logic or known historical facts
> by assuming that the Founding Fathers *intended* . . . (c) to
> empower the Court to serve as the Founders' surrogate for the
> indefinite future—interpreting the Constitution not as they
> themselves would have directed if they had been consulted in
> 1787, but as is thought right *by men who accepted the Founders'
> political philosophy—their commitment to self-government and the
> open society—and consider themselves obligated to effectuate that phi-
> losophy in the America of their own day.*[85]

This assumes the answer to the very question in issue: did the
Framers empower the judges to revise the Constitution. It assumes that the Framers handed the constitution-changing function to a "surrogate," whose crystal-gazing as to effectuation of
their "political philosophy" is made a substitute for the express
terms of the Constitution. Such divination recalls the Chinese
emperor's "mandate from heaven." Lusky's assumption does in
fact do "violence . . . to known historical facts."

He considers that Marshall "unfolded the doctrine of implied
powers" in *M'Culloch v. Maryland,* drawing on Marshall's statement that, given ample powers, the government "must also be

84. Lusky, 270, 318.
85. Id. 21.

entrusted with ample means for their execution."[86] But ample means to execute *existing* powers cannot stretch to their expansion or to creation of *new* powers. Marshall himself disclaimed "any extension by construction of the powers of Congress"; he held that the judicial power "cannot be an assertion of a right to change" the Constitution.[87] The generation that framed the Constitution was devoted to a "fixed constitution"; courts "were not regarded as instruments of social change."[88] Judicial participation in legislative policymaking was forthrightly rejected; despite arguments by George Mason and James Wilson that judicial review confined to violation of some constitutional provision would not allow judges to set aside oppressive though constitutional laws, the Framers would not, as Elbridge Gerry stated, make judges the "guardians of the people."[89] Now Lusky would have it that the Framers turned policymaking over to the judges in toto, constituting them a superlegislature, notwithstanding Hamilton's reassuring quotation of Montesquieu: "of the three powers—the judiciary is next to nothing."[90]

Hamilton alone presents an insuperable obstacle to the Grey-Lusky theories. Presumably inspired by States' Rights distrust of a federal judiciary,[91] he averred that the Constitution is "binding" on all, including the peoples' representatives, who

86. Id. 81.

87. Supra at notes 10–18.

88. Supra Chapter 16 at note 33. In the North Carolina Convention Timothy Bloodworth stated, "I wish to leave no dangerous latitude of construction." 4 Elliot 50. Elbridge Gerry stated in the First Congress, "The people of America can never be safe, if Congress have a right to exercise the power of giving constructions to the Constitution different from the original instrument." 1 *Annals of Congress* 523. Chief Justice Marshall was well aware of the continuing vitality of such fears. Supra at notes 14–16.

89. Supra Chapter 16 at note 8.

90. Federalist No. 78 at 504n.

91. Supra at note 50; see also Berger, supra note 62 at 263, 267–269.

have no "warrant" to make "a departure" from it "until the people" have changed it by a "solemn and authoritative act,"[92] that is, by amendment. He stated that "the intention of the people ["ought to be preferred"] to the intention of their agents." That he meant to leave no room for displacement of that "intention" by the Justices is underscored by his scornful dismissal of the notion that "the courts on the pretense of a repugnancy may substitute their own pleasure [for] the constitutional intentions of the legislature."[93] As Lusky himself comments, this "is hard to square with anticipation of judicial constitution-making power."[94] It is not "hard to square," it is impossible—as Hamilton's further statement that judges would be impeachable for "deliberate usurpations on the authority of the legislature"

92. Supra Chapter 17 at note 15.

93. Federalist No. 78 at 506, 507.

94. Lusky 72. Lusky's reliance on the practice of "successive generations of Justices," id. 95, does not advance his argument because: (1) no chain of argument is stronger than its weakest link—the original source of the power; (2) what a wielder of power claims is but "feeble proof of its legality," supra at note 8; and (3) usurpation is not legitimated by repetition. Powell v. McCormack, 395 U.S. 486, 546–547 (1969). His reliance on United States v. Curtiss-Wright Corp., 299 U.S. 304 (1936), for a theory of "implied power," Lusky 90, leans on a case that has been widely criticized, and as Justice Jackson pointed out, proceeded under a delegation from Congress. Youngstown Sheet & Tube Co. v. Sawyer, 343 U.S. 579, 635–636 note 2 (1952), concurring opinion; David Levitan, "The Foreign Relations Power: An Analysis of Mr. Justice Sutherland's Theory," 55 Yale L. J. 467 (1946); Raoul Berger, "War-Making by the President," 121 U. Pa. L. Rev. 29, 69–75 (1972); C. A. Lofgren, "United States v. Curtiss-Wright Export Corporation: An Historical Reassessment," 83 Yale L. J. 51 (1973).

Lusky handsomely discloses that some of his "most perceptive Columbia colleagues" view his "implied power" theory skeptically because "(1) it affirms the legitimacy of constitutional rules not rooted in the constitutional text. (2) . . . it suggests . . . that the Court . . . can itself initiate changes in the law." Lusky 25. He advances his theory "not because it is more nearly 'correct' but because it is more *useful*." Id. 26 (emphasis added).

confirms. What "usurpations" could there be if judges were empowered to act as "surrogates" of the Founders or to enforce the wide-open spaces of "natural law"? Both the Grey and Lusky theories set at naught the "limits" so carefully framed by the Founders; both would circumvent the Article V method of change by amendment.

22

"Trial by Jury": Six or Twelve Jurors

THE increasingly free and easy judicial revision of constitutional norms is strikingly exemplified by *Williams v. Florida*,[1] wherein the Supreme Court, for the first time in our history, held that a 6-man jury satisfies the requirement of trial by jury. By Justice White's own testimony a 12-man jury has been the invariable common law practice since "sometime in the 14th century"—600 years. The Court held in 1930 that "it is not open to question . . . that the jury should consist of twelve men, neither more nor less."[2] But because history furnishes no explanation why the number 12 was chosen, Justice White dismisses it as "an historical accident, unrelated to the great purposes which gave rise to the jury in the first place."[3]

---

1. 399 U.S. 78 (1970).

2. Patton v. United States, 281 U.S. 276, 288 (1930). Among the remarkable aspects of Florida v. Williams is that Chief Justice Burger, appointed by President Nixon as a "strict constructionist," "join[ed] fully in Mr. Justice White's opinion for the Court." 399 U.S. at 105. Yet on the very same decision day, he stated in Coleman v. Alabama, 399 U.S. 1, 22 (1970), dissenting opinion, "While I do not rely solely on 183 years of contrary constitutional interpretation, it is indeed an odd business that it has taken this Court nearly two centuries to 'discover' a constitutional mandate to have counsel at a preliminary hearing," a statement even more applicable to the "discovery" that the 12-man jury was not an essential component of trial by jury.

3. 399 U.S. at 89–90.

Adherence to a practice for 600 years renders its "accidental" origin irrelevant, for as Coke stated, "usage and ancient course maketh law"[4]—all the more when that usage is embodied with full awareness in a written Constitution. The case for the practical wisdom of 12 jurors has been made by Hans Zeisel, Leonard Levy and others,[5] so I shall focus on Justice White's extraordinary approach to constitutional interpretation.

From Chief Justice Marshall onward the meaning of common law terms or institutions, which had a fixed content at the time they were incorporated into the Constitution, is to be ascertained by resort to that content.[6] With little short of disdain Justice White rejects that meaning as representing "mystical or superstitious insights into the significance of '12.' "[7] "Typical" of such "superstition" is a dithyramb by that great "mystic" Lord Coke, in his crabbed explication of Littleton on Tenures: "it seemeth to me, that the law in this case delighteth herselfe in the number of 12; for there must not onely be 12 *jurors* for the tryall of all matters of fact but 12 judges of ancient time for tryall of mattters of law *in the Exchequer* Chamber . . . And that *number of twelve* is much respected in *holy writ,* as in 12 *apostles.*"[8] When men are moved to make exalted, mystical-religious explanations, it is because they deeply venerate the established practice.

---

4. 1 Coke, *Institutes of the Laws of England* 155a (London, 1628–1641).

5. For citations and discussion, see Levy, *Against the Law* 270–276.

6. See Chapter 20 notes 38, 39; Chapter 21 at note 24. In Townsend v. Sain, 372 U.S. 293, 311 (1963), the Court stated that the "historic conception of the writ [of habeas corpus] anchored in the ancient common law and in our Constitution . . . has remained constant to the present day." See infra note 42, and supra Chapter 11 note 5, Chapter 20 note 39.

7. 399 U.S. at 88. Compare with Justice Holmes, supra Chapter 17 note 32.

8. Supra note 4. Justice White notes that "The singular unanimity in the selection of the number twelve to compose certain judicial bodies, is a remarkable fact in the history of many nations." 399 U.S. at 89 note 23.

Trial by jury was a central pillar of the society the colonists sought to erect; for centuries it had served as cherished buffer against oppressive prosecutors and judges.[9] Blackstone, whose *Commentaries* were widely circulated in the colonies, and whose influence on this issue can be traced into the very terms of a number of State constitutions and utterances of the Founders, stated, "the liberties of England cannot but subsist so long as this *palladium* remains sacred and inviolate."[10] The North Carolina Constitution of 1776 provided that "the ancient mode of trial by jury . . . ought to remain sacred and inviolable."[11] Massachusetts, New Hampshire, Pennsylvania, and Vermont provided that it "shall be held sacred";[12] Georgia, South Carolina, and New York, that it was "inviolate forever."[13] In the Virginia Ratification Convention the Wythe Committee recommended an amendment: that "the ancient trial by jury is one of the greatest securities to the rights of the people, and is to remain sacred and inviolable."[14] George Mason in Virginia termed it "This great palladium of national safety," and James Iredell in North Carolina referred to it as "that noble palladium of liberty."[15] No element of judicial proceedings or power aroused such anxious inquiry as did trial by jury. Every facet of an institution held "sacred" by the Founders, therefore, needs to be approached with respectful regard.

9. 399 U.S. at 87.

10. 4 Blackstone, *Commentaries on the Laws of England* 350 (London 1765–1769).

11. Article XIV, 2 Poore 1410. For complete discussion of colonial and State sources, and Founders' utterances, see F. H. Heller, *The Sixth Amendment to the Constitution of the United States,* 16–34 (1951).

12. Massachusetts (1780), Article XV, Declaration of Rights, 1 Poore 959; New Hampshire (1784), Article 20, 2 Poore 1282; Pennsylvania (1776), Article XI, 2 Poore 1542; Vermont (1777), Chapter I, Sec. XIII, 2 Poore 1860.

13. Georgia (1777), Article LXI, 1 Poore 383; South Carolina (1790), Article XI, Sec. 6, 2 Poore 1633; New York (1777), Article XLI, 2 Poore 1339.

14. 3 Elliot 658.

15. Mason, id. 528; Iredell, 4 Elliot 148.

Except for partial rejection of a jury of the "vicinage," of which more hereafter, there is no indication that any incident of trial by jury was to be more "sacred and inviolate" than another. To the contrary, the First Continental Congress laid claim to the "inestimable privilege of being tried by their peers of the vicinage, according to the due course of the common law";[16] this was repeated in the Maryland Constitution of 1776.[17] South Carolina provided that "the trial by jury, as heretofore used . . . shall be forever inviolably preserved."[18] That usage had been described by Coke as already "very ancient"[19] and was reformulated in Bacon's Abridgment as calling for a "petit jury . . . precisely of twelve, and is never to be either more or less," as Chief Justice Matthew Hale had earlier stated.[20] This "most transcendent privilege," Blackstone stated, required a jury of 12.[21] In the Virginia Ratification Convention, Governor Edmund Randolph said: "There is no suspicion that less than twelve jurors will be thought sufficient."[22] Julius Goebel adverted to "popular sensitivity regarding any tampering with the 'inestimable right of jury trial,' " and concluded that "any suggestion that the jury system as then entrenched might be amended in any detail was beyond tolerance."[23] In the Virginia Ratification Convention, Grayson, for example, stated that "it is generally thought by Englishmen, that [trial by jury] is so sacred that no act of the [omnipotent] Parliament can affect

16. Resolve of October 14, 1774, quoted in Duncan v. Louisiana, 391 U.S. 145, 152 (1968).

17. Declaration of Rights, Article III, 1 Poore 817: "according to the course of that [common] law."

18. Supra note 13. For similar provisions, North Carolina (1776), Article IX, 2 Poore 1409; Pennsylvania, Article IX, Sec. 6, 2 Poore 1554.

19. Supra note 4 at 155b.

20. Bacon's *Abridgment,* "Juries" (A) at 234; 2 Hale, *History of the Pleas of the Crown* 161 (1736).

21. 3 Blackstone 379; see also id. 358, 365.

22. 3 Elliot 467.

23. Julius Goebel, *Antecedents and Beginnings to 1801, History of the Supreme Court of the United States,* vol. 1, pp. 141, 493 (1971).

it."[24] How can this be reconciled with Justice White's refusal to "ascribe a blind formalism to the Framers"? Far from being "wholly without significance 'except to mystics,' "[25] the Framers would have regarded tampering with the number "12" as shaking the very pillars of the temple.

A Jury of the Vicinage

Justice White attached great weight to the Framers' refusal to embody in the Constitution a traditional component of trial by jury—that the jury be drawn from the "vicinage," the "neighborhood, or in medieval England, jury of the county."[26] Article III of the Constitution provides that the jury trial "shall be *held* in the State where the said Crimes shall have been committed"; it does not purport to direct how the jury shall be drawn, and no illumination is furnished by the "very scanty history" of the provision.[27] It received opposing interpretations in the Virginia Ratification Convention: Madison met an objection "that there was no provision for a jury from the vicinage" with the reply "if it could have been done with safety, it would not have been opposed,"[28] implying that Article III did not require that jurors be drawn from the vicinage. On the other hand, Randolph, who also had been a delegate to the Federal Convention, stated in Virginia, "nor is a jury from the vicinage in criminal cases excluded. This house has repeatedly resounded with this observation—that where a term is used, all its concomitants follow."[29] In the upshot, the Virginia Convention attached to its approval an amendment proposing trial by a jury

24. 3 Elliot 569.
25. 399 U.S. at 103, 102.
26. Id. 93 note 35.
27. Id. 93.
28. 3 Farrand 332; cf. infra note 34. Grayson, a Virginia opponent of adoption, charged that Article III abandoned "vicinage," 3 Elliot 568–569, a view shared by Holmes in the Massachusetts Convention, 2 Elliot 109–110.
29. 3 Elliot 573.

of the vicinage.[30] And Justice White remarked that "concern" over failure to "preserve the common law right to be tried by a 'jury of the vicinage' . . . furnished part of the impetus for introducing" the Sixth and Seventh Amendments.[31]

In the First Congress, Madison proposed a jury "of the vicinage, with the requisite unanimity for conviction, of the right of challenge, and other accustomed requisites."[32] It passed the House but was rejected by the Senate; went to Conference and emerged in what ultimately became the final version of the Sixth Amendment: a "jury of the State and district wherein the crime shall have been committed." This Justice White properly views as "a compromise between broad and narrow definition" of the term "vicinage."[33] The compromise sprang from the fact noted by Madison that "In many of the States, juries . . . are taken from the State at large; in others, from districts of considerable extent; in very few from the County alone. Hence a dislike to the restraint with respect to *vicinage*."[34] What this history proves, is that the "vicinage" States did not have the votes to overcome a constitutional modification of the common law *in this respect*. Does it follow that the Founders meant also to curtail the right to challenge jurors, for example, which the Virginia Ratifiers were assured had been left intact by Article III,[35] or to abolish the "mystic" number "12"?

Justice White draws three negative implications, which cast

30. Id. 658.

31. 399 U.S. at 93–94.

32. Quoted, id. 94.

33. Id. 94–96.

34. Quoted, id. 95 note 39. In the Pennsylvania Ratification Convention James Wilson had stated, "there is no particular regulation made, to have the jury come from the body of the county in which the offense was committed; but there are some States in which this mode of collecting juries is contrary to their established custom . . . In some states, the juries are not taken from a single county." 2 Elliot 450.

35. See infra note 39.

"considerable doubt on the easy assumption in our past decisions that if a given feature existed in a jury at common law in
1789, then it was necessarily preserved in the Constitution."[36]
First, "the mere reference to 'trial by jury' in Article III was not
interpreted to include" vicinage.[37] But there was more than a
"mere reference": trial by jury was qualified by "shall be held in
the State," which raised differences of opinion whether or
not vicinage was affected. At most, Article III modified the
common law in that respect alone. Second, "provisions which
would have explicitly tied the 'jury' concept to the 'accustomed
requisites' of the time were eliminated." Justice White recognizes that this elimination is "concededly open to the explanation that the 'accustomed requisites' were thought to be already
included in the concept of a 'jury.' But that explanation is no
more plausible than the contrary one: that the deletion had
some substantive effect."[38] The assumption that the "accustomed requisites" already were thought to be included in the
concept of a "jury" was not left to speculation. The Ratifiers
had been assured again and again in Virginia by John Marshall,
by Edmund Pendleton, the Mentor of its highest court, and by
Randolph, that the words "trial by jury" embraced all its attributes, such as the right to challenge jurors.[39] Curtailment of the
vicinage requirement responded to the preponderant State practice; but the nonvicinage States were no less attached to a jury of

36. 399 U.S. at 92–93.
37. Id. at 96.
38. Id. at 96–97.
39. Pendleton: "It is strongly insisted that the privilege of challenging, or
excepting to the jury, is not secured. When the Constitution says that the trial
shall be by jury, does it not say that every incident will go along with it?" 3 Elliot 546; see also id. 547. Marshall re right of challenging: "If we are secure in
Virginia without mentioning it in our Constitution, why should not this security be found in the federal court?" Id. 559. Randolph: "That the incident is
inseparable from the principal, is a maxim in the construction of laws." Id.
463; and see supra at note 29.

"12" than the "vicinage" adherents,[40] so that curtailment of vicinage does not argue for abandonment of "12." In *Pierson v. Ray* the Supreme Court refused to read *comprehensive* language to abolish a much less treasured common law practice in the absence of a specific expression of intent to do so.[41] Here, where ratification by the people is involved, it is even more important to demand a specific expression of intention to discard the treasured unanimous verdict by a jury of 12. Nothing in the Sixth Amendment phrase "a jury of the State and district" warned the people that by ratification they would surrender those attributes of a jury trial. Then, too, although the Founders, in framing the treason clause, had drastically narrowed the definition of "treason," Chief Justice Marshall looked to the common law for other aspects of "treason."[42] Like Marshall, we may conclude that a partial departure from the common law with respect to vicinage does not spell wholesale repudiation of other concomitants of trial by jury, that to embrace the contrary view is to do violence to the Framers' reverence for the institution.

Third, Justice White reasoned, "where Congress wanted to leave no doubt that it was incorporating existing common law features of the jury system, it knew how to use express language to that effect. Thus, the Judiciary Bill . . . provided in certain cases for the narrower 'vicinage' requirement which the House had wanted to include in the Amendment."[43] Now, as Justice White noticed, "the Senate remained opposed to the vi-

---

40. "The States which had adopted constitutions by the time of the Philadelphia Convention in 1787 appear for the most part to have either explicitly provided that the jury would consist of 12 . . . or to have subsequently interpreted their jury trial provisions to include that requirement." 399 U.S. at 98 note 45. Cf. Parker v. Munday (N.J. 1791), 1 Coxe's L. Rep. 70, 71 (1816).

41. See supra Chapter 1 note 57.

42. United States v. Burr, 25 F. Cas. (No. 14,693) 55, 159 (C.C. Va. 1807): Treason "is a technical term . . . It is scarcely conceivable that the term was not employed by the framers of our constitution in the sense which had been affixed to it by those from whom we borrowed it." See also supra note 6.

43. 399 U.S. at 97.

cinage requirement, partly because in their view the then-pending judiciary bill—which was debated at the same time as the Amendments—adequately preserved the common law vicinage feature—making it unnecessary to freeze that requirement into the Constitution."[44] "Vicinage" was specifically named because compromise of a disputed point so required. So, too, Justice White reads the Seventh Amendment provision that in civil cases "no fact tried by a jury, shall be otherwise reexamined in any Court . . . than according to the common law" against adoption of the 12-man jury.[45] Again this arose out of the need to resolve a particular controversy. Strenuous objections had been made in the Ratification Conventions to the provision for the Supreme Court's appellate jurisdiction of "questions both of law and fact" on the ground that facts found by a jury should be unreviewable. No aspect of judicial review excited greater opposition;[46] as Patrick Henry stated in Virginia: "The unanimous verdict of twelve impartial men cannot be reversed."[47] From settlement of a particular controversial issue it cannot be deduced that the Framers thereby intended to discard rights that had not once been challenged. Justice White, in my judgment, did not succeed in justifying a departure from the rule that common law terms must be given the meaning they had at the time of adoption.[48]

When Madison sought to explain the relation of Article III to vicinage, he said: "It is a misfortune in any case that this trial should be departed from, yet in some cases it is necessary."[49] There the real "necessity" was that Virginia stood in a decided minority in its attachment to "vicinage"; it could not muster votes to overcome resistance to *this* aspect of jury trial. Since

44. Id. 95.

45. Id. 97.

46. For citations, see Raoul Berger, *Congress v. The Supreme Court* 286–287 (1969).

47. 3 Elliot 544.

48. Supra note 42.

49. Quoted in 399 U.S. at 93 note 35.

trial by jury was a fabric woven of many strands—a "seamless web"—we should be slow to countenance a rent, particularly one not dictated by the most urgent need. What necessity impelled the Court to jettison the "very ancient" 12-man jury?

The Court had painted itself into a corner when it held that the Fourteenth Amendment made the "trial by jury" provision of the Bill of Rights mandatory on the States,[50] a position, as we have seen, that is without historical warrant. Since some States employed less than 12 men, the Court, as Justice Harlan observed, recognized that the " 'incorporationist' view . . . must be tempered to allow the States more elbow room in ordering their own criminal systems."[51] The Burger Court is presently retreating from the Warren Court's imposition of federal requirements on State practice,[52] and it might well have concluded that the quite recent extension of the Sixth Amendment's trial by jury to the States was ill-considered and, therefore, as Justice Harlan stated, the Burger Court's decision in *Duncan v. Louisiana* should be overruled.[53] Instead, it chose to rupture a 600-year practice in order to adhere to a dubious decision, illustrating what Washington and Hamilton had warned against: a usurpation to meet a great emergency breeds usurpations where no emergency exists.

50. "In Duncan v. Louisiana, 391 U.S. 145 (1968), we held that the Fourteenth Amendment guarantees a right to trial by jury in all criminal cases that, were they to be tried in a federal court—would come within the Sixth Amendment's guarantee." 399 U.S. at 86.
51. 399 U.S. at 118, dissenting opinion.
52. Supra Chapter 18 note 3.
53. 399 U.S. at 118.

23

Conclusion

THE historical records all but incontrovertibly establish that the framers of the Fourteenth Amendment excluded both suffrage and segregation from its reach; they confined it to protection of carefully enumerated rights against State discrimination, deliberately withholding federal power to supply those rights where they were not granted by the State to anybody, white or black. This was a limited—tragically limited—response to the needs of blacks newly released from slavery; it reflected the hagridden racism that held both North and South in thrall; nonetheless, it was all the sovereign people were prepared to do in 1868.

Given the clarity of the framers' intention, it is on settled principles as good as written into the text. To "interpret" the Amendment in diametrical opposition to that intention is to rewrite the Constitution. Whence does the Court derive authority to revise the Constitution? In a government of limited powers it needs always be asked: what is the source of the power claimed? "When a question arises with respect to the legality of any power," said Lee in the Virginia Ratification Convention, the question will be, "*Is it enumerated in the Constitution?* . . . It is otherwise arbitrary and unconstitutional."[1]

1. 3 Elliot 186.

Or, as James Iredell put it, a law "not warranted by the Constitution . . . is bare-faced usurpation."[2] Hamilton made clear that action not warranted by the Constitution is no less a usurpation at the hands of the Court[3] than of a President. The suffrage-segregation decisions go beyond the assumption of powers "not warranted" by the Constitution; they represent the arrogation of powers that the framers plainly *excluded*. The Court, it is safe to say, has flouted the will of the framers and substituted an interpretation in flat contradiction of the original design: to leave suffrage, segregation, and other matters to State governance. It has done this under cover of the so-called "majestic generalities" of the Amendment—"due process" and "equal protection"—which it found "conveniently vague," without taking into account the limited aims those terms were meant to express. When Chief Justice Warren asserted that "we cannot turn back the clock to 1868,"[4] he in fact rejected the framers' intention as irrelevant. On that premise the entire Constitution merely has such relevance as the Court chooses to give it, and the Court is truly a "continuing constitutional convention," constantly engaged in revising the Constitution, a role clearly withheld from the Court. Such conduct impels one to conclude that the Justices are become a law unto themselves.[5]

Can it be, then, that in a civilized society there exists no means of ridding ourselves of such a blight as segregation? No cost, it can be argued, is too high to be rid of the incubus. Archibald Cox observes: "To have adhered to the doctrine of 'separate but equal' would have ignored not only the revolution sweeping the world but the moral sense of civilization. Law must be binding even upon the highest court, but it must also meet the needs of men and match their sensibilities," and it is

2. 4 Elliot 194.
3. Supra Chapter 17 at note 15.
4. Supra Chapter 7 at note 61.
5. "[T]he Justices have given serious cause for suspicion that they have come to consider the Court to be above the law." Lusky vii; and see id. 101. See Levy, supra Chapter 14 note 136; Murphy, supra Chapter 15 note 13; and Lewis, supra Chapter 17 note 56.

for judges to "make law to meet the occasion."[6] But, as Cox recognized, these "libertarian, humanitarian, and egalitarian" impulses "were not shared so strongly as to realize themselves through legislation," still less through an amendment. They were only realized through the "fate which puts one man on the Court rather than another."[7] I cannot bring myself to believe that the Court may assume a power not granted in order to correct an evil that the people were, and remain, unready to cure. Justification of judicial usurpation—the label Hamilton attached to encroachments on the legislative function—on the ground that there is no other way to be rid of an acknowledged evil smacks of the discredited doctrine that "the end justifies the means."[8] John Stuart Mill cautioned against man's disposition "to impose [his] own opinions . . . as a rule of conduct on others."[9] The Inquisition burned heretics at the stake to save their souls.

Then there are the costs to constitutional government[10] of countenancing such usurpation. As the Court itself has demon-

6. *The Role of the Supreme Court in American Government* 110 (1976). Cox does not regard the segregation decisions as "wrong even in the most technical sense," id. 109, although he states, "Plainly, the Court was not applying customary constitutional principles." Id. 60.

7. Id. 35.

8. Lord Chancellor Sankey stated, "It is not admissible to do a great right by doing a little wrong . . . It is not sufficient to do justice by obtaining a proper result by irregular or improper means." Quoted by Chief Justice Warren in Miranda v. Arizona, 384 U.S. 436, 447 (1966). Levy observes that scholars "cannot be ignored and cannot be gainsaid when they insist that any means to a justifiable end is, in a democratic society, a noxious doctrine." Levy, *Warren* 190.

9. More fully quoted, infra note 20.

10. Cox states, "Nearly all the rules of constitutional law written by the Warren Court relative to individual and political liberty, equality, criminal justice, impress me as wiser and fairer than the rules they replace. I would support nearly all as important reforms if proposed in a legislative chamber or a constitutional convention. In appraising them as judicial rulings, however, I find it necessary to ask whether an excessive price was paid for enlarging the sphere and changing the nature of constitutional adjudication." Cox, supra note 6 at 102.

strated, unconstitutional action to cure a manifest evil establishes a precedent, as Washington and Hamilton warned, that encourages transgressions when such urgency is lacking. Time and again the Justices themselves have accused their brethren of acting without constitutional warrant. So to act is to act unconstitutionally; in another field the Court itself branded its own course of conduct over a hundred-year span as "unconstitutional."[11] "In a government of laws," Justice Brandeis cautioned, "existence of the government will be imperilled if it fails to observe the law scrupulously."[12] Justice Frankfurter added that "Self-willed judges are the least defensible offenders against government under law."[13] How long can public respect for the Court, on which its power ultimately depends, survive if the people become aware that the tribunal which condemns the acts of others as unconstitutional is itself acting unconstitutionally? Respect for the limits on power are the essence of a democratic society; without it the entire democratic structure is undermined and the way is paved from Weimar to Hitler.[14]

11. Erie Ry. Co. v. Tompkins, 304 U.S. 64, 77–78 (1938).

12. Olmstead v. United States, 277 U.S. 438, 485 (1928).

13. "From the Wisdom of Felix Frankfurter," *Wisdom,* vol. III, No. 28, p. 25 (1959), quoted by Kathryn Griffith, *Judge Learned Hand and the Role of the Federal Judiciary* 209 (1973).

14. As Professor Charles Black stated, when urging noninterference with the Warren Court, "constitutional legality is indivisible . . . the right to wound one part of the body as you may desire is the right to destroy the life." *The People and the Court* 190 (1960). Madison said, "It is our duty . . . to take care that the powers of the Constitution be preserved entire to every department of Government; the breach of the Constitution in one point, will facilitate the breach in another." 1 *Annals of Congress* 500.

In a review of Alexander Bickel's last work, *The Morality of Consent,* Professor Alan M. Dershowitz states that Bickel saw "the Nixon Presidency and Watergate as the 'utterly inevitable' consequence of the undisciplined liberalism and 'result-orientation' of the Warren Court." Dershowitz comments, "A strange relationship, probably wrong and surely overstated." "Book Reviews," *The New York Times Book Review,* September 21, 1975, at 1. But Nixon's "idea" man, Donald Santarelli, quite plainly had learned from the Warren Court. Supra Chapter 17 at note 59.

Proponents of the "original understanding," Sanford Levinson justly charges, are rarely prepared to press it all the way: "Thus opponents of the [Vietnam] war eager to return to the original understanding of the War Power are not likely to be eager to return to what was probably the rather conservative initial understanding of freedom of speech."[15] Rigorous constitutional analysis halts at the door of particular predilections. Setting practical considerations aside for the moment, intellectual honesty demands that the "original understanding" be honored across the board—unless we are prepared to accept judicial revision where it satisfies *our* predilections, as is the current fashion. But that is to reduce "law" to the will of a kadi. The list of cases that would fall were the "original understanding" honestly applied is indeed formidable. As Grey summarizes, "virtually the entire body of doctrine developed under the due process clauses of the 5th and 14th amendments," the core "requirement of 'fundamentally fair' procedures in criminal and civil proceedings," and "everything that has been labeled 'substantive due process' would be eliminated," even though it "must constitutionally free the federal government to engage in explicit racial discrimination," for "there is no textual warrant for reading into the due process clause of the fifth amendment any of the prohibitions directed against the states by the equal protection clause." He adds, "there is serious question how much of the law prohibiting state racial discrimination can survive honest application of the interpretive ["original understanding"] model. It is clear that the equal protection clause . . . was *not* intended to guarantee equal political rights, such as the right to vote or to run for office, and perhaps in-

---

Jefferson "foresaw that if the Constitution were ever destroyed, it would be destroyed by construction or interpretation, in final analysis, by the federal judiciary." Caleb P. Patterson, *The Constitutional Principles of Thomas Jefferson* 70 (1953).

15. S. Levinson, "Fidelity to Law and the Assessment of Political Activity," 27 Stan. L. Rev. 1185, 1200 note 68 (1975).

cluding the right to serve on juries."[16] But because repudiation of the cases would have undesirable consequences, it does not follow that the prior determinations were authorized by the Constitution.[17] Whatever may be the merit of Judge Joseph Hutcheson's method of decision in common law cases—first a "hunch," then a hunt for legal rationalization—[18] such reasoning backward in constitutional cases displaces choices already made by the framers. It perilously resembles the subordination of "law" to the attainment of ends desired by a ruling power which was the hallmark of Hitlerism and Stalinism.

Had it fallen to me, therefore, to decide some of the "substantive due process" and "equal protection" cases *ab initio*, I should have felt constrained to hold that the relief sought lay outside the confines of the judicial power.[19] It would, however, be utterly unrealistic and probably impossible to undo the past in the

16. Grey, "Do We Have an Unwritten Constitution?," 27 Stan. L. Rev. 703, 710–712 (1975). An earlier illustrative list had been furnished by Bork, "Neutral Principles and Some First Amendment Problems," 47 Ind. L.J. 1, 11–12 (1971). If effect be given to the framers' intention, the decision in Strauder v. Virginia, 100 U.S. 303 (1879), that Negroes must be permitted to serve as jurors, was wrongly decided. See Chairman Wilson, supra Chapter 2 at note 26, the colloquy between Wilson and Delano, and remarks by Moulton and Lawrence, supra Chapter 9 at notes 25–27.

17. Supra Chapter 14 at notes 103–104.

18. J. C. Hutcheson, "The Judgment Intuitive: The Function of the 'Hunch' in Judicial Decision," 14 Cornell L. Q. 274, 287 (1929). See also Martin Shapiro, *Law and Politics in the Supreme Court* 15 (1964).

19. Justice Stevens recently expressed a similar view. Runyon v. McCrary, 96 S. Ct. 2586 (1976), presented the issue whether the federal Act of 1866 prohibits private schools from excluding qualified children on racial grounds:

There is no doubt in my mind that that construction of the statute would have amazed the legislators who voted for it . . . [S]ince the legislative history discloses an intent not to outlaw segregated schools at that time, it is quite unrealistic to assume that Congress intended the broader result of prohibiting segregated private schools. Were we writing on a clean slate, I would therefore vote to reverse.

Concurring opinion.

face of the expectations that the segregation decisions, for example, have aroused in our black citizenry—expectations confirmed by every decent instinct. That is more than the courts should undertake and more, I believe, than the American people would desire. But to accept thus far accomplished ends is not to condone the continued employment of the unlawful means. If the cases listed by Grey are in fact in contravention of the Constitution, the difficulty of a rollback cannot excuse the *continuation* of such unconstitutional practices.

This is not the place to essay the massive task of furnishing a blueprint for a rollback. But the judges might begin by curbing their reach for still more policymaking power, by withdrawing from extreme measures such as administration of school systems —government by decree—which have disquieted even sympathizers with the ultimate objectives. Such decrees cannot rest on the assertion that the *Constitution demands* busing, when in truth it is the Justices who require it[20] in contravention of the framers' intention to leave such matters to the States. The doctrinaire extension of false doctrine compounds the arrogation. So too, greater restraint in reapportionment matters, the return of the administration of local criminal, libel, and obscenity law to the States would not only respond to constitutional limitations but to preponderant public sentiment. Judges should take to heart Justice Holmes' admonition in *Baldwin v. Missouri:*

> we ought to remember the great caution shown by the Constitution in limiting the power of the States, and should be slow to construe the cause in the Fourteenth Amendment as committing

20. Cf. Lino A. Graglia, *Disaster by Decree* (1976). Justice Rehnquist reminded us of John Stuart Mill's statement, "The disposition of mankind, whether as rulers or as fellow citizens, to impose their own opinions and inclinations as a rule of conduct on others, is so energetically supported by some of the best and some of the worst feelings incident to human nature, that it is hardly ever kept under restraint by anything but want of power." Mill, *On Liberty* 28 (1885), quoted in Furman v. Georgia, 408 U.S. 238, 467 (1972), dissenting opinion.

to the Court, with no guide but the Court's own discretion, the validity of whatever laws the States may pass.[20a]

His counsel is heavily underscored by the manifest intention of the framers to limit federal intrusion into State internal affairs to a plainly described minimum.

All this may seem like idle theorizing in light of Justice Stone's famous dictum that "the only check upon our own exercise of power is our own sense of self-restraint."[21] Were this true, it would offend against one of the most fundamental premises of our constitutional system. "Implicit in the system of government [the Framers] designed," Alpheus Thomas Mason stated, "is the basic premise that unchecked power in any hands whatsoever is intolerable."[22] "Unchecked power" emphatically was not confided to the judiciary; as Hamilton wrote in Federalist No. 81, the Justices may be impeached for usurpation of legislative power.[23] President Taft, no wild-eyed radical, acknowledged in 1911 that the judicial system was not working as it should, and stated, "Make your judges responsible. Impeach them. Impeachment of a judge would be a very healthful thing in these times."[24] Cumbersome as impeachment is, it is yet not so difficult as amendment, which requires approval by three-fourths of the States. At one time Brandeis and Frankfurter, it needs to be remembered, favored an amendment that would remove the due process clause from the Constitution al-

20a. See supra Chapter 21 at note 41.

21. United States v. Butler, 297 U.S. 1, 79 (1936), dissenting opinion.

22. "Myth and Reality in Supreme Court Drama," 48 Va. L. Rev. 1385, 1405 (1962).

23. Quoted supra Chapter 15 at note 50.

24. Quoted in Joseph P. Lash, *From the Diaries of Felix Frankfurter* 113 note 3 (1975). See also Lusky 80. The Supreme Court, by Justice Frankfurter, stated, "Restraints on our jurisdiction are self-imposed only in the sense that there is from our decisions no immediate appeal short of impeachment or constitutional amendment." Rochin v. California, 342 U.S. 165, 172 (1952).

together.[25] But such heroic measures would be unnecessary in the face of an aroused public opinion, a mighty engine, as President Nixon learned after the "Saturday Night Massacre."[26] "The Court," wrote Charles L. Black, "could never have had the strength to prevail in the face of resolute public repudiation of its legitimacy."[27]

A prime task of scholarship, therefore, is to heighten public awareness that the Court has been overleaping its bounds. "[S]cholarly exposure of the Court's abuse of its powers," Frankfurter considered, would "bring about a shift in the Court's viewpoint."[28] Such awareness is a necessary preliminary for, as Mason observed, "only that power which is recog-

25. Louis Jaffe, "Was Brandeis an Activist? The Search for Intermediate Premises," 80 Harv. L. Rev. 986, 989 (1967). In 1924 Frankfurter stated that "The due process clause ought to go." "The Red Terror of Judicial Reform," 40 *New Republic* 110, 113, reprinted in Frankfurter, *Law and Politics* 10, 16 (Macleish and Pritchard eds. 1939).

The requirements for amendment or impeachment, it may be suggested, are so onerous as to render the Court's decisions all but irrevocable. "[I]f the policy of the government is to be irrevocably fixed by the decisions of the Supreme Court," said Lincoln in his First Inaugural Address, "the people will have ceased to be their own rulers." Quoted in Morton Keller, *Affairs of State* 17–18 (1977).

26. Attorney General Elliot Richardson resigned rather than discharge Special Prosecutor Archibald Cox at the insistence of President Nixon. Deputy Attorney General William Ruckelshaus was discharged for refusal to discharge Cox.

27. *The People and the Court* 209 (1960).

28. Quoted in Lash, supra note 24 at 59. Rodell referred to "the reverential awe-bred-of-ignorance, with which most Americans regarded the Court" in 1937. *Nine Men* 247 (1955). Professor Charles Black urges that lawyers "never cease to call the Court to account, and to urge reason upon it. Inadequate reason, lack of responsiveness to counter-argument [as in Reynolds v. Sims] —these are self-wounding sins in any court." Address, "The Judicial Power as Guardian of Liberties," before a Symposium on "The Supreme Court and Constitutional Liberties in Modern America," Wayne State University, Detroit, Mich., Oct. 16, 1976, at 9. Arrogation of power withheld is far worse.

nized can be effectively limited."[29] Calls for disclosure of the Court's real role have been made by both proponents and opponents of judicial "adaptation" of the Constitution. Justice Jackson, it will be recalled, called on the Justices in the desegregation case to disclose that they were "making new law for a new day"; and Judge Learned Hand declared that "If we do need a third [legislative] chamber it should appear for what it is, and not as the interpreter of inscrutable principles."[30]

Forty years ago the philosopher Morris R. Cohen wrote to Professor Frankfurter, "the whole system is fundamentally dishonest in its pretensions (pretending to say what the Constitution lays down when they [the Justices] are in fact deciding what [they think] is good for the country.)"[31] But Martin Shapiro argued: "Suicide is no more moral in political than in personal life. It would be fantastic indeed if the Supreme Court, in the name of sound scholarship, were to disavow publicly the myth on which its power rests . . . If the myth . . . is destroyed . . . the Court loses power."[32] Power in the service of moral imperatives must not rest on a sham.[33] It is not "scholarship," but obedience to constitutional limitations that calls for a halt. "The foundation of morality," said Thomas Huxley, "is to

29. Mason, supra note 22 at 1405. Mason states, "once the public recognizes the personal nature of the judicial power, it would become difficult for the judiciary to function at all." Id. 1399.

30. *The Bill of Rights* 70 (1962); see also A. S. Miller and R. F. Howell, "The Myth of Neutrality in Constitutional Adjudication," 27 U. Chi. L. Rev. 661, 695 (1960).

31. Letter to Felix Frankfurter, January 27, 1936, L. C. Rosenfield, *Portrait of a Philosopher: Morris Raphael Cohen in Life and Letters* 270 (1962), quoted in Lash, supra note 24 at 55. There is a "credibility gap between the Court's pretensions and its actions." P. B. Kurland, *Politics, the Constitution and the Warren Court* xxiii (1970).

32. Supra note 18 at 27; see also supra Chapter 7 at notes 56–57.

33. Cf. Paul Brest, *Processes of Constitutional Decisionmaking: Cases and Materials* 1146 (1975).

have done, once and for all, with lying."[34] On a practical level, as Presidents Lyndon Johnson and Richard Nixon learned, nondisclosure to the people creates a credibility gap.[35]

The nation cannot afford to countenance a gap between word and deed on the part of its highest tribunal, a tribunal regarded by some as the "national conscience." It should not tolerate the spectacle of a Court that pretends to apply constitutional mandates while in fact revising them in accord with the preference of a majority of the Justices who seek to impose *their* will on the nation. Richard Nixon learned at last that even a President cannot set himself above the law, that he is obliged " 'to take Care that the Laws be faithfully executed.' It is necessary and right that the nine Justices be held to a like standard."[36] "The people," in the words of five early State Constitutions, "have a right to require of their . . . magistrates an exact and constant observance" of the "fundamental principles of the Constitution."[37] Among the most fundamental is the exclusion of the judiciary from policymaking.

Let it not be said of us as Gibbon said of Rome: "The *image* of a free constitution was preserved with decent reverence. The Roman senate *appeared* to possess the sovereign authority, and devolved on the emperors all the executive powers of government."[38] Here no Senate devolved the policymaking powers on the Court; they are self-conferred and survive only because the

---

34. Quoted in H. T. Mencken, *Treatise of Right and Wrong* 197 (1934).

35. "The contrast between morality professed by society and immorality practiced on its behalf makes for contempt of law." On Lee v. United States, 343 U.S. 747, 758–759 (1952), Justice Frankfurter, dissenting opinion.

36. Lusky 20.

37. Supra Chapter 15 at note 18.

38. 1 Gibbon, *The History of the Decline and Fall of the Roman Empire* 215 (Nottingham Soc. undated) (emphasis added). He said of the Roman emperors that "they surrounded their throne with darkness, concealed their irresistible strength, and humbly professed themselves the accountable ministers of the senate, whose supreme decrees they dictated and obeyed." Id. at 303.

American people are unaware that there is a yawning gulf between judicial professions and practice. An end, I would urge, to pretence. If government by judiciary is necessary to preserve the spirit of our democracy, let it be submitted in plainspoken fashion to the people—the ultimate sovereign—for their approval.

Appendix I
Van Alstyne's Critique of
Justice Harlan's Dissent

P ROFESSOR Van Alstyne's article[1] constitutes the most extended attempt to refute
Justice Harlan's dissent in *Reynolds v. Sims*.[2]
In the course of my discussion of suffrage, reapportionment, and the
"open-ended" theory I sought to take account of his views. That portion of his article which dealt with the "remedy" aspect of Harlan's
analysis has in part been discussed in connection with Justice Brennan's
adoption of the Van Alstyne argument.[3] Van Alstyne also attributes to
Harlan the view that "§2 equally precludes the application of any earlier provisions of the Constitution to state voting rights."[4] He considers that "there was probably no reliable understanding whatever that
§2 would preclude Congress (or the courts) from employing sources
of constitutional authority other than §2 to affect state suffrage"[5] and
spends many pages demonstrating that there was no such consensus.

Now Harlan was not at all concerned with "other" constitutional
provisions; save for a footnote reference to Bingham's explanation of a
"republican form of government."[6] Harlan concentrated on the Fourteenth Amendment. Here is his thesis in his own words: "The history

1. "The Fourteenth Amendment, The 'Right' to Vote, and the Understanding of the Thirty-Ninth Congress," 1965 S. Ct. Rev. 33.
2. 377 U.S. 533, 589 (1964).
3. Supra Chapter 5 at notes 102–106.
4. Van Alstyne 39.
5. Id. 45.
6. Quoted id. 41.

of the adoption of the Fourteenth Amendment provides conclusive evidence that neither those who proposed nor those who ratified the amendment believed that the Equal Protection clause limited the power of the States to apportion their legislatures as they saw fit."[7] Apparently Van Alstyne bases his inference of preemption of "other" provisions on Harlan's statement that "§2 expressly *recognizes* the States' power to deny or, in any way, abridge the right" to vote.[8] To recognize a State power falls short of holding that the Amendment "precludes the application of any earlier provisions of the Constitution." So to hold would imply that "earlier provisions," if any, had been repealed by implication. It cannot be presumed that Harlan was unaware of the elementary proposition that repeals by implication are not favored and require evidence that a repeal was intended.

Apart from a few radical dissentients,[9] there was a wide consensus that control over suffrage had from the beginning been left with the States, as was categorically stated by Stevens, Fessenden, Conkling, Bingham, and many others.[10] To placate the dissentients there were assurances that the "representation" provision left other provisions, if any, untouched; in other words, they were not repealed by implication. A typical colloquy between Higby and Stevens is cited by Van Alstyne. Higby objected that the "representation" proposal "gives a power to the States to make governments that are not republican in form," and asked Stevens

> if it does not acknowledge a power in a State to do such a thing.
> MR. STEVENS. Yes, sir, it does acknowledge it, and it has always existed under the Constitution.
> MR. HIGBY. I do not acknowledge that it is in the Constitution as it now is.
> MR. STEVENS. Then we do not give it to them.

Van Alstyne finds Stevens' response "confusing."[11] To "acknowl-

7. 377 U.S. at 595.
8. Van Alstyne 39.
9. Cited id. 49–51.
10. Supra Chapter 4.
11. Van Alstyne 50–51; *Globe* 428. This exchange occurred early in the session. Higby profited from the debates and later stated, "The Government of the United States does not propose or attempt to go into every one of the States now in close fellowship with the Government and represented here, and

edge" that States *have* a power is not to *give* it to them. At another point Stevens stated, "the States have the right . . . to fix the elective franchise," and the representation provision "does not take it from them."[12]

Rejection of the dissentient appeal to "other" constitutional sources for federal power over suffrage[13] is demonstrated by the fact that a subcommittee of the Joint Committee reported an Amendment "Congress shall have power . . . to secure . . . the same political rights,"[14] thereby expressing its view that Congress did not enjoy that power. And it is confirmed by the passage of the Fifteenth Amendment.[15] If there were "other" constitutional powers for the purpose the Fifteenth Amendment was superfluous. From 1789 to 1866 it was generally accepted that suffrage had been left to regulation by the States,[16] a view reiterated in 1875 by Chief Justice Waite:

> The Fifteenth Amendment does not confer the right of suffrage upon any one. It prevents the State from giving preference, in this particular, to one citizen of the United States over another on account of race. Before its adoption this could be done. It was as much within the power of a State to exclude citizens from voting on account of race . . . as it was on account of age, property, or education. Now it is not.[17]

---

say to them that all classes of citizens without distinction of race or color shall vote. It is true that the general principle has been to leave the question to each of the States." *Globe* 2252.

12. *Globe* 536.

13. Chief of these was the guarantee of "a republican form of government"; Van Alstyne 50.

14. Quoted id. 48 note 46.

15. Auerbach states, "Students of the history of the Fourteenth Amendment agree that the 'congressional understanding of the immediate effect of [the Fourteenth Amendment] enactment on conditions then present' was that it would not deal with the right of suffrage. Otherwise the Fifteenth Amendment would not have been necessary, as Mr. Justice Harlan pointed out." "The Reapportionment Cases: One Person, One Vote—One Vote, One Value," 1964 S. Ct. Rev. 1, 75. The point was made by the Court in Minor v. Happersett, 88 U.S. (21 Wall.) 162, 175 (1874).

16. Supra Chapter 4 at notes 42, 43, 45–48, 57, 64; Chapter 5 at note 49.

17. United States v. Reese, 92 U.S. 214, 217–218 (1875). Looking at "equal protection" in 1964, Auerbach considers it an "astonishing result" that would

Of course, this does not dispose of the question: were there such other powers? Van Alstyne, however, makes no attempt to demonstrate that there were. My study of the guarantee of a republican form of government, upon which the dissentients cited by Van Alstyne heavily rely, led me to doubt their existence.[18] Those doubts were strongly reinforced by the historical materials Justice Stewart collected in his opinion in *Oregon v. Mitchell*.[19] In any event, Van Alstyne's elaborate argument that the Fourteenth Amendment does not preclude the application of "other" provisions of the Constitution does not shake Harlan's demonstration that suffrage was excluded from the Amendment itself.

Van Alstyne's attempt to downgrade Stevens' testimony stands no better. Stevens did not consider Negroes prepared for suffrage, nor the North ready to accept it; he had stated that the right of a State to disfranchise "has always existed," that the proposed "representation" provision "does not take it from" the States.[20] One could hardly ask for greater clarity. Against this, Van Alstyne quotes Stevens, "If any State shall exclude any of her adult citizens from the elective franchise . . . she shall forfeit her right to representation in the same proportion,"; and asks whether this evidences Stevens' understanding "that an exception was to be read into the unqualified language of §1 and that the Equal Protection Clause could not be applied against par-

---

read "equal protection" to allow a State to deny "the right to vote in a state or local election . . . for reasons which have nothing to do with race, color . . . but which nevertheless result in an arbitrary classification." Auerbach, supra note 15 at 77–78. But that view is a product of our times, not at all responsive to the intention of the framers, either in 1787 or in 1866. See supra Chapter 5 after note 77. In New York v. Miln, 36 U.S. (11 Pet.) 102, 139 (1837), the Court declared, "a State has the same undeniable and unlimited jurisdiction over all persons and things, within its territorial limits, as any foreign nation, where that jurisdiction is not surrendered or restrained by the Constitution of the United States." For the standard of proof required to establish such "surrender" see supra Chapter 1 note 57.

18. Fessenden commented on Article I, §2(3), re qualifications of electors in each State, "it has always been considered that the clause . . . acknowledged the rights of the States to regulate the question of suffrage. I do not think it has ever been disputed." *Globe* 1278.

19. 400 U.S. 112, 288–291 (1970), concurring and dissenting in part.

20. Supra Chapter 4 at notes 25, 64, 46.

tial and oppressive laws denying the freedmen their voice in the government."[21] This quotation did not address that issue; but the above quotations plainly indicate Stevens' view that suffrage was to remain the province of the States; that is an "exception" built into "equal protection" by the entire Republican leadership. Bingham stated: "The amendment does not give . . . the power to Congress of regulating suffrage in the several States."[22] Senator Howard explained that "the first section of the proposed amendment does not give . . . the right of voting."[23] Toward the close of the session Senator Sherman said, "we have refused" to require the rebel "States to allow colored persons to vote."[24] And after passage of the "equal protection" clause, Bingham lent his aid to Tennessee's exclusion of black suffrage, notwithstanding "we are all for equal and exact justice, but justice for all is not to be secured in a day"[25]—eloquent testimony that "equal protection" was not viewed as a bar to denial of suffrage.

Van Alstyne's statement that Stevens "greatly favored Negro suffrage and constantly supported all efforts to that end, to the extent he thought them politically feasible"[26] is not very revealing. In fact, as C. Vann Woodward wrote, "Stevens was not yet prepared to enfranchise the Negro freedmen . . . apart from political reasons he had other doubts about the wisdom of the measure . . . he doubted that the freedmen were prepared for intelligent voting."[27] Eric McKitrick stated, "beyond doubt" Stevens "tipped the balance . . . Being none too keen on direct enactment of Negro suffrage."[28] It was on Stevens' motion that the Joint Committee on Reconstruction preferred a reduction of representation proposal to one prohibiting discrimination, by a vote of 11 to 3.[29] He was taunted during the final debate by Charles A. Eldredge, a Democrat from Wisconsin: "Why is it that the gentleman from Pennsylvania gives up universal suffrage . . . It is . . . for the

21. Van Alstyne 56. But see Bickel, supra Chapter 6 at note 27.
22. *Globe* 2542.
23. Id. 2766.
24. Id. 3989.
25. Id. 3979.
26. Van Alstyne 46.
27. *The Burden of Southern History* 92 (1960); supra Chapter 4 at note 25.
28. *Andrew Johnson and Reconstruction* 348 (1960).
29. Kendrick 51.

purpose of saving their party in the next fall election."[30] Another Democrat, Andrew Rogers, asserted, "The committee does not dare submit the broad proposition to the people . . . of negro suffrage."[31] In September 1866, when the Amendment was a campaign issue, Stevens assured the Pennsylvania voters that the "Amendment does not touch social or political rights."[32]

It is Van Alstyne who would "read into" the words "equal protection" the very suffrage so unmistakably excluded by the framers. For centuries the canon of interpretation has been that a thing may be within the language and yet not within the intention of the framers and therefore not "within the statute."[33] "Equal protection" had limited scope for the framers; it barred discriminatory laws with respect to specified "fundamental rights"—no more.[34]

The difficulties that confront Van Alstyne's attack on Harlan's analysis may be gathered from his own statement. He makes

> several observations generally in agreement with Mr. Justice Harlan's view of what was implied by §2. First, the fact that the Joint Committee considered an amendment to prohibit voting discrimination on racial grounds [and let it wither on the vine] does seem to imply that it otherwise regarded state laws providing for such discrimination as constitutional. Second, the fact that a more limited reduction-of-representation-basis alternative was simultaneously considered and adopted, that the

30. *Globe* 2506.

31. Id. 2538. See Van Alstyne's Summary, supra Chapter 4 at note 16.

32. James 201. Van Alstyne cites a Stevens statement of two years later: "Since the adoption of the fourteenth amendment . . . I have no doubt of our power to regulate the elective franchise." Van Alstyne recognizes that such a "retrospective view . . . must, of course, be discounted to that extent"; Van Alstyne 64–65; it was in flat contradiction of representations made to secure adoption. Such retrospective statements are to be totally discounted. See supra Chapter 3 at notes 51–52; see also Raoul Berger, "Judicial Review: Counter Criticism in Tranquillity," 69 Nw. U. L. Rev. 390, 399–401 (1974). In any event, Stevens' later views did not carry the day because Congress passed the Fifteenth Amendment to fill the gap.

33. See supra Chapter 1 note 24; Chapter 10 at note 94. See also Pierson v. Ray, discussed supra Chapter 1 note 57.

34. See supra Chapter 10.

proposal to prohibit discrimination on the basis of race was not adopted [such proposals were voted down by the Senate by very heavy majorities] appears to imply that §2 itself recognizes the exclusive power of states over suffrage qualifications. Beyond this, the speeches by Stevens and Conkling in support of H. R. No. 51 [a predecessor provision cast in terms of racial discrimination] initially appear to the same effect.[35]

To the "speeches by Stevens and Conkling" should be added those of other prominent leaders, Fessenden, Bingham, Howard and still other Republicans, copiously quoted in Chapters 3 and 4 supra, and unmistakably confirmed by the Joint Committee Report. How Van Alstyne can extract from these statements the conclusion that "its [§2] principal proponents emphasized that it did not acknowledge the constitutionality of state disenfranchisement laws"[36] escapes my grasp.

Among the facts Van Alstyne musters to counteract an "initial favorable" impression is his "package" argument. In demonstrating that §2 illuminated the exclusion of suffrage from §1 of the Amendment, Justice Harlan stated: "the Amendment is a single text. It was introduced and discussed as such in the Reconstruction Committee, which reported it to Congress. It was discussed as a unit in Congress and proposed as a unit to the States, which ratified it as a unit."[37] This is one of the "serious exaggerations" Van Alstyne lays at Harlan's door: "Far from being a single text . . . the Fourteenth Amendment was a package of proposals, the more significant of which were pieced together from independent bills by different men at different times and originally debated as wholly separate amendments."[38]

Let it be admitted that the different bills were "'*originally*' debated as wholly separate amendments"; but down the line they were "discussed as a unit" in the form of an amendment combining five sections, and "ratified . . . as a unit" by the States. And though the several sections were introduced "by different men at different times," they were debated in the very same Congress and same short space of

---

35. Van Alstyne 48–49.
36. Id. 44.
37. 377 U.S. at 594.
38. Van Alstyne 42–43.

time.[39] Members turned from one subject to the other and then back again, time after time. Throughout the debates discussion of "representation," which became the subject of §2, alternated with discussions of the Civil Rights Bill and the Bingham amendment, the antecedents of §1. Explicit recognition that Negro suffrage was beyond the achievable was the leitmotiv of all the discussions. Are we to assume that the members of Congress erased from their minds all reference made to suffrage because made in the context of the Bill or alternately in that of "representation"? Men do not thus insulate important discussions in airtight mental compartments. For example, Stevens referred in the course of the debate on the Amendment to the Black Codes and stated, "I need not enumerate these partial and oppressive laws," patently because they had been frequently mentioned, and to underscore the obvious said that the "civil rights bill secures the same thing."[40] With respect to Howard's proposal that citizenship be defined in §1, Fessenden said, "I should like to hear the opinion of the Chairman of the Committee on the Judiciary [Senator Trumbull], who has investigated the civil rights bill so thoroughly, on the subject."[41] Certainly Bingham regarded the Amendment as a "unit," for he said, "The second section excludes the conclusion that by the first section suffrage is subjected to congressional law."[42] Howard said that "the theory of this *whole* amendment is to leave" suffrage with the States.[43] Van Alstyne himself states that "the brevity of the three-day House debate on . . . the packaged Fourteenth Amendment bill, is probably attributable to the fact that its most significant components

39. For example, §2 "was debated in the Senate in February and March of 1866," id. 43. In February Bingham reported the Joint Committee resolution, H. R. No. 63, a progenitor of the §1 "privileges or immunities" and "equal protection" provisions and explained them, Bickel 33; *Globe* 1033–1034, "while Trumbull's bills on the same subject of civil rights were prominently before Congress and the country." James 83. TenBroek, 226, states that the "speeches in the May and June debates which deal with the meaning of §1 (whether for or against) other than by specific allusion to the Civil Rights Act do so precisely in the terms employed in the February debate."

40. *Globe* 2459.

41. Id. 2893.

42. Id. 2542.

43. Id. 3039 (emphasis added).

had previously been considered at length."[44] That no recapitulation of these "components" was deemed necessary is underscored by the frequent statements that the Amendment was designed to constitutionalize the Civil Rights Act. In short, Congress was thoroughly aware of a common purpose to exclude Negro suffrage that animated discussion of the Civil Rights Bill, and of Sections 1 and 2. On Van Alstyne's own reading of Justice Harlan, §1 was "understood at the time of its promulgation not to apply to suffrage qualifications as determined by the states";[45] it is therefore *in pari materia* with §2 which exhibits a similar understanding. Because "they relate to the same thing, they ought all"—Civil Rights Bill, sections 1 and 2—"to be taken into consideration in construing any one of them."[46] Plainly Van Alstyne's "package" analysis does not vitiate Harlan's documentation.

Finally, Justice Harlan correctly stated that the Joint Committee on Reconstruction, which fashioned the §2 "representation" provision, "regularly rejected explicitly enfranchising proposals in favor of plans which would postpone enfranchisement, leave it to congressional discretion, or abandon it altogether." And, as he pointed out, "the abandonment of negro suffrage as a goal exactly corresponded with the adoption of provisions to reduce representation for discriminatory restrictions on the ballot."[47]

44. Van Alstyne 43. He considers that §2 "became a part of the Fourteenth Amendment largely through the accident of political exigency rather than the relation which it bore to the other sections of the amendment"; id. 43–44. The central "relation" was that Negro suffrage was unacceptable, both in §1 and §2, and those sections could be "packaged" in a unit that was understood by all. As the Joint Committee report stated, the §2 "representation" provision was adopted because an outright grant of suffrage proved unacceptable. Supra Chapter 5 at note 49.

45. Van Alstyne 38.

46. United States v. Freeman, 44 U.S. (3 How.) 556, 564 (1845). The rule is centuries old: "If any part of a statute be obscure it is proper to consider the other parts; for the words and meaning of one part of a statute frequently lead to the sense of another." Matthew Bacon, *A New Abridgment of the Laws of England,* "Statute," I(2) (3d ed. 1768).

47. Oregon v. Mitchell, 400 U.S. 112, 170–171 (1970), dissenting opinion.

Appendix II
Judicial Administration
of Local Matters

In a recent evaluation of the Court's assumption of the policymaking role, Archibald Cox wrote:

[W]here the older activist decisions merely blocked legislative initiatives, the decisions of the 1950's and 1960's forced changes in the established legal order. The school desegregation cases overturned not only the constitutional precedents built up over three quarters of a century but the social structure of an entire region . . . The one man, one vote rule asserted that the composition of the legislatures of all but one or two of the 50 states was unconstitutional and had been unconstitutional for fifty or a hundred years [or more] . . . *New York Times Co. v. Sullivan* overturned the law of libel as it had prevailed from the beginning.

Cox comments:

Decisions mandating reforms in the on-going activities of other branches of government often require affirmative action. The affirmative action can be secured [lacking voluntary cooperation, only] by the courts themselves embarking upon programs having typically administrative, executive and even legislative characteristics heretofore thought to make such programs unsuited to judicial undertaking [and arguably therefore never comprehended in the original grant of judicial power].

The most prominent examples are the school desegregation cases. The court determines which students will be assigned to each school, how teachers shall be selected, what security measures shall be adopted, and even where new schools shall be built. When transportation is required, the court directs the expenditure of hundreds of thousands of dollars.

428

. . . In Boston, for example, the city was induced by fear of fiscal disaster to plan the elimination of 191 teachers. The federal court went down the list, school by school, even hearing the personal pleas of individual teachers, and decided to allow 60 layoffs and disallow 131.

Desegregation decrees have all the qualities of social legislation . . . I can think of no earlier decrees with these characteristics in all constitutional history.

Archibald, Cox, "The New Dimensions of Constitutional Adjudication," 51 Washington Law Review 791, 802, 814–815 (1976).

All this on the theory that "the Constitution requires busing"!

A summary of judicial takeovers of legislative and executive prerogatives is furnished in the following article by Wayne King, *The New York Times,* November 13, 1976, pp. 1, 38.

A Federal court ruling ordering Mobile to scrap its city government and replace it with a new one more favorable to blacks has generated a storm of protest in this city, including a petition drive to impeach the judge.

"This is the first time," said Mayor Lambert C. Mims in an interview, "that the Federal Government has told a free people what kind of government they must have."

"If they can do that, they can tell you what time to go to bed, what time to get up, and whether to have pork and beans for lunch."

Yesterday, a newly formed group called the Constitutional Crisis Committee began distributing petitions calling for the impeachment of Federal Judge Virgil Pittman of the Southern District of Alabama.

Judge Pittman two weeks ago ruled in a class-action suit brought by city blacks that the Mobile system of government, a three-member city commission, with each member elected by citywide vote, "precludes a black voter from an effective participation in the election system."

He ordered that in the municipal election next year the commission was to be replaced by a mayor elected by citywide vote and nine council members elected from single-member districts.

Given the city's racially polarized voting pattern, this would likely result in the election of at least three and possibly four blacks.

The court found that the vote of Mobile's blacks, 35 percent of the population, was "diluted" by the white majority, making it unlikely to elect a black in a citywide vote.

The ruling is believed to be the most extensive intrusion by the courts
so far into legislative and executive affairs. The Mobile City Commission was established under legislative power of the State of Alabama in
1911 and has twice been retained by popular vote of the city's voters.

There have been a number of recent examples of state and Federal judicial action taking over prerogatives normally reserved to the executive or legislative branches of Government.

In Alabama, Mississippi and Louisiana, Federal courts have ordered
state prisons to be brought up to standards set by the courts, in most
cases involving large expenditures of state funds.

In New York City, a Federal court ordered the aging Tombs Prison
closed and a new facility built.

In New Jersey, a state court in effect ordered the Legislature to enact
an income tax by declaring the closing of public schools until adequate
financial support was made available—possible only through enactment
of the income tax.

In Chicago, a Federal court ordered affirmative action in the hiring of
policemen, a step that has also been taken in numerous other places.

In Boston, parts of the operation of public schools have been directed
by Federal Judge Arthur Garrity in an effort to correct racial imbalances.

These are part of the growing trend toward "activist" court decisions
forcing the requirements of the judiciary onto other branches of Government.

Besides the question of separation of powers among the legislative,
executive and judicial branches, these and similar court actions have
raised the question of "accountability" of judges—most of whom, particularly those on the Federal bench, are not elected but appointed for
terms up to life without review.

In a speech to the new Constitutional Crisis Committee, Mr. Mims,
the current Mayor under a rotation system among the commissioners,
said: "This decision, if not reversed, could be the beginning of the end
for local government and the open door for complete Federal takeover
of community affairs."

The city has set aside $500,000, including $200,000 in Federal
revenue-sharing money, to fight the decision.

Eugene McKenzie, a furniture store owner who is head of the crisis
committee, said in an interview that the petitions for impeachment of
Judge Pittman were based on "usurpation of the voters' right to choose
their form of local government as guaranteed by the Alabama Constitution."

The petition also maintains that the 10th Amendment of the United
States Constitution delegating certain powers to the Federal Govern-

ment and reserving others to the states had been breached by the ruling.

Mayor Mims said in an interview that the issue was not racial. "If we'd been bad to blacks, been mean old honkies, then maybe we'd deserve this," he said. "I just hope that blacks will realize that the issue is if a judge can order this, he can order Ku Klux Klansmen into city government."

In his ruling, Judge Pittman observed that "there is no formal prohibition against blacks seeking office in Mobile" and that "since the Voting Rights Act of 1965, blacks register and vote without hindrance."

However, the judge found that "one indication that local political processes are not equally open is the fact that no black person has ever been elected to the at-large city commission."

Although the judge found no current examples of "overt gross discrimination" in city services, he said in his ruling that there were "significant differences and the sluggishness" in responding to needs in black areas as compared to white areas.

Moreover, he found significant racial imbalances in city administrative agencies appointed by the city commissioners.

Mayor Mims said that while such imbalances appear to exist, blacks did have minority representation on all such boards and said that appointments were made according to qualifications and not according to race.

Judge Pittman's ruling is being appealed to the Court of Appeals for the Fifth Circuit in New Orleans. No hearing date has been set, and no ruling is expected before the date of the municipal elections next August. The city will ask for a stay of the order, if necessary, to continue to elect the commissioners as its form of Government. The Mayor also said that the city would continue its appeals to the United States Surpeme Court if necessary.

Bibliography

BOOKS

Acheson, Dean. *Morning and Noon* (Boston, Houghton Mifflin, 1965).

Adams, John Quincy. *Life in a New England Town: 1787, 1788. Diary of John Quincy Adams* (Boston, Little, Brown, 1903).

Allen, Sir C. K. *Law in the Making,* 6th ed. (Oxford, Clarendon Press, 1958).

Bacon, Matthew. *A New Abridgment of the Laws of England,* 8 vols., 3d ed. (London, 1768).

Baldwin, Henry. *A General View of the Origin and Nature of the Constitution and Government of the United States* (Philadelphia, J. C. Clark, 1837).

Bemis, Samuel F. *John Quincy Adams and the Foundation of American Foreign Policy* (New York, Knopf, 1949).

————. *John Quincy Adams and the Union* (New York, Knopf, 1956).

Benedict, Michael Les. *A Compromise of Principle: Conservative Republicans and Reconstruction 1863–1869* (New York, Norton, 1975).

Berger, Raoul. *Congress v. The Supreme Court* (Cambridge, Mass., Harvard University Press, 1969).

————. *Executive Privilege: A Constitutional Myth* (Cambridge, Mass., Harvard University Press, 1974).

————. *Impeachment: The Constitutional Problems* (Cambridge, Mass., Harvard University Press, 1973).

Bickel, Alexander M. *The Least Dangerous Branch* (Indianapolis, Bobbs-Merrill, 1962, paperback ed.).

Black, Charles L., Jr. *The People and the Court* (New York, Macmillan, 1960).

433

Blackstone, William. *Commentaries on the Laws of England* (London, 1765–1769).

Brest, Paul. *Processes of Constitutional Decisionmaking: Cases and Materials* (Boston, Little, Brown, 1975).

Brock, W. R. *An American Crisis: Congress and Reconstruction* (London, Macmillan, 1963).

Brodie, Fawn M. *Thaddeus Stevens: Scourge of the South* (New York, Norton, 1959).

Brooks, Van Wyck. *Days of the Phoenix* (New York, Dutton, 1957).

Butterfield, Sir Herbert. *George III and the Historians* (New York, Macmillan, 1969).

Cardozo, Benjamin N. *The Nature of the Judicial Process* (New Haven, Yale University Press, 1921).

Coke, Edward. *Institutes of the Laws of England,* 4 vols. (London; 1628–1641).

Commager, Henry Steele. *Documents of American History,* 7th ed. (New York, Appleton, 1963).

Corwin, Edward S. *American Constitutional History,* A. T. Mason and G. Garvey, eds. (New York, Harper & Row, 1964).

––––––. *The Doctrine of Judicial Review: Its Legal and Historical Basis and Other Essays* (Princeton, Princeton University Press, 1914).

Cover, Robert. *Justice Accused: Antislavery and the Judicial Process* (New Haven, Yale University Press, 1975).

Cox, Archibald. *The Role of the Supreme Court in American Government* (New York, Oxford University Press, 1976).

Donald, David. *Charles Sumner and the Coming of the Civil War* (New York, Knopf, 1960).

––––––. *Charles Sumner and the Rights of Man* (New York, Knopf, 1970).

––––––. *The Politics of Reconstruction* (Baton Rouge, Louisiana State University Press, 1965).

Elliot, Jonathan. *Debates in the Several State Conventions on the Adoption of the Federal Constitution,* 4 vols., 2d ed. (Washington, D.C., J. Elliot, 1836).

Elliott, Ward E. Y. *The Rise of a Guardian Democracy* (Cambridge, Mass., Harvard University Press, 1974).

Fairman, Charles. *Mr. Justice Miller and the Supreme Court* (Cambridge, Mass., Harvard University Press, 1939).

_____. *Reconstruction and Reunion 1864–1878,* vol. 6, part 1, of *History of the Supreme Court of the United States* (New York, Macmillan, 1971).

Farrand, Max. *The Records of the Federal Convention of 1787,* 4 vols. (New Haven, Yale University Press, 1911).

The Federalist (New York, Modern Library ed., 1937).

Flack, Harry. *The Adoption of the Fourteenth Amendment* (Baltimore, Johns Hopkins University Press, 1908).

Frankfurter, Felix. *The Commerce Clause Under Marshall, Taney and Waite* (Chapel Hill, University of North Carolina Press, 1937).

_____. *Law and Politics,* A. Macleish and E. F. Prichard, eds. (New York, Harcourt Brace, 1938).

_____. *Mr. Justice Holmes and the Supreme Court* (Cambridge, Mass., Harvard University Press, 1938).

_____. *Of Law and Men,* Philip Elman, ed. (New York, Harcourt Brace, 1956).

Freedman, M., ed. *Roosevelt and Frankfurter: Their Correspondence 1928–1945* (Boston, Little, Brown, 1967).

Gibbon, Edward. *The History of the Decline and Fall of the Roman Empire* (New York, Nottingham Society, undated).

Gillette, William. *The Right to Vote: Politics and the Passage of the Fifteenth Amendment* (Baltimore, Johns Hopkins University Press, 1965).

Goebel, Julius. *Antecedents and Beginnings to 1801,* vol. 1 of *History of the Supreme Court of the United States* (New York, Macmillan, 1971).

_____ and T. R. Naughton. *Law Enforcement in Colonial New York (1664–1776)* (Montclair, N.J., Patterson Smith, 1970).

Graglia, Lino A. *Disaster by Decree* (Ithaca, Cornell University Press, 1976).

Graham, Howard Jay. *Everyman's Constitution* (New York, Norton, 1968).

Griffith, Kathryn. *Judge Learned Hand and the Role of the Federal Judiciary* (Norman, University of Oklahoma Press, 1973).

Gunther, Gerald, ed. *John Marshall's Defense of McCulloch v. Maryland* (Stanford, Stanford University Press, 1969).

Haines, Charles G. *The Revival of Natural Law Concepts* (Cambridge, Mass., Harvard University Press, 1930).

Hale, Sir Matthew. *History of the Pleas of the Crown* (London, 1736).

Hamilton, Alexander. *The Papers of Alexander Hamilton,* H. C. Syrett and J. E. Cooke, eds. (New York, Columbia University Press, 1962).

———. *Works,* H. C. Lodge, ed., 12 vols. (New York, Knickerbocker Press, 1904).

Hand, Learned. *The Bill of Rights* (Cambridge, Mass., Harvard University Press, 1962).

———. *The Spirit of Liberty,* Irving Dillard, ed. (New York, Knopf, 1952).

Harris, Robert J. *The Quest For Equality* (Baton Rouge, Louisiana State University Press, 1960).

Hart, Henry M., and Albert Sacks. "The Legal Process: Basic Problems in Making and Application of Law" (unpublished mimeographed edition, 1958).

Hauser, Arnold. *The Social History of Art,* 4 vols. (New York, Vintage Books, undated).

Heller, Francis H. *The Sixth Amendment to the Constitution of the United States* (Lawrence, Kan., University of Kansas Press, 1951).

Himmelfarb, Gertrude. *Victorian Minds* (New York, Knopf, 1968).

Hockett, H. C. *The Constitutional History of the United States, 1826–1876* (New York, Macmillan, 1939).

Holmes, Oliver Wendell, Jr. *Collected Legal Papers* (New York, Harcourt Brace, 1920).

———. *The Common Law* (Boston, Little, Brown, 1881).

Horwitz, Morton J. *The Transformation of American Law* (Cambridge, Mass., Harvard University Press, 1977).

Howe, M., ed. *Holmes-Laski Letters: The Correspondence of Mr. Justice Holmes and Harold J. Laski* (Cambridge, Mass., Harvard University Press, 1953).

Hughes, Charles Evans. *The Autobiographical Notes of Charles Evans Hughes,* D. J. Danielski and J. S. Tulchin, eds. (Cambridge, Mass., Harvard University Press, 1973).

———. *The Supreme Court of the United States: Its Foundation, Methods and Achievements, an Interpretation* (New York, Columbia University Press, 1928).

Hurst, James Willard. *The Legitimacy of the Business Corporation in the Law of the United States* (Charlottesville, University of Virginia Press, 1970).

Hyman, Harold M. *A More Perfect Union* (New York, Knopf, 1973).

Jackson, Robert H. *The Struggle for Judicial Supremacy: A Study of a Crisis in American Political Power* (New York, Knopf, 1941).

James, Joseph B. *The Framing of the Fourteenth Amendment* (Urbana, Ill., University of Illinois Press, 1965).

Jefferson, Thomas. *Writings,* P. L. Ford, ed., 10 vols. (New York, Putnam, 1892–1899).

Keller, Morton. *Affairs of State* (Cambridge, Mass., Harvard University Press, 1977).

Kendrick, Benjamin. *The Journal of the Joint Committee of Fifteen on Reconstruction* (New York, Columbia University Press, 1914).

Kent, James. *Commentaries on American Law,* 9th ed. (Boston, Little, Brown, 1858).

Kluger, Richard. *Simple Justice* (New York, Knopf, 1976).

Kurland, Philip B. *Politics, the Constitution and the Warren Court* (Chicago, University of Chicago Press, 1970).

Lacy, Dan. *The White Use of Black in America* (New York, Atheneum, 1972).

Lash, Joseph P. *From the Diaries of Felix Frankfurter* (New York, Norton, 1975).

Lerner, M., ed., *The Mind and Faith of Justice Holmes* (Garden City, N.Y., Halcyon House, 1943).

Levy, Leonard. *Against the Law: The Nixon Court and Criminal Justice* (New York, Harper & Row, 1974).

————. *Judgments: Essays in American Constitutional History* (Chicago, Quadrangle Books, 1972).

————, ed. *Judicial Review and the Supreme Court* (New York, Harper & Row, 1967).

————, ed. *The Supreme Court Under Earl Warren* (New York, Quadrangle Books, 1972).

Lusky, Louis. *By What Right?* (Charlottesville, Michie Co., 1975).

McClellan, James. *Joseph Story and the American Constitution* (Norman, Okla., University of Oklahoma Press, 1974).

McCloskey, Robert G. *The American Supreme Court* (Chicago, University of Chicago Press, 1960).

McIlwain, Charles H. *Constitutionalism: Ancient and Modern,* rev. ed. (Ithaca, Cornell University Press, 1947).

McKitrick, Eric L. *Andrew Johnson and Reconstruction* (Chicago, University of Chicago Press, 1960).

McRee, G. J. *Life and Correspondence of James Iredell,* 2 vols. (New York, Appleton, 1857–1858).

Madison, James. *Writings,* G. Hunt, ed., 9 vols. (New York, Putnam, 1900–1910).

Mason, Alpheus T. *Harlan Fiske Stone: Pillar of the Law* (New York, Viking Press, 1956).

———. *Security Through Freedom: American Political Thought and Practice* (Ithaca, Cornell University Press, 1955).

———. *The Supreme Court: Palladium of Freedom* (Ann Arbor, University of Michigan Press, 1962).

——— and W. M. Beaney. *American Constitutional Law* (New York, Prentice-Hall, 1954).

Mencken, Henry T. *Treatise of Right and Wrong* (New York, Knopf, 1934).

Mendelson, Wallace. *Justices Black and Frankfurter: Conflict in the Court* (Chicago, University of Chicago Press, 1961).

———. *The Supreme Court: Law and Discretion* (Indianapolis, Bobbs-Merrill, 1967).

Miller, Charles A. *The Supreme Court and the Uses of History* (Cambridge, Mass., Harvard University Press, 1969).

Morison, Samuel Eliot. *The Oxford History of the American People* (New York, Oxford University Press, 1965).

Muller, Herbert. *Uses of the Past* (New York, Oxford University Press, 1952).

Murphy, Paul. *The Constitution in Crisis Times, 1918–1969* (New York, Harper & Row, 1972).

Paludan, Phillip S. *A Covenant With Death* (Urbana, University of Illinois Press, 1975).

Patterson, Caleb P. *The Constitutional Principles of Thomas Jefferson* (Austin, Texas, University of Texas Press, 1953).

Pendleton, Edmund. *Letters and Papers,* D. J. Mays, ed. (Charlottesville, University of Virginia Press, 1967).

Poore, Ben P. *Federal and State Constitutions, Colonial Charters,* 2 vols. (Washington, D.C., Government Printing Office, 1877).

Powell, Thomas Reed. *Vagaries and Varieties in Constitutional Interpretation* (New York, Columbia University Press, 1956).

Randall, J. R. *The Making of the Modern Mind* (Boston, Houghton Mifflin, 1940).

Richardson, James O. *Compilation of the Messages and Papers of the Presidents, 1789–1897,* 10 vols. (Washington, D.C., Government Printing Office, 1897).

Roberts, Owen. *The Court and the Constitution* (Cambridge, Mass., Harvard University Press, 1951).

Rodell, Fred. *Nine Men* (New York, Random House, 1955).

Rutherforth, Thomas. *Institutes of Natural Law,* 2 vols. (Cambridge, J. Bentham, 1754–1756).

Samuels, Ernest. *Henry Adams: The Major Phase* (Cambridge, Mass., Harvard University Press, 1964).

Shapiro, Martin. *Law and Politics in the Supreme Court* (New York, Free Press of Glencoe, 1964).

Smith, Homer W. *Man and His Gods* (Boston, Little, Brown, 1953).

Smith, Page. *John Adams,* 2 vols. (Garden City, N.Y., Doubleday, 1962).

Smith, Zephaniah. *A System of Laws of the State of Connecticut* (Windham, Conn., Z. Smith, 1795–1796).

Stampp, Kenneth M. *The Peculiar Institution* (New York, Vintage Books, 1956).

Story, Joseph. *Commentaries on the Constitution of the United States,* 2 vols., 5th ed. (Boston, Little, Brown, 1905).

Strickland, S. P., ed. *Hugo Black and the Supreme Court: A Symposium;* Foreword by C. L. Black (Indianapolis, Bobbs-Merrill, 1967).

TenBroek, Jacobus. *Equal Under Law* (London, Collier Books, 1965).

Tocqueville, Alexis de. *Democracy in America,* 2 vols. (New York, Colonial Press, 1900).

Twiss, Benjamin R. *Lawyers and the Constitution* (Princeton, Princeton University Press, 1942).

Washington, George. *Writings,* J. Fitzpatrick, ed., 39 vols. (Washington, D.C., Government Printing Office, 1940).

White, G. Edward. *The American Judicial Tradition* (New York, Oxford University Press, 1976).

Wilson, Edmund. *Europe Without a Baedeker* (New York, Farrar Strauss, 1966).

———. *Patriotic Gore* (New York, Oxford University Press, 1962).

Wilson, James. *Works,* R. G. McCloskey, ed., 2 vols. (Cambridge, Mass., Harvard University Press, 1967).

Wood, Gordon. *The Creation of the American Republic 1776–1787* (Chapel Hill, University of North Carolina Press, 1969).

Woodward, C. Vann. *The Burden of Southern History* (Baton Rouge, Louisiana State University Press, 1960).

Wright, Benjamin F. *The Growth of American Constitutional Law* (Boston, Houghton Mifflin, 1942).

ARTICLES

Allen, Francis. "The Constitution: The Civil War Amendments: XIII–XV," in Daniel Boorstin, *An American Primer* 165.

Arnold, Thurman. "Professor Hart's Theology," 73 Harvard Law Review 1298 (1960).

Auerbach, Carl. "The Reapportionment Cases: One Person, One Vote–One Vote, One Value," 1964 Supreme Court Review 1.

Bell, Derrick. "Book Review," 76 Columbia Law Review 350 (1976).

———. "The Burden of Brown on Blacks: History Based on Observations of a Landmark Decision," 7 North Carolina Central Law Journal 25 (1975).

Berger, Raoul, "Constructive Contempt: A Post-Mortem," 9 University of Chicago Law Review 602 (1942).

———. "Judicial Review: Counter Criticism in Tranquillity," 69 Northwestern University Law Review 390 (1974).

———. "War-Making by the President," 121 University of Pennsylvania Law Review 29 (1972).

Bickel, Alexander M. "The Original Understanding and the Segregation Decision," 69 Harvard Law Review 1 (1955).

———. "Is the Warren Court Too 'Political'?" The New York Times Magazine, September 25, 1966, in L. Levy, ed., *The Supreme Court Under Earl Warren* 216 (1972).

——— and Harry Wellington. "Legislative Purpose and the Judicial Process: The Lincoln Mills Case," 71 Harvard Law Review 1 (1957).

Bishop, Joseph W., Jr. "The Warren Court is Not Likely to be Overruled," The New York Times Magazine, September 7, 1969, in L. Levy, ed., *The Supreme Court Under Earl Warren* 93 (1972).

———. "What is a Liberal—Who is a Conservative?" 62 *Commentary* 47 (September 1976).

Bork, Robert J. "Neutral Principles and Some First Amendment Problems," 47 Indiana Law Journal 1 (1971).

Braden, George D. "The Search for Objectivity in Constitutional Law," 57 Yale Law Journal 571 (1948).

Burns, James McGregor. "Dictatorship—Could It Happen Here?" in C. Roberts, ed., *Has the Court Too Much Power* 234 (1974).

Cahn, Edmond. "Brief for the Supreme Court," The New York Times Magazine, October 7, 1956, in L. Levy, ed., *The Supreme Court Under Earl Warren* 28 (1972).

———. "Jurisprudence," 30 New York University Law Review 150 (1955).

Chayes, Abram. "The New Judiciary," 28 Harvard Law School Bulletin 23 (1976).

Claggett, Bruce M. "Book Review," 27 Harvard Law School Bulletin 3 (1976).

Commager, Henry Steele. "Constitutional History and the Higher Law," in C. Read, ed., *The Constitution Reconsidered* 225 (1939).

———. "Judicial Review and Democracy," 19 Virginia Quarterly Review 417 (1943).

Cooper, Tim. "Freund: 40 Years of Supreme Court History Recalled," 64 Harvard Law School Record 1 (1977).

Corwin, Edward S. "The Decline of Due Process Before the Civil War," 24 Harvard Law Review 460 (1911).

———. "The 'Higher Law' Background of American Constitutional Law," 42 Harvard Law Review 149 (1928).

Cox, Archibald. "The New Dimensions of Constitutional Adjudication," 51 Washington Law Review 791 (1976).

Curtis, Charles P. "A Better Theory of Legal Interpretation," 3 Vanderbilt Law Review 407 (1950).

———. "Review and Majority Rule," in E. Cahn, ed., *Supreme Court and Supreme Law* 170 (1954).

———. "The Role of the Constitutional Text," id. 64.

Dahl, Robert, "Decision-Making in a Democracy: The Supreme Court as a National Policy-Maker," 6 Journal of Public Law 279 (1957).

Dershowitz, Alan M. "Book Review," New York Times Book Review, September 21, 1975, at 1.

Dixon, Robert. "Reapportionment in the Supreme Court and

Congress: Constitutional Struggle for Fair Representation," 63 Michigan Law Review 209 (1964).

Douglas, William O. "Stare Decisis," 49 Columbia Law Review 735 (1949).

Downing, Rondel G. "Judicial Ethics and the Political Role of the Courts," 35 Law and Contemporary Problems 94 (1970).

Ely, John Hart. "The Wages of Crying Wolf: A Comment on Roe v. Wade," 82 Yale Law Journal 920 (1973).

Fairman, Charles. "Does the Fourteenth Amendment Incorporate the Bill of Rights?," 2 Stanford Law Review 5 (1949).

Finn, Chester E. "Book Review," Commentary 78, April 1, 1976.

Frank, John. "Review and Basic Liberties," in E. Cahn, ed., *Supreme Court and Supreme Law* 109 (1954).

Frankfurter, Felix. "John Marshall and the Judicial Function," 69 Harvard Law Review 217 (1955).

———. "Memorandum on 'Incorporation' of the Bill of Rights into the Due Process Clause of the Fourteenth Amendment," 78 Harvard Law Review 764 (1965).

———. "The Supreme Court and the Public," 83 Forum 329 (1930).

Frantz, Laurent B. "Congressional Power to Enforce the Fourteenth Amendment Against Private Acts," 73 Yale Law Journal 1353 (1964).

———. "Is the First Amendment Law?—A Reply to Professor Mendelson," 51 California Law Review 729 (1963).

Grant, J. A. C. "The Natural Law Background of Due Process," 31 Columbia Law Review 56 (1931).

Grey, Thomas C. "Do We Have an Unwritten Constitution?" 27 Stanford Law Review 703 (1975).

Hamilton, Walton H. "The Path of Due Process of Law," in C. Read, ed., *The Constitution Reconsidered* 167 (1938).

Hand, Learned. "Chief Justice Stone's Conception of the Judicial Function," 46 Columbia Law Review 696 (1946).

Hawkins, Vaughan. "On the Principles of Legal Interpretation, with Reference Especially to the Interpretation of Wills," 2 Juridical Society Papers 298 (1860).

Henkin, Louis. " 'Selective Incorporation' in the Fourteenth Amendment," 73 Yale Law Journal 74 (1963).

———. "Some Reflections on Current Constitutional Controversies," 109 University of Pennsylvania Law Review 637 (1961).

Hooker, Roger W. "A 'Quiet, Undramatic' Leader," The New York Times, August 19, 1976.

Horn, Robert H. "Book Review," 88 Harvard Law Review 1924 (1975).

Horwitz, Morton J. "The Conservative Tradition in the Writing of American Legal History," 17 American Journal of Legal History 275 (1973).

———. "The Emergence of an Instrumental Conception of American Law, 1780–1820," in 5 Perspectives in American Legal History 287 (1971).

Hurst, James Willard. "The Role of History," in E. Cahn, ed., Supreme Court and Supreme Law 60 (1954).

———. "The Process of Constitutional Construction," in id. 55.

Hutcheson, Joseph C. "The Judgment Intuitive: The Function of the 'Hunch' in Judicial Decision," 14 Cornell Law Quarterly 274 (1929).

Jaffe, Louis. "The Supreme Court Debated—Another View," The New York Times Magazine, June 5, 1960, in L. Levy, ed., The Supreme Court Under Earl Warren 199 (1972).

———. "Was Brandeis an Activist? The Search for Intermediate Premises," 80 Harvard Law Review 986 (1967).

Jurow, Keith. "Untimely Thoughts: A Reconsideration of the Origins of Due Process," 19 American Journal of Legal History 265 (1975).

Kauper, Paul. "Penumbras, Peripheries, Emanations, Things Fundamental and Things Forgotten: The Griswold Case," 64 Michigan Law Review 235 (1965).

———. "Some Comments on the Reapportionment Cases," 63 Michigan Law Review 243 (1964).

Kelly, Alfred H. "Clio and the Court: An Illicit Love Affair," 1965 Supreme Court Review 119.

———. "Comment on Harold M. Hyman's Paper," in H. M. Hyman, ed., New Frontiers of the American Reconstruction 41 (1966).

———. "The Fourteenth Amendment Reconsidered: The Segregation Question," 54 Michigan Law Review 1049 (1956).

Korman, Edward R. "Book Review," 4 Hofstra Law Review 549 (1976).

Levinson, Sanford. "Fidelity to Law and the Assessment of Political Activity," 27 Stanford Law Review 1185 (1975).

Levitan, David. "The Foreign Relations Power: An Analysis of Mr. Justice Sutherland's Theory," 55 Yale Law Journal 467 (1946).

Lewin, Nathan. "Avoiding the Supreme Court," The New York Times Magazine, October 17, 1976 at 31.

Lewis, Anthony. "A Man Born to Act, Not to Muse," The New York Times Magazine, June 30, 1968, in L. Levy, ed., *The Supreme Court Under Earl Warren* 151 (1972).

——. "A Time to Celebrate," The New York Times, May 13, 1974, p. 29.

——. "Historical Change in the Supreme Court," The New York Times Magazine, June 2, 1962, in L. Levy, ed., *The Supreme Court Under Earl Warren* 77 (1972).

——. "What Qualities for the Court?" The New York Times Magazine, October 6, 1957, id. 114.

Linde, Hans. "Judges, Critics and the Realist Tradition," 82 Yale Law Journal 227 (1972).

Lofgren, Charles A. "United States v. Curtiss-Wright Export Corporation: An Historical Reassessment," 83 Yale Law Review 51 (1973).

McCloskey, Robert G. "Due Process and the Supreme Court: An Exhumation and Reburial," 1962 Supreme Court Review 33.

McDougal, Myres, and Asher Lans. "Treaties and Congressional-Executive or Presidential Agreements: Interchangeable Instruments of National Policy," 54 Yale Law Journal 184 (1945).

McGovney, D. O. "Privileges and Immunities Clause, Fourteenth Amendment," 4 Iowa Law Bulletin 219 (1918).

Mason, Alpheus Thomas. "The Burger Court in Historical Perspective," 47 New York State Bar Journal 87 (1975).

——. "Myth and Reality in Supreme Court Drama," 48 Virginia Law Review 1385 (1962).

Mendelson, Wallace. "Mr. Justice Black's Fourteenth Amendment," 53 Minnesota Law Review 711 (1969).

——. "Mr. Justice Frankfurter: Law and Choice," 10 Vanderbilt Law Review 333 (1957).

Miller, Arthur S. "An Inquiry into the Relevance of the Intention of the Founding Fathers, With Special Emphasis upon the Doctrine of Separation of Powers," 27 Arkansas Law Review 584 (1973).

Miller, Arthur S., and Ronald F. Howell. "The Myth of Neutrality in Constitutional Adjudication," 27 University of Chicago Law Review 661 (1960).

Morrison, Stanley. "Does the Fourteenth Amendment Incorporate the Bill of Rights?," 2 Stanford Law Review 140 (1949).

Neal, Phil C. "Baker v. Carr: Politics in Search of Law," 1962 Supreme Court Review 252.

Newmeyer, Kent. "Book Review," 19 American Journal of Legal History 66 (1975).

Nye, R. B. "Comment on C. V. Woodward's Paper," in H. M. Hyman, ed., *New Frontiers of the American Reconstruction* 148 (1966).

Packer, Herbert. "The Aim of Criminal Law Revisited: A Plea for a New Look at 'Substantive Due Process,'" 44 Southern California Law Review 490 (1971).

Pollak, Louis. "The Supreme Court Under Fire," 6 Journal of Public Law 428 (1957).

Pound, Roscoe. "Common Law and Legislation," 21 Harvard Law Review 383 (1908).

Richardson, H. G., and G. O. Sayles. "Parliament and Great Councils in Medieval England," 77 Law Quarterly Review 213 (1961).

Rodell, Fred. "The Crux of the Court Hullabaloo," The New York Times Magazine, May 29, 1960, in L. Levy, ed., *The Supreme Court Under Earl Warren* 192 (1972).

————. "It is the Warren Court," The New York Times Magazine, March 13, 1966, id. 136.

————. "The 'Warren Court' Stands Its Ground," The New York Times Magazine, September 27, 1964, id. 209.

Rostov, Eugene V. "The Democratic Character of Judicial Review," 66 Harvard Law Review 193 (1952).

————. "The Japanese-American Cases—A Disaster," 54 Yale Law Journal 489 (1945).

Shattuck, Charles E. "The True Meaning of the Term 'Liberty' in Those Clauses in the Federal and State Constitutions which Protect 'Life, Liberty and Property,'" 4 Harvard Law Review 365 (1891).

Sowell, Thomas. "A Black 'Conservative' Dissents," The New York Times Magazine, August 8, 1976, p. 14.

Steel, Lewis M. "Nine Men in Black Who Think White," The New York Times Magazine, October 13, 1968, in L. Levy, ed., *The Supreme Court Under Earl Warren* 82 (1972).

Stephenson, D. G. "Book Review," 61 Virginia Law Review 1338 (1975).

Sutherland, Arthur E. "Privacy in Connecticut," 64 Michigan Law Review 283 (1965).

Thayer, James Bradley. "The Origin and Scope of the American Doctrine of Constitutional Law," 7 Harvard Law Review 129 (1893).

Van Alstyne, William W. "The Fourteenth Amendment, The 'Right' to Vote, and the Understanding of the Thirty-Ninth Congress," 1965 Supreme Court Review 33.

Warren, Charles. "The New 'Liberty' under the Fourteenth Amendment," 39 Harvard Law Review 431 (1926).

Wofford, John. "The Blinding Light: The Uses of History in Constitutional Interpretation," 31 University of Chicago Law Review 502 (1964).

Woodward, C. Vann. "Seeds of Failure in Radical Race Policy," in H. M. Hyman, ed., *New Frontiers of the American Reconstruction* 12 (1966).

Wright, J. Skelly. "Professor Bickel, The Scholarly Tradition, and the Supreme Court," 84 Harvard Law Review 769 (1971).

MISCELLANEOUS

Act of April 9, 1866, Ch. 21, 14 Statutes 27.

1 *Annals of Congress,* vol. 1 (1789), 2d ed. (Washington, Gales & Seaton, 1834, print bearing running head "History of Congress").

2 *Annals of Congress,* vol. 2 (1791), id.

Charles L. Black, Jr., Address, "The Judicial Power as Guardian of Liberties," before a Symposium on "The Supreme Court and Constitutional Liberties in Modern America," Wayne State University, Detroit, Mich., October 16, 1976 (unpublished).

Congressional Globe, 39th Congress, 1st Session (1866).

———. 39th Congress, 2d Session (1867).

———. 40th Congress, 3d Session (1869).

———. 42d Congress, 1st Session (1871).

Hearings on Executive Privilege before the Senate Subcommittee on the Separation of Powers, 92d Congress, 1st Session (July 1971).

Hearings on the Supreme Court before the Senate Subcommittee on the Separation of Powers, 90th Congress, 2d Session (June 1968).

General Index

Note: for members of the Congress, a * before the name indicates Senator; a † indicates Representative.

Freund, Paul A., 335, 369

Fugitive Slave Act, 222, 226, 254

Fundamental enumerated rights: protection against discrimination, 15, 18-19, 64, 96, 102-103, 153, 167; scope of, 20-22, 24-36, 120-121, 161-165, 174, 211; and citizenship, 39-46, 48; and equal protection, 111, 133, 140-141, 169-183; and due process, 141-142, 208-214; and "persons" and "citizens," 215, 219-220; "fundamental" as Supreme Court label, 274, 279; nonenumerated, 388-389. *See also* Privileges and immunities

†Garfield, James A. (Ohio), 23, 40, 55, 59, 67, 181, 190, 208

Garrison, William Lloyd, 58, 230, 234

Georgia, 72, 399

Gerry, Elbridge: on Bill of Rights, 135; and Council of Revision, 301-302, 334, 379, 394; on representatives of people, 303; on amendment process, 317-318, 354

Gettysburg Address, 85, 348

Gibbon, Edward, 307, 417

Gibson, Justice (Pa.), 296-297

Gillette, William, 71

Goebel, Julius, 196, 291, 400

Goldberg, Justice Arthur J., 324; on opponents of 14th Amendment, 159; on original intent, 367-368; and 9th Amendment, 389

Goodwin, Richard, 333

Gorham, Nathaniel, 301

Government by consent, 295-296

Graglia, Lino A., 413

Graham, Howard Jay: on Civil Rights Act and 14th Amendment, 23; on *Corfield* "protection," 33; on racial

discrimination, 36; on Trumbull's 1871 remarks, 49-50; on framers' federalism, 63; on school segregation, 119, 127, 131, 288; on Bill of Rights, 146; interpretations of due process, 204-208 *passim;* abolitionist theory, 230-242 *passim,* 391; defends judicial change, 282; cited, 5, 10, 28, 51, 120, 222, 250, 254, 333, 334, 348

Grand jury, 151, 152, 156

Grant, J. A. C., 250

Grant, Ulysses S., 50, 322

Gray, Justice Horace, 367

Grayson, William, 400

Great Britain, 380

Grey, Thomas C.: critique of Supreme Court, 283-284, 319; on judicial review, 351; and judicial revision, 373, 387-391, 393; on original understanding applied, and Supreme Court cases, 411-412, 413; cited, 99, 137, 198, 231, 243

Griffith, Kathryn, cited, 223, 259, 330, 333, 354, 410

*Grimes, James W. (Iowa), 60, 235

†Grinnell, Josiah B. (Iowa), 27, 125

Gunther, Gerald, 377, 378

Haines, Charles G., 249, 250, 252, 257

Hale, Sir Matthew, 20, 400

†Hale, Robert S. (N.Y.), 61, 112, 182, 226; on blacks, 11; on State protection, 144, 153-154, 177, 178; and Bingham, 145-146, 171, 172, 181, 186-187, 217-218; on Bill of Rights power, 184

Hamilton, Alexander, 132, 191, 251, 252, 257, 260, 261, 292, 318, 322, 335, 356, 410; on due process, 194, 196, 198, 205, 385; and courts'

Index of Cases